MURDERED BY MUMIA

MURDERED BY MUMIA

A LIFE SENTENCE OF LOSS, PAIN, AND INJUSTICE

Maureen Faulkner
and
Michael A. Smerconish

THE LYONS PRESS
Guilford, Connecticut
An imprint of The Globe Pequot Press

To those who have suffered the unending pain inflicted on them by a loved one's killer, only to be victimized again by our appellate process. Be strong. You are not alone in your pain or in your struggle for justice.

To buy books in quantity for corporate use
or incentives, call **(800) 962–0973**
or e-mail **premiums@GlobePequot.com.**

The Lyons Press is an imprint of The Globe Pequot Press.

All photos courtesy of Maureen Faulkner unless otherwise noted.

Library of Congress Cataloging-in-Publication Data is available on file.

ISBN 978-1-59921-376-7

Printed in the United States of America

10 9 8 7 6 5 4 3 2 1

CONTENTS

CONTENTS

FOREWORD

On a hot August afternoon in the summer of 1995, I wandered four blocks from my law office in the Beasley Building on Walnut Street to Philadelphia's fabled City Hall, located where Broad meets Market Street. Upon entering the ornate building, I climbed to the second floor using one of the circular staircases located in each of the four corners of the building. Although showing signs of age and neglect, City Hall remains a grand and formal building. My kids have likened some aspects of it to Hogwarts in the Harry Potter movies. It's difficult to believe that construction of any one municipal building could take three decades—that is, until you walk into this structure, which occupies an entire city block and encompasses twenty-seven acres of floor space. That makes it larger than every other municipal seat in the nation, including all fifty state capitols and the national Capitol. When it was finally completed in 1901, it featured a 548-foot tower—surpassing all the cathedrals of Europe—topped by the largest statue on any building, anywhere: a thirty-seven-foot-high William Penn, the city's founder, standing as tall as a town house. It is said to have the largest clocks of any building; it would loom over Big Ben.[1] The behavior I was about to witness in a second-floor courtroom stood in stark contrast to the formal setting in which it occurred.

In Courtroom 253, there appeared a complete lack of solemnity, much to the displeasure of the Honorable Albert F. Sabo, the presiding judge. For Judge Sabo, it must have seemed like a bizarre time warp to a period thirteen years prior. He found himself positioned on the same high perch, hearing testimony about the same underlying facts for the same case over which he had presided more than a decade earlier. The high-ceilinged room was much like a church on a wedding day, where friends and family of the bride are on one side of the aisle and the groom's party sits opposite. Only this was no joyous occasion for any of the assembled. On one side sat the widow of a slain police officer, surrounded by members of her family and an extended family of men in blue uniforms. On the other side sat those more loosely associated with the man convicted by a jury of murdering the cop. I surveyed the room and quickly took my seat on the side of the "bride," sitting close enough to offer support but sufficiently far away so as not to intrude. From my vantage point, I had a clear view of the profile of the widow, Maureen Faulkner, then just shy of her fortieth birthday. She was already more than ten years into a vigil of support for a husband to whom she'd been married only a year and, on the day of my courtroom visit, she could not have known just how far from the end of the road she still was regarding this ordeal. Her stoic demeanor gave no hint of the degradation she was then enduring. Spite emanated from the other side of the aisle where friends and supporters of Mumia Abu-Jamal gathered in solidarity for a man who by now was an international cause celebre, despite his conviction for the first degree murder of Maureen's husband. Some in the cast of characters who assembled daily at this appellate hearing in support of Abu-Jamal had been going out of their way to make life unpleasant for Maureen, much like they had in the original trial. Many stared at her and tried to intimidate her with menacing looks; others taunted her in the hallway, yelling banalities such as, "We're glad your husband is dead. He got what he deserved." One day in the original trial, someone went so far as to spit on her. But their enmity was not evenly distributed. While openly and vocally displaying their fierce disrespect for the judicial process, they would respectfully treat any appearance in the courtroom by Abu-Jamal as the Second Coming. I found it mind-boggling. It was unlike anything I had witnessed during my career as a lawyer and all my time spent in courtrooms, albeit my experiences as a litigator involved civil trials. Here, the stakes were not large sums of money, but a man's life. And today I was only an observer.

Amidst this sea of spite and seething animosities coolly sat Maureen. She had traveled from her comfortable home and new life in California to once again carry the flame in Danny's honor. It occurred to me that most people would have given up by this time. How many of us might have stayed on the West Coast and moved on with our lives, taking the necessary steps to block out the most gruesomely traumatic episode anyone could possibly experience? But, as I was learning, Maureen is not most people. Although Maureen and I had met not long before this, when I interviewed her in my role as a guest host on talk radio station WWDB-FM, this was one of my first views of her immeasurable strength. My observations of her calmness under fire that day in court caused me to lend my hand to her efforts in the name of her slain husband.

Today I no longer practice law. A few years ago I reversed careers. Whereas I had been a lawyer who was also a talk radio host, today I am a talk radio host who happens to be a lawyer. I am also a columnist for the *Philadelphia Daily News* and the *Philadelphia Inquirer*, the city's two major newspapers. You can't do talk radio in this town or write columns without having something to say about the case of Mumia Abu-Jamal. It would be like hosting a show in Boston and remaining silent about the scandal that rocked the Church. Or being on the air in L.A. but having nothing to say about Rodney King. My radio career began with guest appearances and fill-in hosting in the late 1980s and since that time this case has been a constant topic of conversation. And not just here in Philadelphia. In Hollywood, too, and overseas.

I myself got a glimpse of Abu-Jamal's worldwide celebrity one year after watching Maureen suffer in City Hall, when I traveled to England with my father. Dad was not supposed to join me; the trip was intended to be a belated honeymoon with my wife. We'd been married two years before, but by the time of the vacation, she was pregnant and enduring morning sickness. The trip was paid for, so, as I like to joke, "Dad and I honeymooned." I have always loved London, in particular, and while we were in that city we enjoyed the usual tourist haunts: Churchill's Cabinet War Rooms, Westminster Abbey, the Imperial War Museum, dinner at Rules. We had a blast. On a rare, sunny London afternoon, we decided to walk from our hotel just off of Green Park into Piccadilly Circus. The bright neon lights of Piccadilly Circus are one of the most recognized nighttime photographic images in the world. We, however, were there for a daytime stroll. And so we walked, talked, and window shopped. Three thousand, five hundred miles from home, we were approached by a woman standing beside a card table, peddling something for the Communist Party. I think it was a subscription to the *Daily Worker*. She engaged us in conversation. We were thoroughly disinterested in buying her wares but somewhat amused by the fact that, from so many, she had singled us out. Hearing our American accents, she asked us where we were from and, when one of us responded "Philadelphia," she very quickly raised the name of Mumia Abu-Jamal. I asked her what she knew of the man and without missing a beat, she replied, "That he is a political prisoner in your country, of course." Her comment put a damper on what had been until then one of my all-time great days, although I should not have been surprised. By the time of my trip to London, the man who had more than a decade before murdered a Philadelphia police officer in cold blood had become a worldwide phenomenon and by then I was well acquainted with the facts of his case. I did not make known my knowledge to the young woman who talked with us. I was determined not to let her further sour the afternoon. It was probably the only time I have bit my tongue when opportunity has presented itself to set someone straight about what happened to Danny Faulkner.

What's notable about Abu-Jamal's support is that it grows in strength the farther one gets from Philadelphia. Being approached in London is understandable but, in Philadelphia where the murder occurred, it would be more of a rarity. Support for Abu-Jamal in the City of Brotherly Love has never been strong, except in the most radical of circles. Consider that one of the first groups to publicly defend Abu-Jamal was a group of New York Trotskyites called the Partisan Defense Committee (PDC). The same group had supported members of the so-called back-to-nature group MOVE, which was responsible for the murder of a Philadelphia police officer named James Ramp in a siege of the group's compound in 1978. Nine MOVE members were convicted of third degree murder for his slaying. There was a second catastrophe on May 13, 1985, wherein MOVE was responsible for one of the darkest days in Philadelphia history, resulting in the deaths of eleven people, five of them children. The PDC's support for MOVE morphed into support for Abu-Jamal, himself a MOVE defender. The point is, they were out-of-towners, not locals. Same thing with an outfit called the Quixote Center based in Hyattsville, Maryland, best known for sending money to Nicaragua when the Reagan administration was backing the Contra rebels. More interlopers, now supporting a cop killer. Also along the way came National Public Radio (NPR); it signed Abu-Jamal to do radio commentaries from behind bars while he was on death row. Meanwhile, back in Philadelphia, Temple University radio station affiliate WRTI-FM refused to air them! In the early nineties, Abu-Jamal hired a high-profile but nevertheless out-of-town lawyer, Leonard Weinglass. Weinglass, in turn, recruited celebrity supporters based in California: Mike Farrell, Ed Asner, Ossie Davis, and many others. Again, no Philadelphia heavyweights were featured among the cast of characters. To complete this out-of-town guest list, Farrell and Davis chaired a New York–based Committee To Save Mumia Abu-Jamal; the Committee, too, boasted more non-Philadelphians, including Whoopi Goldberg, E. L. Doctorow, Ruby Dee, and David Mamet.

When a publishing house decided to print a book of Abu-Jamal's thoughts penned while he was in prison, it wasn't Philadelphia-based Running Press, but rather one based in Massachusetts called Addison-Wesley. On a number of occasions Abu-Jamal has been welcomed, via audiotape, as a commencement speaker, but never amongst Philadelphia's many colleges and universities. Instead, those invites have come from campuses like Evergreen State College in Olympia, Washington, and Antioch College in Yellow Springs, Ohio. When his Hollywood pals, including Alec Baldwin, Roger Ebert, Spike Lee, Paul Newman, Tim Robbins, Susan Sarandon, and Oliver Stone decided to fund an ad in support of Abu-Jamal, they didn't engage the locals in the *Philadelphia Inquirer* or *Daily News*, publications that would best reach those in the judicial system in whose hands Abu-Jamal's fate might rest, but decided instead on the *New York Times*. Similarly, when Rage Against the Machine and the Beastie Boys played before sixteen thousand people in a benefit for Abu-Jamal, it was not held in Philadelphia's Spectrum or the Wachovia Center, home of the Flyers and the 76ers. Instead, they chose the Continental Airlines Arena in northern New Jersey. And it was the far-off City by the Bay, San Francisco, not Philadelphia, that named a day in Abu-Jamal's honor and, similarly, it was Oakland that closed its schools for a day to teach children about the "travesty" of Abu-Jamal's conviction. That would never have happened in Philadelphia. Overseas, in the City of Lights, a bulb dimmed and failed when Paris adopted the convicted cop killer as an "Honorary Citizen." *Quelle horreur!* At home, he is better known as the most dishonorable of residents.

My keen awareness of this global Mumia mania is the reason my street-walking encounter in London, however disturbing, was not a total shock. I have always attributed this lack of support at home to the fact that people here have been presented with a more steady and balanced view of the evidence than those Hollywood types who have been offered only snippets of misleading information and have then glommed onto sound bites generated to build support for an anti–death penalty effort. Generally speaking, in the city where the murder occurred most people are of the opinion that the guy who did it is where he belongs, if not six feet above where he ought to be.

I confess that my instincts have always been supportive of law enforcement. Chalk it up to my upbringing, my environment, and my general view of the world. In the conventional police shooting of an unarmed man where there is later a dispute as to whether the officer's life was threatened, I am inclined to believe the police officer until proven otherwise. I choose to tell you this quite candidly at the outset of this book. I have always respected the uniform and those who voluntarily wear it to protect and to serve. And so, to the extent I was predisposed here, it was toward Maureen Faulkner, Danny Faulkner's widow. Without digging too deep, there has always been plenty of evidence available to me and anyone else with a modem to suggest that Abu-Jamal murdered her husband: There were several eyewitnesses; the murder weapon was Abu-Jamal's; the ballistics matched; Abu-Jamal confessed; people of color were part of the jury; and Abu-Jamal was a known agitator who had advocated violence toward law enforcement (he wrote "Let's Write Epitaphs for Pigs, Signed, Mumia" in a Black Panther publication in April of 1970[2]). Moreover, Abu-Jamal has never explained what took place that night (which is certainly one of the most puzzling aspects of the case if one is inclined to side with him) and his own brother, William Cook, who was present at the murder, has himself never testified on Abu-Jamal's behalf. Common sense dictates that if one brother is on death row for a crime the other brother knows he didn't commit (because the second brother was himself present), he'd say so. But not William Cook. His silence has been deafening. Incredibly, this has never seemed to matter to Abu-Jamal's celluloid supporters.

My command of these basics along with my predisposition toward Maureen combined to inspire a more than decent talk radio conversation on the murder when I first came on the airwaves in the early 1990s, a time when I was both an aspiring host and full-time attorney. But I decided to take it up a notch after the day I first walked into City Hall during the summer of 1995 and bore witness to the degradation she was experiencing at the hands of Abu-Jamal supporters during the Post-Conviction Relief Act (PCRA) hearing. What I saw was appalling and deeply offensive to my sense of justice, logic, and morality; I was galvanized to get off the sidelines and into the game. My commitment became one of educating myself as to the facts surrounding the case and then assisting Maureen as she defended the honor of her husband. The stakes were high for her, and for society.

Lawyers have an ethical responsibility to do pro bono work, meaning to work for no fee for people in need. As I sat and watched the PCRA hearings, I realized that I had found someone in need—Maureen Faulkner—and I was prepared to donate whatever time I could make available to assist her cause, Danny's cause. I knew she did not need me as a lawyer as much as she did as an advocate in the battle of public relations. Her legal interests were more than ably represented by an extraordinary team of people from the Philadelphia District Attorney's Office led by Lynne Abraham, who never wavered in the face of a constant onslaught of chicanery brought by Abu-Jamal's lawyers. These folks are real heroes. People like Joe McGill who prosecuted the case originally, and Hugh Burns, who has held the verdict thereafter. I believe that many of those who have for years labored on behalf of the Commonwealth of Pennsylvania through the DA's office could most certainly double their earnings in private practice and yet they willingly forgo the money and notoriety often given to their pinstriped counterparts. These prosecutors are the backbone, the foundation of our criminal justice system. They have served Maureen, and Danny, and all law-abiding citizens very well. Besides, I am not a criminal lawyer. I'm a civil trial lawyer and my knowledge of criminal legal process is limited to the basics I learned in law school and what I've acquired since then by being a careful observer of American jurisprudence. However, I know a lot about public relations and that's where I perceived Maureen's efforts to be lacking. That is not to say that she wasn't making waves on her own; indeed, she was. She has never faltered in her support for Danny and in her willingness to go anywhere and do anything to stave off the ugly forces of untruth. I was simply coming in for reinforcement.

Although Maureen had done a great deal on her own, she was working with her own money and very limited funding from friends. She was also out-gunned by the organized leftists with celebrity, if only titular, leadership. She was the proverbial one-armed paperhanger, and I was concerned that there should be a more concerted approach to defending Danny's cause, including some fund-raising. The Abu-Jamal defense had always been funded through an apparatus that I believed to be on very shaky ground legally and I did not want to see Maureen fall into that trap. It was important that she establish a tax-exempt not-for-profit 501(c)(3) entity to support her efforts and I was willing to undertake the effort to get that done. Together with a legal colleague, Michael Katz, and with the support of the chairman of our firm, James E. Beasley, we made that happen. I also saw the need to conduct regularly scheduled, well-publicized events in which the story of Danny's murder could be told. I was more than willing to use the fifty thousand watts of power that stood behind my own radio program on WWDB-FM (and more recently on the legendary CBS station now called the Big Talker, 1210-AM) to spread the word and promote these events. First things first, though. In order to be of value to Maureen, I recognized that I needed to know the case in its entirety. Cold.

So, here's what I did. I reached out for Mike Foley, Maureen's brother and stalwart supporter of Danny's memory, and asked that he provide me with a complete copy of the trial transcripts. They were not easy to find but Mike managed to obtain them. He walked into my law office one day with about thirty volumes, each approximately two inches thick. They represented the five thousand or more pages of trial testimony in the 1982 case of *Commonwealth of Pennsylvania v. Mumia Abu-Jamal*. For months, I would pick up each binder, one after the other, in the dated sequence of the trial testimony, and read them, in total, for a full appreciation of what had transpired at that trial. Night after night, I took home separate binders. I put down the Nelson DeMille and Dominick Dunne on my nightstand and picked up trial transcripts. Not only did I read but I also tabbed and highlighted passages that were particularly significant. It was time well spent. The more I read, the more I became sickened by the plain picture that emerged from trial testimony. My readings starkly revealed that Abu-Jamal murdered Danny Faulkner in cold blood and that the case tried in Philadelphia in 1982 bore no resemblance to the one being home-cooked and served hot by the Abu-Jamal defense team. My nights spent knee-deep in papers and Post-its confirmed that my predisposition toward Maureen was more than justified by the clear, hard facts presented at trial.

I've done a fair amount of public speaking about this case over the years and, in so doing, have tried to skip any unnecessary hyperbole and focus on the facts. In my prepared remarks, I rely on the actual trial testimony, which even supporters of Danny are generally unfamiliar with. The essence of my remarks is drawn from what is now the Appendix to this manuscript, which I encourage you to read. The eyewitness accounts and indisputable facts in those pages will leave no doubt as to the propriety of the jury's unanimous guilty verdict. This book is intended not so much as the definitive evidentiary record of the case as it is the story of one woman's incredible fight for her husband. Still, the Appendix should be your starting point.

After reading the Abu-Jamal trial transcripts, I did a radio show I will never forget. I told my audience what I'd been up to and said that I wished that everyone in the world had been given the same access as I was to the core information—i.e., the trial transcripts. A rather naïve thought then occurred to me, which I voiced on the air. What if I could get thirty typists together, hand each of them one of the trial transcript volumes and have them come back to me with a floppy disk with their efforts? We would then be able to assemble all the disks and have the entire transcript ready to upload onto the Web. I solicited volunteers; within minutes, I had more than one hundred volunteers for Danny Faulkner. All that typing wasn't necessary, however, because a radio listener of mine named Dan Hiltwine called on behalf of a guy who owned a scanning company, Scott Mackin, and within twenty-four hours, they enabled us to post a complete record of the trial testimony at www.danielfaulkner.com. How curious, I thought, that in all the years the Abu-Jamal forces had been howling the cry of injustice and insisting that Mumia had been railroaded at trial, they had never undertaken such an effort on their own despite the presence of more than a hundred of their Web sites in many different languages. Their inaction was telling.

Clearly, my friend in Piccadilly Circus had not fully acquainted herself with the case. She was not alone; many have been drawn to Abu-Jamal with no thought of the facts of the case and, worse, with no thought of what Maureen Faulkner has had to endure for a quarter century. This book seeks to change that. What follows is the story of one woman's successful battle against the self-described intelligentsia, the media elites, and professional leftists. I am no longer content to tell people that Maureen Faulkner is an amazing individual. Or that she is a person of rare substance. And courageous. Loyal. Indefatigable. It is time to assist her in telling the world her story so as to document what many of us who are close to her have witnessed.

Ten years ago, I told Maureen Faulkner to write this book, never intending a role for myself. She had the best of intentions but could not commit the time necessary to tell the story while also fighting Danny's continued battle. In the meantime, I've had success in writing two books, *Flying Blind: How Political Correctness Continues to Compromise Airline Safety Post-9/11* and *Muzzled: From T-Ball to Terrorism, True Stories That Should Be Fiction* (a *New York Times* bestseller), and decided that I was in a position to play scribe for her. My motivation in assisting is to offer an antidote to the lies and misinformation that have been spread about this case over a quarter century and to tell the story of an amazing American woman. Such is my agenda that I am not benefiting financially from this manuscript. One hundred percent of my author's proceeds are being given to Justice for P/O Daniel Faulkner, the not-for-profit Maureen established in Danny's name to provide scholarships to the children of murder victims in Philadelphia.

Years ago, the Hollywood left embraced the man who murdered her husband. In movie terms, it's time for the sequel. Maureen Faulkner is now ready for *her* close-up. What follows is her story, told to me twenty-five years after the murder of her husband. She's in my study as she begins to relate the painful details of a night a quarter century ago, a night that started as any other but ended in surreal horror, a night that changed her life forever. Maureen has recounted most of these events to me many times before, but this time, she knows I want all the details; these fine points will enable you to finally hear her story. The whole story.

—MICHAEL A. SMERCONISH, ESQ.
December 9, 2007
Philadelphia

1

THE PREMONITION

We were both excited about the weekend, even though it would be the first in roughly a year of marriage that we would not be together. Danny was happy about his long-planned annual hunting trip; I was anxious to entertain my mother in our home. Every year, Danny would travel about two hundred miles north of Philadelphia via the Pennsylvania Turnpike to reach Sullivan County. He loved to hunt and to spend time with friends, mostly fellow cops like Hugh Gallagher. Hugh's father had a small cabin where he loved to go for a few days at a time. They'd track the deer, probably have a beer or two, and, knowing Danny, I'm sure they'd spend lots of time swapping stories while trekking in the cold mountain air. Danny loved to tell stories. Stories about his work as a cop. Stories about growing up in Philadelphia. Stories about his family. And stories about life in general. I knew I'd miss his company for two nights, but I was also looking forward to my mother's company. My mother was going to make the forty-five-minute drive from where my parents were living as caretakers in the historic Valley Forge area into the city and, although she had visited our home before, this time she was going to spend the night. I was hoping it would be time spent together doing the things that moms and daughters don't often get to do when a husband enters the picture.

I was content with my life at that time and wanted very much for my mother to see and experience my surroundings. She was a consummate worrier and I was anxious for her to see that, at age twenty-five and married, I was getting along just fine in the world. I was very proud of the modest, comfortable little house Danny and I called home and I spent time before her arrival making sure everything looked just right. My mother was disappointed that Danny was leaving on his trip before she would arrive. They had a terrific relationship. At first, Mom had been wary of him as my choice of a spouse, not because of who Danny was but, rather, what he did for a living. Police work was dangerous, she often warned, as if telling me something new. But her concerns about his profession soon succumbed to her fondness for the tall, personable, handsome young man with the shy smile I had fallen in love with. Both my parents loved Danny like another son.

It was the early 1980s. Stamps were 20 cents; Luke had finally married Laura on *General Hospital*; Olivia Newton-John's "Physical" was atop the charts. President Reagan was nearing the end of his first year in office. CDs, pagers, fax machines, laptop computers, and cell phones did not exist yet. MTV was in its infancy and rap music almost unheard of. Danny spent his Sunday afternoons watching another Dan—Dan Fouts—throw touchdowns for the team in San Diego. And I, contentedly nestled in my small house in southwest Philadelphia, was confident that bloody shoot- 'em-ups and tragedy were merely the stuff of TV dramas like *Magnum, P.I.* as I vacuumed the living room and excitedly prepared to entertain my mom that December day.

My mom said good-bye to my father and drove down to my home, in southwest Philadelphia. We had a terrific time together doing things that would seem inconsequential to an outsider. I remember we sewed curtains for my windows. The small house was cozy, nothing extravagant about it, but it was the kind of place where both Danny's and my families and all our friends always felt welcome.

Saturday night was all that I had hoped it would be. The conversations with my mother were nothing short of hilarious; we joked and reminisced, had fun, and stayed up late. But things changed on Sunday morning. When Mom woke up, there was a marked change in her demeanor that she refused to discuss. As we had coffee in the kitchen, I could sense her uneasiness. But despite my prodding, she just wouldn't share what was troubling her.

By Sunday afternoon, she was ready to spill. She told me she had not slept well the night before. When I asked why, she finally said that she'd had a horrible nightmare that frightened and depressed her. Her peaceful slumber was disturbed by a vision of one of her boys on the pavement, bleeding. "One of my boys" is how she put it, meaning to me, and to her, one of my four brothers: Jim, Mike, Lawrence, or Francis.

The nightmare continued to gnaw at my mother's sense of ease as the cheerful tenor of the weekend was transformed by her looming anxiety. She was uncomfortable until the time she left for home. I remember that when a neighbor's dog started howling late that afternoon, she was frightened enough to say, "Maureen, I don't like this feeling of doom—I'm sure something terrible is going to happen to one of the boys." My mom was so concerned about my brothers that she called each one of them from my house and told them to be very careful because of what she had dreamt.

Mom's premonition was half-right. My brothers remained healthy and fine, but her dread and anxiety were founded. One week after her nightmare, I experienced my own when my husband, Danny, was found dead, murdered in the line of duty. Mom's divination of doom was transformed into a sad still frame of reality when, on the night of December 9, 1981, the innocent blood of the man I loved soaked the cold pavement of a frozen Philadelphia street.

2

THE KNOCK

The knock. That rap on the door that is the dread of all of the spouses of people who put their lives on the line—cops, firefighters, EMTs, the military, each profession with its own protocol. I got that knock in the early morning hours of a bitter-cold Wednesday, December 9, 1981, when my fitful slumber was interrupted by the thud of destiny.

That night I had trouble sleeping, so I went down and fell asleep on the couch in front of the TV. I was awakened by the sound of a rap on the door. It was a gentle tapping but it sounded like a cannon shot to me. I quickly looked at the clock and saw that it was a little after 4:00 a.m. I got up and looked through the window to where a police officer was standing on the step. With his shiny adornments glistening against the dark night, I thought maybe I was dreaming. My heart pounded furiously against my ribcage and my knees felt weak as I opened the door. There was not one police officer but three standing there, two men and a woman. I let them into the living room and one of the men solemnly spoke. "Your husband has been shot and they've taken him to Jefferson Hospital." I felt disconnected from my body as I darted up the steps to put on some clothes. As we headed out the door, somebody said, "Why don't you call Danny's mother." I replied that she had a bad heart and I didn't want to call his mom until I knew he was OK. At the time, Danny's brother Joe was quite sick, so I wasn't sure she could take any bad news on the phone. I called my own mother instead. The familiar sound of her voice pierced the surrealism of the night and sent me into a sharp panic. My throat went completely dry. In halting phrases, I finally got it out that Dan had been shot and I was going to Thomas Jefferson University Hospital. My words came spastically as the telephone rocked in my trembling hands. I'm sure she thought of her premonition, but not a word was mentioned of it at the time.

Within minutes, the female cop and I were in a marked police car racing into Center City. No sirens, just the piercing lights. I heard the police radio blasting but it was quickly turned off. This was no dream and, in the silence of the ride, I was forced to confront the reality of the situation. My thoughts were racing all over the place yet fiercely focused on my husband, and I was thinking about our last few days together. Danny had gone to work on his normal midnight to 8:00 a.m. shift on Monday night. When he got home Tuesday morning, I was still home, which was not our usual routine. I had been sick for a few days and had finally stayed home from work, hoping to shake off whatever it was. He was so happy to see me there, I almost forgot about how bad I felt.

Normally, when Danny worked the night shift, we just missed each other. I'd be in my car on the long commute to the suburbs by the time he walked through the front door. This day, however, we got to have breakfast together for a change. Afterwards, he handed me $200, a significant portion of his $900 monthly salary, to do some Christmas shopping when I was feeling better. After breakfast, I decided to keep him company as he sat at the dining room table and paid the monthly bills.

It was unusual for him to stay up instead of going right to bed. I remember him going over the household expenses before organizing the dining room and living room drawers. When I questioned him regarding his puzzling burst of enterprise, he simply retorted that "it ought to be done." Later on, he took a short nap. When he got up, he was thinking about taking the next shift off. *A Chorus Line* was playing in Philadelphia and we wanted to see it. He said, "You know what, Hon, since you're feeling better, let me see if I can get off from work and we can go see the show." He called the theater and found that the only seats available were up in the rafters. "Well, if we do go to the show, we should have good seats, so I'll just go to work," he reasoned. After going to the store to buy a couple of things, he cooked dinner for us, the last meal that we would have together.

After dinner, I sat on the couch with him. He decided he would go upstairs and sleep for a couple of hours before he had to go back to work. I remember him saying, "Come on up and lie down, too—you know I can't sleep without you." I remember that the two of us went up to bed and slept from probably 8:00 until the alarm went off around 10:00. We had a clock radio and I'll never forget that, when the radio alarm came on, we were lying in each other's arms and Barbra Streisand was singing "Coming In and Out of Your Life." That song has never stopped haunting me.

Listening to the song in a disoriented state of half-wakefulness and half-sleep, I was suddenly jolted by what I thought was a gunshot. I jumped up in bed in panic. When I told Danny that I thought I'd heard a gunshot, he calmly smiled back with gentle amusement, saying, "What are you talking about?" I now wonder if this was the same kind of premonition my mother felt, like something bad was going to happen. In retrospect, there were many curious events that foretold the harm that was to come his way. This was just another of them.

Danny was running late and decided that he'd better get dressed at home. Normally, he'd keep his uniform at work and dress at the district, but this night he dressed before he left. Unfortunately, his bulletproof vest was not at home, and he dressed for work without it. I sat at the edge of the bed and gave him a hug and kiss; he looked so great in his uniform. His quick kiss good-bye was the last moment I shared with my living husband—my kind, loving, irreplaceable husband who had little more than four hours to live. I missed him, as always, the minute he walked out the door.

Danny was a patrolman who worked the city's Sixth District, comprised of what the locals call "Center City" Philadelphia, where he policed the city's governmental, financial, and entertainment hub. After hours, certain streets turned a little ominous, and some slices of the city's less desirous underbelly were his responsibility. Together with his partner, Garry Bell, Danny "worked the wagon"—a two-man job unlike driving a patrol car, which was duty for one. Police wagons were used for transporting suspects and involved the type of risk that required two men. On this particular night, the wagon was "down on a mechanical." Garry later told me that he and Danny had flipped a coin to see which one would get to cruise the city streets in a warm patrol car and who would work on foot. Danny won the toss. He picked the patrol car.

Somehow, a news truck beat the squad car carrying me to Jefferson Hospital and the emergency room area was bustling with media. When we arrived, the female cop and I walked briskly through the automatic doors so we didn't have to talk to anyone. I was escorted to the policeman in charge and the woman who had driven me disappeared without a word. Come to think of it, I don't think we talked to each other at all. Unbeknownst to me, the female officer was just twenty-three years old at the time. She had been called by her lieutenant, Larry McShane, who was responsible for notifying me of the situation. They were both cops in the Twelfth District where Danny and I lived. Lieutenant McShane thought it appropriate to have a woman be part of the detail that came to tell me, and Cathy Kelley (née Clarkson) was the officer he asked. She was fresh out of the Police Academy, having graduated only three months earlier. She was from Narberth, out on Philadelphia's privileged Main Line, and despite becoming a police officer and being married to a cop, she was still unaccustomed to the perils of the job. Very quickly, she has since said, she learned how to "be stone-faced and cry in private." For her, having to notify me was a "9/11-like experience."

At Jefferson Hospital, I was escorted by a policeman into a room where Garry Bell and another friend, Eddie McGrory, sat waiting for news. Garry had not only seen the badly wounded body of his partner, he'd also seen the man who shot him, Mumia Abu-Jamal, and, as he would later attest, he'd heard Abu-Jamal admit that he shot Danny and add that he "hope[d] the motherfucker dies." When he heard that, Garry told Abu-Jamal that if Danny died, he would die. He was so rattled about what he had seen, and by this exchange, and no doubt concerned about me, that it would take him a while to remember those words, and of course, Garry told me none of this at the time. Thankfully, he was not the only one to hear Abu-Jamal's confession; a Thomas Jefferson employee heard it as well. That would all be discussed for years to come, but at that particular moment in the ER, it was hard to talk at all and we sat silently together, waiting for news of Danny's condition.

Although frightened at the prospect, I wanted desperately to see Danny. Somebody told me he was "being worked on" in the next room and I couldn't see him yet. Resigned to perhaps a long wait, I decided to go for a bathroom break. Walking down a hospital corridor, I heard a loud voice echoing from an adjacent area. I remember hearing the voice, not because of any words being said, but because of the man's shouts of defiance as opposed to cries of pain.

There was a lot of commotion besides the guy screaming. Somebody said, "That's the shooter." I couldn't make out what he was saying; I could just hear him yelling in anger. I never saw him that night. I would later learn that Abu-Jamal had refused treatment after arriving at the hospital. Finally, after talking to his own family and to surgeons, he allowed doctors to remove the bullet from his stomach. An attorney representing Abu-Jamal would later say that he'd been beaten, that there were bruises on his face, but a police spokesman, Detective Jerrold Kane, immediately refuted this claim, as did the physician who treated him that night at Jefferson.[3] Two Philadelphia police officers, John McGurk and Daniel Sobolewski, later testified that as they carried a struggling and angry Abu-Jamal to a police van after the shooting they accidentally struck his head against a pole on Locust Street.[4] Some would try to claim that was police brutality. But, Dr. Anthony Colletta, a surgical resident at Jefferson, would later testify that Abu-Jamal had lacerations on his forehead and lip and swelling on his neck and under his left eye, which were consistent with the officers' descriptions of what they say occurred when they took Abu-Jamal into custody.[5] Prosecutor Joe McGill went so far during a pre-trial hearing as to borrow a billy club from an officer in the courtroom and ask Dr. Colletta if the injuries were consistent with what a billy club might do, and the doctor said, "I would think that instrument would do more injury."[6] Moreover, a subsequent police brutality inquiry found no evidence of any such conduct.

Soon, Police Commissioner Mort Solomon arrived at the hospital, and later, so did Mayor William (Bill) Green. Green had replaced Frank L. Rizzo after he served two terms as mayor. Rizzo was, of course, the man who rose from patrolman to police commissioner. After he ran the city for eight years, he was prevented by the City Charter from seeking a third consecutive term. Mayor Green was appropriately solemn and compassionate. My interaction with Police Commissioner Solomon was not as staid as my discussion with Mayor Green. With regard to Commissioner Solomon, I became livid at the sight of the man who, to my mind then, was partly responsible for Danny's injury. See, Danny had recently complained to me about Commissioner Solomon's change in rules that governed the use of deadly force, restricting a police officer's ability to use a weapon. In "policespeak" they called it Police Directive 10, and it had gone into effect in 1980. At that minute, I did not yet know the circumstances surrounding Danny's shooting but found myself standing up to Solomon, holding his face, crying and saying to him, "You, with your deadly force restriction!" Too late, I realized I had unintentionally scratched his face. I was sorry immediately for my unrestrained emotion, which only added to the agony of us all that miserable night. I knew it was not so much the policy, but the confusion it caused when it went into effect, that caught the ire of cops like Danny. This was the first time deadly force was formalized into a directive. Initially there were a lot of questions and confusion on why it was being done. Police Directive 10 was viewed by the cops as limiting their ability to defend themselves. Danny had the perception that "our hands are being tied." In spelling out when they could or could not shoot, the general feeling was that there was no room for mistakes, and whoever made one would be in trouble. This was also the same time frame in which a less powerful bullet was adopted for use by the police department, which also had the guys riled up. That too was on my mind, given that Danny got off one shot on Abu-Jamal. Nevertheless, I was sorry, and remain sorry, for accidentally scratching the commissioner's face.

After this unexpected encounter that surprised even me, I was afraid I was losing control and returned to the private area where I could wait for news with Garry and Eddie. Danny's mom was then living with Danny's brother Ken; when the telephone rang to alert the Faulkners, Kenny had answered. They told him something had happened, that Danny had been shot. They did not want to tell him his condition but, when Kenny asked where he'd been shot, they told him "in the face." Kenny hadn't known it, but his mother had picked up an extension and when she heard the conversation, screamed in pain. Within minutes, other family members' phones were ringing with the news of Danny's predicament. Another brother, Pat, got his call from Kenny: "Danny's been shot, we don't know how bad, and we're all headed to Jefferson." Hoping for the best, Pat Faulkner jumped in his car for the twenty-minute ride to the hospital and tuned in to KYW Newsradio. He heard a report that the officer who had been shot was dead. Danny Faulkner was not named, but that's the way Pat learned of his baby brother's death. Imagine what it must have been like for him, driving alone in the middle of the night, racing to the hospital to see a dead brother.

At the hospital, his doctor soon walked in, wearing a white coat splattered with ominous patches of blood. I was seated with Garry Bell and Eddie McGrory. Nobody moved. He came directly over to me. I looked up as he quietly said, "I'm sorry, he's gone." That was it. He delivered the earth-shattering blow of my life, then turned away and left the room. It was about 5:00 a.m.

That's how I learned my relationship with Danny of 913 days, 396 of which we were married, was over. The horrors of the night had started with a knock and ended with a scream. I remember shrieking and crying and thinking I was in a nightmare, hoping I could be dreaming and it wasn't true. Then, my parents walked through the door and brought reality with them. It was the first time in my life I ever saw my dad, a hardened WWII vet, cry. In twenty-five years, I had never seen him break down, but I remember that he sat there with his head in his hands, his tears hitting the floor. We all—the Foley and Faulkner families—just sat in that anteroom and held hands and cried as my new world turned in slow motion.

They then asked me if I wanted to see Danny. I went to the door of the room where they had cleaned him up—and I remember seeing what seemed like a vision of him lying on the table. I wanted desperately to help him but I couldn't go near him. I was too scared. Still disbelieving, I guess. I thought that if I went near him, I would snap and lose all control. I was in a state of shock. Everybody was crying and I remember saying that I didn't want to go back home. By now it was daylight, so I went with Mom and Dad and spent the day with them at their place. My parents were in their bedroom, and I remember I was so devastated over losing my husband that I crawled in between my mom and dad and went to sleep. I was twenty-five years old, an adult, out in the world. I was married and I had started a new life with a husband I deeply loved. But when you have something so devastating happen to you, you just need to be with your parents.

The next day, I returned to the house Danny and I had shared in southwest Philadelphia. A steady procession of family and friends began to gather to grieve and comfort me, and each other. Suddenly, my ten-year-old nephew, Jimmy, shouted, "Look, Aunt Maureen, Uncle Danny's not dead, he's right here." For an instant, my heart raced. When I looked up, I saw Danny's good friend Thom Hoban in his Philadelphia police uniform, there to pay his respects. For just a split second, I actually entertained the thought that Danny had walked in. That's how crazy and in a state of shock I was in: I was willing to believe he was still alive a day after seeing his body in the hospital. I remember how difficult it was for me to see any man in a uniform after that.

When it happened, the story of Danny's murder in what was then the nation's fourth-largest city dominated the local news for days. He was killed in the early hours of the morning of December 9, and somehow they were able to get it on the cover of that day's *Philadelphia Daily News*. I was numb to the coverage at the time and the newspapers were kept from me by friends. In fact, I remember when I first looked at the press coverage— it was New Year's Eve going into 1982. I was alone in my parents' home— they were going out with close friends Frank and Peg Salerno. I was getting panicked as the clock moved closer to midnight. I did not want to be alone. I remember running to get the telephone to call my parents at the Salerno's, and in reaching into a drawer for their phone number, I suddenly came upon a picture of Danny in the casket. They had taken it at the viewing and hidden it from me until more time passed. I was shocked, and started to scream. Thank goodness, my brother Michael arrived at that moment and took me into his arms. After I calmed down, I went back, that night, and read all of the stories about the murder. For me, New Year's Eve has always been the most difficult. Not Christmas. For me it remains New Year's Eve.

Over the years I have often gone back and re-read the clips saved for me by friends. One edition ran with the full-front-page headline: "Cop Shot to Death; Newsman Arrested; Mumia Abu-Jamal Held in Killing."[7] Next to the headline was a large picture of Danny, identifying him as a five-year veteran. It was his official police photo and, although no one could have known it at the time, that picture would become the symbol of decades of battle in his honor.

Inside the front cover, the *Daily News* reported that Danny had been shot at Thirteenth and Locust Streets and that he died at Thomas Jefferson

University Hospital from two gunshot wounds. The suspect was identified as "Wesley Cook, 27—who used the name of Mumia Abu-Jamal."[8] I had never heard of him before, but the news stories gave details about the crime and his checkered past.

> Police piecing together the details of the shooting said that, at 3:45 a.m., Faulkner apparently stopped for investigation a car driven by Wesley Cook's brother, William Cook, and ordered William Cook out of the car. Moments later, Wesley Cook apparently approached on foot and saw the confrontation between the two, police said. The shooting followed.
>
> One witness told police he saw Wesley Cook fire one shot as he ran across the street toward his brother and Faulkner. The witness reportedly said Faulkner, apparently hit by the shot, crumpled to the sidewalk and that Wesley Cook then stood over him and fired another shot at him point-blank. The witness was not able to say when Faulkner fired his gun.
>
> Police said five shots had been fired from the gun they believe to be Wesley Cook's. Faulkner had fired his gun once.
>
> Wesley Cook of 17th Street near 66th Avenue was widely known for his support of black activist causes. He was a leader of the local Black Panther Party while still a teenager.[9]

. . .

> Up until November, Abu-Jamal had served as president of the association [Philadelphia Association of Black Journalists] for a year and during his tenure, said *Daily News* City Hall reporter Linn Washington, Abu-Jamal urged the organization to become "more active and out front."
>
> Abu-Jamal most recently had been a radio stringer for radio station WDAS. Before that, he worked with WUHY radio as a reporter and commentator. He left the station in March after a disagreement with news director Nick Peters.
>
> Peters said Abu-Jamal agreed to leave his position after disagreements between the two men over Abu-Jamal's trouble showing objectivity and fairness on several stories over a period of months.
>
> Abu-Jamal often reported on housing, prisons, and other stories involving poor people and minorities. "Anyone who knows him knows he has a lot of talent; he had an incredible voice, he was a very good writer and could do wonders with a microphone," Peters said.[10]

. . .

One of the subjects about which Abu-Jamal had difficulty maintaining objectivity was his coverage of the radical, back-to-nature group MOVE. MOVE had a violent stand-off with police at its Powelton Village compound in 1978 which resulted in the death of a police officer named James Ramp. It was reported that, as Abu-Jamal covered MOVE, he also grew close to the group, and when several MOVE members went on trial for manufacturing bombs the previous summer, Abu-Jamal was seen in the City Hall press room selling copies of the group's newspaper called "First Day."[11]

Abu-Jamal's fondness for black radical politics was also noted in the coverage following the murder:

In 1970, while attending Benjamin Franklin High School, Cook, then a member of the Black Panther Party, was dismissed and transferred for circulating pamphlets calling for "black revolutionary student power."

"He was a very bright student," said Dr. Leon Bass, principal of Franklin. "He was very articulate and could write well. But he was very radical. His radical views were disruptive."

Abu-Jamal and three other students who were dismissed filed suit on the ground that their right to free speech had been denied. A Common Pleas Court judge upheld the dismissal.

In a 1970 interview, Jamal said: "Black people are facing the reality that the Black Panther Party has been facing: political power grows out of the barrel of a gun."[12]

The clips from those first few days remain a good insight into Abu-Jamal. According to the articles, Abu-Jamal had become enamored with the Jamaican-based Rastafari religious movement, which worshipped the late Ethiopian King Haile Selassie as a deity and advocated the frequent use of marijuana. It was reported that Abu-Jamal was a member of the board of directors of the Marijuana Users Association of America, a group based in Philadelphia with the goal of legalizing marijuana use. The group had apparently broken up earlier in the year because of a lack of funds. Most menacing was his association with the MOVE group, a radical back-to-nature outfit that was responsible for the 1978 murder of Philadelphia police officer James Ramp.

Elsewhere, Danny was remembered as a man who had "won citations." One day after his murder, on page one, the *Philadelphia Inquirer* told about his recent hunting trip with Hugh Gallagher. They wrote that he would have turned twenty-six on December 21, twelve days after he was murdered, and that we had recently signed up for a ski trip that winter and a Bermuda cruise in the spring. That's true, and we had been excited about both. On what would have been his birthday, I went to St. Barnabas Church with my friend Carol McCann and lit a candle for Danny—she shared his birthday. The coverage of Danny also noted that he was raised in southwest Philadelphia in a house with five brothers by a father who worked for the old Philadelphia Transportation Company (SEPTA's forerunner), and that his adolescence was spent at West Catholic Boys and Bartram High Schools and was followed by brief service in the army. Family members and police officials told the newspaper that Danny received numerous citations for his police work and finished second in his class at the Police Academy in 1976. Our neighbors along Harley Avenue said he used to play baseball with the local youngsters during the summer.[13]

"He was a good guy, one of the best guys in the squad. He was a normal guy, just one of the guys. As far as police work, he was tops. He loved police work and he was one of the best I've seen at it," Sergeant William Ryan was quoted as saying in the Daily News. Sgt. Ryan remembered that Faulkner had ambitions of "moving ahead in the department."[14] An elderly man who lived down the street from Danny and I said that the police officer was a "nice guy" who "used to come out on the stoop to talk in the summertime."[15]

It is interesting now to go back and look at the details of the murder that were reported in those first few days. In 1981, Philadelphia was a four-newspaper town: the Inquirer, Daily News, the Philadelphia Journal, and the legendary Evening Bulletin. The latter reported the most detailed account of the murder from an eyewitness who had not yet been identified. From his sworn statement and trial testimony, the man is now easily recognized as Robert Chobert. "Slain Policeman Had No Chance, Eye-Witness Says," read the banner headline. Chobert was able to provide the grisly details. It was painful for me to read this then, and it is painful for me to read now. While cruising the area in his cab, Chobert witnessed Danny being knocked to the ground and the "gunman" standing over him firing three more shots. Little is left to the imagination. Danny's last moment was looking through the barrel of a gun. Holding that weapon was the man who infamously had said that "political power grows out of the barrel of a gun."

> "That cop ain't had a chance against that man," said the witness, who told a reporter he was driving by in a cab when the shooting occurred. The policeman, Daniel Faulkner, was shot in the head at close range after being knocked to the ground by a bullet in the back, officials said . . .
>
> "The guy was holding the cop on the arm," he said. "The guy walked over and went Pow! Pow! Pow! . . . I saw the flame come out of the gun."
>
> As the assailant stumbled away, he looked "like he was drunk or something," the witness said.
>
> The cab driver said he didn't see the policeman fire, "All I seen was that guy shooting," he said.
>
> The cab driver said the officer and his assailant appeared to be "about face-to-face" when he first saw them.
>
> A third man [William Cook] was standing on the sidewalk near the wall "like he was froze," the cab driver said.[16]

The news coverage in the immediate aftermath of the murder has withstood the test of time. It's the same picture that would later emerge at the trial. This is the heartbreaking tale of a young cop, deeply committed to his role as community protector, who was robbed of his promising future and his life with me, his young bride. The suspect was cast as a bright and formerly respected newsman whose attitudes transformed with his deepening fascination and involvement with radical politics. The facts sounded pretty straightforward. Multiple eyewitnesses, close to the murder itself, had seen Abu-Jamal shoot Danny at close range after Danny stopped Abu-Jamal's brother while presumably driving the wrong way down a one-way street. Most significantly, with a bullet to Abu-Jamal's stomach, Danny told us all the identity of his killer before he left this earth. Someone once said to me that Danny left his burr in his killer. Between those lines, and under the microscope of a quarter century of reflection, it is clear to me now that the seeds were already being sewn on the local level for what this case was to become internationally.

I did not know, or pay attention to it at the time, but immediately after the murder, the Philadelphia chapter of the Association of Black Journalists issued a statement saying that it "supports our president, Mumia Abu-Jamal.

He is our leader, our colleague and our brother. We're concerned about stories that have been printed and broadcasts that portray him in an inaccurate and unfair light. We offer our condolences to both families involved in this tragedy. We will continue to monitor news reports of this incident."[17]

I also later learned that City Councilman Lucien Blackwell went on television and expressed his concern about the defendant getting a fair trial. Mjenzi Kazana, a community activist who worked out of State Representative David Richardson's office, set up the Abu-Jamal Defense Committee and held meetings in the community. He also asked then Philadelphia District Attorney Ed Rendell to drop the charges until a "more thorough review" could be accomplished.[18] Rendell, the future mayor and future governor of Pennsylvania, declined. Present at a news conference for the group was Jerome Mondesire, future leader of the Philadelphia NAACP, who then represented Congressman Bill Gray, himself the future head of the United Negro College Fund. Claude Lewis, a columnist for the *Evening Bulletin*, suggested that a special prosecutor be appointed "as one way of convincing the community that justice in this case will be done."[19]

To the extent that in these initial developments there was a sign of what this case was to become, I surely did not see it at the time. What should have been a simple story of senseless murder and young life lost would eventually assume a much larger cultural significance. Still, in the early days after the murder, nobody who read about the events in Philadelphia could have predicted that Abu-Jamal would become the poster boy for an international anti–death penalty campaign. Why should he? He murdered my husband.

3

WITH HIS BOOTS ON

Danny's funeral service took place five days after he was killed, on December 14, 1981, when he was laid to rest at Glenwood Memorial Gardens in Broomall, Pennsylvania. Driving out of the city to the cemetery, I was amazed at the number of people lined up on the streets holding flags and who, as the funeral passed them, would bless themselves. The procession probably held traffic up a couple of hours getting out there.

Police from approximately 150 different departments in Pennsylvania, New Jersey, and Delaware came to pay him honor; as a result, there was a long delay before the burial could commence because the number of cars overwhelmed the available parking spaces in the small cemetery. At the end of the ceremony, the honor guard removed the folded American flag from the casket and handed it to Police Commissioner Morton Solomon who, in turn, handed it to me. Forgotten for the time being was the incident in the hospital emergency room. I gave it to Danny's mother, Mary. Then the twenty-one rifles sounded their salute, the bugle sent its mournful farewell, and the crowd of police and others who had attended the graveside service departed, leaving us with only the flowers that had witnessed the events of that dreary day.[20]

Earlier, a Mass of Christian Burial was said at St. Barnabas Roman Catholic Church at Sixty-third Street and Buist Avenue in Philadelphia, followed by a procession through the streets of the city's southwest section. The night before the burial, an estimated five thousand people came to pay their respects despite the bitter cold. The local merchants were giving out free hot coffee to keep people warm. The Faulkner family stood for close to six hours to greet the mourners. I remember clearly how the viewing had begun at the church Danny attended as a young boy after the passing of his father. (Initially, the family worshipped at Most Blessed Sacrament, which I think was then the largest parish in the country.) I am sure it was the conviction of their faith that enabled them to survive this ordeal.

I personally selected Danny's pallbearers. One was Danny's partner and friend, Garry Bell. The others were Ed Frederick, Jude McKenna, Jason Clark, Danny McCann, Eddie McGrory, Hugh Gallagher, Glenn Shiffler, and Mark Moger. We called these men the "Bailey Boys"—I think because of their fondness for Baileys Irish Cream. They liked to hang out at the Irish Pub on the 1100 block of Walnut Street. That place has often served as clubhouse for friends of Danny, both before and after his death. While the nine pallbearers are now spread throughout the country, they have always managed to make it back to Philadelphia to be there for me when I have needed them most.

Despite its geographical size and population, Philly is really a small town made up of many neighborhoods, and Danny's friendships resembled those you'd find in countless small communities across the country. Eddie and Danny became friends through Garry Bell when Eddie and Danny went to the Academy together. At the time I first met Garry, he was tall, good-looking, blond, well built, and about twenty-two years old. He was pretty quiet. In a nutshell, I guess you'd say he was the strong, silent type. Garry was very nice, easy to talk to and warm, but a no-nonsense kind of guy. He had a sense of humor, but he wasn't a prankster. He was already in the department when I met him with Danny. I always found him to be a straight shooter. He and Danny became very close friends after they became partners. They had shared a house down at the Jersey Shore and lived the twentysomething bachelor life together. The guys loved St. Patrick's Day. It was Danny's favorite day of the year. Every St. Patrick's Day, Garry and Danny would spend the day at Froggies Bar in Center City, making corned beef and cabbage.

Ed Frederick was on the stakeout unit in Danny's precinct the night he was killed. They saw each other that night when they spoke at Broad and Race Streets, just like any other night on the job. Ed said that Danny had to leave around 2:00 or 3:00 a.m. to do "club checks" when the bars let out. That was the last Ed heard from him.

After hearing of the murder, Eddie McGrory immediately came to be with me at the hospital and stayed around the clock, as a friend and also as a representative of the Fraternal Order of Police (FOP); he was the executive trustee of the FOP at the time. He was the person who put Danny's uniform on him for the funeral and was at my side the entire time. All of these guys, the pallbearers and many, many more who would have loved the honor of being a pallbearer for Danny, got me through this ordeal.

We had laid Danny out inside the church for the mass. It was a biting-cold night. I went into the church accompanied by Gregore Sambor, then a high-ranking cop and the future police commissioner. I had thought about having a closed casket because Danny was shot in the face and I was still numb and confused and not thinking straight—I really did not want to see him dead, did not want to realize he was actually gone from my life forever. But Gregore told me, "You need to see him, Maureen, you need to see him one last time, and understand that he is gone." I remember going into the church that night and standing in the vestibule—and feeling I couldn't walk up to his casket. I just couldn't do it. Then, Gregore asked two police officers to escort me up the aisle to where Danny lay, and they literally had to pick me up and carry me to the open casket. Gregore, who would later lose his own son in a murder, was really a pillar of strength for me. He knew how to talk to me and pull me together as far as emotionally possible.

I looked in Danny's casket and noticed he was wearing shoes. I told them he never wore shoes, he always wore boots. Everyone was momentarily stunned; then, one of the police officers took off *his* boots, removed Danny's shoes, and put the boots on him in the casket. Danny's law enforcement brothers went to enormous lengths to try to help me get through the worst torment of my life, and I am forever grateful for their concern.

As per Danny's wishes, I refused to have him buried in the city. That caused a bit of controversy, but he had explicitly told me what to do if anything ever happened to him. For some reason, he wanted to be buried out in the countryside. I remember going to the cemetery in Delaware

County and arranging his burial on a hillside, under a tree. The cemetery had not yet opened that particular section but when I said I would really like him buried there, they honored my request. They now call it the Mountain of Youth because of the many young people, including Danny, who are buried there. I broke ground in that part of the cemetery.

Frank Dougherty of the *Daily News* did a nice job capturing the solemn nature of the moment:

> Faulkner's brown metal casket, draped with an American flag, was carried out of the church by eight uniformed patrolmen. All eight officers work out of the 11th and Winter Streets police station where Faulkner, a patrolman for five years, had been assigned since 1979.
>
> The casket was placed in a black Cadillac Fleetwood hearse as the Police and Firemen's band played "Holy, Holy, Holy" to the measured beat of the pallbearers' steps.
>
> The band switched to "Onward Christian Soldiers" as Faulkner's wife, Maureen, his mother, Mary, his five brothers, Thomas, Joseph, Lawrence, Patrick and Kenneth, and a sister, Joanne Bell, entered two long gray sedans for the trip to Glenwood Memorial Park. The couple had no children.[21]

Mayor William Green, former mayor Frank Rizzo, then Managing Director and future mayor Wilson Goode, and Fire Commissioner Joseph Rizzo, brother of Mayor Rizzo, all attended the funeral services. Mayor Green said that being there was the worst aspect of being mayor, the worst thing he ever had to do: "I feel as if I had just lost a brother." Commissioner Solomon echoed the sentiment: "It's a sad day for all police officers. Any killing is a sad thing, especially when it's a policeman who was only doing his duty."[22] I remember Mayor Rizzo taking me into his big frame and telling me, "Maureen, you are part of our family, and if there is anything I can ever do for you, just ask." He was a bear of a man and yet so appropriately tender at that moment.

Today I hardly recognize myself in the grainy, yellowed photos of the funeral. But there I am in my cloth coat, sobbing and shivering. I completely lost it when I heard the police band playing "God of Our Fathers." Danny's mother, Mary, my own family, and Danny's siblings with their spouses soon joined me on the steps. Our little band of mourners—who comforted each other in shock and grief that day as we clung together in the sorrowful act of burying our beloved one who died too soon—had no way of knowing that the man who murdered my husband, their son, their brother, would end up outliving many of us.

4

FACTS

I could write several volumes on the facts of Danny's murder. I hope that, someday, someone will do that, but it is not my place here. My aim is to recap my twenty-five-year fight for Danny's honor in a way that exposes the many who irresponsibly rushed to support his killer without any understanding of what the case was all about. I recognize that in order for me to do that, I must first supply readers with some basic understanding of what occurred the night Danny died. And so I offer the following summation of the facts surrounding Danny's murder, free of hyperbole and entirely substantiated by sworn testimony.

Shortly before 4:00 a.m. on December 9, 1981, my husband was working the midnight–8:00 a.m. shift as a patrolman in Philadelphia's Sixth District. Danny, driving alone in radio patrol car 612, pulled over a light blue, beat-up Volkswagen, with its license plate hanging by a thread, on a one-way street in Center City.[23] This was the heart of Philadelphia's red-light district, and it was the wee hours of morning. It is presumed that Danny stopped the Volkswagen for turning into traffic against the direction of a one-way street, but that was never established at trial.[24] Danny used his police radio to make the normal call for a backup before getting out of his car, and then changed his request, saying to the dispatcher, "on second thought send me a wagon."[25] The driver of the Volkswagen was William Cook, brother of Wesley Cook, aka Mumia Abu-Jamal.

Witnesses reported that William Cook had opened the door of the Volkswagen and stepped out before Danny even approached his automobile.[26] One witness testified that Cook was directed by Danny to stand spread-eagle up against the Volkswagen. Then, with Danny behind him, Cook turned around and punched Danny in the face.[27] After Danny was struck by Cook, he responded, and they got into a scuffle, and Danny struck Cook, probably with his flashlight, which was found at the scene with a broken lens. (William Cook subsequently pleaded guilty to assault for this incident.) Across the street at the time of the traffic stop was Cook's brother, Abu-Jamal, working as a taxi driver. Abu-Jamal once had a promising career as a journalist and had a history of involvement with the Blank Panther Party, and in that role, he had glorified violence toward police officers in his writings.[28] That night, Abu-Jamal was armed with a weapon he had lawfully purchased from a Philadelphia sporting goods store almost two years prior.[29] Two eyewitnesses (Robert Chobert and Cynthia White) testified at his trial that they saw Abu-Jamal run across the street and fire at Danny, then saw Abu-Jamal fire down at Danny as Danny lay on the sidewalk, and then saw Abu-Jamal, himself shot, slump on the curb.[30] For those witnesses, Abu-Jamal never left their sight. (At the 1995 PCRA hearing, another witness, Robert Harkins, provided additional testimony corroborating Chobert's and White's accounts. Ironically, Harkins was called by the defense supposedly to prove that the police were pressuring witnesses. He instead complained that defense investigators had misrepresented what he had told them and proceeded to testify that, after the shooting, the perpetrator went over to the curb and sat down.[31] This of course is where two responding police officers found Abu-Jamal.)

Another eyewitness (Michael Scanlan) saw William Cook strike Danny as they stood at Thirteenth and Locust Streets after the traffic stop. He said he saw Danny defend himself with a flashlight or billy club just before a man ran across the street and killed Danny. Scanlan testified at trial to having seen a man run across the street and raise his hand. He said he heard a shot, but did not see a gun. Then, he said, he saw the man point down toward Danny and saw two flashes. Scanlan positively identified the coat that Abu-Jamal was wearing when he was arrested as the coat worn by the shooter but could not identify Abu-Jamal as the shooter.[32] A fourth eyewitness (Albert Magilton) testified at trial and identified Abu-Jamal as the man who ran across the street; he did not see the gun that fired the shots, but he heard five of them.[33] (I have always said that if you put those four eyewitnesses together—Chobert-White-Scanlan-Magilton—you would have a time sequence that shows exactly what happened, almost the way you forward through images to assemble an animated movie.)

The ballistics evidence in the case showed that the bullets in Danny's body matched the gun purchased by Abu-Jamal, a .38-caliber Charter Arms, which was recovered at the scene along with five cartridges, all of which had been fired.[34] Abu-Jamal's revolver contained what are called "plus P" high-velocity bullets, a particularly lethal form of ammunition. The bullet recovered from Danny's brain was too deformed to be linked to a particular weapon; however, it was consistent with Abu-Jamal's gun.[35] Danny died from two gunshot wounds he sustained—one to the center of his face and the other to his upper back. Both bullets were fired from less than twenty inches away.[36] One expert witness said the bullet that passed through Danny's jacket was fired within twelve inches, and that the bullet that hit him in the face was also fired at very close range.[37] Wounded by Abu-Jamal, but prior to his death, Danny was nevertheless able to get off a shot of his own and he struck Abu-Jamal in the stomach. The bullet that struck Abu-Jamal was determined to have been fired from Danny's police-issued .38-caliber Smith & Wesson gun.[38]

In addition to the trial testimony of four eyewitnesses to the murder, there was testimony of Abu-Jamal's hospital confession. Given the proximity of Thomas Jefferson University Hospital to the shooting scene at 1234 Locust Street, both Danny and Abu-Jamal were taken to the same emergency room. In the ER, Abu-Jamal was heard by two eyewitnesses to shout defiantly, "I shot the motherfucker and I hope the motherfucker dies."[39] William Cook, Abu-Jamal's brother, was not so talkative. The only thing William Cook has ever said to the authorities is, "I ain't got nothing to do with this."[40] He has never testified on his brother's behalf.

Abu-Jamal had a three-week trial for first degree murder in Philadelphia in 1982, in front of a jury that he personally helped select, which was made up of nine men and three women—ten whites and two blacks. There were originally three blacks on the jury, but one was jointly excused by counsel. The jury got the case at noon on July 2, 1982, and returned with a unanimous first-degree conviction by 5:00 p.m. The same jury then deliberated on Saturday, July 3, for about four hours before returning a sentence of death.

As Paul Harvey might say, "now you know the rest of the story" about a man named Wesley Cook aka Mumia Abu-Jamal. It was really that simple. But it surely didn't end there. Read the Appendix to this book for more sworn testimony, and visit www.danielfaulkner.com if you wish to read the entire trial record of this case.

5

SPIN

A cop is murdered by a man he never knew while patrolling the streets in the ordinary course of his duties. Period. End of story. An unfortunate yet simple tale. Or so it should have been. Instead, this ostensibly uncomplicated scenario has been subjected to more manipulation than any other murder in the United States. Without foundation, it has been transformed into a sensationalized saga of persecution and injustice that has attracted support from, among others, a large group of Hollywood sympathizers.

The farther away from Philadelphia you get, the more support Wesley Cook aka Mumia Abu-Jamal seems to garner. From Piccadilly Circus to Paris to the Pacific shores, Abu-Jamal has earned the perverse distinction of being a political prisoner. Petitions are circulated demanding his release, his honor is extolled, and his words, spoken and printed from behind bars, are broadcast and cherished by his supporters. In a media circus of sorts, Abu-Jamal has somehow emerged as a victim of prejudice and unfortunate circumstances. The face of a murderer has become the symbol of a campaign for social justice. So unfounded in reality and so anti-establishment have been some of the Abu-Jamal efforts that sometimes I wonder whether some of his supporters secretly harbor a belief that he really did murder Danny, but argue in support of his innocence nonetheless.

Within the Pennsylvania legal apparatus and around the globe, not six months have passed in the last twenty-five years without a new installment of the Abu-Jamal saga emerging and capturing the airwaves and newsprint. Inevitably, each has ended with Abu-Jamal's defense being embarrassed by a theory gone south and correspondingly needing to reinvent its case yet again. I could give you countless examples, and many will emerge in the pages that follow, but my personal favorite is the Arnold Beverly story. I think it says a lot about what a farce this case has become.

Eighteen years after Abu-Jamal murdered Danny, a man named Arnold Beverly surfaced, declaring that he knew who really committed the crime. He said *he* did it! This guy's story was that he and another man received money from the Mob to do the hit at the behest of cops at the top of the Philadelphia Police Department. Where he'd been for the nearly two decades since he "committed the crime" was anybody's guess. When Beverly came forward, Abu-Jamal was being represented by Leonard Weinglass and Dan Williams. Weinglass was a nationally recognized defense lawyer best known for his prior representation of the Chicago Seven; Williams was Weinglass's second seat and earning stripes of his own in equally liberal circles. Weinglass was hired by Abu-Jamal in 1992. You're probably thinking that Arnold Beverly's "admission" was welcome news to Weinglass and Williams. You'd be half right. Even these defense lawyers (at least Williams) knew the story was preposterous and were reluctant to run with it, but that didn't stop others in the Abu-Jamal legal camp from wanting to capitalize on it for Abu-Jamal's benefit. Jonathan Piper and Rachel Wolkenstein, two other lawyers for Team Mumia, must have been positively giddy about Beverly's admission of guilt.

How do we know this? Well, Dan Williams wrote a book and told us. In *Executing Justice: An Inside Account of the Case of Mumia Abu-Jamal*, Williams wrote, "I have to admit, I wasn't about to embarrass myself by running with such a patently outrageous story on the most visible death-penalty case in the world." Leonard Weinglass's analysis of this situation is less well known but he ended up with the same conclusion: If Mumia wanted the witness, he'd have to get another lawyer to present him.[41] Well, Williams's candor marked the end of his representation of Abu-Jamal. In April of 2001, Abu-Jamal hired a new legal team, which made clear that part of the reason for the change was the success Weinglass and Williams had had in convincing Abu-Jamal not to rely on Arnold Beverly's confession.

When the newest version of Team Mumia showed up in federal court in the summer of 2001 to press for habeas corpus relief, they resurrected

Arnold Beverly's "confession." They asked the federal judge to delay the appeals process until the Pennsylvania courts could hear Beverly's testimony. Here is what their petition stated: "Attorneys Weinglass and Williams told Petitioner they were unwilling to present the evidence concerning Arnold Beverly without further investigation."[42] However, it was revealed in Williams's book that he and Weinglass never had any intention of going forward with this evidence, instead maneuvering from the beginning to "push this witness onto the trash heap."[43] An oral argument on this issue occurred in state court on August 17, 2001, and a brain trust of Abu-Jamal sympathizers was present, including Jesse Jackson, Ossie Davis, and comedian Dick Gregory. Ultimately, this effort failed, as had the many that came before it. The willingness of Abu-Jamal himself to advance what was so obviously a bogus claim is, in my opinion, typical of what has enabled this case to clog up our court system for the past twenty-five years.

The Beverly fiasco's pure idiocy is almost matched by another embarrassing episode for Team Mumia in the mid-1990s. In the midst of a post-conviction hearing, Abu-Jamal's lawyers called witnesses to suggest that someone other than Abu-Jamal committed the crime. As I sat in the courtroom, I listened to one of those witnesses, William Singletary, who remembered seeing Abu-Jamal in Arab costume and a police helicopter at the scene (which quite simply did not exist), also claim that, after he had been shot, Danny spoke to Abu-Jamal, telling him "to get Maureen . . . get the children."[44] There were a few problems with Singletary's testimony—namely, that the assistant medical examiner testified that Danny died instantly from head wounds he sustained after being shot point-blank. Additionally, we never had children! In other words, Singletary, this alleged eyewitness to my husband's murder (according to Abu-Jamal's attorneys and supporters) purported to provide evidence of Abu-Jamal's innocence by saying that he spoke with a *dead* man about children with which we were never blessed.

And so it has gone for me for twenty-five years. Apparently, this sort of news is slow to make its way from Philadelphia to Hollywood, or overseas to Paris.

6

THE TRIAL

When Pulitzer Prize–winning journalist Buzz Bissinger (author of the bestseller *Friday Night Lights*) profiled Danny's murder for *Vanity Fair* in the summer of 1999, he asked Ed Asner if he'd read the original trial transcript. In an unfeeling reply, Asner asked, "Could I stay awake?"[45] That answer speaks volumes.

Yes, Lou Grant, the five thousand pages that tell the story of how Abu-Jamal murdered my husband would keep you awake. Lord knows, the case has prevented me from sleeping for two and a half decades. I have always been shocked by the readiness of Asner and others from the Hollywood left to attach their names to a murder case without reading every scrap of paper suggesting who did it. I think it is essential to read and appreciate the evidence in order to understand the extent to which the myth of Mumia Abu-Jamal separates from reality. Only ignorance of the true nature of the tragedy could lead anyone to conclude that Danny's murder is an "unsolved" mystery. The trial testimony and pre-trial statements from the eyewitnesses to the murder, which are attached to this book as an Appendix, all provide lucid and consistent confirmation of Abu-Jamal's conduct. And they barely scratch the surface of the information that is publicly available. These statements illustrate a high degree of specificity, recounting such details as Abu-Jamal's brand of car, color of shirt, and style of hair. The pre-trial statements from eyewitnesses are elaborated upon in the subsequent trial transcripts, and then in those of countless appellate hearings.

Through this collection of documents, we learned that, on the night of the murder, the flashes of the shots were seen, the suspect was identified, and the image of a triumphant killer standing over his victim was captured by the minds and memories of multiple eyewitnesses, none of whom was more than sixty feet from the shooting. And yet—somehow—the illusion and the myth remain. It certainly was not born of anything I witnessed at the trial of the case. It's like that old Nazi propagandist said, if you tell a lie, tell it big enough, tell it often enough, it becomes truth.

I first laid eyes on Abu-Jamal at the preliminary hearing for him and his brother, William Cook, in the courtroom of the (then) presiding judge, the Honorable Paul Ribner, in the Philadelphia Court of Common Pleas. I have to admit I was emotional, upset, and very angry. I will never forget that first time I spied Abu-Jamal: the cocksure way he would strut around; his dreadlocks a little bit shorter than his shoulders; how he liked to swing his head and acknowledge his supporters. He had a loud, obnoxious demeanor. A few times, while the judge was speaking, he would say, "No Judge, I am not doing that! Go to hell!" He actually told Judge Ribner to go to hell!

After the preliminary hearings, there was a lonely and unsettling six-month period between the crime and the trial. To help me through this bleak time, a friend of mine I met at work named Donna Dunne moved in with me. She lived in the Valley Forge area with her parents but wanted to stay with me to give me moral support. We lived comfortably at my place and it really helped that we could travel back and forth to work together. Donna proved to be a very good friend at a very bad time. And I must also tell you that our employer, AMP Special Industries, was very, very good to me, always very supportive. The Human Resources people couldn't do enough for me. When the trial began, I took a leave of absence. Even later, if I ever needed a day off, they understood. They were great people to work for.

The assistant district attorney, the prosecutor assigned to the case, Joseph McGill, was in his ninth year of work in the DA's office. He had won five death penalty convictions before this case. The man was an absolute saint in his dealings with me. He sat down with me and pretty much told me what was going to take place. Still, I never really could have envisioned what was actually going to happen when the trial started. He explained how they would select the jury and then how the trial would proceed and about the eyewitnesses who were prepared to testify. Some of the police officers were sequestered because they were the ones who arrived at the scene when Danny was killed. I remember the first day I went to court for the actual trial and the halls were lined with people who supported Abu-Jamal, some in dreadlocks. The MOVE people were standing outside. They would sit and eat their fruit, then throw it on the ground. I remember the stench of their body odor was so bad at one point that they had to lower the air conditioner in the courtroom into the sixties to reduce the nauseating smell. It was Courtroom 253. It is a courtroom I have now spent decades visiting.

My appointed seat in the 1982 trial was in the front row on the left side. My mother usually sat next to me, then my father, next to Mrs. Faulkner, who was in her sixties, and whichever of the Faulkner brothers, Joanne Bell, and sisters-in-law were able to make it to court. Danny's brothers Pat and Kenny drove with Mrs. Faulkner each day. The whole group of us usually took up two rows. There was also space for some more of my family, my brothers or nephew, whoever showed up. Many of Danny's friends were there, including Pete Daley, Thom Hoban, Eddie McGrory, and Danny McCann.

On the defendant's side were Abu-Jamal and his lawyer, Anthony Jackson. MOVE member Pam Africa (all MOVE members adopted the surname Africa) was usually running back and forth with the Abu-Jamal team often talking with Abu-Jamal's mother, Edith, and older sister, Lydia, both of whom came to court quite a bit. Abu-Jamal himself was constantly whispering to his lawyer.

The jury was off to the left. So, as you looked on, the jury sat on the left and, in front of them, was Joe McGill, then Abu-Jamal, with Jackson and the trial judge, the Honorable Albert Sabo, straight ahead. Every seat in the courtroom was taken every day of the trial, and there was a line outside to get in. The trial lasted about three weeks, including Saturdays. Unlike what was to come, there was no celebrity factor for Abu-Jamal in the initial trial. The MOVE organization was always there, of course; Pam Africa was with Abu-Jamal a lot, talking to him, whispering back and forth all the time. I remember seeing Ramona Africa, too.

I mentioned that the preliminary hearing was presided over by Judge Ribner, but the trial judge was Judge Sabo who, contrary to the characterization by Abu-Jamal supporters, was reserved and dignified. He demanded respect in his courtroom. I remember him telling the spectator-supporters:

"If you don't want to stand when I enter the courtroom, then leave and come in after I am in the courtroom." But they refused to do that. What they did was stand up and turn their backs towards the bench, or they would just sit. Sometimes they would thrust Nazi salutes at Judge Sabo.

Other than Danny, Judge Sabo is arguably the most maligned person in this entire debacle. He was a man born of working-class stock, raised on the tough streets of the city's Northern Liberties neighborhood and educated at the Wharton School and the University of Pennsylvania Law School, one of the nation's finest law schools. He served his country in World War II and became an Under Sheriff in Philadelphia. He joined the bench in 1973, was elected to a full term in 1974, and was retained by the voters in 1983. He was a religious man, very proud of his Slovak heritage, who regularly attended St. Agnes Church. Judge Sabo was very workman-like, and not at all glib, which kept him from becoming a media darling. I think some people mistakenly believed him to be dull-witted, but anyone who spent the kind of time I did watching him manage his courtroom would assuredly say otherwise. He had a very sharp intellect and was very thoughtful. His docket was dominated by homicide cases and, consequently, he earned a reputation for being a no-nonsense judge. Judge Sabo also had a reputation for being very seldom reversed on appeal, due, I suspect, to his knowledge and understanding of criminal law.

Judge Sabo was not the kind to do lunch in one of Center City's fancy restaurants. He was known for preferring to stay in his chambers and reading the advance sheets of cases recently decided by the appellate courts. One of his clerks once told me he had a slight heart condition and his lunch was invariably cottage cheese and papaya juice, followed by a short walk around City Hall. He was on the bench early and worked a full day. He did not engage in the extracurricular activities other judges enjoyed. He was old school, nose to the grindstone. I watched him closely over a long period of time—longer than I would have liked to be sitting in his courtroom or any other courtroom. He struck me as a person who had plenty of street smarts and could smell deceit a mile away. There was a lot of that in this case. (Consider Arnold Beverly and William Singletary!) The judge was a slight man with the heart of a lion. He could not be intimidated by any lawyer; the best of them took a run at him. The reason was simple: This man knew the law.

Years later, in addition to maligning Judge Sabo, Abu-Jamal supporters would try to blame his defense counsel, Anthony Jackson, for ineffective representation. In truth, Abu-Jamal was his own worst enemy in that courtroom. He was cautioned repeatedly by Judge Sabo about impeding his own legal representation. Initially, Abu-Jamal wanted to defend himself—which was allowed until he proved too incompetent and disruptive to provide a sensible, substantive defense. Anthony Jackson was appointed by the Court, after having been interviewed and personally selected by Abu-Jamal, as his backup counsel (with his counsel fees and costs paid by the City, a common practice for defendants who elect to represent themselves).

Jury selection took seven days and was completed by June 16, 1982. I was there every day with my parents, Danny's mom, and members of both of our families. There were many disruptions during jury selection, as there would be at trial, and often they started with MOVE members. After refusing to stand and acknowledge the court, they decided that they would stand and turn their backs or leave the courtroom when Judge Sabo entered, and then come back in after he was seated, just so they would not have to show him and the system any level of respect. Initially, Abu-Jamal was insistent on representing himself, which raised concerns not only from Judge Sabo but also from the prospective jurors. One of the jurors expressed the old concern about Abu-Jamal's desire to represent himself, namely, that "one who acts as his own counsel has a fool for a client."[46] In fact, even before jury selection began, Judge Sabo had similarly warned Abu-Jamal that "if you choose not to drink at the fountain of knowledge, you do so at your own peril."[47] Another juror admitted that she was scared to death during the qualification process when Abu-Jamal questioned her. When yet another potential juror found him intimidating, Judge Sabo discontinued Abu-Jamal's questioning of the jury candidates because he thought it was in Abu-Jamal's best interest. Although Abu-Jamal took great umbrage, Anthony Jackson took control of jury selection to expedite the process, but the defendant was still his own counsel. Abu-Jamal wrote questions to be asked to prospective jurors and Jackson asked them. But

Abu-Jamal was making all the jury selection decisions. Pennsylvania law required that each prospective juror be interviewed individually in all trials that could result in imposition of the death penalty.[48] It was a slow, laborious process. In the first three days, fifty prospective jurors were interviewed and only two jurors were selected.[49] Many were dismissed "for cause" because they said they were opposed to the death penalty.

The jury selection process would later become one of the many angles the Abu-Jamal defense would pursue to overturn his conviction. One of the often repeated canards is that somehow Joe McGill had stacked the jury with whites. Among other things, this overlooks the fact that the very first person selected for the jury was a black woman from southwest Philadelphia. Abu-Jamal was still acting as his own lawyer at this point and asked the woman, "Is there anything about how I look that offends you or turns you off?" I guess that was a question about his dreadlocks. She answered, "No, you look like people to me." She was the very first person selected with McGill's approval.[50]

It would take the screening of 157 potential jurors to identify the twelve jurors, plus four alternates, who would hear the case. Of the twelve primary jurors, nine were white and eight were male. Four of the primary jurors came from northeast Philadelphia, and one each from Germantown, Roxborough, Tacony, Fairmount, west Philadelphia, Harrowgate, southwest Philadelphia, and Strawberry Mansion. Four were retired, two were unemployed, two worked as mechanics, one was a letter carrier, one a telephone lineman, one a supervisor with the federal government, and one a mail clerk. One of the jurors, an unemployed baker, attended Benjamin Franklin High School at the same time that Abu-Jamal did. Another was the head of the Philadelphia chapter of an organization of Vietnam veterans.[51] They were a very diverse jury—representing people who were white, people of color, men, women, differing professions, and from different neighborhoods.

With the jury finally seated, opening arguments were supposed to begin on June 18, 1982. They didn't, because Abu-Jamal was ejected after causing a melee. Not only was he thrown out, but so too was his brother, William Cook, and another man identified as his brother, Wayne Cook aka Ron Ali. Both of them had been seated in front of their mother when their outburst began. Remember, William Cook was the guy whose traffic stop began the sequence that culminated in Danny's murder. That day in court he shouted, "This is a fuckin' railroad."[52] Curiously, he's had nothing further to say about the case in twenty-five years, and like Abu-Jamal, did not testify at trial, nor any of the proceedings since. A brawl erupted when the sheriffs moved in to remove the brothers, and both William and Wayne were held in contempt of court.[53] When the fight broke out the sheriff's deputies tried to take them away, but they refused to leave. The next thing I knew, in a moment of sheer madness the courtroom was transformed into a scene of anarchy, complete with things flying through the air. People everywhere were hurling objects in the courtroom and I remember trying to seek refuge under a chair. There was absolute bedlam in the courtroom—screaming, fighting, and yelling. The court attendants escorted my family and the Faulkner family out of the room and downstairs to the Judge's chambers, after which they put us in a wagon with bars for the trip back to the district attorney's office. They thought it wise to put us all in one of the caged vans because, as we left the courtroom, the mob continued to threaten in passionate shrieks that they were going to "get" us.

The entire trial was punctuated by Abu-Jamal's many outbursts. He caused so much delay that Saturday sessions became necessary to move the trial along. Like a latter-day Charles Manson, Abu-Jamal was disruptive from day one and his unruly behavior caused chaos in the courtroom on multiple occasions. It would begin the moment Judge Sabo would enter the courtroom and a bailiff would announce, "All rise." Everyone except MOVE and Abu-Jamal. At least then he was quiet. Much more disruptive were his shouted outbursts directed toward Judge Sabo. On the first day, he harangued the judge for not allowing non-lawyer MOVE founder John Africa (aka Vincent Leaphart) to sit at his table and "represent him." Finally, after the entire first day was spent arguing, Judge Sabo relieved Abu-Jamal of his self-representation duties and called Anthony Jackson off the bench, a decision made after he concluded that Abu-Jamal's major intent was to disrupt the trial. Justice James T. McDermott of the state Supreme Court upheld that ruling just before opening arguments got underway, but not before Abu-Jamal would shout at McDermott, "Where are you going motherfucker?"[54] No wonder Judge Sabo warned Abu-Jamal that if he kept up his antics, he would be removed from court.[55] Abu-Jamal did not heed Judge Sabo's warnings and was subsequently thrown out of court the next day after again disrupting proceedings with verbal abuse hurled at the judge for not allowing him to have John Africa as his counsel. He's recorded as yelling, "You're afraid to have John Africa represent me. I have a right to the defense of my choice. I want John Africa to represent me."[56] However, since John Africa was not an attorney, such a request could not be honored under Pennsylvania law. Abu-Jamal was removed from the courtroom again on June 21 after he continually interrupted proceedings by insisting on being reinstated as his own counsel.[57] I think that he missed about half the trial because of behavior such as this.

Outside the courtroom, the corridors of City Hall were perpetually filled with a cacophony of shrieks, taunts, and cries of defiance. Inside and out of the courtroom, as I sought justice for Danny, I watched and lived a daily free-for-all. Despite the chaotic climate, Judge Sabo and the bailiffs were able to restore order and the trial had moments of poignancy and clarity. Most of the people who provided pre-trial eyewitness statements delivered meaningful courtroom testimony as well. The accounts elicited from the witnesses by prosecutor Joe McGill over the course of the trial intertwined and overlapped, creating a comprehensive and consistent sequence of events.

Finally things got started. Joe McGill began the presentation of the prosecution case by having me identify Danny's police hat, which he was wearing when murdered, and some of his other personal effects. My own trial testimony was limited. Joe McGill asked me just a few questions, which were primarily about the night that Danny was killed, what he was wearing when he left, and how long he was in the police department. Then Anthony Jackson got up and asked me a very odd question. He asked me if Danny owned a camera. I said he did.[58] It was very strange. After me came Danny's brother Patrick. Pat told of identifying Danny's body in the office of the medical examiner. McGill also called Robert Shoemaker, the first police officer to arrive on the scene. Shoemaker testified that when he arrived, Abu-Jamal had his hands on his chest. He said that he ordered Abu-Jamal to freeze, but that he started moving toward what the officer recognized as a revolver, and so he kicked Abu-Jamal to prevent him from shooting him. Shoemaker and his partner, James Forbes, both told of finding William Cook, who at the murder scene said, "I ain't got nothing to do with this." Forbes testified that he retrieved two guns at the scene, and that Danny's had one spent cartridge, while Abu-Jamal's had all five cartridges spent.[59]

One early, important witness was Robert Chobert, the man whose account was detailed right after the murder in the *Evening Bulletin*. He was a cab driver who had just dropped off a fare and was about two car lengths from the murder when it happened. He told the jury about Danny being shot repeatedly and falling to the ground. "I know who shot the cop, and I ain't going to forget it," he testified. He then pointed at Abu-Jamal in the courtroom and announced that the individual who shot the cop was sitting in the courtroom in a "long shirt, a tee shirt, and a beard and long natty hair . . . That's the man all right. I got no doubt," Chobert proclaimed.[60] The testimonies of Cynthia White, Michael Scanlan, and Albert Magilton supported his account. White was a prostitute then in her early twenties (remember, Thirteenth and Locust at 4:00 a.m. was not a place you'd find priests and choir boys) who also saw the murder. She testified that she saw Danny pull over William Cook's Volkswagen and that Cook then struck Danny on his right cheek. She said that Danny then spun Cook around so as to handcuff him, and then she saw a man she now identified as Abu-Jamal run toward the two of them from a parking lot across the street. When Abu-Jamal got to be about three feet from Danny, she saw him fire "once or twice" and hit Danny in the back. Then she saw Danny stagger "as if to grab for something" and then he fell, at which point Abu-Jamal fired down at him on the sidewalk.[61] She looked at Abu-Jamal in the courtroom and said, "There's no doubt, it's him."[62]

The same day Cynthia White testified, Joseph Kohn took the stand. He was a gun salesman for Pearson Sporting Goods and he said that in 1979, he sold Abu-Jamal the gun used in Danny's murder. He had with him papers with Abu-Jamal's signatures that had the serial numbers of the gun.[63] It was an emotional day, to say the least. It was also a day when I left the courtroom crying after Danny's bloodstained police shirt was admitted into evidence. To see the bloody clothing worn by Danny when he died was just too much for me. And all the while, Abu-Jamal was watching me.

As the evidence handler left the evidence table after making the identification and went back to sit down, Abu-Jamal smiled at me in a way that shocked me to the core. Abu-Jamal was in the habit of turning toward my mother and me and looking at us for long periods, sometimes grinning, sometimes not. He was positioned about fifteen feet away from where I sat. Sitting beside me, my mother would usually say, "Don't look at him" or "Stop looking at him; you're just upsetting yourself." But I couldn't help seeing him and what he was doing—he was so close.

I need to clear something up here and now. In an interview many years later, I once made the mistake of saying that Abu-Jamal smiled at me during the testimony of the ballistics expert. That was not correct. He actually did this when I first saw the horrible condition of Danny's clothes that he was wearing at the time that he died. The clothing was shown twice in court, once by the evidence handler and once by the ballistics expert. I got them confused. On June 21, it was the evidence handler who brought the clothing out of the bag and identified each piece. I remember seeing it and thinking, "Oh, my God, his bloody clothing." You could actually smell the stench of dried blood on those clothes. They had his shirt and police jacket, and the pants. I remember the nylon police jacket that he wore that night but the thing I remember most was his shirt, drenched in blood and pungent with the smell of death.

I remember Abu-Jamal turning towards me as he had before. I remember looking at him that day and starting to feel faint. My head began to ache and my heart was pounding as I watched them take Danny's clothing out of the bag. And then there was Abu-Jamal, calmly sitting with his arm over the chair, grinning at me as usual. The word "smirking" would better describe it. Despite my mother's persistent instructions not to look at him, I became so upset I had to get up and walk out or I knew I'd pass out. I got out of my chair and feebly walked towards the exit, but when I got to the back of the courtroom, I was overcome with dizziness and started to fall. I held onto the wall. I remember crying and not feeling well, and that they decided that I should go to the hospital. I don't remember what actually happened, but they did take me to Jefferson Hospital where they kept me for a while in the emergency room. My blood pressure was high. I had to remain there for about three hours and, as a result, missed part of the trial on that one day. When they finally released me, I went home.

I was certain that Abu-Jamal had smirked at me during the exhibition of Danny's bloodied police uniform but my memory was later challenged by Abu-Jamal's supporters. Years later, in 1998, Leonard Weinglass and other Abu-Jamal sympathizers took issue with my recounting in the *Washington Post* of the behavior of Abu-Jamal in their response to a report on KGO-TV in San Francisco. That TV show had not gone as they hoped; many of Team Mumia's assertions were contested and proved faulty, which really seemed to incense them. I think they thought they were going to get a free ride from the San Francisco–based station, which, instead, looked at their efforts to discredit me with a critical eye. Anyway, the bloody clothing became a focal point. They claimed that the day the clothes were shown to the jury by the ballistics expert (June 26, 1982) happened to be a day on which Abu-Jamal was thrown out of the courtroom due to unruly behavior. Therefore, they said, Abu-Jamal could not have smirked at me during the exhibition of the clothes. In their estimation, this proved that I am a liar. Unfortunately for the Abu-Jamal defenders, the bloody clothing episode which occurred on June 21, 1982 was captured in print at the time it occurred. I may have later mixed up the exact date, but a reporter saw it happen and the court record verifies that Abu-Jamal was in court that day. The *Philadelphia Inquirer*'s Marc Kaufman wrote this on June 22, 1982:

> Earlier in the day, Maureen Faulkner, the officer's widow, left the courtroom crying after her husband's blood-stained shirt was admitted as evidence.[64]

For me, the eagerness of Abu-Jamal's lawyers to question whether he was even present when the bloody clothing came into court was one of the low points—of which there were many—made by the Abu-Jamal defense. I never wavered in my conviction in what I had seen. To this day, I have a vivid recollection of the progress of the trial that I attended every day accompanied by my mother and father, who were then in their sixties. God, it was rough on them.

Each day, my parents would drive to southwest Philadelphia to pick me up. We'd get in my dad's Ford and, on our way to the courthouse, talk about what was going to happen that day, or what we thought might happen. I was always apprehensive about having to see Abu-Jamal again. That was the one thing about the trial that really unnerved me. My dad would usually park in the lot near the district attorney's office and, most of the time, we'd pick up the attorneys and all walk over to the courthouse together. We never missed a day, and we weren't alone. My brothers and other members of the family, plus Danny's mother and brothers and sister and their families, were there every day as long as their work schedules permitted.

As the trial slowly progressed, Abu-Jamal was again thrown out of the courtroom. I think he ended up missing half the trial because of his unruly behavior in court. This time it was on the day a ballistics expert (Anthony Paul) said a bullet found in Abu-Jamal came from Danny's gun, and that while the fatal bullet that struck Danny's brain could not definitely be linked to any specific weapon because it was so badly damaged, it did come from the same kind of gun wielded by Abu-Jamal, a Charter Arms–type weapon. Paul also said that the bullets fired from Abu-Jamal's gun were "plus P" bullets, which are loaded with additional gunpowder for extra velocity.[65]

Priscilla Durham worked as a security guard at Thomas Jefferson University Hospital. She added a chilling component to the aftermath of the murder. Here is an amazing footnote to Danny's murder: Durham had encountered Danny that night, prior to his death, when he had brought a seven-year-old rape victim into the emergency room for treatment.[66] That is one of the more telling and underreported aspects of the case. Here was my husband on the night he would be murdered, escorting a child—an African-American rape victim—to the same hospital where, in a few hours, he would be pronounced dead. Two hours later, Durham was still on duty in the emergency room when both Danny and Abu-Jamal were delivered after the incident. At the trial, she recounted Abu-Jamal's infamous confession: "I shot the motherfucker and I hope the motherfucker dies." She said that Abu-Jamal sounded boastful.[67] Durham reported what she had heard to hospital officials the following day. Durham also testified that when Abu-Jamal admitted killing Danny, she heard Bell respond, "If he dies, you die."[68] Bell, Danny's partner, who rushed to the hospital as the police van was taking Danny there, confirmed Abu-Jamal's emotionally charged declaration of guilt, but unlike Durham, he did not immediately report it.

There has always been controversy about the fact that Garry Bell did not immediately offer his recollection, but after the dust settled concerning the murder, he recounted: "I wanted to see who did it, who shot him. I looked at him and he looked at me. He said, 'I shot the motherfucker and I hope the motherfucker dies.' Those were his exact words to me." In response to these rants, Bell said he responded, "He shouldn't be the one that dies, you should," which is essentially what Priscilla Durham said she heard. When Garry Bell testified, he was asked in his cross-examination why he did not recollect his exchange with Abu-Jamal until two months later. He testified that he "wasn't thinking clearly" during that time, and "I watched my best friend die before my own eyes. I put it [the exchange with Abu-Jamal] in the back of my mind at the time."[69] There is something else that I think people need to know, and that is that there had also been testimony at a preliminary hearing when Abu-Jamal was still acting as his own lawyer. Thomas Gray, a police officer from the Ninth District, explained that he was in the Thomas Jefferson ER and handcuffed Abu-Jamal to a hospital gurney. As detailed by *Philadelphia Inquirer* columnist Dorothy Storck, Gray testified in response to an Abu-Jamal question: "The cop looks at the man questioning him. His face shifts slightly. The muscles around his jaw harden. 'He said . . . you said . . . "I'm glad." You said, "If you let me go, I'll kill all you cops." ' "[70]

A witness named Michael Scanlan testified to seeing William Cook strike Danny as they stood at Thirteenth and Locust after the traffic stop, and that Danny hit Cook back with a flashlight or billy club just before a man ran across the street and killed Danny. He could not say whether it was Abu-Jamal.[71] But Scanlan noted that the killer wore a striped jacket or sweater and had dreadlocks, just as Abu-Jamal did the morning he killed Danny. Another witness named Albert Magilton said he saw a man he could identify as Abu-Jamal run across the street to the spot where William Cook's car was stopped, but he then lost sight of the man and heard the shots fired.[72] Sitting in court, I thought it was like we had two pieces of film, and that if you just spliced them together, you'd have a picture of

Abu-Jamal killing Danny, just as two prior eyewitnesses (Chobert and White) had said.

At this stage, I was numb from the emotional nature of the testimony. Listening to what was being said was both mentally and physically taxing. But I thought the case was convincing. As far as I was concerned, Joe McGill had already established that three people saw Abu-Jamal do it—four if you count Magilton who temporarily looked away. The ballistics matched, and Abu-Jamal had used his own gun. Plus the confession. And now they were about to hear the grisly details of death.

Dr. Paul Hoyer, the assistant medical examiner who performed Danny's autopsy, also offered convincing evidence during his testimony that bolstered with scientific fact the observational evidence reported by the eyewitnesses. Dr. Hoyer reported that, according to his postmortem examination of Danny, external evidence of injury included a five-and-a-half-inch-wide, eight-inch-high area of focal thermal burns and mechanical injuries from unburned and partially burned powder particles centered about the entrance of the wound. According to Dr. Hoyer, this was strong evidence of a gun being within twenty inches of the target. In other words, he said that Abu-Jamal shot Danny in the head from less than two feet away. The trial testimony of Dr. Charles Tumosa, supervisor of the police crime lab, confirmed Hoyer's medical determination of a close-range shooting. Relying on findings related to the comparison of the primer lead around the bullet hole, Tumosa estimated a more specific distance of twelve inches or less between shooter and victim. In referring to the jacket that was identified as Danny's, Tumosa concluded that the primer lead residue on the back of Danny's jacket was evidence of an even closer range for that particular shot—probably around six to nine inches.

Prosecutor Joe McGill's case was strong. And he remained outstanding throughout the entire trial. He was also terrific in his demeanor with me. In the mornings before we left for court, he'd brief us about upcoming events that day. He'd give a quick review of what was on the agenda and prepare me, insofar as possible, for events that might elicit a strong emotional response, such as the day of the bloodied clothes. With his customary sensitivity, Joe would gently tell me things like, "They are going to be displaying his clothes today," or, "They are going to be talking about the ballistics and how Danny was shot." For example, the assistant medical examiner's testimony would involve discussion of the parts of Danny's body ravaged by bullets, such as how he was shot between the eyes, and that the bullet had lodged in my dear husband's brain. Joe told me that, if the assistant medical examiner was going to have to discuss such things, I should leave if I thought I could not handle it. I was grateful to Mr. McGill for the warnings, but I never left. I stayed all day, every day, except for the one when I had to go to the emergency room.

My family and Danny's were not the only ones present in Courtroom 253 on the second floor of Philadelphia's City Hall. Abu-Jamal's mother was not far from us as the case unfolded. In the beginning, when the trial first started, I sort of felt sympathy for Edith Cook, thinking about a mother whose son murdered my husband and who now had to also endure the anxieties of trial. She raised Abu-Jamal, a twin brother Wayne, their brother William, and sister Lydia. Apparently his father died when he was a young boy. My sympathies ended, however, the day Edith revealed a nasty disposition. While walking down the courthouse corridors one day, I was startled by a loud calling from down the hallway: "Make sure you search that woman!" Edith barked, "that woman" meaning me. After that, I knew she was hostile. Her son murdered my husband and now she was screaming for me to be searched! It was hard to fathom. Her demand was completely uncalled for, since we were all searched. In any event, the incident soured my impression of Edith and undermined my previous sympathies for her difficult position.

One day, I needed to leave the room during court. Outside, there were hordes of unruly people trying to get into the crowded courtroom. I was walking down the hall when one of the MOVE people spit on my leg. "That's what you deserve, you little bitch. Your husband's in the grave and that's exactly where he belongs." And, "Oh, poor widow! It's such a shame what happened to her pig husband." I could not believe what I'd heard. It was an unfortunate episode in an upside-down world; the victim had been transformed into bad guy! My first instinct was to unleash my furor and scream something back, but there really was no possible reply—no convincing—no room for reason. I strode forward while fighting back tears, looking for a place where I could be alone for a few minutes. As I quieted my mind, I thought, "God, help me! Why me? Why Danny? Our lives are shattered and now blame is being hurled atop tragedy." I didn't want anyone to know I was devastated and thus give the Abu-Jamal supporters their victory. Instead, I feigned composure and forced myself to walk calmly back to the courtroom. The fracas continued, but I was able to ignore it.

Abu-Jamal's supporters, MOVE and otherwise, taunted me every chance they got. I have to admit now that it was sometimes intimidating. There was no official help then, no Victim's Unit at the District Attorney's Office, so I had to improvise and do the best I could to keep away from confrontation. The trial did not provide security for the participants, unlike the later 1995 hearings. I remember that most of the time we tried to walk the halls together and ride the elevator in a group. I had a scare one time when everyone else got on a full elevator and the doors closed before I could get in. I took the next one, filled with MOVE people. As expected, they harassed me the entire ride. Uncomfortably wedged in this elevator surrounded by Danny haters, I felt as if I might be gobbled by spite.

I have rehashed the trial many times over the years with Joe McGill. He is always quick to point out that among the many murder cases he tried, Abu-Jamal's was far from the closest case based on the facts. Like the rest of us, he had no idea in 1982 what the trial would become. And I know that he was taken aback by Abu-Jamal's refusal to recognize our legal system, the rule of law, and the judge. McGill worked hard and successfully established that Abu-Jamal had an anti-police, anti-establishment, anti-government philosophy that accounted for his desire to murder Danny. After all, it was Abu-Jamal who was fond of saying that "political power grows out of the barrel of a gun." He disrupted the trial at least seventeen times by McGill's count. As a result of Abu-Jamal's behavior, the courtroom was very tense and his supporters were very aggressive.

Abu-Jamal's lawyer, Anthony Jackson, did the best he could with facts that did not support the innocence of his client. Of course, over time, his successors as Abu-Jamal's lawyer would attempt to throw him under the bus and blame him for the conviction. But it was different back at the time of trial. Consider this: Immediately after the jury verdict, upon watching her son proclaimed guilty of murdering a Philadelphia policeman, Edith Cook said, "I think Tony Jackson is an excellent attorney."[73] Again, Edith

Cook is Abu-Jamal's mother. Jackson's problem was that the facts were not on his side. By the time he opened his case, three eyewitnesses had testified to having seen Abu-Jamal run across the street after his brother's car was stopped, and shoot Danny in the back and then in the head as he lay wounded on the sidewalk. A fourth eyewitness said he was sure Abu-Jamal was the man who ran across the street toward Danny, although he was not able to see him fire the fatal shot because he looked away for an instant. Put that together with the ballistics and the confession and you have a pretty compelling case. Jackson put Dessie Hightower on the stand. Hightower did not see the murder; he just witnessed its aftermath. He said several officers hit Abu-Jamal with nightsticks. Hightower added that after the shooting, he saw a figure run from the scene. But he just wasn't credible. Joe McGill brought out the fact that the geography at the scene, the buildings, would have prevented him from seeing what he claimed. Hightower also said that Danny's gun was still in its holster when he was carried from the scene. Nobody was buying that.

Jackson also called Veronica Jones to testify. She was another prostitute close to the murder scene. She said she was drunk at the time of the shooting and high on marijuana on the day she was interviewed by police. Whereas she had earlier told police she saw two black men at the scene who walked across Locust Street and then start jogging from the spot where Danny was killed, now she changed her story and testified that she did not see two men running away from the scene of the shooting. This was a big setback for Jackson, who was no doubt counting on her saying that perhaps Danny's killer and another man had fled. Even worse for the defense, she said that she had known Danny and that he once saved her from being beaten and once from being robbed. Like I said, Jackson tried, but just didn't have the facts on his side. Michael Sokolove covered much of the trial for the *Philadelphia Daily News* and at the time wrote, "Most courtroom observers felt Jackson put up an able defense for Jamal under difficult circumstances."[74] When all else failed, he attempted to portray Abu-Jamal as a peaceful man by calling a half dozen character witnesses, including poet Sonya Sanchez. Even then, Joe McGill beat him to the punch, pointing out that Sanchez was also supportive of Joanne Chesimard, who was convicted of killing a New Jersey cop years before and was now a fugitive.

Joe McGill took one hour to give his closing argument to the jury. Anthony Jackson took about ninety minutes. I remember Joe saying to the jury, "Nobody asked Danny Faulkner if he wanted an attorney." Anthony Jackson, in his closing speech, tried to point a finger at Abu-Jamal's brother, William Cook. I was shocked. He was actually insinuating that William Cook killed Danny, not Abu-Jamal. Of course, by now all the evidence was in and neither of them had testified themselves. Jury deliberations began at noon on July 2, 1982, and at around 5:20 p.m., after considering two and a half weeks of testimony, the jury of nine men and three women announced its verdict. I remember the heightened anticipation as the foreman stood up and Judge Sabo asked him if they had a verdict. The foreman was George W. Ewalt, a telephone lineman. He gave the judge an envelope as I clenched my hands to keep from crying out. They had *unanimously* found twenty-eight-year-old Mumia Abu-Jamal guilty of first degree murder. It was at this moment that I shed tears of relief and gratitude to those good people who served in judgment, which is an immense responsibility. After the verdict was made known, I looked at the man just convicted of murdering my husband. He was initially motionless, slouched in his chair.[75]

After the proclamation of "guilty," the courtroom erupted into chaos, with a lot of screaming and yelling from Abu-Jamal's supporters. As the rage erupted, I just sat there quietly. I was able to maintain my composure. I remember Lydia, Abu-Jamal's older sister, loudly protesting the verdict: "I can't believe it. This is injustice!" At that point, we got up and left the courtroom. I tried not to show any emotion one way or the other. The sentencing hearing was yet to come and I'd been told by numerous people not to show emotion, which might prejudice the sentencing hearing. I was very careful to keep my thoughts private.

As we filed out of the courtroom, bedlam ensued. Abu-Jamal was escorted from the courtroom by the sheriff's deputies, shouting: "Long live John Africa. This system is finished."[76] MOVE member Jeannette Africa immediately started yelling at Anthony Jackson: "You're a traitor. You're going to pay for this." Jackson told her not to touch him as she bumped into him. He seemed upset by the accusations and the unwarranted treatment of his defense. "I'm disappointed. I'm hurt. But the jury has spoken and there's nothing more to say."[77] Assistant District Attorney McGill noted calmly: "I'm especially proud of the courage of the jury. To stand up to the shouting and the antics that have gone on in this courtroom takes something special."[78]

Sentencing came a day later, on July 3, 1982, marking the first and only time that Abu-Jamal would claim innocence in the death of Danny but without offering any explanation of the events surrounding the murder. In other words, he did not offer an account of what happened on December 9, 1981. After the jury verdict on guilt, but before the jury made a decision as to life or death, there was a brief sentencing hearing. In speaking as a witness on his own behalf, Abu-Jamal delivered a bitter and defiant statement to the jury, accusing the police of "trying to execute me in the street." Abu-Jamal continued, "This trial is a result of their failure to do so. I am innocent of these charges that I have been tried for and convicted of. And despite the connivance of Sabo, McGill and Jackson to deny me my so-called right to represent myself . . . I am still innocent of these charges."[79]

"I am still innocent of these charges." Those would be the only words Mumia Abu-Jamal would utter under oath about his role in connection with Danny's death. Never, in twenty-five years and despite a worldwide campaign on his behalf, has he offered an explanation of what occurred on December 9, 1981. More than a few legal observers have noted that even Abu-Jamal's proclamation of innocence is not what it appears on the surface: Perhaps when he says he is innocent of the charges on which he was tried and convicted, he is taking the position that, while he did indeed take Danny's life, he is guilty of something less than murder in the first degree.

After Abu-Jamal was finished delivering his statement during the sentencing phase of the trial, prosecutor Joe McGill finally had the opportunity to cross-examine him. There was then a tense discussion between the two, with Abu-Jamal sitting at the bar and McGill standing a few feet away near the witness stand. The exchange focused on Abu-Jamal's courtroom behavior and his past. "Why don't you stand when Judge Sabo comes into the courtroom?" "Because Judge Sabo deserves no honors from me," Abu-Jamal said. "This courtroom is run on force, not honor. He is an executioner, a hangman." McGill brought out the fact that Abu-Jamal was third in command of the Philadelphia Black Panther Party in 1970, and asked him in reference to an article Abu-Jamal had written for the Black Panther

Party, "Did you ever say that political power grows out of the barrel of a gun?" Abu-Jamal replied: "That's a quote from Mao Tse-Tung. It's America that seized the land from the Indian race and it was not done through preaching Christianity, or civilization. I think America has proven that quote to be the truth." And so it went for about fifteen minutes with Abu-Jamal demanding to read the entire article in question out loud, which McGill did not object to and which demonstrated the hostility between the police and the Panther party. When it ended, Abu-Jamal declined to call any other witness to testify about "mitigating circumstances" and mentioned not a word about his wife and the five children he "has claimed responsibility for." I was surprised, but he did not ask anyone from the local Association of Black Journalists to speak on his behalf.[80]

Abu-Jamal was sentenced to death on July 3, 1982, a Saturday, in the middle of the July Fourth weekend, by the same jury that one day before had found him guilty of murder in the first degree. It took them under four hours to decide his fate. Unlike the previous day, the scene was less emotional. A few police officers stood around clenching their hands. Justice served could not bring back my husband, but I was relieved. Judge Sabo talked about how Abu-Jamal would be put into the electric chair. At the time, I think they even said something about an electric current going through his body, something like that. When they gave him death, I remember Abu-Jamal just sitting there impassively. As I stared at him, unexpected tears started to stream down my face. I found myself crying at the futility of the senseless deadly crime and all its victims. There was, as usual, a lot of commotion going on in the courtroom. I remember some woman standing up in the back of the courtroom saying "Happy Birthday, America." She started singing "God Bless America." For some reason, her haunting hymn has always remained etched in my memory.

Abu-Jamal left the courtroom shouting: "On the MOVE, long live John Africa!" At that point, I thought my days in the courtroom were over and that the nightmare was drawing to a close. Afterwards, all our friends and family went to the Irish Pub on Walnut Street, on the second floor, where we gathered together to remember Danny and had sandwiches and talked about the trial. The *Philadelphia Inquirer* quoted me as follows: "I'd just like to thank the jury for being so courageous. At least I'll be able to sleep again at night. But nothing—not the conviction or the penalty—will bring back Danny."[81] I wasn't the only one quoted that day. Danny's brother Kenny told the *Inquirer*, "Thank God that Danny shot him, got a bullet in him so he couldn't run away, or else we'd never have gotten him at all. This verdict was important to the city of Philadelphia and to the 7,500 police officers in the city." Garry Bell, Danny's friend and partner, was also quoted. His words remain, unfortunately, the most prophetic: "This man will have appeals and appeals, and I really don't think he'll ever be electrocuted."[82]

Months later, at the formal sentencing that was held on May 25, 1983, Judge Sabo affirmed the will of the jury. Moments later, Abu-Jamal shouted at Judge Sabo, "Judge, you have just sentenced yourself to die. You have just convicted yourself and sentenced yourself to death. Long live John Africa." Also during the formal sentencing, Abu-Jamal referred to his defense attorney as "a baboon, a shyster."[83]

Looking back, I'm grateful that, in death, Danny was afforded the best of Philadelphia's legal talent. I know that Assistant District Attorney Joseph McGill was top shelf at trial. So too, have been Hugh J. Burns Jr. and the other appellate lawyers who have been keepers of the flame; Arlene Fisk and Joey Grant are two deserving of special mention for their in-court action. Ron Eisenberg, too, is due my thanks for his skillful behind-the-scenes efforts running the DA's appellate unit. I am forever indebted to two Philadelphia District Attorneys—Ed Rendell, now governor of Pennsylvania, on whose watch the murder occurred, and Lynne Abraham, who has defended Danny's memory against a decades-long appellate charade. Ed Rendell and Lynne Abraham have never wavered in their support of Danny Faulkner in the face of some very ugly criticism leveled at them at times by the Mumidiots.[84]

7

DANNY AND ME

I was born Maureen Foley on October 29, 1956, and raised in a typical Philadelphia row house in the Juniata Park section of the city. "Typical" is a lovely word when it means that particular place and time. The youngest of five children, I grew up in a traditional Irish-Catholic family. Holy Innocents Elementary and Little Flower Catholic Girls High were my schools. I graduated in 1975. My dad, Jim Foley, was a plant supervisor for more than forty years for Philco Ford. My mom ran the house. It was a wonderful young life I knew.

We lived around the corner from my elementary school. I was very much involved in sports—you name it, I played it. I loved basketball, softball, and riding my bike around. You could say I was a tomboy, I guess. We lived in an area where you could get on your bike at eight in the morning, tell your folks you'd be home for dinner, and nobody had to worry about you all day long. In the winter we'd sled and, in the summer, my brother Michael was into horses. He taught me how to ride horseback at a young age. We had a place in Sea Isle City, New Jersey, where we used to go and spend our summers. The day after we'd get out of school, Mom would pile us into the car and we'd head to the beach and stay there practically all summer. Then, the day before school started, we'd come home.

My brothers and I were raised very strict Catholics. Every Sunday, our normal routine was to attend Mass at Holy Innocents, come home and have a big breakfast together. My mother was family focused and created a loving, if somewhat regimented, structure in the house, with plenty of rules and regulations. Weekdays, we went to school and then we would sit around the dining table and do homework together during the evening, followed by dinner. During the week, there was no TV. After dinner, it was baths and off to bed. The weekends were more relaxed, but not much. Only then did the TV get turned on. Sunday was our Walt Disney night. Every week, my dad would walk to the corner store and get ice cream and, at 7:00 p.m., we'd sit and watch Walt Disney. I know it sounds a little hokey, but it wasn't. Looking back, I wouldn't trade my nights of *Peter Pan* and mint chocolate chip ice cream for anything.

My dad, a WWII veteran, was a quiet man who was loved by many people. Although somewhat reserved, he was also the sort of guy who, if he got mad, nobody would get in his way. If he confronted us in times of seriousness, we kids knew to straighten up because when Dad got mad, we were in trouble. He was gentle at heart and would never hit us, or anything like that, but he demanded respect, which we were happy to offer him. My mother was the real day-to-day disciplinarian.

After graduation from high school in 1975, I went to work in the accounting department of Westinghouse Electric and later moved to their computer department. I was in accounts payable and handled pricing problems for customers and did some light typing and a little filing. Three years later, I moved to AMP Special Industries in suburban Berwyn, where I was an accounts receivable clerk. My responsibilities were varied and ranged from handling payment-related problems to processing checks for payment. I also did credit inquiries for corporations. I often ran TRW searches and set credit limits for commercial accounts. The work was a bit predictable, but the people were extremely nice. They were incredibly kind to me when Danny was murdered. Their patience and understanding with me is something I will never forget.

As you can imagine, growing up in the Foley household, I didn't date much. Then came a time when my parents started to spend a couple months a year outside the city. They'd go to a big estate in Valley Forge, the Butt Estate, where they were caretakers, and I would go with them. They finally moved to Valley Forge and it was while living there, at age twenty-one, that I had my first real dating experience. I had always wanted to fly and being a pilot seemed within my abilities at the time. I began flying lessons at the small airport in nearby West Chester where I met a flight instructor named Ed who I dated for a couple of years. Ed would sometimes fly to different parts of the state and occasionally would fail to show up when we had a date. Ed showed up at the house one day after one of these episodes of dating truancy and my brother Lawrence told me that I could not leave the house. Lawrence walked outside and had a few words with him. I'm not sure exactly what was said, but I never heard from Ed again. That's the way my brothers took care of things. I was always the little sister.

My lifetime love of the Jersey Shore led me to Danny Faulkner. After I ended my relationship with Ed, my girlfriend Joan Gluch invited me to go with her to Avalon for a weekend. Joan, Lynn Gavin, and I headed to the Shore together and went out on a friend's boat for hours. With the sun beating intensely in the early afternoon and reflecting off the water, and without the proper protection, all of us were treated to vicious early-season sunburn. I mean, we were really sick! But, before we left for home that Sunday night, we decided to go to Jack's Place, one of our favorite haunts in Avalon. How well I remember the date! It was June 10, 1979.

I had on a halter top, which revealed a very red back. We were standing in line getting roast beef sandwiches and somebody behind me said, "Excuse me, do you have any idea how sunburned your back is?" I turned around and saw a guy with beautiful blue eyes looking down at me. Oh my gosh. My heart skipped a beat as Danny said, "How about if I run down the street and get you a little Solarcaine to spray on your back." I told him no, that I was OK. Of course, it was a pickup line. My friends and I got our sandwiches and, with beef and beer in hand, surveyed the room for a place to sit. Danny, Garry Bell, and Billy Dorsch were there together that day and asked us to sit at the table with them. Of course we did. From that day, Joan Gluch started dating Garry Bell, Lynn Gavin dated Billy Dorsch, and I dated Danny. Their relationships didn't last. Mine did.

I remember us sitting around a table at Jack's and talking about the trivial and mundane happenings of the day. All the while, I snuck furtive glances at Danny, giddy about how much I liked my newest prospect. Danny was very funny and personable, and I remember laughing a lot that night. But more than anything else, I think I fell in love with his beautiful blue eyes. On that June day, I was twenty-two; Danny Faulkner was twenty-three. He had been a police officer for just two years and was working in the Sixth District with Garry Bell.

Danny was no stranger to Avalon or Jack's Place. He and his buddies on the force found in Avalon their summer paradise in the late 1970s into the early '80s. This is where Danny met some of his closest friends. Ed Mc-Grory still tells me the story about how he met Danny at their summer digs on Twenty-second Street and First Avenue. "We automatically hit it off the day we met in Avalon. We ended up playing cards all night," recalls Ed.

Jack's Place was like another home to Danny and his buddies. Mike "Bean" McCullough told me how they all had Jack's Place T-shirts in hopes they would be confused for employees and not have to pay the cover at the bar. Dan McCann remembers fondly the Sunday afternoon talent shows at Jack's. "The House of the Rising Sun," Dan recalls with a laugh. Danny's friends all tell me of the countless Sunday talent shows spent listening to Danny bellow out the chorus of his favorite song.

The mere mention of "House of the Rising Sun" still causes Michael Petrucci, another of Danny's cop buddies, to offer another story. In the Sixth District where they worked together, it was almost a regular routine after working the 4:00 p.m.–midnight shift to end up at a watering hole called Joe's Bar at Eleventh and Race Streets. That was just two blocks from the district. The owner, whose name was actually John, was what they called "cop friendly." He had one of those clocks that never seemed to have a closing time on it and it was not uncommon for patrons, including Michael and Danny, to leave into the morning sun. On one of their more memorable outings, Michael has a clear picture in his mind of Danny holding a microphone for a prop, while the jukebox blasted "Sun." Danny was in rare form that night and Michael tells me that to this day, when he hears the song he thinks of Danny. Anyone who actually listens to the song can attest that the words are not easy to conquer—Michael claims to have done just that, and credits Danny.

"Bean" told me this story about a trip back from Avalon late one night:

> Danny was always a responsible driver. When he was tired, he would pull over to the side of the road and get some rest. This backfired when we went down the Shore to look at rentals for the coming summer. There were five of us with Danny on this particular trip. Danny, becoming tired, pulled off the road and fell asleep. Unfortunately, he had pulled into a bank drive-in lane. Sometime around 6:00 a.m., I awoke to find the car surrounded by four cops pointing shotguns at Danny's car, not a

pleasant feeling since I was the first one to wake up. The cops must have thought we were going to rob the place. Knowing it was time to play the cop card, I immediately woke Danny to hopefully resolve the situation. Danny came through, proudly announcing he was a Philly cop and had merely stopped to rest rather than to drive on recklessly tired.

Danny's adventurous spirit never failed to result in a good story. Danny McCann and Thom Hoban still remember Danny as the "camp counselor." "On Sunday mornings, Danny would try to get people up for a softball game even after a late Saturday night," Thom reminisced with me. And Dan McCann adds, "He would walk around the house with that army bag, giving us wake-up calls before our Sunday game."

Thom Hoban lit up as he told me about his favorite memory of his Avalon days with Danny. "It was Labor Day weekend, 1981. We had sun, softball, kegs of beer, champagne, and a double-header of softball. It was the best day of the whole summer." That was Danny's last summer with the gang in Avalon.

I'll tell you something that I don't believe has ever been printed about Danny: He was married before he met me. Briefly, to a woman named Daisy. He didn't talk about her much; I believe the marriage lasted under two years and I really don't know a great deal as to why it didn't work out. He told me about it early on in our relationship and it was of little or no consequence to me.

Danny and I dated for about a year after that first meeting at Jack's. That very day we had decided we would meet there again the following weekend. Danny and I started dating after that. At one point in the summer, I went to Georgia to visit my brother and sister-in-law and, when I came back the following week, Danny was at Jack's Place talking with someone else—a female someone else! I remember going to Jack's Place and looking for him to give him a kiss and Danny drawing away and complaining that he just had root canal work. He didn't fool me with that line and I was confused until I spotted his companions.

Later in the evening, he left the someone-else standing there as he walked over to me and said, "Look, I thought you were still away on vacation." By then, we had only gone out a couple of times and weren't yet a long-term item. He said, "I'm sorry, I have a friend with me but I will stop over to see you tomorrow." I turned to him and said, "If you want to come see me, you put her on a bus home." You know what, the next day he came to see me! There was no way I was going to answer that door; I wouldn't go near him. He came back again the following week and I told him plainly, "If you want to date me, that is fine with me, but you're not going to play games because I won't put up with it." We dated from then until November of 1980, when we were married, about a month after Danny completed a career development program in basic supervision at the Police Academy.

Danny and I were married on November 8, 1980, at the Butt Estate in Valley Forge, Pennsylvania. On our wedding day, we vowed always to kiss each other good-bye. Danny said it made him feel happy to kiss me before leaving to start his day. We always kept that vow until his last kiss. We invited 125 friends and family to the wedding. Danny's best man was Hugh Gallagher; my maid-of-honor was Joan Gluch, who had been with me when I first met Danny. Joan was a friend since first grade. There wasn't room for many friends at the reception at the Kimberton Inn because most of the tables were taken up by our large families. Our honeymoon in San Francisco and Hawaii is etched in my memory forever.

After Danny and I got married, we lived in the same neighborhood and right around the corner from the rest of the Faulkner family. Danny and I could always stop by, and Trish, our sister-in-law, would have something cooking. If you walked in, you couldn't leave without having a meal first. Trish Faulkner, Mary Faulkner, and I were really close and would often have tea together. Trish was like a big sister to me, as she still is today. Sundays were all special days, especially during football season. A Sunday in the fall meant church, football, and dinner, all with family. Friends were always welcome, but with the Faulkners, it was all about family.

I moved into Danny's house. He was earning about $900 per month as the low man on the totem pole in the police department but he loved being a patrolman. My hope of becoming a commercial pilot had been shelved because of the after effects of a major back surgery and, frankly, higher priorities. Our plan was that I would continue to work at AMP, as I really enjoyed it and had moved up in a couple of different departments in the company. I wanted to go back to school and eventually start a family. We both wanted to have children, several of them. When Hugh Gallagher had his first daughter, Kelly, Danny was the godfather; after that, we started to seriously talk about having a baby. But Danny thought we should wait a couple of years until we had a little money in the bank. The first year we were married, we managed to save a couple thousand dollars that would be the down payment on a property.

My parents loved Danny dearly. They just adored him and we were all very close. In the fall of 1981, Danny went out and bought my mother a pair of diamond earrings and, for some reason, he gave them to her right away. He had intended to give them to her at Christmas, which he never lived to see, but he decided to give them to her on her birthday, October 18, instead. I'm glad he got to do that before he died.

Danny's upbringing was similar to my own. Both of Danny's parents were born in the United States to parents of Irish heritage. His father, Thomas, worked as a trolley driver and died of heart and liver ailments when Danny was only ten years old. (He died on Danny's brother Larry's birthday and Larry never again would recognize the day.) His mother, Mary, was widowed at a young age and left with seven children to raise: Thomas Jr., Joseph, Joanne, Lawrence, Patrick, Kenny, and Danny. Because Danny was the youngest, everyone heaped attention upon him. Tommy, Danny's oldest brother, and his wife, Trish, lived around the corner when he was growing up and were particularly close to Danny. His mom worked several jobs at a time, sometimes as a waitress, and brought up her seven children pretty much alone. In fact, her mother, Danny's maternal grandmother, had died at a young age and Mary raised that family, too.

In Philadelphia, people like to use the expression: "good people." Well, if you are wondering what it means, the Faulkners are a great example. They went to church. They loved one another and looked out for one another. They worked hard. Nothing was handed to them. They stayed out of other people's business and kept within the law. They were "good people." Tommy was a cop for five years but was injured. He ended up working for a private security firm. Joseph worked for a cement company and battled many physical problems during his life. In fact, Joe was on a kidney dialysis machine when Danny was killed, and, when his mother received the telephone call that jolted her awake that night, her first thought was that something had happened to Joe. Joanne was a waitress. Lawrence was a bartender. Patrick has spent forty years working for Acme, the supermarket. Kenny worked a variety of jobs, including bartender. Perhaps the most painful part of this entire story is that while all of Danny's siblings were alive at the time of his tragic death, now only Larry and Pat remain. My parents are gone. Mrs. Faulkner is gone. And so are four of Danny's siblings. Abu-Jamal, the heartless executioner, has outlived them all.

When Danny Faulkner was growing up in the city of Philadelphia, it was a place where you still identified yourself by your Catholic parish. In his case, he was proud to say Most Blessed Sacrament located at Fifty-sixth Street and Chester Avenue, then the largest parish in the United States. His first address was at 1219 South Wilton Street, a modest home where the brothers doubled up. Later, the family moved to 6113 Glenmore in St. Barnabas Parish. Both neighborhoods were Irish, blue-collar, middle-class. He attended Most Blessed Sacrament Elementary School and attended West Catholic Boys High School and John Bartram High School. He went into the army from 1972 to 1974, was Honorably Discharged and recognized for having received a National Defense Service Medal. He also received a sharp-shooting award for his rifle shooting. He ultimately received his GED on September 23, 1974, before beginning work on an associate's degree. He worked briefly as a prison guard in Delaware County before deciding to join the Philadelphia Police Department, where he was appointed to the Academy in May of 1976.

His first assignment was in the Twenty-third District at Seventeenth and Montgomery in north Philadelphia, where he worked with his close friend Hugh Gallagher. Danny received numerous commendations. He remained in this district for a few years before being transferred to the Sixth District based at Eleventh and Winter Streets. The new territory encompassed Center City Philadelphia, which represented quite a change from where he had been, in north-central.

I have to tell you a funny story about Danny's police work. In the summer of 1980, a photograph of him in uniform was in the *Philadelphia*

Inquirer. We never let him forget it. He was photographed while on duty at a beauty contest! It was sponsored by a short-lived Philadelphia newspaper called the *Philadelphia Journal.* Feminists tried to stop the pageant but, in the end, the show went on, at JFK Plaza, next to City Hall. There were about one thousand men on hand ogling a group of shapely contestants and, the next day, Clark DeLeon wrote one of his funny columns about it in the *Inquirer.* There is a hysterical picture on top of the column showing the back of a woman's thigh and, in the foreground, a Philadelphia police officer with his arms folded and left hand on his face in a serious and attentive pose. "He was listening to his ear piece," Bill Dorsch jokingly tells me. There were no earpieces being used in the summer of 1980! Well, he wasn't identified in the story or under the picture, but it was Danny! Actually, it is a great picture of Danny and it captured his very funny personality.

Not that his police work was a laughing matter to him. In fact, I am proud to possess a few of the commendations he earned while on the job. For example, on November 3, 1976, he was given a Commendation of Merit as a result of his "aggressive patrol procedures," which resulted in the arrest at Berks and Gratz Streets of Myron Cherry who, ten minutes earlier, had robbed people inside a grocery store at 1800 West Montgomery Avenue. He received another Commendatory Letter noting that on December 11, 1976, "as a result of your alert and aggressive patrol procedures, you and Officer Snow apprehended the defendant Earl Johnson at Myrtlewood and Master Streets. He had, accompanied by three other men, robbed the complainant, an elderly man, as he crossed the intersection of Hollywood and Thompson Streets at 6:40 a.m." He was given a Citation of Merit for his work on August 26, 1978, for having "pursued and apprehended the defendant, Michael Jones, as he and an accomplice fled the scene of a robbery that they had perpetrated against an elderly man at Thirtieth Street and Girard Avenue." On November 5, 1979, Danny earned a Commendation for Merit as a result of having been on patrol: "You were informed by a witness that a robbery was in progress on the subway platform at Broad Street and Girard Avenue. You immediately proceeded to the location and apprehended two suspects trying to flee the scene. You also searched the area and found a revolver, which was taken from the complainant. The defendants were charged with Robbery, Theft and other related offenses. Action such as this on your part reflects credit on the entire Police Department. Notation of this commendation will appear on your official record." And, on April 8, 1980, he received a Commendatory Letter for having "observed three males exiting the store at 1001 Chestnut Street after the building had been closed. Spotting you, the suspects tried to flee the scene. You alighted from your vehicle and apprehended the three males. The defendants were later charged with Burglary, Theft and other related offenses."

There is another document related to Danny's police work that I treasure. After Danny's murder, I received a letter from David F. Michelman, an assistant district attorney. He wrote to me:

> I only worked with Dan once, but I immediately came to like and admire him. I worked with him on his first big case, involving a frail eighty-year-old man who was beaten to death by two men who broke into his home to rob him. Dan almost managed to arrest them both himself but had to stop chasing one in order to help and protect his partner, a woman, who had been knocked down by the other one. Dan's identification of these two men, who both had long criminal records for violent crimes, caused them to be convicted and sent away for a long jail sentence. One of these men was so brutal and vicious that his mother almost asked the Judge to send her son to jail to protect her and the rest of the family from him. Because of the devoted, thorough and professional manner in which Dan did his job as a police officer, many other people who never had a chance to meet him personally have lived safer lives. I know how important this goal was to Dan and that he believed that it was worth the price that he paid to try to accomplish it.

Danny was revered by his friends as a good cop. Ed Kelly tells me about his compassion as he actively looked after the elderly residents in the Sixth District: "He was aggressive too. Danny was always the first to race in and get the guy—we called him 'Flash.'"

Danny was not content to be the cop on the beat. He was the driven type who wanted to be commissioner. Danny attended Philadelphia Community College and took courses in Criminal Justice to further his career. Danny was a goal-oriented person. The best proof of that comes from Dan

Sobolewski, who tells a pretty insightful story about his last conversation with Danny. It was just twenty minutes before Danny was murdered, and the two cop friends were parked in their police cars, side by side: "We talked about playing ball, the job, and Danny's craving for a Nick's roast beef sandwich. Sitting there in his patrol car, Danny had his books with him; he was studying for the Sergeant's test." Danny was always focused on his objectives. In his early twenties, he purchased his own home in southwest Philadelphia, close to his family. When I met him in 1979, he was trying to get ahead in life. He was very intelligent; straight-A-super-smart, really. I think he was bored with school, to be honest with you, and just wanted to get moving in the world. Danny was a street-smart man. No one was going to fool him, whether it was in his initial job as a prison guard or when he joined the police department.

Danny was also compassionate. When Jerry Lewis would run his annual telethon for Muscular Dystrophy, Danny supported it by running marathon softball games at the Regent Playground. Danny would work tirelessly for those three-day weekends, giving fifty to sixty hours of his time to raise money for kids afflicted with Muscular Dystrophy. He would get all his buddies to support him.

Which reminds me that Danny's family and friends all agree that Danny was a real character growing up, which doesn't surprise me because that is the Danny I knew and loved. He was usually the focal point of a conversation. Gregarious. Inviting. Always thinking. And always hustling. Danny was a worker. In his neighborhood, growing up, he worked at a local corner market called Nick's. By his mid-teens, he would practically run the place. Pat Faulkner fondly remembers that, when Danny was only sixteen, before he had access to a car, he bought tickets to an Elvis concert for him and his girlfriend, and they took the trolley to the show. That sounds like Danny.

Danny was a little over six feet tall. He weighed about two hundred pounds and kept himself in shape. Bill Dorsch recalls Danny's competitive edge. Having heard that Bill would sometimes ride his bike all the way to the Shore, Danny just had to try it too. "I gave him a bike to ride to the job, but he had to compete [with me]. He made it [to Avalon] in six hours." It was always an adventure with Danny. He loved that bike and was a devoted rider long before it caught on and became a fad. He liked to play poker with his friends and used to have great games for hours at a time at our house. Danny's competitive side, however, would sometimes land him in trouble. Jude McKenna was quick to tell me about a memorable afternoon in the Barefoot Bar at the Jersey Shore. The guys decided to hold an eight-ball tournament and Jude was partnered with Danny.

Jude explained: "After we played several games, beating all challengers, Danny stood on the footrest at the bottom of the bar and raised both hands in the air, proclaiming victory. Well, having been there as long as we were, Danny started to lose his balance and reached for something to steady himself. The only thing close was a large Slushy container. He reached out, grabbed the Slushy machine, fell backwards and spilled it all over himself. Needless to say, we were asked to leave. We had a blast!"

Another passion of Danny's was deer hunting. He and Hugh Gallagher went to Sullivan County during deer season every year. He loved to travel and delighted in planning our trips to places we hadn't been before. He had planned a cruise for us in the spring of 1982, with several other couples who were good friends, but we never made it.

I'll tell you something else nice about Danny. He attracted many kinds of friends. Some were cops like him, but people of all backgrounds and personalities gravitated to him—accountants, attorneys, guys who sold insurance. He was very close to a couple of his cousins who were investment advisors. I already said that Thom Hoban and Dan McCann called him the camp counselor; well, I called him the "social director." He was always organizing something—a softball game, basketball game, fishing, or crabbing trip, anything that would bring his friends together.

He was just a happy-go-lucky guy. He liked to sing. He sang in the shower all the time and liked to get up on the stage at Jack's Place. He had a pretty good voice. He was an entertainer; he liked being around people. He enjoyed having get-togethers at our house and was a great cook, much better at it than I. He was very kind. My perception is that Danny was a very good, very caring police officer, a fact proven to me the night of his funeral when a gentleman came up to me to talk about my husband. He was terribly upset and actually sobbed as he told me that he had no family and that Danny was one of the few friends he did have. He owned a hot dog stand in Center City and Danny would always stop and ask him how he was doing. "He talked to me and seemed to really care about me." That didn't surprise me—that's the type of person Danny was.

Danny also had a keen interest in current affairs. He was a smart and ambitious young man who was very aware of the world around him. As I mentioned before, Danny went to community college night school while in the police department. What's interesting is, a couple months before he was killed, he wrote a paper about capital punishment. It is pure fiction about a young girl who was brutally beaten and raped and, when the case got into court, the guy was acquitted. After his acquittal, her father was so incensed by the outcome that he shot and killed the suspect. The gist of the paper centered on whether the father would be charged with murder for shooting the alleged perpetrator or be judged temporarily insane because he just went crazy over his daughter being the victim of a brutal crime committed by a man who was subsequently acquitted. He went into the whole capital punishment situation, which he thought was ultimately just. He believed that when someone decided to take a life, that person deserved to lose his own life.

I told you that Danny loved being a cop and wanted to further his career in the police department. He also thought of becoming an attorney, maybe even working out of the District Attorney's Office. He wanted to do something worthwhile, to "amount to something," as our mothers used to say. He took courses in Criminal Justice. He might have stayed a police officer, but I think that working in the District Attorney's Office was really what he wanted to do.

Life in 1980 and 1981 was simple and happy. We got along very well. During the summer of 1981, Danny and I spent some quality time in the Pocono Mountains and as many weekends as possible "down the Shore," as Philadelphians like to say, in Avalon, New Jersey. Our social circle was composed usually of Garry Bell (Danny's partner), Pete Daley, Danny Sobolewski, Danny and Carol McCann, Billy Dorsch, and Eddie McGrory. Joan Gluch was always there, too. There was a whole crowd of us that were always getting together and doing things. We went to dinner, played softball, went to the beach—all those fun, summer-down-the-Shore things people do. Danny and Garry were very close friends as well as partners, so we saw each other outside of the police department. Working a wagon together or cruising in patrol cars was their usual duty.

All told, Danny and I were married just fourteen months. After Danny's passing, I did the calculation about how many days we'd known each other and how many we'd been married: way too few. At first it was only my mother who was concerned about my marrying a police officer. I remember her saying to me, "You know, he is out protecting the public," or, "What would you do if anything ever happened to him?" I always assured her, "Oh mom, he'll be fine." I believed it. My biggest concern was the odd hours he had to work, the different shifts that kept us apart.

Then, a friend of Danny's was hurt on the job and it began to hit home that something could possibly happen to him. One day, I got a telephone call from Danny reporting that Pete Daley had been badly injured and taken to Guiffre Medical Center (St. Lukes) at Eighth and Girard. Danny came home and picked me up. He said, "We have to go and see Pete." I protested, "We can't—we won't be able to see him until he's stable, there's still too much going on." I knew he was in surgery and we couldn't see him for quite a while. Danny said, "No, we have to go right now. We definitely have to go." We were driving down there, talking about it, and it began to dawn on me finally that being a police officer was dangerous work. I remember telling Danny, "I don't know what I would do if you were ever killed." He answered without skipping a beat, "If anything ever happens to me, life goes on. You would know I died doing what I loved most. I love being a police officer and there is nothing that is going to stop me from doing what I enjoy; it's my life." Then we arrived at the hospital and went to Pete Daley's room. When I saw Pete, I just could not believe his injuries—and that the house he had been going into was booby-trapped. I think he opened the door and it exploded. A wave of fear started to rise in me; we didn't explore that topic again after that. Danny was the type of person who didn't talk about police work. He was usually silent about his job. If you ever had met Danny, you would never have known he was a police officer.

Danny and I were never together enough. The last week of his life, we spent as much time together as work allowed. My day started at 7:00 in the morning so I could be at work by 8:30, while he worked rotating shifts, most of the time from midnight to 8:00 a.m. There seemed to be no reason to rush Christmas—the Earth had circled the sun one time since we married and was preparing for another turn. Our world was traveling along just as it should, pretty much according to plan, and we saw no need to speed it up. No one could have known that our world was about to end and Christmas would never come.

The weekend before Danny died, we went out and got a Christmas tree but never put it in the house. It just sat on the front patio and became an unadorned reminder of special times that would never be. We did some Christmas shopping downtown at John Wanamaker's, where we picked up a few things, and we got in some early holiday grocery shopping. Danny brought some of the Christmas stuff out of the basement because we were thinking about starting to decorate the tree. But we never got that far, just brought up the boxes of decorations that weekend. He had just come back from deer hunting with Hugh Gallagher in Sullivan County and they had hardly unpacked and gotten back to their post-vacation schedules. He was happy and full of stories. I was happy because he was happy. Although common wisdom says that if something is too good to be true, it probably is, this didn't apply to Danny and me. Our life together was better than we ever thought it could be—until it came to its abrupt and unfathomable end.

Of course, no remembrances of Danny from me or his buddies would be complete without the words of Garry Bell, his partner. Garry's a private guy who likes to keep things, as they say, "close to the vest." But in 1996, he penned some thoughts about Danny at the request of Monsignor Howard of the Philadelphia Archdiocese. I think that he was a bit too shy to then read them publicly at Mass, so Sister Joanne read his thoughts aloud. Some of this you just heard from his other friends, but Garry's words are beautiful, and so I offer them here unedited:

> Daniel Faulkner was born on December 21, 1955. He attended West Catholic and John Bartram High Schools; he served his country in the United States Army from 1972 to 1974. He was appointed to the Philadelphia Police Academy in May of 1976.

I first met Danny at the Fraternal Order of Police during a Union meeting. He walked over to a group of us, introduced himself, shook everyone's hand, and a friendship was forged. Danny was a very outgoing person; he had a warm and giving personality, and would go out of his way to make you feel comfortable. His sense of humor would always bring a smile, and make you laugh. Danny was the friendliest, most fun-loving person I have ever met in my life.

Danny had a love for life. He loved being a police officer and took his job very seriously. He was aggressive and firm when he had to be, and caring and compassionate, depending upon the circumstances. He was always a professional; law enforcement was his life. He set his sights high—he dreamed one day of being police commissioner. Danny was attending Philadelphia Community College, taking courses in Criminal Justice, in order to further his career. Knowing Danny, he was destined for the top; he would not settle for anything less.

Danny loved his family, especially his many nieces and nephews. He often had them at his house, playing ball in the backyard. He looked forward to having a family of his own after he married.

Dan loved the Jersey Shore in the summertime. A large group of us would rent a house in Avalon. Throughout the summers of 1978 to 1981, we would fish, go crabbing, and barbeque every chance we had. Dan and I were out one Sunday when he met Maureen. I truly believe it was love at first sight for both of them. I know from our conversations he adored Maureen, and they married in November of 1980. I remember when Dan picked up Maureen's engagement ring at the jeweler. He came back to the Sixth District, where we were all assigned, to show everyone the ring. He had a smile on his face from ear to ear; he was so happy, proud as a peacock. The ring was a beauty. After Danny and Maureen married, they had a next-door neighbor named Jim Sheehan. Because Danny was allergic to grass, he made a deal with Jim. Jim would cut the grass at both houses in the summer, and Danny would shovel the snow for both houses in the winter—because Jim was allergic to snow!

Danny had a nickname at the Shore—we called him the "social director." He was always organizing a softball game, basketball game, fishing and crabbing trips—anything that would bring groups of people together to have fun. He always succeeded.

One of my most precious memories of Danny is that every Labor Day weekend no matter what we had planned at the Shore, he would leave all of his friends to make the trip back to his southwest Philly neighborhood to help organize a softball marathon to benefit the Muscular Dystrophy

Foundation (Jerry's Kids). Danny would work tirelessly on those three-day weekends, giving fifty to sixty volunteer hours of his time in order to raise money to help kids afflicted by MD. He did this from the generosity of his heart, without a thought of seeking recognition or reward.

This was Danny Faulkner.

8

TIME TO REBUILD

I think I hit rock bottom the summer of 1983, a year and a half after Danny's murder. It just kept getting harder and harder, worse instead of better as the event became further back in time. My routine consisted of nothing but empty time, occupied only by a grief that I could not share with anyone. The pain became unbearable, and I felt very alone.

I took a place down the Shore with our friends—some married, some single—everybody together. My friends were my support system that summer. Saturday afternoons at the beach were times of particular vulnerability. I would lie there listening to my friends making plans for the night, where they were going to go for dinner and what they were going to do afterward. It was grueling to absorb the permanence of loss and the hard fact that I wasn't part of a couple anymore. It was difficult for me to be enthused about doing things with my friends who were coupled up. I lay in the hot sun, with my sunglasses hiding my perpetual tears, thinking *Here I am, lying on this beach, odd person out, everyone talking about their date night, which used to be my date night with Danny.* I felt so far removed from those other happy young couples, knowing my next encounter with my soul mate would be in the privacy of his gravesite.

As bad as things were, one thing I thought I could count on was that Abu-Jamal had been dealt with and I would not have to have anything more to do with him. I remember that I asked a few friends if there was any kind of lawsuit I could bring to stop Abu-Jamal from making money from behind bars. Back then, we were all young and naïve, and didn't know much about the law. They said they didn't think there was, but—hey, he's on death row. He's going to be put to death. You don't have to worry about him anymore. He won't cause you any more trouble and neither will his supporters from the trial.

Then, not long after the trial, the phone calls came. Somehow, somebody got my unlisted phone number and I started to get strange telephone calls late at night. One night when the phone woke me up, I heard the caller say "Hi—Maureen?" in a somewhat pleasant voice. When I said I was Maureen, he started to whine, "It's Danny. Help me. Help me. I want to come home. Help me." A couple of times a caller said, "You're fighting for the wrong reason. Mumia Abu-Jamal is an innocent man. He did not do this." I don't know how they got my number. Sometimes Donna Dunne, a close friend from work who was living with me, would answer and they would say things to her, thinking it was me. It was suggested to me that somebody in Abu-Jamal's family worked for the telephone company, but I really do not know. The harassing phone calls thankfully didn't come too often, but when they did, they shook me to the core. It was too soon after Danny was killed.

After the trial, I had sold our house and bought a home in northeast Philadelphia, this time just a small bungalow. I wasn't at all sure what I wanted to do with myself and took a leave of absence from work to think things over. My cousin, Roseanne McGovern, worked for Trans-World Airlines (TWA) in New York and asked me to come visit her and maybe even get a job. I started at TWA and shared an apartment with her in Queens during the week, returning to my own house in Philly on the weekends. Working for the airline gave us travel privileges, which we used to the best of our advantage.

By 1984, I needed a change. When layoffs hit TWA, it was time to move. At this point, I looked west with no inkling of where the Abu-Jamal case was headed. I believed all that was behind me. I moved to just about as far from Philadelphia as I could get and still stay in the United States: golden California. Why California? I felt I just could not stay in Philadelphia. It was the same old refrain: too much pressure, too many memories. Too much of Danny would haunt my psyche as long as I stayed put. When I went into Center City, I'd be aware I was in the Sixth District where Danny was killed. If I went there for dinner or anything else, I couldn't enjoy myself. Also, many of our friends were getting married and having children. I was a widow, and widows are usually not included in social circles. Time went on and my friends and I had less and less to talk about.

And then there were the people I didn't know, people who knew the name of Daniel Faulkner because he was killed in Philadelphia. So often when I went shopping and used my credit card, people would ask if my husband was Daniel Faulkner, the murdered cop. "Are you the girl that lost her husband?" It upset me every time I heard it as I'd start remembering all over again the tragedy that had taken Danny away from me forever. I definitely needed a fresh start, preferably far away.

My brother Jim, his wife, Cathy, and their two children lived in California, where I had visited them courtesy of the airline. After the major downsizing at TWA, my cousin was transferred to Florida, and I decided to try California for a few months to see what it would be like to live there. I stayed with my brother's family the summer of 1984 and found I liked it very much. In August, I called my mother and told her I had decided I wanted to move permanently. I went home long enough to pack up my house; my brother and one of his friends drove my belongings across the country to my new town house in Southern California.

Not long after I arrived in California, my brother, sister-in-law, and I opened a small deli. I was happy that no one knew me and that my past was no longer an issue. I rarely discussed my personal life with anyone. I think a couple of people who were regulars knew my history because Jim had befriended them and told them a little. At times, someone would ask if I was single or married, and he'd say that I was a widow. But no one really discussed it and it wasn't brought up that often. It was great to be off the hook because it helped me heal. Hard work keeps you from sitting around and dwelling on your loss. I really believe that when someone loses a loved one, he or she needs to keep busy and stay occupied constantly. For me, I found it to be the best kind of therapy.

Things gradually seemed to be getting easier. Right after Danny was killed, to ease the pain, I would occasionally go to a friend's house for a drink. I would drink and cry and, in the morning, I would have to face the day all over again and feel absolutely wretched from drinking the night before. My routine every single day for months on end was to get up, go into the shower, and cry. Then get out of the shower, get dried off and dressed, and go to work at AMP. It was always the same sad sequence of events. I don't know why, but something about the shower triggered it—the water, the cleansing—it always made me cry. Since then, I have talked to a lot of police widows who said they have done the same thing; they get into the shower and cry. In retrospect, that's really the best place to do it. You're alone, away from other people; it's the perfect time to let out all the anger and sadness. You then rinse off your face and start the day. Sorrow never gets boring so you keep on doing the same thing. That routine, living that life, had to change, and I knew it.

Someone at the police department suggested that I see a psychiatrist. I went just once. As I sat and talked to him, he began to tell me his problems: how he accidentally backed into his mother-in-law and knocked her over with the car, almost killing her. I decided to forget it. I wasn't going to a psychiatrist anymore. I knew I didn't need therapy to get over what happened to Danny. He was murdered. It happened. It was tragic. No amount of therapy would change anything. I didn't need to talk to someone so far removed from the events. All I needed was time, time and that deli. I do believe that time heals people. And, at my sandwich shop, customers needed service, crusts needed cutting, and bills needed to be tabulated. My mind was kept busy and I had little time to think.

We did pretty well with the deli, but after a while we just got tired of it. We had that place from '84 until '87, then sold it because it was too much work, six days a week, morning, noon, and night.

Many Hispanic construction workers came into the deli on a daily basis and I'd talk to them about their lives. One guy told me about a place in Mexico that he said was the most beautiful place in the world. At his suggestion, I booked my flight. He was right—it was perfect. I stayed at a condo on the beach, my first taste of the solitude that I so desperately needed. I then bought what would become my little safe haven, my own condo on the beach. After we sold the deli, I lived down there on the beach, eating fish, swimming and running by the sea. I had guests every once in a while, but mostly it was a place where I could go and get my thoughts together. I lived in Mexico for months and then came back to California.

Upon my return to California, a friend of mine introduced me to a physician just out of residency who was looking for an assistant. I went to work for him and he pretty much took me under his wing. In 1988, I went to work for two physicians, Howard Mandel M.D. and Stuart Fischbein M.D. who had done their residency at Cedars Sinai Hospital and are now in private practice. I learned more from them and I also went back to school to learn medical technology. In 1996, Dr. Fischbein and I opened a new practice with two certified nurse midwives. A second office followed in 1997. I managed both offices until 2007, when I left to work on this book.

At the beginning, I did not discuss my past with my coworkers. No one knew a thing. And for a few years I had peace and quiet as I tried to rebuild my still-young life in California.

9

THE *YALE LAW JOURNAL*

Ten years after Danny's murder, the effort to renew my life was interrupted by a sinister jolt from the past in an unlikely form: the *Yale Law Journal*. I was a decade removed from the slaying of my husband and totally unprepared for the nasty media surprises that the next few years would bring. I knew that Abu-Jamal's case was on appeal. I also knew that he had been building support behind bars amongst death penalty opponents and some pretty politically extreme groups. But I was caught off guard when in January of 1991 the *Yale Law Journal* decided to publish an article authored by Mumia Abu-Jamal entitled "Teetering on the Brink: Between Life and Death." Unbeknownst to me, Abu-Jamal had been a prodigious writer behind bars. His writing was primarily about prison life and had been published in *The Nation*. This particular essay was an examination of the life of a prisoner on death row according to the "Death Row Extraordinaire," Abu-Jamal.

In the opening paragraph of the essay, Abu-Jamal quotes Camus: "For there to be equivalence, the death penalty would have to punish a criminal who had warned his victim of the date at which he would inflict a horrible death on him and who, from that moment onward, had confined him at his mercy for months. Such a monster is not encountered in private life."[85] This was the first time that I encountered Abu-Jamal in print. I had received a telephone call from a friend of mine who heard about it and told me that Abu-Jamal had written an essay. I immediately telephoned Yale and their law school, and someone told me that the person responsible was the essays editor, named Robert Gulack. They actually gave me his home number, so I rang him there. Gulack told me that yes, Abu-Jamal did write the essay. He then made me the most remarkable offer—that if I wanted to write something, he would be more than happy to publish my work, also. I told him I wasn't asking for equal space. The point was that he was publishing the work of a murderer.

The ten pages that comprised Abu-Jamal's contribution to the law review publication were but a mere prologue to the media madness that would come in the next decade, thus marking a new season of dread in the Abu-Jamal saga. It was immediately apparent that I was not rid of the man the jury determined had murdered my husband. Was he destined to remain a part of my life until death did us part? Further fueling my fury, Abu-Jamal was receiving top billing in a credible publication without having to offer an account of what he claims not to have done on December 9, 1981. He was being cloaked in the respectability of an Ivy League school despite his refusal, by omission, to offer an explanation of his conduct on the night Danny was murdered. That seemed to be unimportant to his editors, as would be the case for the many others who would be drawn to his "cause" in the years to come. This perplexing void in the "Save Abu-Jamal" lore is one facet of Abu-Jamal's sordid tale that continues to mystify me: How could so many people give their support to a man who was convicted by a jury and who has never offered an explanation of his conduct at the time of the murder? Cast in this light, the essay was a preview of a "new and improved Abu-Jamal"—an Abu-Jamal as a positive figure despite his conviction. In the glossy pages of the *Yale Law Journal,* Abu-Jamal was welcomed, not scorned. The convicted cop killer was recast as a victim of circumstance and a pseudo-intellectual worth fighting for. In this ludicrous distortion of truth, the *Yale Law Journal* was making Abu-Jamal a martyr.

The *Journal* bestowed the mark of intellect upon Abu-Jamal despite his Slip Mahoney–like prose. Slip Mahoney was a character in the 1940s series *The Bowery Boys* whose butchery of the tongue was a recurring part of the story line. Abu-Jamal's verbiage was more precise but out of place in his short discussion about the state of the death penalty in America: "Hurled by judicial decree into this netherworld of despair, forcefully separated from relationships, overcome by the dual shame of their station and the circumstances of the crime which led them to death's door, a few succumb to the shady release of suicide."[86]

The *Yale Law Journal* essay also sounded the starting gun for a major playing of the race card, which thereafter would be a constant theme of the

Abu-Jamal defense. Consider the lengthy footnote on the first page of the essay, which offered a one-sided bio of the author:

> Mr. Abu-Jamal is an African-American on Death Row in Pennsylvania. He was sentenced to death in 1982 for the shooting and killing of a police officer. During the incident, Mr. Abu-Jamal suffered a serious gunshot wound and was badly beaten. At the time, he had no police record and was a prominent radio journalist in Philadelphia and the president of the local chapter of the Association of Black Journalists. Mr. Abu-Jamal was a member and spokesperson of the Black Panther Party in the early 1970s and has been a supporter of the MOVE organization. He has challenged his conviction and sentence on numerous grounds, including: the prosecutor's use of peremptory challenges to exclude Black jurors and the court's refusal to permit Mr. Abu-Jamal's challenge for cause of a juror who admitted uncertainty as to whether he could be open-minded; the court's permitting the prosecutor to conduct a cross-examination of a character witness about her "sympathy to cop killers"; the court's permitting the prosecutor to present Mr. Abu-Jamal's political views and controversial group associations to the jury (the ACLU and National Conference of Black Lawyers submitted an *amicus curiae* brief challenging these references on First Amendment grounds); the prosecutor's closing argument asking for the death penalty in which he told the jury that Mr. Abu-Jamal would have "appeal after appeal" and that the jury was not being "asked to kill anybody." This past summer the Partisan Defense Committee organized a series of international protests on Mr. Abu-Jamal's behalf. Over 35,000 people have signed petitions to the Governor of Pennsylvania urging clemency. Hundreds of prominent individuals have written letters on his behalf, including U.S. Representative Ron Dellums, Amnesty International Executive Director John Healey, Southern Christian Leadership Conference President Rev. Joseph Lowery and Philadelphia Union Local 1034 President Charles Valenta. The Supreme Court denied Mr. Abu-Jamal's petition for *certiorari* and, at present, he is preparing a petition for postconviction [*sic*] relief. Since his incarceration, he has written articles on legal and social issues and prison life for several newspapers and periodicals, including *The Nation.*–Ed.[87]

This warrants some comment from me. To begin with, missing in the biography, as it often would be in the years to follow, was any mention of the man murdered by Mumia Abu-Jamal, my husband, Danny Faulkner. Danny's name was never seen in print. This is another aspect of the case that has always troubled me: This has become the cause and the case of Mumia Abu-Jamal, not the matter concerning the death of Danny

Faulkner. Abu-Jamal is a household name, Danny Faulkner is not. It is almost as if Danny became a prop in Abu-Jamal's story. Then, there is the first description offered about the convicted murderer: "Mr. Abu-Jamal is an African-American on Death Row in Pennsylvania."[88] Yes, should the reader have any doubt, the *Yale Law Journal* thought it most important that you immediately know he is black! As the years went by, efforts were made to paint me as a racist. When asked, I have consistently stated that Abu-Jamal's race is inconsequential to my view of the case and that I would wish the same outcome for an assailant of any race, creed, or circumstance. Years after the Yale publication, a group called The National Association for the Advancement of White People made an unsolicited contribution to our not-for-profit in Danny's name; I immediately insisted that it be returned.

Over the years, there have been many attempts by Abu-Jamal's supporters to portray Danny as a racist rogue cop who pulled William Cook over just to beat him up. Abu-Jamal lawyer Leonard Weinglass wrote in his book that William Cook was being "brutally beaten" by Danny and the strong insinuation was that it was racially motivated. Overlooked in all this racism ballyhoo is the actual racial composition of the key players who objectively determined Abu-Jamal's fate. Two of the black eyewitnesses, Cynthia White and Veronica Jones, one of whom would be called as a defense witness, both stated that they knew Danny and that he was a good cop. Jones stated that Danny "saved" her from her pimp who was beating her. Indeed, the young rape victim Danny delivered to the emergency room on the night of his own death, the same emergency room in which he would later be pronounced dead, was black. Danny stayed a few extra minutes with her in the hospital just to make sure she felt safe. Nevertheless, the Abu-Jamal forces have argued that the District Attorney's Office, the court, and the police "orchestrated a racist frame up." This preposterous subterfuge ignores the fact that prosecutor Joe McGill selected four blacks to be on the jury when he still had five unused peremptory challenges; that the first person seated on the jury was black; that the lead investigative officer was black; that lead prosecutor at the 1995 PCRA hearing, Joey Grant, is black and that Cynthia White and Priscilla Durham, eyewitnesses to the shooting and to Abu-Jamal's hospital outburst, respectively, who voluntarily testified against him, are black. The accusers also choose to forget the two blacks on the jury who were among the twelve who unanimously convicted Abu-Jamal and sentenced him to death. "Racist" is the presumption that, had more blacks been on the jury and seen and heard the same evidence as the two blacks who *were* on the jury, they would have chosen to *not* convict him. Why would they? Simply because he is black? Abu-Jamal and his supporters (including Amnesty International) appear to be arguing that if you put enough blacks on a jury you're sure to find one, or even a few, who will turn a blind eye to the evidence and choose to acquit just because the defendant is black. What they really seek is jury nullification, and that is real racism.

In the *Yale Law Journal*, after the mention of race, came this: "He was sentenced to death in 1982 for the shooting and killing of a police officer. During the incident, Mr. Abu-Jamal suffered a serious gunshot wound and was badly beaten."[89] Stop the press. What about the fatal wound inflicted on Danny at point blank-range? And then there was this: "At the time, he had no police record and was a prominent radio journalist in Philadelphia and president of the local chapter of the Association of Black Journalists."[90] This is in stark contrast to the real facts of Abu-Jamal's life—namely, that after having been touted as a rising star, he had lost his way in life and, by 1981, was no longer in journalism. He was an out-of-work writer, struggling as a cabbie just to make ends meet. Looking back, I believe that his article in the *Yale Law Journal* represented the beginning of the campaign to make Abu-Jamal, not my husband, the victim. Abu-Jamal was quick to thank John Africa, "my loving reverence."[91] Remember, John Africa was the leader of the group MOVE, which caused the shooting death of a fifty-two-year-old Philadelphia police officer named James Ramp in August of 1978.

Let me give you a more accurate description, which should have appeared in his printed bio:

> Wesley Cook is the author of this piece. He wrote it while sitting on death row. Why is he there? Well, he had a trial in front of a jury of his peers in 1982 and they unanimously concluded that he was solely responsible for the execution-style murder of a twenty-five-year-old police officer named Daniel Faulkner. During the incident Officer

Faulkner, while defending himself, managed to fire off a gunshot that struck Abu-Jamal in the stomach. This shot would effectively tell the world who was responsible for his death. Unfortunately, the assailant lived. At the time of the murder, Abu-Jamal had squandered a once-promising future as a journalist; he was a broken-down, out-of-work radio commentator working as a taxi driver.

I made sure the *Yale Law Journal* editors heard from me and, as a result of my objection and inquiry, I received a letter dated April 3, 1991, under the signature of Robert Gulack, telling me: "The editing committees for Vol. 101 of the *Journal* ought to be selected soon. Please feel free to send your contribution to the Vol. 101 Essays Committee for consideration for publication in 1991–1992." I never submitted an essay. It seemed pointless. The damage was done. Already, with the *Yale Law Journal*'s seal of approval, Abu-Jamal's name quickly hijacked the public consciousness. The article was a huge coup for Abu-Jamal and his camp as far as making his voice heard. Unfortunately, it wasn't the last time that his written word would find an audience.

1 0

RADIO WAVES

Like a cancer that first presented itself in an Ivy League law journal, support for Abu-Jamal soon metastasized to National Public Radio. NPR, the longtime publicly owned bastion of politically correct thought, decided to offer airtime to a man convicted of murdering a public servant. Apparently, one of Abu-Jamal's prison essays, either the *Yale Law Journal* piece or one published in *The Nation*, caught the attention of Noelle Hanrahan, a San Francisco radio producer, who was inspired to record him.

Of course, Abu-Jamal's association with broadcast journalism began long before his incarceration for the murder of Danny. Prior to his arrest, Abu-Jamal was a journalist with various Philadelphia radio stations, last employed by an NPR affiliate, WHYY. His work caused him to be recognized by *Philadelphia Magazine* as "One to Watch" in 1981.[92] Watch indeed! The *Philadelphia Magazine* article was published at the outset of the same year he shot Danny. A former Black Panther (he became a founding member of the Black Panther Party's Philadelphia Chapter in 1969 when he was fifteen) and commentator on issues ranging from racism to city government, Abu-Jamal was touted as a "voice of the voiceless" and had become president of the Philadelphia Association of Black Journalists prior to being fired from WHYY in March of 1981.[93] That termination coincided with Abu-Jamal's increasing flirtation with radical politics. Colleagues of Abu-Jamal's at the time of *Philadelphia Magazine*'s accolade questioned the recognition; some even theorized that it was a misplaced attempt by the publication to include a person of color.

Abu-Jamal covered the contentious trial of nine MOVE members convicted in the 1978 murder of police officer James Ramp. That trial dragged on from late 1979 until the spring of 1980, and during its course Abu-Jamal became increasingly sympathetic to the group. Years later, his supporters would argue that he was convicted of Danny's murder because of his outspokenness against the police at the trial, but there is no evidence that he ever reported on the subject of police brutality. Nevertheless, his connections to MOVE strengthened with time and serious questions arose about the impartiality of his reporting. According to one coworker, Abu-Jamal's behavior at the radio station "really started getting out of control. He looked like a guy who was high all the time. He acted like a guy who was high."[94] The "voice of the voiceless" lost credibility quickly. In reality, nobody could be heard above the din of MOVE members when they were having a media moment; the truly voiceless were the property owners in MOVE's largely African-American neighborhood in west Philadelphia who couldn't get help from anyone in evicting the lawless, smelly, and dangerous group. An exploding bunker, complete with gun gallery to provide a clear line of fire, finally put them all out on the streets in 1985, but not before eleven died, including several children.

Danny died young but outlived Mumia's media career. In March 1981, Abu-Jamal was fired from his job as reporter. As Abu-Jamal lost credibility and friends in the industry, he turned to other means of employment and at the time of Danny's murder in December of 1981, his primary source of income was driving a taxi. Despite a less than illustrious professional tale, Abu-Jamal's occupation would later be sanitized and subjected to a complete Hollywood makeover. The Mumia Abu-Jamal template for Amnesty for Anarchists that emerged—the so-called gifted orator and social commentator, the intellectual exposer of all injustice—was destined to become the champion of anti–death penalty advocates. While the celluloid creation now known only as Mumia surged forward en route to celebrity, the real Abu-Jamal aka Wesley Cook, the taxi driver and aspiring black radical, was casually cast into the periphery, fading into the background, forgotten and ignored.

The blame for Abu-Jamal's reemergence in broadcast journalism while on death row lies primarily with Hanrahan, an activist and Stanford University graduate, who was director of something called Prison Radio. She must have been absolutely tickled to find what superficially seemed like her perfect poster child for the anti–death penalty forces. Prison Radio, as directed by Hanrahan, sought to: "Challenge mass incarceration and racism by airing the voices of men and women in prison by bringing their voices into the public dialogue on crime and punishment . . . and to have listeners question the costs to society of mass incarceration and the increasing use of the death penalty."[95] Hanrahan met Abu-Jamal one year after the *Yale Law Journal* article was published, in 1992, when she asked him to comment about his experiences during nine years on death row as a follow-up to KPFA's coverage of Robert Alton Harris, the first person executed in California in twenty-five years. Hanrahan has been quoted as saying she clearly remembers the thunderclap of the doors clanging shut behind her when she entered the Pennsylvania facility where he was housed. "As a radio person, I'm always listening for the sounds of a prison," she intones. She admits to being captivated by how talented Abu-Jamal seemed. "I didn't realize until I met him that he was a trained broadcast journalist of the highest quality. The timbre of his voice is amazing."[96] Starting shortly after this initial meeting, Hanrahan began recording for posterity Abu-Jamal's countless broadcast commentaries.[97]

After being discovered behind bars by Hanrahan, Abu-Jamal started broadcasting essays and social commentaries on issues ranging from the rise of Peruvian President Alberto Fujimori[98] to reading recommendations for his younger listeners.[99] The excerpts were aired every Wednesday on *Flashpoints,* a program on Pacifica Radio Network in 1992.[100] The exposure Abu-Jamal received through his weekly shows caught the attention of others in the broadcast world. Ellen Weiss, executive producer of the NPR program *All Things Considered,* claims she first heard Abu-Jamal on one of his weekly broadcasts and was impressed by what she heard: "He is a good writer and brings a unique perspective to the air."[101] This "sufficient uniqueness" was apparently enough for Ms. Weiss to include a murderer's commentaries in the afternoon portions of her program.

After the Pacifica broadcasts, Abu-Jamal was contracted by NPR to record and broadcast oral essays describing his perceptions of life on death row, which were scheduled to be aired beginning on May 16, 1994, during the *All Things Considered* program.[102] His first commentary described the interactions between prisoners and guards when a thunderstorm cut short recreation time. NPR planned to broadcast one commentary each month for at least six months.[103] In anticipation of launching the program segments, each about three to four minutes long, NPR compiled ten recordings taped in the visitor's area of the state prison in Huntington, Pennsylvania, where Abu-Jamal is incarcerated. His salary at the standard rate of $150 per segment[104] came as news to the Pennsylvania Department of Corrections, which had not been informed by NPR that Abu-Jamal had been retained as a commentator. The Department of Corrections declared that prison policy specifically precluded Abu-Jamal from receiving any form of compensation for such work.[105]

Thankfully, not everyone had lost their minds; a public backlash soon arose.

Arnold Gordon, the first assistant district attorney of Philadelphia, wrote a great letter to Delano E. Lewis, president and CEO of NPR, on the day that Abu-Jamal's commentaries were set to be aired. In the letter, First Assistant Gordon wrote: "Because you have chosen to bestow upon Mr. Abu-Jamal a privilege not given to most good citizens of this Commonwealth let alone convicted cop killers, I thought that you should be aware of the nature of his actions and the evidence produced at his trial lest you labor under the misguided notion that perhaps, despite his conviction, he was in fact innocent."[106] Then, after painstakingly spelling out the evidence supporting Abu-Jamal's conviction and death sentence, Mr. Gordon concluded by saying: "You have rewarded this murderer of a twenty-five-year-old police officer who left a grieving widow, and a mother, by giving him a platform from which to address perhaps millions of listeners. Who is your next media star—Sirhan Sirhan? John Hinckley? Jeffrey Dahmer? Have you no sense of decency, no sense of what is right and what is wrong? Your decision to provide this opportunity to Mr. Abu-Jamal constitutes an insult to police officers and families of murder victims nationwide as well as to the millions of law-abiding citizens who will no doubt be repulsed by your actions. I urge you to reverse your misguided and inappropriate decision with regard to your future programming."[107]

Another friend, Michael Lutz, then an FOP leader, was extremely upset by the decision to air the musings of a cop killer and expressed the following thoughts: "I was under the impression he [Abu-Jamal] was supposed to be punished. This man is a cold-blooded killer whose appeals went to the highest court in the land, and he's getting a radio show out of the deal. It's not fair to the family of the slain officer to have this going on."[108]

I first heard of the NPR debacle from a relative on the East Coast. My uncle Bill sent me a clip that Abu-Jamal was going to do commentaries on NPR. I remember I opened my mail that night around 9:00 p.m. Upon receiving the news, I nearly vomited. I was overcome with anger, betrayal, and seething animosity. First Yale, and now NPR. I was so upset about it that there was no hope of sleep. I stayed up all night pacing, wondering how I could stop it from happening. I was disgusted. It was so wrong. Abu-Jamal had taken Danny's voice from him. He could not live his life, or go to school, or have children. But this man, this evil man who silenced Danny in the most cold and callous way, was going to be given the opportunity to justify himself and his radical viewpoints to national audiences. It really infuriated me, and the adrenaline pumped at a rate I had never felt before. I stayed awake all night and called Rich Costello, another FOP leader, the next morning. Rich knew about it and said, "Don't worry about it, Maureen, I already have the wheels turning."

Rich Costello and others in the Philadelphia FOP, and Danny's friends in the police department, were all very angry about this. Costello vowed to take action, and Rich, who as a cop took a bullet in the head, cowers in front of no one. At that time, I was working for the doctor and he, too, was disgusted at the thought of Abu-Jamal on the radio, especially since he was a contributor to NPR, as were many of his acquaintances. He offered to try to obtain a list of people who contributed to National Public Radio who I could contact to get out the word that NPR had embarked on this sinking ship.

Both the FOP and I collected names of people who supported National Public Radio and we sent to those people hundreds of protest letters.[109] I informed NPR contributors of the ill-advised decision to air the thoughts of a cop killer and to let them know that they were supporting him as well as NPR by their contributions. To the argument that Abu-Jamal was protected by the First Amendment, my reply was always: What about my husband who is six feet under? He's lost his freedom of speech.[110] Ultimately, I think that the efforts of so many contributors to National Public Radio who threatened their non-support was what really started the ball rolling; plus the fact that the FOP sent out letters putting additional pressure on them.

I took my boss up on his offer to find out the names of larger contributors that we could contact. Momentum was mounting fast. Someone did send a list of big contributors and I didn't hesitate to send more letters. I also personally expressed my revulsion to NPR regarding their celebration of Abu-Jamal. Were they completely morally bankrupt? How could they let a convicted killer talk to the populace? A public broadcasting system has responsibility to its listeners; I was quick to remind them of this fact.

It didn't take long before NPR revisited its programming decision. A groundswell of opposition arose across the country at the idea that a man who murdered a cop was about to get a platform from behind bars, and NPR scrapped the project. The letters had their impact! Friends, the FOP, and everyone I talked to personally put pressure on NPR. I received a call shortly before 6:00 a.m. on the morning the commentaries were supposed to air. "Is this Mrs. Faulkner?" The caller identified herself as Ellen Weiss, the producer of the program *All Things Considered.* "You got your wish," she curtly reported, with no apology, and hung up the phone.

NPR explained that their change of heart was due to "serious misgivings about the appropriateness of using as a commentator a convicted murderer seeking a new trial" because they "had not arranged for other commentaries or coverage on the subject of crime, violence and punishment that provided context or contrasting points of view."[111] NPR News managing editor Bruce Drake talked about being disturbed at calling a convicted murderer a "commentator." "It's not that I oppose having the voices of people in prison on the air. What my problem was, was the special niche of Commentator."[112] The reversal caused consternation among supporters of Abu-Jamal who claimed that they viewed NPR's action as a blow to free speech. Ellen Weiss also expressed disappointment insofar as she believed that Abu-Jamal's commentaries would have been an interesting aspect of a larger overall report by the program on the issue of crime from various perspectives.[113]

Abu-Jamal's attorneys filed suit against NPR, claiming that the public radio giant had violated his constitutional rights and infringed upon his right to free speech. A federal judge would eventually throw out the suit in August of 1997, finding that NPR was not a government entity and, therefore, did not fall under the jurisdiction of the courts in regard to constitutional issues. The judge also threw out Abu-Jamal's other claims that the recordings were never returned and that Abu-Jamal was not sufficiently paid for his work.[114] His lawyers vowed to file another suit, insisting that NPR's actions were a form of censorship and thus a clear violation of his First Amendment rights.[115]

Unfortunately, Abu-Jamal was not completely silenced by NPR's decision to cancel his proposed commentaries. Shortly after NPR's cancellation, Pacifica Radio—the same group that had aired segments by Abu-Jamal on its *Flashpoints* program—decided to air the already taped segments that had been banned from NPR.[116] This came as no surprise to anyone familiar with Pacifica Radio, which first went on the air in 1949 in Berkeley, California. Founded during World War II by a group of conscientious objectors, Pacifica has a history of broadcasting far-left-leaning programming from the heart of California. According to the statement of policy of the Pacifica Foundation (composed of five member stations in Berkeley, Los Angeles, District of Columbia, New York City, and Houston), Pacifica seeks to stand apart from traditional corporate-governed radio:

> The Pacifica Foundation was founded in 1949 as a visionary alternative to commercially-driven media. We pioneered listener-sponsored, community radio and have been a beacon for noncommercial, free media. Pacifica's mission is to promote peace and justice through communication between all races, nationalities and cultures. We strive to contribute to the democratic process through public discourse and promotion of culture. Unbeholden to commercial or governmental interests, we recognize that use of the airwaves is a public trust.[117]

Among the high points in its history, Pacifica did a live interview with Che Guevara in 1967; broadcast Abu-Jamal's banned NPR work in May 1994; and launched *Democracy Now!* hosted by Amy Goodman on February 19, 1996. *Democracy Now!* would later become a clearinghouse to disseminate Abu-Jamal disinformation. It is a doctrinaire program for left-wing political views with production values reminiscent of the movie

Wayne's World. Watch it and you will swear that it is being televised from Amy Goodman's garage or rec room.

When this all happened, I looked into Pacifica Radio's founding and learned that it was created in March of 1946 by Lewis Hill, a conscientious objector confined during World War II. When Hill was released, he believed there was no media outlet for his point of view, so he founded a radio station to provide a platform for left-wing thinkers. Pacifica Radio has continued to grow over the years; it is now the most prominent far-left station in the United States. It received syndication mostly on college campuses and in California, where it is heard loud and clear from San Diego to San Francisco, and probably farther. In this way, Pacifica Radio became a key facilitator in propagating the "Myth of Mumia" and helped reinforce Abu-Jamal's growing support among college students. After he made his first Commentary on *Democracy Now!* on February 24, 1997, the centrality of the Abu-Jamal movement was sealed. College campuses soon became hotbeds of Abu-Jamal support. Fueled by the unfortunate spread of misinformation, earnest and idealistic kids were manipulated by these messages of so-called injustice and crusaded with the misguided hope of rectification.

Even after we managed to get Abu-Jamal off NPR, I still was not aware of the relationship between him and Pacifica Radio. I thought we'd won that battle and he would not have access to the airwaves. Well, I was wrong. I'll never forget the dagger in my heart when I first discovered this. I was driving on the 101 freeway on my daily morning commute to work when an odious voice filled my car. It was a voice I thought I would never have to hear again, the unmistakable snarl of Mumia Abu-Jamal. I had been flipping through the stations as I drove, and all of a sudden the voice came booming through my car. I had gone to the next station but quickly reversed the dial upon my recognition of the speaker. My whole body violently shook, and I actually had to pull off to the side of the freeway. I sat there with an overwhelming sense of defeat, weighed down by the futility of all I had tried to do to keep Abu-Jamal's voice off the air, to keep him voiceless. All the effort had been for naught. It had been so hard to counteract NPR and win. And now this radio station hijacked our campaign and allowed Abu-Jamal's crazy ideas an outlet and audience. I cried in frustration.

I regained composure and got to work. After recovering from my initial shock, my anger turned to action. I knew I had to do something to stop this madness. To bestow a killer with celebrity status would not be tolerated. What qualifies this outspoken cop hater, with no discernable compassion or qualifications, to suddenly become a philosopher and orator? I was completely bewildered. At that time, I could not comprehend the mindset of those on the far left.

I did the only thing I could think of. I had to contact Pacifica Radio. I sent a statement to management about their decision to pinch-hit for NPR. I presented the facts of the case and stated unequivocally that my main objection to Abu-Jamal being on the air was not because he had killed my husband or because he had inflicted immense pain on our families, but because of the savage nature of the crime he committed and his general "contempt for a society he hated and still hates, but whose charity he now solicits." I justify my determination to see this case to "Abu-Jamal's end" for this very reason.[118]

To this day, believe it or not, Abu-Jamal remains a commentator on Pacifica Radio.

11

HARRISBURG

Despite being sentenced to death in 1982, Abu-Jamal's death warrant had not been signed by any Pennsylvania governor for more than a decade after the trial. With the *Yale Law Journal* and NPR battles very much in mind, not to mention the celebrities now flocking to Abu-Jamal's side, I decided to organize a trip to Harrisburg, Pennsylvania's state capital, to change that. It was 1994 and I was supported and encouraged by state legislators like Dennis O'Brien to do so. Denny is known as a fighter for kids and crime victims. He's a straight shooter and largely non-partisan. As a matter of fact, in 2007, Denny, a Republican, was elected Speaker of the House by a *Democrat*-controlled legislature.

Abu-Jamal's supporters had been united by a rising opposition to the death penalty. As I prepared to go to Harrisburg, it occurred to me that Abu-Jamal himself was an active supporter of the death penalty, at least as a means of defending himself. It had been established at the trial that Abu-Jamal had bought the weapon he used to shoot Danny about two years prior from the famous Philadelphia sports store Pearson Sporting Goods, and, although his supporters would insist that he purchased the gun ostensibly to wave in a robber's face without intending to use it, I'm certain he bought it fully resolved to shoot and seriously injure or kill someone. Don't forget, the trial testimony was that Abu-Jamal loaded this gun with special high-velocity ammunition that is "devastating" to whoever is shot with it. Abu-Jamal's protectors have tried to assert that he purchased the gun to defend himself against bandits who had robbed him in the past, but even operating under this bogus assumption, his choice of ammunition clearly indicates that his self-defense tactics involved not merely wounding any potential robber but the execution of anyone who crossed his path.

In Harrisburg, a Democrat who was opposed to the death penalty was occupying the Governor's mansion. A conservative Catholic, Robert P. Casey was the Commonwealth's chief executive from 1987 to 1995.

By the time I decided to campaign for the signing of Abu-Jamal's death warrant, I had strengthened my ties with the Pennsylvania Fraternal Order of Police under the leadership of Mike Lutz. Over what would unfortunately stretch into decades, Lutz would prove himself and his organization to be tireless advocates for Danny's memory. Lutz organized the trip to Harrisburg that would involve delivering to the Governor's Office petitions with signatures of people who wanted Abu-Jamal's death sentence carried out. The plan was to deliver these petitions on April 12, 1994. When all was ready, our supporters filled two buses for the two-hour drive from Philadelphia to Harrisburg. When our group arrived in Harrisburg, we were greeted by more than two hundred Abu-Jamal supporters. The situation quickly turned into quite a confrontation.

The Free Mumia crowd had staked out the Main Rotunda of the Capitol. Our group of law enforcement and supporters of law enforcement was based in the New Capitol Rotunda. Their group was chanting "Free Mumia" and ours began responding in kind, "Kill Him Now." Passions were raging and hostilities were mounting. It wasn't pretty, and it was on the brink of getting worse. When I said that my expectation was to personally deliver the petitions we had brought to the Governor's Office, there was concern among the Capitol Police, who thought the entire situation could easily ignite. You must understand the climate of chaos at this point. The screaming in the Capitol was so loud from the competing sides that I am sure you could have heard it down on the banks of the Susquehanna River, blocks away. As we made our way toward the Governor's Office, the groups collided. I remember being with Denny O'Brien, my point of contact in the Legislature; Mike McGeehan; Mike Lutz; and Garry Bell, Danny's partner, among others. Years later, this same group, along with State Senator Hank Salvatore and State Representative George Kenney, was instrumental in getting Roosevelt Boulevard in northeast Philadelphia renamed Daniel Faulkner Boulevard. There are no shrinking violets in that group! The pro-Abu-Jamal folks were accompanied by William Cook, Abu-Jamal's brother, whose traffic stop precipitated the entire showdown on the night of the murder. That's the same William Cook who has never offered an accounting of what happened on December 9, 1981. At one point, Mike Lutz was chest-to-chest with William Cook and I was convinced it was about to become a full-fledged riot. Garry Bell had his hand on a stair rail and said to Denny O'Brien, "If any of them come near me, I will launch them over," meaning over the railing. Then, one of the MOVE members in the Abu-Jamal group began to taunt Denny O'Brien by revealing his home address. Denny told me that the guy actually said to him, "You live at XYZ address, and you will be killed." I do not take those threats from MOVE lightly, as they have proven to be a very dangerous group.

My statement that MOVE is a perilous group is based on the role nine MOVE members played in the murder of James Ramp in 1978, as well as the conflagration they caused leaving eleven dead on Osage Avenue in 1985, and what I have learned from a former MOVE member named Tony Allen. Allen was once an adherent of the authoritarian cult and at one time he dedicated his life to defending Abu-Jamal. He even lived in a MOVE house in Chester, Pennsylvania, with the group's Minister of Information, Ramona Africa. He himself spent time on the Internet attacking and smearing anyone who criticized his cop-killer idol, Abu-Jamal. Eventually he turned against MOVE and now works to educate people about MOVE and the dangers of authoritarian sects. His decision to extricate himself from the group came after the 2002 murder of a man named John Gilbride, the ex-husband of MOVE leader Alberta Africa. Now he runs Web sites (http://antimove.blogspot.com and www.themoveorganization.com) where he exposes the group and its connection to Abu-Jamal. Due to threats against his life from his former comrades, Tony Allen must keep his location and that of his family a well-guarded secret. This did not stop him from sharing insights with me in the preparation of this book regarding the support that the group offered to Abu-Jamal.

He told me that on the night that Abu-Jamal shot Danny, MOVE founder John Africa immediately sent MOVE members Pam Africa and a number of others to the hospital and subsequently ordered Pam to lead the support network for Abu-Jamal. That is a task she has done at various levels of dedication and success throughout the years.

He also said that, during the time he was in the Free Mumia movement, from 1995 to 2004, I was regarded as one of the chief enemies of the
movement and there were no kind words spoken about me. He said that I
was cast as a villain and referred to in the vilest terms imaginable. He said
that I was not viewed as a victim or even the spouse of a victim but, rather,
as an active participant in the "conspiracy" to kill Mumia. The fact that I
was Danny's widow was something that mattered little to the core Abu-
Jamal people. As Tony Allen has explained: "It is not hyperbole to say that
they hated Maureen and spun wild tales about her as a means of discrediting her and making her seem like a vulgar opportunist whose sole ambition
was to profit off of her late husband's death. I heard this theme repeated numerous times over the years." Tony Allen also told me the following:

> We were told that you had re-married and were flying around on FOP-
> paid-for planes, and you were being paid for your anti-Mumia work by
> the FOP directly and the U.S. Government indirectly.
>
> We were told that Daniel Faulkner was known as a wife-beater and that
> the night that he was killed, you celebrated. One MOVE member named
> Carlos Africa was particularly fond of telling a tale that had you closing
> the blinds in your house and celebrating your husband's death because he
> had so violently abused you.
>
> We were told by MOVE members that you knew Mumia was innocent
> but because of fear of the FOP and because of the money you were being
> paid, you could not come clean about your true feelings.
>
> Finally, we were told that Daniel Faulkner was a "pimp" of sorts down
> around the area where he patrolled and that Veronica Jones in particular
> had relations with him and could recognize aspects of his anatomy (if
> you know what I mean). We were told that you knew about his illicit re-
> lationships with prostitutes, etc.
>
> I realize that all of this is rather repugnant and seemingly unbelievable,
> but I swear to you on the life of my child that what I am writing is the
> truth.

Now you know what I was dealing with that day in Harrisburg. Governor Casey was not in the Capitol; his chief of staff received us. We told
him we wanted to know whether the governor would be signing death warrants. The meeting was cordial but yielded no result. By the time we were
ready to leave, the situation outside the Governor's Office had deteriorated.

I sensed the Abu-Jamal people were angry that I was being given some kind of audience not afforded to them. The Capitol Police told me that they would give me an escort to an elevator so that I did not have to pass the Abu-Jamal people on my way down the stairs. I refused. There was no way I would let them dictate my path.

Don't misunderstand: On the inside I was shaking. I was frightened to death about walking down those stairs, but something came over me and I thought that to do anything less was an insult to Danny's memory. As soon as they saw me approaching, the noise subsided. The screaming stopped. And everyone gave me the foot or so of clearance that I needed to descend. It was a little bit surreal. When I got to the bottom of the stairs, I felt a great sense of accomplishment, and I remember Denny O'Brien leaning over and saying to me, "You have more guts than brains."

That same day Denny O'Brien got a call from the governor who was, by now, very ill. He was in desperate need of a double transplant, heart and liver. He told Denny that he would meet with us on a coming Saturday, when things would be quiet in the Capitol, and we quickly agreed. Now fewer in number, but including prosecutor Joe McGill, we went back to Harrisburg and met with Governor Casey. I remember that he really did not look well. But when he asked me, "Maureen, do you have children?" I lost it. I knew he had no intention of playing on my emotions, but that is one subject that has always been guaranteed to bring me to tears regarding Danny and me, and it did, right there in front of the governor. "You don't understand," I told him. "I never had a chance to have children with my husband." That day, Governor Casey, despite his death penalty opposition, assured me that he would sign Abu-Jamal's death warrant before he left office. But he never did.

Something very positive did come out of that trip to the capital of Pennsylvania. My visit to Harrisburg made national news and further galvanized emotions on both sides of the controversy surrounding Abu-Jamal. As the convicted cop killer drew strength from the likes of the *Yale Law Journal* and NPR, I attracted support from rank-and-file police officers across the country and victims' rights organizations that existed on a grassroots level from coast to coast. Pam Lychner, the victim of an attempted sexual assault who narrowly escaped her attacker, ran such an organization in Texas. She watched me with great interest as her local TV station broad-cast my battle in Harrisburg. Our relationship grew from that event.

In June of 1993, after several brutal crimes in the Houston area, Pam Lychner and Dianne Clements, along with several friends, formed the or-ganization they called Justice For All to remind people about the victims of violent crime. Justice For All took the lead in an effort for important vic-tims' rights legislation to be implemented in Texas. Its members were re-sponsible for a new Department of Corrections policy allowing victims' families to view executions, habeas corpus reform law, curtailment of Texas's "good time" policies for inmates, averting a policy to allow inmates access to telephones, and curtailing inmates' lawsuits against victims. Vic-tims are now allowed to address the perpetrators after sentencing in many Texas courts.[119] Pam Lychner personally provided "court support" to many victims of violent crimes, attending trials with them, helping them to know what to expect, and speaking to the media on their behalf during the trials, which is usually the second worst time in a victim's life.

Pam was a fighter. From halfway across the country, she saw television news footage of my trip to Harrisburg to solicit Governor Casey's support in signing Abu-Jamal's death warrant. Pam contacted me after she saw the vocal abuse hurled against me during the trip and told me I didn't have to endure such treatment. She recommended that I file restraining orders to protect myself. I remember that when she first called me, we ended up talk-ing for quite a long time. After that, we would get on the phone and talk for three or four hours at a time. Later, she came to Philadelphia and spoke in support of victims. No one who was there will ever forget her appearance.

That ceremony was called the Living Flame Memorial, and it was or-ganized by Rich Costello and Lodge 5 of the Philadelphia FOP. The cere-mony occurred on September 16, 1995, just after a major Abu-Jamal hearing, the first of several such hearings under a law called the Post-Conviction Relief Act (PCRA), had ended. In a group of powerful speak-ers and in front of five thousand supporters of Danny, Pam Lychner stole the show.

Pam became deeply devoted to Danny's cause. When I say that Pam supported me, well, there are lots of people who support me, in theory, both emotionally and financially, but Pam became a role model for me because in her I saw a person like myself who was confronted with similar circumstances. Pam wasn't willing to back down. I aspired to emulate her resilience. When Pam approached me, she introduced Dudley Sharp, a victims' right advocate. I remember him telling me: "You need to understand what you are up against. You need to know what you're doing. You need to realize that this is bigger then just some little thing in Philadelphia. They are very well financed." Dudley was right. I was up against a beast but, like Pam, I was not willing to succumb.

Sadly, Pam Lychner's crusade for justice was cut tragically short when she died aboard the fireball that was TWA Flight 800 on July 17, 1996, accompanied by her daughters, ten-year-old Shannon and eight-year-old Katie. I attended her funeral along with many other crime victims Pam had aided in their time of need. Pam's insight, vision, and friendship continue to shape my initiative today.

12

TOM SNYDER

It did not take the television world long to realize the inherent appeal of Danny's murder. It had all the elements: white cop, black defendant, young life lost, a death sentence, prostitute witnesses, and the backdrop of Philadelphia, which the media was quick to point out as the city in which patrolman Frank Rizzo rose to the position of mayor. (I always thought that spoke well of both Rizzo and the City of Philadelphia.) In this passion play, I was quickly cast as the "sympathetic widow," or much worse.

As a growing list of liberal elites championed the cause of Abu-Jamal, it became an inescapable element of my existence to contend with the incessant mentioning of the case on national outlets, including the *CBS Evening News* and *Good Morning America.* Almost always, I did not like what I saw. In every instance, the murder of Danny seemed like a sub-plot or afterthought to a main story about Abu-Jamal. The omnipresent echo of "well-respected journalist" saturated the airwaves. "Cab driver who, as a Black Panther, advocated 'Death for Pigs'" was a title never mentioned. Why this case? Why now? I repeatedly asked myself these questions and concluded that the most satisfactory explanation was inextricably linked to the Hollywood support that existed for the man convicted of murdering my husband. Ed Asner. Mike Farrell. Whoopi Goldberg. Ossie Davis. They had all climbed aboard the Free Mumia effort. Inevitably, one of their faces would make the televised story. Most distressing of all, friends of mine began mentioning with increasing frequency that they had seen something about the case on TV or in the paper. Although I understood that they had my best interests at heart, I could sense by their questions that they were entertaining lingering doubts about the conviction of Abu-Jamal. Even my friends were not immune to the media indoctrination!

It was hard to hear close friends express doubt. I remember one story that was aired on a major network, either CBS or NBC. I was in the piece. When it aired, Paul Palkovic, by now the new man in my life who I will introduce to you at length soon, watched it at the home of a friend he had known since high school named Ken Franklin. We knew he was a pretty left-leaning guy even though we rarely talked politics. Well, that night, Paul got into a heated debate on the subject of the death penalty and its ramifications, and even though the topic wasn't specific to Abu-Jamal, it was inspired by the TV piece about him. Franklin's attitude was, "this guy sounds like he is innocent and he's been framed. They shouldn't execute him until they figure it out." Three thousand miles from where it happened, there was no escaping the murder, and no escaping the absurd web of craftily contrived lies.

Despite my initial reluctance, it was precisely these kinds of reactions that compelled me to make more media appearances of my own. Motivated by both my love for Danny and a respect for justice, I felt as if I had no other choice if I wanted to protect the integrity of Danny's case and present his true persona. I felt as if I had acquired a vast amount of specialized knowledge about the case over the past ten years. Despite my general discomfort in being in the national spotlight, I was determined to confront the Abu-Jamal propaganda machine. Tom Snyder's *The Late Late Show* offered me one of my first opportunities to emerge from my comfort zone and challenge what had become a preposterous onslaught against truth.

The live broadcast occurred in early August 1995. I appeared via satellite from Philadelphia, where I was for a hearing on the case. At my side was Danny's former partner, Garry Bell. Appearing opposite me was a woman who was associated with *The Nation*, a magazine in which Abu-Jamal had been published. With the klieg lights burning overhead, I must admit, I was scared to death.

Tom Snyder started the interview in a very balanced fashion, questioning each side evenly. He respectfully addressed my fellow guest as "Mrs." whatever her name was, even as she spouted outrageous statements. She even had the gall to mention the often-repeated lie that Abu-Jamal had been convicted by an all-white jury! Tom Snyder pressed her. I remember him saying something like: "Where did you get your facts?" and "How do you know this?" As soon as he started firing the questions, she fell apart. She obviously was uninformed. He didn't let her get away with it and held her accountable for what she was trying to pass off as fact.

I was incredibly nervous at the thought of doing a *live* interview. I found the whole scenario to be completely overwhelming. It was sensory overload. I had to form strong and coherent responses to Tom Snyder's questions while simultaneously focusing my attention on "the little black box." Meanwhile, I was getting feedback in my ear through a little earpiece. Each time I spoke, my own voice also reverberated back into this little earpiece. The process was demanding and unnerving. I could feel my heart thumping and my body heat rising under the uncomfortable glow of the hot lights. Nevertheless I managed to clearly express my distress at the aftermath of Abu-Jamal's conviction:

> Now I cannot live in peace because, when I get in my car and I turn on the radio, I hear the voice of Mr. Jamal. I hear supporters having fundraisers for him. I see posters on walls for him. He's on the TV. He's in the newspaper. And it's haunting me.[120]

Despite the discomfort, it was extraordinarily empowering to finally be able to voice the feelings that had been brewing inside of me since I first learned about the *Yale Law Journal* article. It was a definite turning point. Under the blaze of the bright lights and with the hum of the cameras rolling, I experienced a true moment of clarity. I knew right then and there that I needed to be out on the front lines and that, if I were, this battle could be won, no matter how many Hollywood types supported my husband's murderer. I suddenly realized that, while I lacked the practice and polish of the Hollywood professionals, I could do this. I could fight them in their own environment, under the media spotlights. I was getting ready for *my* close-up.

13

MURDERER'S MANUSCRIPT

My quarrel with NPR had an unintended and unfortunate effect. The police community's outrage over NPR's broadcast proposal, combined with the pro-Abu-Jamal community's outrage over NPR's eventual reversal, converged to elevate the cop killer's profile.[121] This heightened publicity may help explain why a formerly reputable book publisher was soon calling at Abu-Jamal's cell. In the spring of 1995, Mumia Abu-Jamal released what would be his first of many books, *Live from Death Row*, published by Addison-Wesley. With a title reminiscent of *Saturday Night Live*, the book included a collection of writings that he was originally contracted to deliver on-air for NPR. As stated in the book, the project was meant to serve as "a collection of [Abu-Jamal's] prison writings—an impassioned yet unflinching account of the brutalities and humiliations of prison life, and a scathing indictment of racism and political bias in the American judicial system."[122]

Pennsylvania prison officials learned on February 23, 1995, that Abu-Jamal had a book contract.[123] He was subsequently punished for breaking the Pennsylvania Department of Corrections rule prohibiting inmates from engaging in private business. Restrictions were immediately placed upon him with respect to TV, phone calls, and visitors.[124] His punishment also barred him from talking with reporters, something that caused quite a stir among those interested in interviewing the new author. Attorney Jere Krakoff went to federal court on June 27, 1995, for the purpose of forcing the superintendent of Abu-Jamal's prison to allow him to speak.[125]

While Abu-Jamal's cause had raised a significant amount of money by 1995, the publication of *Live from Death Row* proved to be the single biggest boost to his legal fund. With a $30,000 advance and fifty thousand copies sold within the first several months, Abu-Jamal was set to net at least $425,000 based solely on those sales statistics.[126]

Hearing this, I went on the attack. I told the *Philadelphia Daily News*: "The very thought of this convicted killer profiting from the murder of my husband is obscene. Where are their [Addison-Wesley's] morals?"[127] That Abu-Jamal would personally profit from the sale of his book shocked me the most. It was disheartening that a publisher such as Addison-Wesley, which specialized in children's schoolbooks, would be so quick to glamorize and financially reward the pretensions of a convicted cop killer.[128]

I was forced to experience the hurt, shock, and disbelief all over again. As per course, I called Addison-Wesley and spoke to a man named David Goehring. He was the top guy. I asked him if he was the one who made the decision to accept this book and give Abu-Jamal a $30,000 advance. He said, "Well, I feel that he has something to say. He has not lost his freedom of speech." My retort was, "Well, I think he should lose his freedom of speech. He stepped over the line when he murdered my husband and he should be voiceless as a result. My husband is forever voiceless—the grave is a terrible silence. My husband wanted to go to school—why should Abu-Jamal be able to continue his education behind bars? Now he's writing from behind bars, and you are going to give him a $30,000 advance and publish his book!" I told him I was going to get in touch with every school in the United States and let them know what Addison-Wesley was doing. At that time, Bob and Mary Ellen Auman and several other friends of mine back in Philadelphia compiled a list of schools that used Addison-Wesley textbooks. We sent letters out notifying those schools that they were supporting a publisher that was giving thousands of dollars to a man convicted of murdering a cop.

In a Fraternal Order of Police newsletter, I asked for a public boycott of the book *Live from Death Row* and a letter-writing campaign of protest to Addison-Wesley: "The boycotting of the publication of *Live from Death Row* will send a clear message that the public feels a need to enforce strong penalties against violent offenders and it's time to put the rights of the victims ahead of the criminals."[129] Although this campaign may have had some limited effectiveness, I still wasn't convinced that I had gotten the full attention of Addison-Wesley. I realized that when you really want to hurt someone, you hit him in the wallet. You have to get someone's attention to make an impact. I knew there had to be something more I could do to embarrass Addison-Wesley and expose what they were doing. One afternoon, while staring into space, ruminating on this unfortunate predicament, a plane towing an advertising banner flew overhead. I was immediately inspired and decided then and there what I was going to do: I'd hire my own plane with a banner to circle around Addison-Wesley's offices. Public shaming is a tried and true impetus for change.

When I first devised my plan, I did not even know where Addison-Wesley was located. As soon as I found out, I called directory assistance and scoped out all the private airports in the area. I was delighted to find one willing to work according to my plan. Upon talking to the gentleman who answered the phone and informing him of my intentions, the man responded with zeal that it would be his privilege to personally pilot the plane. He was true to his word. He flew that plane in the morning, he flew it at lunch, and he flew it at 5:00 p.m. The idea was to capture the attention of all the rush-hour commuters. The pilot also got special clearance to fly low so that people could read it from the building. It is quite a large building and I soon discovered it was also the biggest employer in that area. People waiting in traffic and driving to work at Addison-Wesley would inevitably see that banner. No sense leaving anything to chance; I made sure that in big, bold letters, the banner would proclaim to all that Addison-Wesley was the supporter of a cop killer.[130] The banner proudly read: "ADDISON-WESLEY SUPPORTS COP KILLER."

The plane flew over Addison-Wesley the first day *Live from Death Row* was released in bookstores across the United States—May 1, 1995. Management at Addison-Wesley was not happy about the surprise in the sky. The pilot told me he saw a man at a window waving at him. We hoped it was an outraged David Goehring. The pilot said that every time he went around the building and saw this guy waving his arms, he puffed smoke out of the plane. You have to love that. It's ironic that now, when the opposition talks about the incident, it always refers to how the FOP hired an airplane to fly around Addison-Wesley. It was not the FOP. I am happy and proud to report that it was me. Only me. The check for services rendered was signed "Maureen Faulkner."

At the time, Addison-Wesley Publisher David Goehring issued a statement concerning the reason the book was chosen: "We were just bowled over by the power of his writing. We take no position on his guilt or innocence, so it's inappropriate for Mrs. Faulkner to point her finger at us. Abu-Jamal has a right to be heard."[131] David Goehring went further by adding: "Here is a writer, writing from a place we have never heard from before. Abu-Jamal tells us what it's like to live on death row. His book can only add to the national debate on capital punishment and the prison system."[132]

If Mr. Goehring's outlandish attempt at justification was not enough, he also called me to add: "Don't take it personal. It's freedom of speech." I don't know who he thought he was talking to, certainly not a dead cop's wife. If that was not sufficiently insulting to me, he offered to send me a copy of the book, insisting, "Once you read it, you'll understand where Abu-Jamal is coming from."[133] Coming from? Mr. Goehring, I am only interested in where Abu-Jamal is going.

After publication of *Live from Death Row*, my lawyers informed me that I had no cause of action against Abu-Jamal or Addison-Wesley because the book contained no specific details about Danny's murder. In February of 1997, Abu-Jamal published another book, *Death Blossoms: Reflections from a Prisoner of Conscience*, which does contain reference to his 1981 crime.[134] And he was not finished. Despite the strong opposition to his writing, he continues to publish to this day. In addition to *Live from Death Row* and *Death Blossoms*, Abu-Jamal has written *All Things Censored, 175 Progress Drive, Faith of Our Fathers,* and *We Want Freedom.*

Still, one thing you will not find in any of Abu-Jamal's books is an accounting of what happened on December 9, 1981. If you did not murder my husband, Mr. Abu-Jamal, why not write a book and tell us in your words exactly what happened that night?

14

WASHINGTON

A beautiful monument called the National Police Memorial is located on Judiciary Square in Washington. It lists the names of over seventeen thousand law enforcement figures who have given their lives in service, the earliest dating back to 1792. Bordering the memorial's well-planted park are two "Pathways of Remembrance" where the names of the fallen officers are engraved. There, on Panel 25, W4, is the name of Daniel Faulkner.

I will never forget the first time I visited the wall where Danny's name appears, prominently displayed alongside the many others who gave their lives in the line of duty. It is a very special, sacred place to go and meditate. My first visit to the memorial was on May 16, 1995. It was a spring day; the flowers were in full bloom and the crisp spring air brought the promise of hope and change, as the change of seasons always does. The beauty of the day combined with the emotional impact of seeing Danny's name on the wall filled me with nostalgia. Although it had been more than ten years since he was murdered, many poignant memories flashed instantly back to me: the thought of Danny leaving the house that night, the doctor coming into the waiting room and saying he was gone, the trial, my moving to California and all the other things that followed—moving around, trying to find a place where I could turn a new leaf in my life. Yes, the cool spring breeze carried with it the past.

I was besieged with interview requests but apprehensive about all the newfound media attention. By now, the Internet was a virtual beehive of pro-Abu-Jamal information. I was still coming to terms with this new information outlet, and I was afraid that even the mainstream news outlets that came to me prior to printing or televising their pieces were doing it only to claim they had a "balanced" report and could spin it any way they wanted because they had talked to me. I was ignorant of how things worked, about who to trust, and aware I was vulnerable. During my visit to Washington, I gave an interview to Megan Rosenfeld of the *Washington Post,* whose lead became a source of controversy. Rosenfeld began her May 18, 1995, coverage this way:

> There is an image from Mumia Abu-Jamal's trial that stays with Maureen Faulkner even now, thirteen years later. Abu-Jamal was charged with killing Faulkner's husband, Daniel, a 25-year-old Philadelphia police-man, by shooting him first in the back and then pumping four bullets into his prone body. When the ballistics expert held up her husband's bloody blue shirt to display the bullet holes, Abu-Jamal, seated at the de-fense table, turned around and looked at Maureen Faulkner. "He smiled at me," she says.[135]

I remember her questions that day and why I told her that story. She asked me if there was anything that happened in the courtroom that stuck in my mind. I told her about Abu-Jamal smirking at me when Danny's bloody shirt was displayed. She printed what I said and that is exactly where a controversy started over whether or not I made it up. The defense has long insisted that on the day when the shirt was introduced, Abu-Jamal was not present, so I must be lying. Leonard Weinglass has stated that Danny's shirt was displayed in the courtroom on June 26, 1982, at which time his client was not present. He once sent a letter (which was published on the Web site of Refuse and Resist) to KGO-TV in response to a San Francisco broadcast he believed to be unfair to his client, and stated, "It would have been helpful if KGO had asked Mrs. Faulkner about a claim she makes that when a ballistics expert held up her dead husband's bloody shirt in the courtroom to display the bullet holes, Jamal turned and smiled at her. This is a real crowd stopper. It seems to capture the very essence of the prosecution's claim that Jamal was a cold-blooded killer. The only problem is, it's not true. A simple examination of the transcript shows that on the day the ballistics expert presented his testimony [June 26, 1982], Jamal was absent from the courtroom." Weinglass went on to say, "In the court of law, the prosecution has had Judge Sabo to protect them. But in the court of public opinion, Mrs. Faulkner has no such protection. Her erroneous statements were quickly exposed."

That's some pretty hard-hitting stuff, and I know I made reference to this incident in the early pages of this book, but I want to clear this up, in detail, once and for all. I misspoke in my interview with Megan Rosenfeld insofar as I tied the introduction of the shirt to the testimony of the ballistics expert, and ever thereafter the Abu-Jamal supporters have deemed me a liar because Abu-Jamal was not in court on the day that ballistics expert testified. I made a simple mistake. I did not mean to refer to a ballistics expert; I meant to refer to the evidence handler. The bottom line here is that contrary to what has been asserted by the Abu-Jamal defense, it is true that Abu-Jamal, the bloody shirt, and I were all in court at the same time and I left the courtroom crying.

The trial transcripts reveal that Danny's bloodstained shirt was displayed in the courtroom on two different days, June 21 and June 26, 1982. With regard to June 21, the transcript reveals this exchange with Officer John Heftner, the court's evidence handler:

> **Joe McGill:** Would you take a look at C-27?
> **Heftner:** Yes.
> **McGill:** Can you identify it?
> **Heftner:** It's Officer Faulkner's shirt.[136]

This verifies that the shirt was displayed in the courtroom on June 21, 1982. Shortly after this exchange, the prosecution called Joseph Kohn, the manager of the gun department at a sporting goods store, as its next witness. Kohn was asked to examine Abu-Jamal's gun, while Prosecutor McGill questioned him concerning the gun's purchasing record:

> **McGill:** Is there a name indicated on the record as the purchaser [of that gun]?
> **Kohn:** Yes, there is.
> **McGill:** And what is his name?
> **Kohn:** Mumia Abu-Jamal.
> **McGill:** Would that be Mumia Abu-Jamal?
> **Kohn:** That is correct.
> **McGill:** Is that the individual in the courtroom today?
> **Kohn:** Yes, sir, it is.
> **McGill:** Would you point him out?
> **Kohn:** Right there, sir.[137]

Which proves Abu-Jamal was in court that day.

Now, as for whether I was led from the courtroom crying, I offer the *Philadelphia Inquirer*, in its coverage the very next day, where reporter Marc Kaufman writes about that fact:

> Earlier in the day, Maureen Faulkner, the officer's widow, left the courtroom crying after her husband's blood-stained shirt was admitted as evidence.[138]

So there you go. This information verifies beyond any doubt that Abu-Jamal was in the courtroom when the bloodstained shirt of his victim was displayed, and that I left crying at that time.

Speaking of reporter Marc Kaufman, late in the summer of 1995 he wrote his own analysis of what was going on, which was published (coincidentally) in the *Washington Post* and entitled "The Rise of Death Row Chic." In it, Kaufman did an excellent job assessing the rise of the Free Mumia movement that was now unfolding all around me, and he highlighted Abu-Jamal's deafening silence in the one area that matters most:

> After the jury imposed the death penalty on Abu-Jamal, this combination of factors—from the history of the Philadelphia police to his obvious intelligence and writing ability—gradually attracted opponents of the death penalty, academics and other leftist groups. By 1992, Abu-Jamal had enough cachet to prompt defense attorney Leonard Weinglass (formerly of the Chicago 7 and Pentagon Papers cases) to visit death row for a job interview. Weinglass was hired, and the Mumia Movement shot into orbit. . . .

> Still, Abu-Jamal has never given his version of what happened the night that Daniel Faulkner died. He instructed his lawyer to argue during the trial that the Pennsylvania definition of murder was unfair. Now that news organizations around the world are clamoring for interviews, Abu-Jamal's attorneys have laid down one ground rule: He cannot be asked about the night of the crime.

> For a man so articulate and surrounded by so many who make their living with words, it is a loud silence.[139]

In Washington, we went to a memorial service for fallen police officers, which was expectedly moving. I could tell that being there and understanding the event's emotional significance really touched Paul Palkovic, the new man in my life, who was still coming to grips with what this case represented. There was a long line of guys in full police dress in their wheelchairs, many of them forced to maneuver their wheelchairs with their tongues or fingertips due to injury sustained in the line of duty and consequent paralysis. There were probably twenty-five of them, all wheeling through the crowd, battered yet proud. Then, the master of ceremonies sent out a blue laser light that ran maybe four or five feet above everyone's heads. They left that light glowing for the week, day and night—emitting light and symbolizing the strength of the force. I was proud to be in the company of such heroes.

15

CALIFORNIA DREAMIN'

By the mid-1990s, more than a decade after the murder, there was no escaping what had become the Free Mumia movement, not even three thousand miles away from Philadelphia. Two particular incidents confirmed this unfortunate reality.

Not long after the trip to Washington, I went to a gas station close to my home. As I pumped the gas, a young man, a white kid who looked college age, pulled up behind me. He was wearing a T-shirt that read "Free Mumia Abu-Jamal," and it immediately caught my eye. I had seen those shirts before when we had court hearings in Philadelphia and they were usually worn by Abu-Jamal's MOVE supporters. But here was a suburban white kid showing support on his chest for the man who killed my husband three thousand miles away.

I walked up to him and asked where he got the T-shirt. He said he was a student at UCLA and they had recently held a rally for Abu-Jamal. Someone who came to talk about the case was selling the shirts. I asked him if he knew anything about the case in which Abu-Jamal was involved. He said, "Well, I know that this guy was a Black Panther who was railroaded. Someone else shot a police officer and he was framed for it." I cringed when he went on with the usual recitation of misinformation being spun by the Abu-Jamal defenders: a peaceful black activist, a social dissident, hostile white police force, FBI surveillance, conned eyewitness accounts, phony ballistics, etc. I heard him out and offered to provide him with the actual facts of the case. He politely declined my offer. Before I left I suggested that when he wore a political statement on his chest he would be well served if he knew his facts, because you never know when you might run into the widow of the officer. I left him in stunned silence.

Not long after the filling-station encounter, I had another shock behind the wheel. One day, my usually monotonous morning drive on the 405 freeway was jolted when my eyes were drawn to a huge concrete retaining wall. There, in big bold lettering and in plain view of tens of thousands of daily commuters, someone had freshly painted "Free Mumia" on the wall. Once again, rage and pain overcame me and I had to pull over to the side of the road to take it all in. Despite the passage of time, each and every episode exalting my husband's murderer fills me with new hurt and pain. It is not the type of thing you can get used to.

Driving down the 405 that morning, I felt as if I were in a bad dream. The *Yale Law Journal.* The radio debacle. Abu-Jamal the author. The celebrities. The trip to Harrisburg. Washington. The kid at the gas station. And now, graffiti on my way to work. I was clear across the country from where Abu-Jamal shot Danny and more than ten years removed from the event but it was still controlling my life, and at an increasing rate.

No wonder the California media soon realized that there was yet another celebrity in their midst, albeit one of widow, not celluloid, fame. On August 7, 1995, I was the subject of a front-page profile in the *Los Angeles Times.* For the first time, my friends and neighbors were now fully in the loop about the dramatic background of a woman they thought they knew. My Philadelphia past was now the stuff of neighborhood conversation. The water-cooler crowd had something new to talk about. Soon, *People* magazine came calling.

One night there was a knock at the door and I opened it to find a gentleman named F. X. Feeney who said he was from *People* magazine. It was a Sunday night, and he just came and knocked on my door and wanted to do an interview right then and there. He was very nice but I was still quite annoyed—I felt like my privacy had been invaded. While my two dogs growled and snarled at the stranger, I heard him out. I asked him how he got my address. He said he had looked me up in public records, adding, "You're tough to find. I have been looking for you for a long time." I was still understandably suspicious of anyone in the media because of how the story had been reported thus far. I told Mr. Feeney that I didn't think it was a good time to visit. His comment was, "Look, you can talk to me or you don't have to talk to me, but I am going to do my story either way. My advice to you is that you talk to me and tell me your side of the story so I can tell it. Otherwise, it's going to be one-sided." This pseudo-threat worked.

I relented when I realized I had to tell my side of the events to this reporter. He promised to write a fair account and, as it turned out, he was a man of his word. What was published was generally fair, focusing, as the title of the magazine would suggest, on the celebrity element more than the facts of the case. Although the article presented the reader with a hearty sampling of "Free Mumia" conspiracy theories, they were told objectively.[140] I was also able to once again express my disgust with Addison-Wesley and their decision to publish Abu-Jamal's book.

I found the article in a box in my garage recently. The pages accompanying the article are decorated with pictures that were then old and new. Danny and I are seen cheek-to-cheek, in blithe spirits and glowing with young love. This picture of youthful cheeriness is in contrast to one of me taken fifteen years later where I am standing alone, arms crossed and with a determined look on my face. These pictures bear testament to the weary passage of time. I had been transformed from doting young wife to a battered yet bold soldier.

16

PAUL

Six years after Danny's murder, my life began to change for the better when I was introduced to Paul Palkovic. I met Paul through my dear friend from home, Anne Ryan, who had moved to California. She accepted my invitation to live with me while going through a transitional period in her life and ended up staying for a couple of months. One day, she told me she had met a really nice guy named Paul, a salesman for the company she worked for, and she thought we should meet. She and I and another friend, Ruth Lomino, who had worked with me at AMP in Philadelphia and who had also moved to California, went to a place called the Bombay Bar & Grill one night. It wasn't really a blind date, just a group of friends getting together to have a few beers and listen to some music. My friend was right—Paul was a nice guy! It soon became clear that Paul and I had a lot of chemistry. By the night's end we were in an intimate conversation about our many mutual interests.

Raised in California's San Fernando Valley, Paul attended Idaho State University on an athletic scholarship. After working several years he took a year to backpack around the world, then returned to Los Angeles and joined a firm where he continues today in sales of middle-market, high-end commercial business insurance products.

Paul has his own vivid recollection of our first meeting. He remembers trying to talk to me but being distracted by an obnoxious guy trying to hit on me. Being sensitive to my clear annoyance, Paul confronted my drunken suitor, saying, "leave my sister alone." We then went through a whole dance with this guy who actually bought into our siblings story! Bonded by the hilarity of this episode, we ended up on the dance floor together later that evening.

Although we were soon seeing each other every weekend, I initially gave Paul no hint as to what I'd been through over the past years. When I finally told him, I said that my husband was a police officer who was killed in the line of duty. Paul was appropriately sympathetic. We didn't dwell on the past, but sometimes the past caught up with us. When we were first dating, Paul took me to see the movie *Colors*, starring Sean Penn and Robert Duvall. At the end of the movie, Duvall is shot and slowly dies on the ground while asking for his wife. I was overwhelmed and started to hyperventilate; we walked out of the movie in stunned silence.

Over time, Paul's sympathy would turn to full-fledged activism as he learned more about the events surrounding Danny's death. Paul's entry into the struggle against Abu-Jamal first came when he accompanied me to the National Police Officers' Memorial Service in Washington, D.C. Many of Danny's and my friends were in attendance, including Thom Hoban, Danny McCann, and some of the other guys Danny worked with on the police force. This was not only the first time that Paul had been around police officers but also his first face-to-face encounter with the many marvelous men who had been so supportive in Danny's absence. "The boys," of course, were eager to meet Paul, assuming a pseudo-big-brother role on my behalf. In this way, the memorial service became Paul's first "family outing," as he was there to experience with us all the hardship, pain, pride, and drama.

That visit was Paul's initiation into a side of my life he never knew in California. I could not have anticipated the enormous role that Paul was about to play in my battle to honor Danny's memory.

Paul's direct involvement as a defender of Danny Faulkner came as a result of the encroachment of the Abu-Jamal defense apparatus into his home area of Southern California. That happened soon after Leonard Weinglass signed on to the Abu-Jamal defense team in 1992.[141] Weinglass was instrumental in cultivating support for Abu-Jamal on college campuses, including the University of California–Los Angeles. In the mid-1990s, Weinglass appeared on campus at UCLA to speak about the case. Paul, now my significant other of some years, still did not know the facts of the murder. Paul heard about the upcoming Weinglass appearance at UCLA on Pacifica Radio. Without telling me, he decided to attend the lecture.

Paul Palkovic was the proverbial sore thumb as he walked into the gathering space at UCLA. At 6 foot 3, balding, and conservatively dressed (he actually showed up in a coat and tie), Paul stood out. It was the beginning of what Paul now calls his "Immersion Project." Paul admits that Weinglass was a captivating storyteller that night, and driving home he remembers wondering if it was possible that I didn't really know what the evidence was, even though he knew I had sat through the trial and many subsequent hearings.

When Paul returned from the lecture that night, he did not tell me where he had been. He waited about a week, until after he had a chance to purchase and read Leonard Weinglass's book, *Race for Justice*. His eventual admission to me regarding his night outing inspired quite a lively discussion. I told him that he could not believe a word from Weinglass's mouth; that the Abu-Jamal defense had been manipulating the evidence since the trial ended and that, if he really wanted to know what happened, he should take the time to read the entire five-thousand-page trial transcript himself. That is exactly what Paul decided to do!

When he finally invested the time to read about the proceedings and learn the facts of the case, he was persuaded by the clear-cut, logical conclusion arrived at by twelve responsible and well-intentioned individuals. Beyond being a pillar of strength for me, Paul then transformed into a dedicated warrior for Danny Faulkner. He undertook responsibility to quietly quarterback many of the efforts initiated for Danny even though he never even had the opportunity to meet him and was now in love with me, his widow. It is Paul who painstakingly created www.danielfaulkner.com, which has become an incredible clearinghouse for facts about the murder. Paul's natural instinct to get the job done is evident through a quick browse of the site, where he has done a comprehensive job dispelling what he calls the "Myths About Mumia" with factual information. Myth by myth, point after point, he shreds the bogus claims asserted on behalf of the cop killer in a cleverly complete fashion. First, he relates the Mumia myth. Then he debunks it. Then he plays devil's advocate with the argument he is debunking. He concludes with even more analysis!

Paul's ode to justice is the product of many sleepless nights and endless hours of self-education. Remember, when he began working on the Myths

About Mumia, he had thousands of pages of transcript to tackle, no legal background, and no basic knowledge of the case. For about nine straight months, we'd be up until 3:00 or 4:00 in the morning, catch a couple of hours of sleep, and then head off to work.

I want you to have a look at Paul's handiwork. This example will not only give you an insight into the love of my life after Danny, but it will also exhibit the way in which the defense of Abu-Jamal has sought to distort an important aspect of the case. The Free Mumia movement has cultivated support for years based on the assertion that the ballistics evidence doesn't support the conviction. Well, take a look at what Paul has appropriately captioned on our Web site as Myth #1. This is Paul's effort to dispel one of many widely circulated falsehoods used to defend Abu-Jamal.

> **Myth #1:** *Those who support Mumia Abu-Jamal often allege that the bullet removed from Officer Faulkner's brain was a .44 caliber. Abu-Jamal's gun, found on the ground next to him at the crime scene, was a .38 caliber revolver. Therefore, his supporters argue, Abu-Jamal couldn't have fired the shot that killed Officer Faulkner.*
>
> *When asked to provide proof to support this allegation, Abu-Jamal's supporters point to a handwritten note made by Assistant Medical Examiner, Dr. Paul Hoyer. The note made by Dr. Hoyer was: "shot .44 Cal."*
>
> *However, Dr. Hoyer's testimony at the 1995 PCRA Hearing explaining his preliminary note sheds light on the subject. He testified, under oath, that the cursory note he made was his first impression of Officer Faulkner's wounds and, when he jotted down his impressions, he was trying to guess, from his examination of the devastation the bullet had caused, what caliber the fatal bullet might have been. This was preliminary, unofficial, not yet subjected to laboratory examination. He made it when he first viewed the fallen officer's fatal wounds, and, as it turned out, it was some period of time later that he was able to start the autopsy. He had scribbled it on a piece of scrap paper that was never intended to be part of his professional findings. Preliminary notes of an investigation never are.*
>
> *Some of Abu-Jamal's supporters, including his attorneys, have now altered this ".44 caliber myth" on the pretext that there may be several fragments of the bullet "missing" and, if these fragments were the correct size and weight, they would prove that the bullet was .44 caliber. But they have never offered evidence of any kind to support this theory of missing pieces.*
>
> **Brief Rebuttal:** *The official ballistics tests done on the fatal bullet verify that Officer Faulkner was killed by a .38 caliber bullet, not a .44 caliber bullet.*

The fatal .38 slug was a Federal brand, Special +P bullet with a hollow base (the hollow base in a +P bullet was distinctive to Federal ammunition at that time). It is the exact type (+P with a hollow base), brand (Federal) and caliber (.38) of bullet found in Abu-Jamal's gun. Additionally, tests have proven that the bullet that killed Officer Faulkner was fired from a weapon with the same rifling characteristics as Abu-Jamal's .38 caliber revolver. Further, Jamal's own ballistics expert, George Fassnacht, conceded in his 1995 PCRA testimony that the fatal bullet was not .44 caliber and that it was "most likely" a .38.

Although the District Attorney's office, in open court, offered to let Abu-Jamal's attorneys test the fatal bullet, that offer was refused by the defense, which has never provided any alternative test results to counter the above evidence. Dr. James Hoyer's hastily written notation on a piece of scrap paper certainly does not constitute such evidence.

Dr. Hoyer, a medical doctor who has had no formal ballistics training, never claimed that he was able to determine the caliber of the bullet. He plainly testified in 1995 that what he wrote was "a guess." Furthermore, Dr. Hoyer testified that, after writing down this guess, he measured the bullet with a standard ruler. Although he acknowledged that this was not the accepted scientific method by which to gauge the caliber of a bullet, his rough measurement was consistent with the slug being a .38 caliber and not a .44. Finally, Dr. Hoyer testified that, at the time he made his .44 caliber guess— while looking at the horrendous wound to Officer Faulkner's head—he was unaware that the killer had been using high-velocity +P ammunition. Had he known this, he would not have assumed that the slug was of an unusually large caliber.

So, maybe the gun the police produced as evidence against Abu-Jamal was thrown there in order to frame him? No. The gun had been legally purchased by Abu-Jamal years prior to the shooting and was registered in his name.

Facts Supporting Rebuttal: *Despite the meaningless nature of Dr. Hoyer's notation, Abu-Jamal's advocates often argue that the jury should have heard about it at the 1982 trial. But, had the defense introduced Dr. Hoyer's notation, there is no doubt that Dr. Hoyer would have been called to testify. What Abu-Jamal's supporters overlook is the fact that this is exactly what happened in 1995.*

At the 1995 PCRA Hearing, Dr. Hoyer appeared as a defense witness. Leonard Weinglass asked Dr. Hoyer about his ".44 Cal" notation:

Weinglass: *What is it, doctor?*
Dr. Hoyer: *It's a notation I made on a piece of paper that was normally— normally discarded.*
N.T. 8/9/95, p. 186

Further questioning by appellate attorney Arlene Fisk, representing the District Attorney's office, showed that Dr. Hoyer readily admitted that he had no formal ballistics training.

Fisk: *Am I correct, sir, that you've never had training in the field of ballistics and firearms identification?*
Dr. Hoyer: *I've never had formal training in that; that is correct.*
Fisk: *And am I correct that in 1981 you were by no means an expert in that field?*
Dr. Hoyer: *That is correct.*
Fisk: *Would I be correct that any statement by you as to the caliber of any projectile would merely be a lay guess and not that—not the valuation of an expert in the field of ballistics?*
Dr. Hoyer: *Correct.*
N.T. 8/9/95, pp. 191–92

What did the Ballistics Reports reveal about the gun and bullet? In the 1982 trial, the prosecution's Firearms Examiner, Anthony Paul, was asked if the bullet removed from Officer Faulkner's brain was consistent with one having been fired from a Charter Arms .38 caliber revolver (the type of gun owned by Abu-Jamal and found next to him at the crime scene). Mr. Paul stated that it was.

Anthony Paul: *It's possible to say that it [the bullet which killed Officer Faulkner] was fired from a revolver with that type of rifling, with the Charter Arms type of rifling.*
N.T. 6/23/82, at 6.110

Later at trial, defense attorney Anthony Jackson asked Anthony Paul if the general rifling characteristics etched on the bullet removed from Officer Faulkner's brain matched the pattern found in the barrel of Abu-Jamal's gun. Mr. Paul stated that they clearly do match Abu-Jamal's gun.

Anthony Paul: *The general characteristics being part of the eight lands and grooves and a right-hand direction of twist, you have a part of that [bullet] still exposed with sufficient quantity to be able to say that a firearm rifled with eight lands and grooves with a right-hand direction of twist discharged that projectile.*
N.T. 6/23/82, at 6.168

Anthony Paul went on to state that there are many .38 caliber handguns with eight lands and grooves and a right-hand twist and that the fatal bullet was so deformed that it could not be scientifically matched to Abu-Jamal's gun to the exclusion of all other firearms. However, he stressed the fact that there was one, and only one, gun with all of these characteristics at the crime scene, i.e., the gun owned by Mumia Abu-Jamal, the same gun that was registered in Abu-Jamal's name and found next to him shortly after the shooting. By any rational standard, the facts show that the fatal bullet was fired from Abu-Jamal's gun.

In addition to matching the general rifling characteristics of the gun used to kill Officer Faulkner, Abu-Jamal's five-shot Charter Arms handgun contained five spent casings from hollow-base, .38 caliber, high velocity Special +P ammunition. The shells found in Abu-Jamal's gun were all Special +P ammunition (4 were Federal brand, 1 was Remington). In 1981, Federal was the only brand of Special +P ammunition with a hollow base. In addition, Anthony Paul acknowledged that the Special +P bullet was a type of ammunition that was rarely seen in 1981. Mr. Paul commented that the Special +P is a unique bullet with an extra heavy load of gunpowder. It so devastates its target that police departments are restricted from using it.

This extensive ballistics evidence clearly ties Abu-Jamal's gun to the murder. But his attorneys and apologists simply ignore this evidence, hide it, or act as if it doesn't exist.

Maybe the gun on the ground next to Abu-Jamal was not his. Anyone who doubts that the gun found next to Abu-Jamal was actually his gun should have a look at the trial evidence. The gun was purchased by Mumia Abu-Jamal and registered in his name. Storeowner Joseph Kohn, testifying in 1982, stated that he sold Abu-Jamal this exact gun on July 17, 1979 (two years before Abu-Jamal became a cab driver). He produced a purchase receipt with Abu-Jamal's signature on it and a serial number that matched Abu-Jamal's gun. Abu-Jamal was wearing an empty shoulder holster when he was apprehended. Even Abu-Jamal's own lawyers admit that he was carrying a gun that morning although they have never explained what he intended to do with it other than murder Officer Faulkner.

Surely the Defense has produced alternative ballistics information. It sounds absurd but, to date, Abu-Jamal's ballistics expert George Fassnacht (the same ballistics expert Abu-Jamal had at the 1982 trial) has refused to even look at the bullet that killed Officer Faulkner, much less run tests on it himself. There is no doubt that if the bullet were not .38 caliber, it would have been a simple matter for Abu-Jamal's ballistics expert to verify that. But then, of course, Abu-Jamal's expert would be required to at least look at the physical evidence. When offered the opportunity to do exactly that at the 1995 PCRA Hearing, Abu-Jamal's expert flatly refused to look at the bullet, while Abu-Jamal's lawyers stood by and said nothing. That refusal to test the bullet gives us all the insight we could ever need into the validity of his bogus ballistics claims.

In July 1995, Assistant District Attorney Joey Grant quizzed Fassnacht:

Grant: *Well, you have opined that since you didn't have a chance to look at the evidence, test the evidence [in 1981], all you did was read a report. Well, we [now] have what you didn't have in 1981. Would you be willing to try a hand at it now?*
Fassnacht: *Would I be willing to reexamine this evidence? No, I wouldn't.*
N.T. 8/2/95, p.150

Further exposing the myth that the fatal bullet was .44 caliber is the fact that George Fassnacht has never stated that he believes the bullet is .44 caliber. Instead, while testifying in 1995, Fassnacht actually agreed with the prosecution's findings:

Grant: *In any event, no matter whether that explains it or not, you know from your own expertise that this is in no way close to being a .44 caliber bullet, don't you?*
Fassnacht: *Yes.*
N.T. 8/2/95, p.158

George Fassnacht again repeated his belief that the bullet was not .44 caliber when he was cross-examined by Assistant District Attorney Grant and asked the following:

Grant: *Considering what you read [the ballistics reports], you must admit to a reasonable degree of scientific certainty that a .44 caliber that [bullet] was not?*
Fassnacht: *Yes.*
N.T. 8/2/95, 160

The Myth Exposed Lives On. The 1995 PCRA Hearing completely refuted the .44 caliber myth. Yet, outside the courtroom, lawyer Leonard Weinglass continues to use this .44 caliber myth to drum up public support for a convicted killer. Despite the fact that his allegation that the bullet was .44 caliber was contradicted by his own ballistics expert, Mr. Weinglass still shamelessly repeats this fiction at his public presentations on the alleged "facts of the case."

Jamal's Lawyer Gets Caught. After a four month investigation of the facts of this case, the ABC News program 20/20 aired a broadcast that looked into this and other myths offered by Abu-Jamal's lawyers as evidence of his alleged innocence. While being interviewed by Sam Donaldson, Leonard Weinglass's obfuscation regarding the caliber of the fatal bullet was captured on film for all to see. Cornered by Donaldson, Weinglass was forced, on nationwide television, to publicly back away from his .44 caliber claim although he continues to say the opposite to this day in his off-camera lectures.

Donaldson: *The police say that that slug has the lands and grooves consistent with being a .38 slug.*
Weinglass: *It does.*
Donaldson: *But if it's a .38, then your contention that it was a .44 is wrong.*
Weinglass: *Well, I think that issue is very much something that should be played out in front of a jury.*

The New Defense Bullet Theory. *Because the testimony of their own ballistics expert publicly refuted the idea that the fatal bullet was .44 caliber, the defense has now added a new spin on the .44 caliber theory. They now claim that there may be a "fragment," or even multiple fragments of the fatal bullet, that are "missing." Though they have never offered any shred of evidence to prove this in court, they claim that, if this supposedly missing fragment just happened to be the right size, it would verify that the bullet was .44 caliber.*

But the new myth continues to be plagued by the problems of the old one, as so often happens when the truth intrudes on fantasy. Like the old myth, the new one directly conflicts with all of the ballistics tests as well as the expert testimony from both the defense and the prosecution.

Further, it is plainly dishonest for Abu-Jamal's attorney to claim that something is "missing" when he never looked for it.

Conclusion Regarding the Caliber of the Bullet: *Officer Faulkner was killed by a .38 caliber bullet from Abu-Jamal's .38 caliber gun.*

Paul continues to update the Web site whenever possible and to support me in every aspect of our lives, yet we are constantly, vaguely haunted by the nearly ten thousand days that have passed that Danny Faulkner never had. What a twist he represents. More than a quarter century after the murder of Danny, his memory and honor are being defended by a man he never met, who has fallen in love with his widow.

In 1990, after a three-year courtship, Paul and I decided that it was time to formally commit to our relationship. However, at the time, Pennsylvania law dictated that if I remarried, I would lose my much-needed health insurance provided to me as the spouse of a slain police officer—a problem, I discovered, common to many police widows and one that could be potentially dangerous for me given some very serious medical issues I was facing. So in 1991, we had our relationship formally blessed. To our families and friends, we were "married," but, legally, and in reality, we are not. Recently, after the plight of so many police widows was made known to the Pennsylvania State Legislature, the law was changed, making it possible for Paul and me to be officially married without losing my insurance coverage. We look forward to finding a place in time in our lives to do so someday soon.

1 7

TOM RIDGE

On June 1, 1995, Pennsylvania Governor Tom Ridge finally signed Abu-Jamal's death warrant. (A former member of Congress from Erie, Pennsylvania, Ridge was tapped by President George W. Bush in the aftermath of 9/11 to be the first Secretary of the Department of Homeland Security.) With a swift stroke of his pen, his decision filled me with the hope that Abu-Jamal's haunting presence would soon fade. How wrong I was. Contrary to expectations, the signing of the death warrant proved to be the starting gun for one of the most raucous summers this case has seen.

When I think back to this time period, I have a recollection that may sound a bit odd. I am one of those people who often associates events with songs, and at the time that Governor Ridge signed the death warrant, the Phil Collins song "In the Air Tonight" was constantly in my head. Even today, I hear those lyrics and they speak to what I was going through.

By Governor Ridge's order, Abu-Jamal was slated to die on August 17, 1995. With the papers signed and the specter of death looming, there was an unprecedented level of combative Abu-Jamal support in the summer of 1995. The president of France and the foreign minister of Germany made public appeals on Abu-Jamal's behalf. In Rome, one hundred thousand people signed a petition to stop his execution. And four American cities— Cambridge, Massachusetts; Ann Arbor and Detroit, Michigan; and Madison, Wisconsin—passed resolutions demanding a new trial for Abu-Jamal.

His defenders, motivated by a tenacious brand of unfounded conviction, threatened to burn down Philadelphia if Abu-Jamal himself "burns."[142] "Fire in the Skies if Mumia Dies" was the banner many of them held.[143]

Late in the summer, in the midst of an important Abu-Jamal appellate proceeding, thousands of Abu-Jamal supporters came to Philadelphia. The rally drew reporters from the Netherlands, Norway, Germany, Japan, and Mexico, and special-interest supporters from unions, socialist organizations, and academia. Police said there were three thousand assembled for the protest (of course, the organizers counted ten thousand).[144]

Looking back now, I would have to say that it was during the summer of 1995 that support for Abu-Jamal achieved its zenith. The cause had assumed truly global proportions. People from all over the world made the pilgrimage to Philadelphia to participate in that August 12 rally, and many others outside of Philadelphia protested in their home cities. From the East Coast to the West, from Germany to South Africa, supporters bellowed, cried, and pleaded for donations with the hope of winning freedom for their beloved cop killer. I remember reading about an incident in London where seven people were arrested while demonstrating their support for Abu-Jamal outside of the Disney Store on London's Regent Street, a location chosen because of its symbolic representation of U.S. corporate interests. It was mind-boggling.

Danny was a wonderful man but he was a cop from Philadelphia, not a player on the world stage. It was astounding to witness the way in which his heinous death became an opportunity to advance a sundry assortment of unrelated agendas. Danny's death became a blank canvas onto which protestors could smear their own homemade "isms" and accusations: racism, classism, police brutality, you name it. They saw in his case whatever they wanted to believe. It's a hard stretch to comprehend how the savage murder of a Philadelphia cop could inspire demonstrators in London to trot around in Mickey Mouse masks and Grim Reaper outfits.[145]

The circus had come to town in the summer of 1995, and it showed no sign of leaving anytime soon.

18

HOLLYWOOD AND
THE *NEW YORK TIMES*

Abu-Jamal's celebrity supporters were not content to allow the legal process to run its course unfettered by their onerous influence. Their ranks were growing and they demanded attention. On August 9, 1995, just as the Post-Conviction Relief Act hearing was in full stride in Philadelphia's City Hall, a full-page advertisement appeared on Abu-Jamal's behalf—not in the *Philadelphia Inquirer*, mind you, but in the *New York Times*. It prominently featured the A-list of Abu-Jamal Hollywood supporters: Alec Baldwin, Mike Farrell, Spike Lee, Susan Sarandon, Oliver Stone. It was a veritable Who's Who of left-wingers and all were willing to lend their names to a man whom a jury concluded had murdered a law enforcement officer.

One month prior to the *New York Times* ad, on July 14, 1995, E. L. Doctorow, a long-time Abu-Jamal supporter, had penned a column of support that also ran in the *New York Times*. Doctorow's Op-Ed read like the Team Mumia Mission Statement. He put forth the usual hackneyed arguments discrediting Abu-Jamal's conviction and disparaging the eyewitnesses. To the well informed, the piece was easily dismissed, but to the uninitiated I suppose it presented a rather compelling portrayal of an innocent man on death row. Doctorow ended the piece by questioning: "Will the pain of Officer Faulkner's widow, who supports Mr. Jamal's execution, be resolved if it turns out that the wrong man has been executed and her husband's killer still walks the streets?"[146]

Doctorow's article was clearly a clever ruse to try to sway the court and manipulate public opinion. Adding salt to my wounds, at this time I had to sit and listen to the Abu-Jamal witnesses tell endless lies in the PCRA hearings and hear so-called character witnesses say what a wonderful man Abu-Jamal was—without any regard for Danny.

The Internet was taking hold about that time and also fueling my fury (at this point we still called it the "World Wide Web"). I remember a reporter once telling me Abu-Jamal was a hero in "cyberspace." I had never even heard the word, and needless to say, I had not yet taken advantage of the Internet as a resource for Danny's cause; however, the Abu-Jamal defenders wasted no time in establishing sites in several languages. As if international celebrity was not enough for the convicted cop killer, he was now also quickly becoming the downtrodden darling of cyberspace, too. This was overwhelming. I went out and spoke publicly, did TV interviews, and spoke on the radio about my feelings and frustrations regarding Abu-Jamal's omnipresent celebrity. I tried to combat the onslaught of misinformation and urged the listening public to read the actual court testimony and not get their information from Ed Asner.

At this point, I truly felt like I had been assigned the task of putting out the fires of hell with a bucket. One thing after another, after another. I was running in a hundred different directions trying to combat the hysteria. I was getting hit from every angle. Fatigued by this seemingly endless assault, I came down with colitis during that Summer of Hell. I was sick and in constant pain, both physically and emotionally, and lost a lot of weight. And, just when I thought it could not get any worse, there came a full-page ad in the *New York Times*, with these words gracing the top of page A-13 on August 9, 1995: "MUMIA ABU-JAMAL MUST HAVE A NEW TRIAL."[147]

The copy continued with an opening sentence that many such writings on Abu-Jamal have replicated. Take a look at the text of the ad:

> Award winning journalist, talk show host, former Black Panther and MOVE supporter Mumia Abu-Jamal was convicted in 1982 of killing a Philadelphia police officer and sentenced to death. As E.L. Doctorow details below, Abu-Jamal's trial was full of gross procedural errors and judicial misconduct. There is strong reason to believe that, as an outspoken critic of the Philadelphia police and the judicial and prison systems, Mumia Abu-Jamal has been sentenced to death because of his political beliefs. Human Rights Watch gave him one of its 1995 awards for authors under political persecution, and Amnesty International stated that the government: "appears to have overtly used Mumia Abu-Jamal's past

political beliefs and affiliations . . . to impose the death penalty." Seven days after his death warrant was signed and two months before his scheduled execution, Abu-Jamal's access to family, legal counsel, and reading and writing materials was restricted in punishment for publication of his book *Live from Death Row.* As Abu-Jamal, known as the "voice of the voiceless," put it, "They don't just want my death, they want my silence."[148]

There you have it. Not one iota of factual information. The ad is awash with speculation and cites a fraudulent tome written by one of their own (Doctorow) as the factual support for its case. I concede that it might sound somewhat compelling to some, especially with the ad's reference to the Human Rights Watch Award and Amnesty International's opinion of his case. Nevertheless, I'm equally sure that none of those who then affixed their names to the above message have ever spent the time to read the five thousand pages of transcript from Abu-Jamal's 1982 trial. I think it is important that I name names. I want there to be a book record of every single person who allowed their name to be set in newsprint on behalf of the man who murdered my husband. Thus, I hereby present you with the official wall of shame:

Adjoa A. Aiyetoro, Shana Alexander, Laurie Anderson,
Maya Angelou, Paul Auster, Alec Baldwin, Russell Banks,
John Perry Barlow, Richard J. Barnet, Derrick Bell,
Dennis Brutus, David Byrne, Naomi Campbell, Robbie Conal,
Denise Caruso, Noam Chomsky, Richard A. Cloward,
Ben Cohen [Ben & Jerry's], Kerry Kennedy Cuomo, Ron Daniels,
U.S. Rep. Ronald V. Dellums, Dominique de Menil,
Jacques Derrida, David Dinkins,
E. L. Doctorow [wrote foreword to Dan Williams's book],
Roger Ebert, Jason Epstein, Susan Faludi, Mike Farrell,
Timothy Ferris, Eileen Fisher, Henry Louis Gates, Terry Gilliam,
Danny Glover, Leon Golub, Nadine Gordimer,
Stephen Jay Gould, Günter Grass, Herbert Chao Gunther,
Jack Healey, Edward S. Herman, Jim Hightower, James Hillman,
bell hooks, Molly Ivins, Bill T. Jones,
June Jordan, Mitchell Kapor, Casey Kasem, C. Clark Kissinger,

Herbert Kohl, Jonathan Kozol, Tony Kushner, John Landis,
Spike Lee, Edward Lewis, Maya Lin, Norman Mailer,
Frederick Marx, Nion McEvoy, Bobby McFerrin,
Susan Meiselas, Nancy Meyer, Pedro Meyer, Jessica Mitford,
Michael Moore, Frank Moretti, James Parks Morton, Paul Newman,
Peter Norton, Joyce Carol Oates, Dean Ornish, MD, Grace Paley,
Alan Patricof, Martin D. Payson, Frances Fox Piven,
Katha Pollit, Sister Helen Prejean, CSJ, Charles B. Rangel,
Adrienne Rich, Tim Robbins, David A. Ross, Salman Rushdie,
Susan Sarandon, Charles C. Savitt, André Schiffrin, Peter Sellers,
Nancy Spero, Art Spiegelman, Bob Stein, Gloria Steinem, Sting,
Michael Stipe, Oliver Stone, Brian Stonehill, Nadine Strossen,
Trudie Styler, William Styron, Edith Tiger, Edward R. Tufte,
Eric Utne, Bill Viola, Alice Walker,
Cornel West, Marc Weiss, John Edgar Wideman, Garry Wills,
Joanne Woodward, and Peter Yarrow[149]

As far as I know, the only one on the above list who ever disavowed his support for Abu-Jamal was Sting. He would later say that he was only an anti–death penalty advocate and had given money to Amnesty International, which, in turn, sent the Free Mumia crowd the names of like-minded celebrities. This all came to light when he was scheduled, a few years after the ad ran, to appear at the Tower Theater just outside of Philadelphia. He offered this excuse to appease police groups who planned a protest at his concert. In this spirit, I must commend the organized efforts of police and Irish groups who have remained amazingly loyal to Danny's cause and have been unwilling to forget or forgive any attacks on the truth of Danny's case. For this, I owe them my deep appreciation. Another Abu-Jamal celebrity supporter to incur the wrath of Philly's finest was Martin Sheen, whose support for Abu-Jamal came in the form of praise for a book he wrote on death row. When Sheen came to Philadelphia in 2001 to appear before an immigration group, a local Irish dance group pulled out in protest of his outspoken support for Abu-Jamal. Whoopi Goldberg is another who has felt the brunt of appropriate criticism. She didn't just lend her name. She has attended fund-raisers for Abu-Jamal at which she has read from his memoirs. She is acknowledged in his book *Live from Death Row,* which mentions "Whoopi, Danny Glover, the dynamic duo of Ossie Davis and Ruby Dee; artists who have evoked imagery of a progressive ethos and who have dared to breach the barriers between art and life, like Ed Asner and Mike Farrell." Well, when Whoopi was in Lancaster County, Pennsylvania, filming *Girl, Interrupted,* local police officers refused to work overtime. Of 137 police officers, 97 responded to a ballot sent out by Chris Erb of the Lancaster City Police Officers Association regarding a proposed boycott. Of the ninety-seven responses, ninety-four were in favor of a boycott.[150]

I bitterly remember and resent each and every celebrity who has proclaimed support for Abu-Jamal. When, in 1996, Bill Clinton invited Whoopi to host his fiftieth birthday party, I was appalled. I fired off a telegram to the White House saying so. I wrote: "My husband, Officer Daniel Faulkner, was killed in the line of duty. His convicted murderer is Mumia Abu-Jamal. Whoopi Goldberg is on the Committee to Free Mumia Abu-Jamal. Do you want someone who supports a convicted cop killer to host your 50th birthday? I know the law enforcement across this country will be appalled." I signed it: "Widow of Officer." Leon Panetta, the President's Chief of Staff, responded this way: "Let me assure you that Ms. Goldberg's participation in the President's birthday does not imply that he endorses her view on this particular matter . . ." I am just glad that there were no memoirs read at the gala.

When a public figure chooses to support a murderer, this is not a decision that should easily fade in the minds and memories of a discerning public. It is not a position in favor of a fashion trend or on one side of a feuding couple. It is a serious political position that threatens undue meddling in the affairs of other people's lives. Given the importance of this stance, it is therefore shocking to realize how willing people have been to overlook celebrities' support for my husband's murderer and celebrate their stardom without any consideration for their publicly proclaimed principles.

With notable exceptions, this has been the case even in Philadelphia. The most glaring manifestation of this tendency was in 2005 when Philadelphia's elite gathered at the newly minted Kimmel Center to fete

Ossie and Ruby with the Marian Anderson Award. It was during this ceremony that Mayor John Street, the very face of Philadelphia, exalted Ossie and Ruby, proclaiming that "they exemplify the power of the artist to change the world. They were among the most vocal Americans in support of the early days of the Civil Rights Movement. They used the power of their roles as critically acclaimed artists to effect change in society in areas where change was most needed."

Shame on you, Mr. Street. Ossie and Ruby were indeed vocal Americans, I do concede. However, short of changing the world for effecting positive change, I only remember Ossie's loud bark as he protested alongside Jesse Jackson in support of Abu-Jamal. I remember his booming assertions as he spoke on Abu-Jamal's behalf at Madison Square Garden. I will never forget Ossie Davis's public pilgrimage to visit Abu-Jamal behind bars. And I will also never forget that it was Ossie who, in 1995, after Governor Ridge signed the death warrant, issued a statement under the letterhead of "Committee to Save Mumia Abu-Jamal" in which he called the fulfillment of the jury sentence "an outrage." I have not forgotten this, Mr. Street. I never will. Why have you?

Each time another glossy talking head spews a new serving of nonsense, I develop a fantasy whereby I would have the opportunity to confront the senseless celebrity and deliver reason. Rarely am I afforded this possibility to enlighten. Michael Smerconish, a radio commentator in Philadelphia, did, however, have the opportunity to question at least one of the best-known celebrity soldiers in Abu-Jamal's force: actor Tim Robbins. Robbins appeared on Michael's morning radio program to promote a then current project called *Embedded*. After discussing that movie, they had the following brief exchange:

> **MAS:** I've got one more topic for you: Mumia Abu-Jamal. Remember you're speaking to a guy in Philly. Your support for him distresses me. Can I ask how knowledgeable you are about the case?
> **Robbins:** It's interesting how many times I've been contacted by those organizations and I don't believe I'm even on a committee. So, I don't know where you get your information from.
> **MAS:** It's in a *New York Times* ad that ran a couple of years ago.
> **Robbins:** I believe the ad said that people should look at a new trial. It

was not for his getting out of jail or anything like that. It was to look at the evidence and advocate for a new trial. It was not for getting him out of jail.[151]

Calling for a new trial but declining to say Abu-Jamal is innocent is, at best, a fuzzy distinction. Mike Farrell has tried the same excuse. The fact is that at the very time the ad ran, Abu-Jamal was being afforded yet another opportunity to "look at the evidence and advocate for a new trial." No, it was not about giving him another court date. It was about *setting free* the man who murdered Danny.

For me, by now, the case had become all encompassing, extending even as far as the local ice-cream parlor.

In the aftermath of the full-page ad supporting Abu-Jamal that ran in the *New York Times* in the summer of 1995, a Philadelphia cop named Al Kukler began an Internet boycott of Ben & Jerry's because Ben Cohen, co-founder of the company, was listed as an Abu-Jamal sympathizer. One day, I was sitting at my desk at work, absorbed in medical billing paperwork, when a woman came in with her young grandson. I heard her tell him that if he was good when she went in for her visit, she would get him some ice cream when she came out. Later, when they were leaving, the little boy was quick to ask his grandmom to deliver on her ice-cream promise. And then I heard him say, "Remember, Gran, not Ben & Jerry's because of what Pop-Pop said." I couldn't believe it! I immediately knew what he was referring to. This was happening in Ventura, California!

Ben Cohen was on that long list of celebrities and business owners who showed support for Abu-Jamal. When asked to explain his involvement in the movement and articulate the rationale behind his support of Abu-Jamal, Cohen was candid: "His trial was unjust," Cohen said flatly. When asked to detail his origins in the Abu-Jamal movement, Cohen replied: "I think I might have been at some conference and saw something on a table. And I think I might have been maybe at some festival and signed a petition . . . I think I saw something about how he and his lawyer didn't get along."[152]

Ben & Jerry's posted a statement about Mr. Cohen's involvement and support for Abu-Jamal. It read: "Ben Cohen, one of our cofounders, acting as a private citizen, joined hundreds of other people in signing a petition four years ago calling for a re-trial. Mr. Cohen made his decision to sign as a private citizen, stating: 'I am in no position to judge his guilt or innocence. For all I know, a new and impartial trial could find him guilty again. But the American system of justice must be fair and must be perceived as fair.'"153

Whatever. I still prefer Breyers. And am grateful to Al Kukler for his work on the boycott.

19

THE 1995 PCRA HEARING

Abu-Jamal murdered Danny in 1981. His trial and sentencing were in 1982. His first state appeal was denied in 1989. His death warrant was signed in June of 1995, and one month later marked the beginning of a proceeding mandated by Pennsylvania law to allow the opportunity to bring any new information before the same judge who presided over the original trial. The Pennsylvania statute affording Abu-Jamal that opportunity is called the Post-Conviction Relief Act. I initially thought this would be a one-and-done process, but nothing in this indefatigable case has ever gone as expected.

Abu-Jamal was ultimately given three PCRA hearings in back-to-back years (1995, 1996, and 1997) and I was present for all of them. This was no small feat for me. Each time it involved putting my life on hold to be in Philadelphia to witness the proceedings. The first PCRA hearing lasted longer than the original trial itself, beginning on July 26 and running through August 15, 1995, with closing arguments on September 11. Despite the duration, when it was over, Judge Sabo did not require much time to render his ruling. In a 154-page Opinion, he rejected Abu-Jamal's petition on September 15, four days after receiving the parties' post-hearing briefs and hearing their closing arguments.

By 1995, the Abu-Jamal supporters were well organized, vocal, and large in number. They wasted no time in making their presence known in Philadelphia. Two days in advance of the hearing, supporters of Abu-Jamal surreptitiously entered City Hall and unfurled a thirty-foot banner that read: "Liberty & Justice for Mumia/No Sabo." Then, on the first day of the hearing, about five hundred of his supporters descended on City Hall. Many lined up at 6:30 a.m. just to get a seat inside. This was to be

Abu-Jamal's first public appearance since his 1982 trial and the first since his newfound celebrity status. The emotion in the building was palpable. I think *Philadelphia Inquirer* reporters Julia Cass and Marc Kaufman did a pretty good job capturing the scene when they wrote:

> Outside the courtroom, Harvard philosophy and religion professor Cornel West likened Abu-Jamal to jazz great John Coltrane and the Rev. Dr. Martin Luther King Jr. New York City lawyer Alton Maddox told supporters to build a tent city at City Hall. And Dick Thompson, a leader of the Bruderhof religious community near Pittsburgh, volunteered to be executed in Abu-Jamal's place.

> West compared the atmosphere in Sabo's courtroom to "Mississippi 1995 . . . It was unbelievable. Philadelphia should be ashamed."

> MOVE member Pam Africa said that she knows where Sabo lives and that "we will be coming to his neighborhood . . . Sabo has to know we're coming after him."[154]

There was something else that ran in the *Philadelphia Inquirer* just as the 1995 PCRA was getting underway—an editorial that summed up my thinking, and reiterates something I have been saying in these pages:

> But through it all, the leaflets, the book, the public readings of Abu-Jamal's tracts, the protest updates on the Internet and the original trial itself, something is missing. Abu-Jamal himself has never given a full accounting—on or off the record—of how it was that on a fateful night 13 years ago, he came to be wounded, his gun nearby, a police officer dying in the street.

> Neither has his brother, William, who was in the car that was stopped.

> That is their right. And no such accounting is required in a court of law, the state having the burden to prove beyond a reasonable doubt that the accused did the crime.

> But this case is being argued, also, far afield of the courtroom. And it would be instructive to hear, just once, from Abu-Jamal how he came to find himself in such an incriminating circumstance.[155]

That editorial appeared in a newspaper that has staffed the case for thirteen years consistently, and has a thorough body of knowledge about the case, a paper traditionally seen as very liberal that brands itself as the voice of the underdog. Of course, the *Inquirer*'s request would go unmet. Neither Abu-Jamal nor his brother would use the PCRA process to offer an explanation of what occurred that night, assuming it was something other than what the jury concluded.

For the 1995 hearings, Abu-Jamal was represented by a legal team headed by famed defense attorney Leonard Weinglass rather than by a court-appointed solo criminal defense lawyer. Contrary to all rumors, Abu-Jamal never had a public defender. Anthony Jackson, who represented him at the 1982 trial, was in private practice and his name did not exactly come out of a hat. Leonard Weinglass, however, was a real force to be reckoned with. His reputation in left-wing circles had been solidified by his representation in some high-profile cases, including the Chicago Seven in 1969–70 and the Pentagon Papers.[156]

I have to admit that hiring Leonard Weinglass in 1992 was probably the smartest thing that Abu-Jamal could ever have done. Weinglass is well connected in the left-winger world as well as Hollywood, and he did a terrific job in making Abu-Jamal the premier case for the anti–death penalty crowd. More than a great lawyer, he was a master propagandist. He traveled all over the world to rally support and was sure to include many college campuses on this worldwide "March for Mumia." Weinglass also used his contacts with the host of Pacifica Radio's *Democracy Now.* Weinglass was on the program all the time discussing the case. In 1995, when he finished a day in court, he would routinely exit the courthouse and make statements to the news media. The media generally reported verbatim whatever he said, and he would then go straight from the steps of the courthouse to broadcast on Pacifica. He would reiterate how he had proven all of his points and how the prosecution had fallen on its face, that Sabo continued to be a racist hanging-judge, and other remarks concerning "evidence" that wasn't there.

Having read Weinglass's bio, I can tell you that he's a graduate of Yale Law School who served as a Captain Judge Advocate in the United States Air Force from 1959 to 1961. At the time of his counsel to Abu-Jamal, he was "Of Counsel" to the firm of Rabinowitz, Boudin, Standard, Krinsky & Lieberman in New York City. In the same year as this first PCRA hearing, he wrote a book titled *Race for Justice: Mumia Abu-Jamal's Fight*

Against the Death Penalty. I read an interview with him that ran in a publication called *The Progressive* where he explained how he became involved in the Abu-Jamal case. The following is an excerpt:

> At the end of 1991, a group of his friends and family members came to New York to talk to me about getting involved in his case. I entered his case in 1992 because Mumia is a political prisoner who is on death row because of his beliefs . . . He had not had good experiences with either his trial lawyer or appellate lawyer. His papers to the Supreme Court were filed without his ever having an opportunity to read them. He was justifiably concerned and suspicious of lawyers. He knew my history, which I think reassured him. We are now as tight-knit a lawyer and client as I have ever been with anyone I've worked with."[157]

That "tight-knit" relationship would not last. Ultimately Abu-Jamal would discard Weinglass.

Ever since the arrival of Leonard Weinglass as Abu-Jamal's lead attorney, a recurring theme of the Abu-Jamal defense strategy has been the vilification of the trial judge, Albert Sabo. The fact that he was presiding at the 1995 PCRA hearing was a subject they tried to invent as a matter of controversy. Weinglass argued that Judge Sabo should remove himself from the proceedings in order to keep an "appearance of impartiality" in the trial.[158] The then seventy-four-year-old Sabo refused. Eventually, the Abu-Jamal supporters went so far as to protest in front of the judge's Philadelphia residence. Eleven individuals were arrested.[159] Judge Sabo did not bend. "No threats, no mob pressure will intimidate this court," he said at the time. "If the day comes when the court responds to that, we are truly in dire straits."[160]

In announcing his plans to remain on the bench throughout the hearings, Judge Sabo said, "I feel that I was fair to him during his trial and I could be fair to him now."[161] I think anyone who takes the time to review the 1982 trial transcript will see that, if anything, Judge Sabo showed amazing patience with Abu-Jamal. Consider the very first day. The transcript of June 17, 1982, which was supposed to be the first day of trial, shows that Judge Sabo pleaded in vain with Abu-Jamal to allow the trial to move forward. He gave Abu-Jamal repeated warnings and directions as to how to address the rulings he made. In turn, Abu-Jamal insulted the judge and suggested that his only intent was to deny him "counsel of my choice," which happened to be non-attorney MOVE founder John Africa (who was then in prison), and to make sure he was convicted:

> **Defendant:** Judge, I have a statement.
> **Court:** If you have anything to say you say it at side bar.
> **Defendant:** I need the microphone at the table.
> **Court:** I don't have one.
> **Defendant:** You can get one.
> **Court:** You should have asked for one before.
> **Defendant:** I need one now.
> **Court:** You have to speak up and if you can't speak up then I may have to remove you and put Mr. Jackson in.
> **Defendant:** I don't care.
> **Court:** You can do whatever you want.
> **Defendant:** You can do whatever you want. I need a microphone.
> **Court:** I do not have a microphone.
> **Defendant:** You can get one, Judge.
> **Court:** Let's go.
> **Defendant:** I need a microphone, Judge.
> **Court:** I'm sorry.
> **Defendant:** You're sorry?
> **Court:** Mr. McGill, please.
> **McGill:** Yes, Your Honor.
> **Defendant:** I'm not finished.
> **Court:** Mr. McGill, please.
> **Defendant:** I need a microphone.
> **Court:** You don't need a microphone now.
> **Defendant:** I do need one.
> **Court:** You're speaking loud enough. I can hear you.
> **Defendant:** I need everyone in the courtroom to hear me. I want everyone on the jury to hear me.[162]

Things got worse later that day. When Judge Sabo finally had enough of Abu-Jamal's disruptions, and ordered that he could not defend himself, Abu-Jamal was afforded an emergency hearing in front of Pennsylvania Supreme Court Justice James T. McDermott. When Justice McDermott ruled against him, he shouted, "Where are you going, motherfucker?"

It seemed to me sitting there thirteen years after the original trial that now it was Weinglass and his colleagues who were misbehaving as much as Abu-Jamal did at the 1982 trial. Once again, Judge Sabo bent over backwards to accommodate a belligerent Abu-Jamal and his lawyers. I am not the only one who thinks so. Three years after the 1995 PCRA hearing, a unanimous Pennsylvania Supreme Court assessed Judge Sabo's handling of this difficult case as follows:

> Our careful review of the proceedings reveals that none of the challenged behavior on the part of Judge Sabo evidences an inability to preside impartially.
>
> While there are certain instances in the record where the judge displays displeasure and/or impatience, those instances were, in large part, a direct result of obstreperous conduct on the part of Appellant's counsel. The record reveals instances where defense counsel refused to accept a particular ruling offered by the court, relentlessly urging the court to reconsider. Although we certainly don't condone unjustified or indiscriminate rhetoric on the part of the presiding judge, we are nevertheless mindful of the fact that judges, too, are subject to human emotion. It simply cannot be denied that this particular case was one that was not only highly publicized, but also highly emotionally charged. As a result, the judge's duty to maintain the judicial decorum of the proceedings, was, at times, met with great resistance. Upon review of the entire record, we cannot conclude that any of Judge Sabo's intemperate remarks were unjustified or indiscriminate, nor did they evidence a settled bias against Appellant.[163]

Bear in mind that as the 1995 PCRA hearing got under way, Abu-Jamal was subject to the death warrant signed by Governor Ridge. So, Weinglass's next move was to ask for a stay of execution for Abu-Jamal in order to allow examination of an Appeals Petition filed on June 5, 1995, by the defense team. Judge Sabo responded by requesting that Weinglass make his case for a stay of execution by bringing in witnesses to show that such a stay was justified.[164] Ultimately, the stay was granted before the PCRA hearing ended.

By now, the original prosecutor, Joseph McGill, was in private practice, affiliated with the prestigious Locks Law Firm and representing severely injured plaintiffs in mass tort litigation, and Ed Rendell was no longer the district attorney. Philadelphia now had its first female district attorney, a woman named Lynne Abraham whose nickname (given to her by former mayor Frank Rizzo) was the "tough cookie." For the Abu-Jamal case, Abraham fielded a top-notch team of prosecutors that included Hugh Burns, Joey Grant, and Arlene Fisk to represent the Commonwealth of Pennsylvania. The three were terrific. And behind the scenes, an unsung hero was a man who has been a tremendous, intellectual benefit to Danny and me in a legal sense: Ron Eisenberg. He is a deep thinker, and in many ways, the brains of our operation. Leonard Weinglass had Dan Williams from Moore & Williams in New York City at his side, as well as Steven Hawkins of the NAACP Legal Defense Fund; Jonathan Piper, an associate attorney at Sonnenschein, Nath & Rosenthal in Chicago; and Rachel Wolkenstein, a staff attorney for the Partisan Defense Committee. I think it is worth noting that the Partisan Defense Committee has been described as "a gathering of New York Trotskyites, carrying on a leftist tradition dating back to when the PDC defended strikers jailed in the 1930s."[165]

While I was sitting in court in Philadelphia, the reverberations of this battle could be heard, or at least seen, back in California. I had asked my boss at the medical office where I was working in California to accommodate a long leave of absence. I volunteered to quit so that I did not have to inconvenience the office, but he told me not to worry, they would find a temp. Not only was the doctor an extraordinarily supportive boss in this regard, but he also became a fierce fighter for Danny's cause. During the PCRA hearing while I was in Philadelphia, he was driving down Santa Monica Boulevard one morning on his way to the office. His commute was disturbed by posters on the lightposts all the way along Santa Monica Boulevard stating FREE MUMIA ABU-JAMAL. Instead of merely pulling down the signs, he fought back. He had stickers printed up that said: OFFICER FAULKNER IS DEAD. EXECUTE HIS CONVICTED MURDERER. He had about two hundred of them made up and posted them all the way down Santa Monica Boulevard, on top of the Abu-Jamal signs. I was both amazed by and deeply appreciative of his efforts.

The scene of the 1995 spectacle was the same courtroom where the original trial had occurred, Courtroom 253 of Philadelphia's City Hall. It was all somewhat surreal; I sat in the same place, in the same room, with the furniture arranged seemingly the same, with the same judges' portraits peering down on me from the wall. Judge Sabo still proudly reigned. Yet, so much had happened in the interim. I would look around me, and there were the family and friends who had been with me in the courtroom in 1982—a little bit plumper, a little grayer at the temples, a few more lines around the eyes—but their support unwavering. The same, yet different in many ways. My dad was gone. Danny's mother was gone, as were Joanne and Joe Faulkner.

To its severe detriment, the Abu-Jamal defense apparatus was hell-bent on turning Judge Sabo's courtroom into a sideshow for ridiculous theories conceived by the uninformed as evidence of his innocence. This was Abu-Jamal's opportunity to present evidence that he'd been wronged in the 1982 trial. Of course, his side vigorously chose to attack his original lawyer, Anthony Jackson. Weinglass & Company argued that Jackson's representation was ineffective at trial in 1982. Now, in 1995, Jackson himself would take the stand. Jackson claimed that he had made numerous mistakes during the trial and that he did not receive enough money for expenses during the trial.[166]

As I sat watching, it seemed that Jackson was trying to walk a tightrope. He wanted to acknowledge that he had been ineffective while maintaining his reputation and his dignity. The straddling of the line between being both ineffective and reputable took its emotional toll on him and he literally broke down on the stand. Part of the reason is that Joey Grant, the prosecutor, was terrific. He's a slightly built African American who is great on his feet. Joey is also a Johnny Cochran protégé. He made short work of Jackson.

Jackson's attempt to testify in support of Abu-Jamal by admitting that he had been an ineffective lawyer is contradicted by the trial record, which unambiguously shows that Abu-Jamal utterly refused to cooperate with him. Before his testimony would finally end, Joey Grant would get Jackson to admit that no matter what level of investigation he could have undertaken, with whatever time and all the resources possible, he still may have found out that there was no evidence which showed Abu-Jamal to be innocent. Jackson agreed. It was a big moment.

That same day, I was verbally assaulted by supporters of Abu-Jamal who demanded that I be thoroughly searched before I entered the courtroom (even though I had already been searched). The altercation brought back memories of the original trial and caused me to leave the courtroom sobbing. I remember going into the courtroom and someone screaming, "You search that bitch! Search that bitch!" I remember running across the hallway into an empty courtroom and sitting in the back convulsing in sobs. Thank goodness that there was a woman with me from the special victim's unit, which had been created since the original trial.

Each day, the scene outside of the courtroom was intense. Day after day, protestors and Abu-Jamal supporters congregated on the City Hall apron. I remember at one point, when the windows were open in the courtroom, somehow—and I'm not quite sure exactly how they pulled this off—supporters of Abu-Jamal were able to communicate with the protestors outside. Every time Joey Grant would get up to speak, there was some kind of a signal for everyone outside to engage in loud singing, drumming, and chanting. Their rambunctious shouts would drown out the prosecution so that no one could hear what was being said. Meanwhile, every time Leonard Weinglass would get up to speak there would be dead silence—nothing from outside—you could hear his every word. This went on repeatedly for days until Judge Sabo finally ordered the protesters to be removed from outside the courtroom window.

The behavior of Abu-Jamal's attorneys was not that much better than that of his boisterous supporters. At one point during the hearing, Judge Sabo was forced to throw defense counsel Rachel Wolkenstein into jail for her churlish conduct. Despite ample warnings, Wolkenstein refused to comply with Sabo's request that she limit her incessant and disruptive complaints about his decisions.[167] Wolkenstein argued: "It's an attempt to intimidate the defense. It's an attempt to railroad Mr. Jamal to death. It is a repeat of the earlier process of what was done to him. We are not going to be intimidated."[168] After being threatened with a fine of $1,000, Wolkenstein returned to court and apologized.

Regarding the incident, Sabo remarked: "I think it is time for the court to take back the reins on the defendant. It's like having a bull untended in a china shop that just goes through and knocks everything down . . . We're not trying this case again."[169]

I had many difficult days in City Hall, matched only by His Honor, Judge Sabo. They were brutal towards him. Many years later, his son, Mark, himself a special agent with the Pennsylvania Office of Attorney General, told me that he remembered walking into City Hall with his father during the 1995 PCRA hearing and that a few of his peers came up to him and told him they would not hear this case if they were in the same situation. He said his dad was defiant and told them "it was my case from the beginning. Who knows it better than me? I never ducked a case in my life and I will not start now." Mark said he also refused to avoid the protestors on his way into City Hall each day. Apparently the sheriffs assigned to him suggested an alternate entrance and he refused. He told them he had entered City Hall the same way for twenty-two years and was not about to stop. So he walked right through the crowd. Mark said he watched as they banged a drum, hung him in effigy, screamed and yelled, and he just walked on by. And here is the kicker, according to Mark Sabo. When he asked his father, "Doesn't that bother you?" his dad replied, "No," and proceeded to defend the right of the Abu-Jamal supporters to do what they were doing!

And then, just when I thought the hearing had reached the pinnacle of pandemonium, Jesse Jackson swooped in. Now all three rings of the courtroom circus were in full operation. Prior to the 1995 PCRA hearing, Jackson had played no discernable role in the Abu-Jamal defense. This changed on August 7, 1995, when Jackson haughtily entered the courtroom, confidently strode to Abu-Jamal's side of the room, and asked the court if he could possibly sit next to Abu-Jamal at the defense table (as if he were some part of the defense team). Of course, Judge Sabo denied such a ridiculous request by a non-lawyer. After Jackson's appearance, one of the news reporters from the local NBC affiliate turned to me and said, "Hey Maureen, are you going to talk to Jesse Jackson?" I said, "No, I have no reason to talk to him. He already has proven to me what side he's on by asking to sit at the defense table. I know where he's coming from—he's supporting Mumia Abu-Jamal, so why should I want to talk to him?" Maybe if he had sat down in the back of the courtroom and hadn't said a word, I would feel differently. The reporter, Bill Baldini, then asked if there were any questions for Jesse Jackson that he could deliver for me. With a moment's contemplation, I responded with an enthusiastic yes. I requested that Jesse Jackson's response be captured on camera. My question was simple: What happened on December 9, 1981? As promised, the cameras rolled as Bill

Baldini coolly asked: "You're telling everyone that Jamal is innocent and you have been disposing that there must be some basis for that, so can you please tell us what happened on December 9, 1981?"

I remember that Jesse Jackson's response was something like, "I really don't know what happened the night the police officer was killed, but I do know that Mumia Abu-Jamal has not received a fair trial. But I don't know what happened that night." He also said that people that he relied on to be accurate and honest, implying Leonard Weinglass, had told him that he was innocent and that he hadn't received a fair trial, and that he believed them. The reporters then went back to me and asked for my thoughts on Rev. Jackson's appearance in the courtroom. I said, "How dare he walk into a courtroom, ask to sit at the defense table and say that he believes Mumia Abu-Jamal deserves a new trial when he doesn't even know what happened the night my husband was murdered."

On August 8, 1995, in the midst of the unfinished PCRA hearing, Judge Sabo granted Mumia Abu-Jamal a stay of his execution, which had been scheduled for August 17. The Abu-Jamal supporters believed this to be a total victory, but given the nature of the proceedings, I think he had little choice at that time under the law given that the PCRA was underway. In commenting on his decision on August 9, Judge Sabo denied that any outside forces had forced his hand in the decision. "I did it because the law required it to be done. Mr. Weinglass, this little old judge in this little old court will not buckle under any pressure—national or international."[170]

Remember, this 1995 PCRA hearing was designed by law to afford Abu-Jamal an opportunity to present new evidence in an effort to prove his innocence. As the hearing unfolded, it became clear that the bulk of this "new evidence" more closely resembled the mad hallucinations of Abu-Jamal zealots than anything grounded in cold, hard fact.

A supposedly big hitter in Weinglass's batting order was Arnold Howard. Some of Abu-Jamal's more ardent supporters had long suggested that the "real killer's" driver's license was found in Danny's front pants pocket the morning he was murdered. Danny's pocket did contain a temporary driver's permit for Arnold Howard, an associate of William Cook. I don't think it is so unusual that Danny had the driver's license given that he had pulled over William Cook's car, but of course, the defense treats this like it is evidence of something sinister. The defense insinuated that this license belonged, or was used by, the "phantom shooter" allegedly seen running away from the scene by four supposed eyewitnesses before the police arrived. To support their assertion, Abu-Jamal's attorneys called Arnold Howard to testify at the 1995 PCRA hearing. On December 9, 1981, the police had interviewed Howard because what was actually his application for a duplicate driver's license had been found in Danny's uniform pants pocket. Some speculate that Danny had decided to arrest William Cook because Cook had given this license application to Danny, trying to pass it off as his own. Howard had a time-stamped receipt from a store on Aramingo Avenue that proved he could not have been near the murder scene when it occurred. He told the police that he had lost his application for a duplicate driver's license in the back of William Cook's Volkswagen when Cook had given him a ride on November 30, 1981. Given the irrelevance of his account, he was not called to testify at trial by either side.

In 1995, however, Howard was cast in the Weinglass theater of paranoia, with the intent of supporting the defense "ABJ" theory (Anybody But Jamal) by suggesting the existence of a phantom gunman. Howard had an impressive record of convictions for forgery, theft by receiving stolen property, and burglary; he also admitted that he had known Abu-Jamal all of his life. He now claimed that, immediately after the murder, the police had held him incommunicado for three days, saying that "by my license being found at the scene of a homicide, that I was somewhat involved in it." Howard also described attending a lineup in the Police Administration Building that featured a stage with one-way glass in which a supposed witness (he implied this was Cynthia White, without ever actually saying so) implicated a man named Howard Freeman. Freeman conveniently happened to be dead.

The prosecution responded by calling two witnesses: Officer Joseph Brown and former Police Captain Edward D'Amato. Officer Brown, the custodian of the sign-in book at the roundhouse, testified that persons who are in police custody and in handcuffs are not brought through the lobby of the Police Administration Building, and do not sign the log. But Howard did. The log showed that Howard had signed in at 12:30 p.m. and signed out at 2:30 p.m. on December 9, 1981. And contrary to Howard's story, there is no lineup facility, or any stage with one-way glass, in the building. Captain Edward D'Amato was the officer who recorded Arnold Howard's statement on December 9, 1981. He confirmed that Howard was questioned because his application for a duplicate driver's license was found at the scene. He testified that Howard had come to the interview voluntarily and was never handcuffed. The interview lasted two hours, not three days. As noted above, Howard had simply reported that he had recently lost the application in William Cook's Volkswagen, that he was not at the murder scene, and that he knew nothing about the crime. He also mentioned that he knew Abu-Jamal because they had "gang warred together." And remember, William Cook never told the police that there was anyone with him in the Volkswagen. Nor did he say anything else in his brother's behalf.

Ultimately, Judge Sabo rejected Howard's new account and credited the testimony of Officer Jones and Captain D'Amato. And so once again, another spectacular witness for Abu-Jamal's supposed innocence had gone nowhere. It was obvious that Howard had invented—and rather ineptly at that—his 1995 story for the benefit of his lifelong friend. Even Dan Williams, one of Abu-Jamal's own lawyers who later wrote in his book about the case, said that the evidence made it highly unlikely that Freeman, the dead man that Howard tried to implicate with his transparently phony lineup story, was the "real" killer.

Dan Williams' discussions about the inner workings of the Abu-Jamal defense apparatus are instructive. His book *Executing Justice: An Inside Account of the Case of Mumia Abu-Jamal* was published in 2001 over Abu-Jamal's objection. Abu-Jamal went to federal court to prevent its publication and ultimately, in March of 2000, fired both Williams and Leonard Weinglass. What accounts for the split? Well, Williams writes of being "saddened by the sharp left turn the 'Free Mumia' movement took in the past year."[171] In his account, he discusses the disagreement amongst counsel over whether to put forth certain witnesses whose credibility was in serious doubt. He wrote that "Rachel [Wolkenstein] and Jon [Piper] held more extreme views; they were convinced—actually to them, it was sacrilegious to believe otherwise—that law enforcement knew Mumia was innocent, knew that the shooter fled the scene, and relished that a conviction and death sentence would be a terrific coup in the city's war against MOVE. Their view was an article of faith that grew out of their ideological zeal. . . . Len [Weinglass] and I nevertheless approached the case from a pragmatic standpoint."[172]

Remember, this is not me talking, this is one of Abu-Jamal's lead lawyers, and he is saying that one-half of the defense team bought into a sick and twisted notion that police want to knowingly kill an innocent man. He also acknowledged that both Wolkenstein and Piper were affiliated with the Partisan Defense Committee, a Trotskyist organization, and that to some in the PDC, "the only justifiable political call was for Mumia's release: no new trial, no calls for a moratorium on the death penalty, no advocacy that he was not a genuine candidate for execution. Mumia must be released, now!—and those holding the reigns of power have to capitulate to this demand of the proletariat."[173] This tension within the defense became exacerbated with the next witness at the hearing in 1995.

William Singletary is another man who was touted by Weinglass as an eyewitness to the crime who would exonerate Abu-Jamal, in that he saw what really happened and that Mumia Abu-Jamal was not the shooter. Needless to say, Singletary had no credibility. No wonder that in his book, Abu-Jamal defense lawyer Dan Williams said there was disagreement amongst counsel as to whether he should be called. He actually wrote that Wolkenstein blundered by submitting Singletary to questioning under oath before a stenographer. Not surprising, in light of what else Williams wrote about the inner workings of the defense team, namely that it was Rachel Wolkenstein and Jon Piper who insisted that he be called to the stand. Why was that a bad move? Well, the details he provided about the murder made absolutely no sense. William Singletary is the guy who claimed that, after being shot in the head, Danny said, "Get Maureen—get the children." But the major problems with that testimony are that the medical examiner testified that Danny died instantly from the shot to his head, and Danny and I never had any children! So the alleged eyewitness, touted by Weinglass in the media for weeks, provided evidence that he had spoken with a dead man about children we never had. No wonder

Williams would later write in his book, "I felt it was a mistake to commit ourselves to such a preposterous version of events."[174]

The defense also sought to score points through Robert Chobert, who really *was* an eyewitness to Danny's murder and had testified at the 1982 trial. In 1982, Chobert spoke directly to Abu-Jamal when Abu-Jamal challenged his claims just as the trial process was beginning. Specifically, at a pre-trial hearing, when Abu-Jamal was representing himself, Abu-Jamal asked Chobert, "You're sure you saw me? You're sure you saw me shoot him? And Chobert responded "I saw you, buddy. . . . I saw you shoot him and I never took my eyes off you."[175] He later said, "I know who shot the cop, and I ain't going to forget it."[176] Now, in 1995, the defense was attempting to exploit that Chobert himself had tangled with the law. He had been placed on probation in 1977 after being arrested on arson charges. The Abu-Jamal defense was attempting to argue that Anthony Jackson was ineffective for not using that as evidence of bias. But Chobert's 1982 testimony at trial demonstrated that he was not fingering Abu-Jamal just so that he could gain points with his probation officer. When his background was brought up in the 1982 trial, Chobert was surprised and questioned why it was relevant.[177] Chobert was not asked about the arson conviction or his probation at the PCRA hearing.

You might be wondering what became of "Wrong-Way Cook," Abu-Jamal's silent sibling whose illegal nocturnal driving directly set the stage for the murder of Danny. William Cook has never cared to testify as to what happened that December night. However, as the 1995 PCRA hearing was drawing to a close, there was increased speculation that he would surface and finally offer an account of what had taken place. In the proverbial eleventh hour, Leonard Weinglass announced he would call him to testify. This happened just at about the time that the attorneys were given approximately two weeks following the hearing to get their closing arguments together. I went home to California and then returned to Philadelphia for the one-day closing arguments held on September 11. It was a fiasco I will never forget. Literally moments before Weinglass was about to finish up his argument, someone ran into the courtroom with a yellow piece of notebook paper, which was handed to Weinglass via the other attorney.

He read the note and then made a striking proclamation to the courtroom and Judge Sabo that William Cook had agreed to testify. The note apparently said that Cook would be willing to come into the courtroom the next morning. A huge gasp overcame the courtroom. Judge Sabo agreed to give Weinglass the evening to get Cook in there and said that court would reconvene the next day at 9:00 a.m.

The next day in the courtroom, we were greeted, not by William Cook, but instead by his attorney, Danny Alva, who reported that William Cook feared that his life was in jeopardy and that Cook would only appear under a very specific set of circumstances. Judge Sabo had been very accommodating in allowing an extra day for the defense to produce Cook, especially because it was on the eve of closing arguments, but, upon hearing this news, he demanded that the defense get him into court immediately. Mr. Alva volunteered to testify on Cook's behalf. Can you imagine? This is a hearing fourteen years after a policeman's murder at which the defense is allowed to present new evidence and they are asking the court to allow a lawyer to speak for an eyewitness to the murder—a witness who himself had failed to "clear" his brother of the crime for which he was convicted, even though the man was "innocent." What a joke. He claimed that, after extensive conversations with Cook, he could anticipate what he would say. Judge Sabo rejected Alva's ridiculous plea and threw him out of the courtroom. This thereby concluded the drama of William Cook's promised testimony. To this day, Cook remains silent.

The closing arguments of the hearing proceeded with the defense and prosecution each being given two hours to summarize their cases. They were held in the city's brand-new $125 million Criminal Justice Center in what was called the "Mob Room" because it has a partition of bulletproof Plexiglas separating the lawyers and defendants from the spectators.[178] It was the first day it had ever been used. I traveled with Paul, who had come in from California, and the family to the back of the courthouse in a police van. As we got out of the van, there was a busload of convicts waiting for trial next to us and they boisterously jeered as we solemnly walked in. No matter, at least we were able to bypass the lengthy line that had formed in front. Metal detectors had been set up but only two of them were working. Consequently, there was a huge backup of people trying to get in, not just for our case but for every case that was going to be heard that day. Mingling among all those people were hundreds of Abu-Jamal people trying to get into the courtroom.

When it was all over, we were not escorted out as we had been escorted in upon arrival that morning and, as we were exiting, we confronted some very angry pro-Abu-Jamal protesters. There were some police officers present but they were largely scattered, leaving us essentially alone and unprotected as we faced the mob. Had we known there was a side entrance to the building, nothing would have happened, but the building was new and unfamiliar to us. Word spread within the Abu-Jamal contingency that I was going down the side street next to the courthouse. Barks, bellows, drums, and whistles clamored excitedly. And then they started to chase us! There were about ten of us, including attorneys and a couple of cops.

Poor Paul, fresh off an airplane from California, at his first hearing, was caught in the eye of the storm. As we arduously attempted to move forward, people with cameras blocked our escape, eager to capture the footage and unwilling to back off. We just couldn't get away. The cameramen then joined the stampede and chased us as well. In the midst of this hysteria, someone tripped me, and I nearly toppled into the street. Then, in one guy's effort to seek refuge, he ended up pushing the guy who tripped me. It was mayhem! As the crowd raged, a guy from CNN fell and broke a very expensive camera lens, and he had the gall to blame me for the mishap. Moreover, he threatened to sue the City and demanded exorbitant fees for the camera lens. I was outraged. I walked up to the female reporter from CNN and said, "I'll tell you what, if you put in a claim about your camera lens, I'm going to put in a claim about me tripping and falling in the street, and hurting my back and my hip, because you wouldn't get out of the way and one of your camera people tripped me." That was the end of the matter.

There was a far more pleasant encounter Paul got to be part of at the time of the PCRA hearing. We once had the good fortune of an impromptu meeting after court with the former district attorney, then mayor (and future governor) Ed Rendell. By happenstance, we bumped into him at City Hall and he recognized us. I think Paul was expecting a hard-core, liberal kind of guy because of Rendell's reputation as a big city Democrat.

Much to Paul's delight, Rendell was a cordial, jovial, welcoming, and low-key kind of guy. We ended up in pleasant conversation about all sorts of things for nearly an hour. Ed Rendell has always been a strong supporter of mine, for which I am deeply grateful. As we were leaving, he beckoned, "Hey, you know what you two ought to do? Let me get somebody to take you up to the top of City Hall." We cheerily took him up on his offer to see the city from the top of the statue of William Penn. The elevator is tiny and the viewing platform is not much larger but, once you get to the top, you have a breathtaking view of Philadelphia. There we stood, just the two of us, caught in the whirlwind of this bizarre saga but enjoying the pristine perfection of our temporary solitude—perched high atop the city where the madness raged below us.

Judge Albert Sabo ruled on Friday, September 15, 1995, that Mumia Abu-Jamal did not deserve a new trial. I know exactly where we were and what we were doing when we heard the news. That day, we were headed to eat pizza at my brother's house. We had been told that it could take a few weeks to hear from Judge Sabo concerning the ruling, so we were caught completely unaware. We were driving from my mom's apartment to Franny's house because we were the ones who were supposed to stop and get the pizza. As we drove along, we were listening to the legendary Sid Mark radio program *Fridays with Frank,* which has been on in Philadelphia for more than fifty years. Well, here we were, listening to Sinatra, enjoying a brief respite from our agonized waiting. Our musical interlude was abruptly interrupted by an announcement of breaking news. Judge Sabo had released the decision on the Mumia Abu-Jamal appeal. He had denied him the right to a new trial. He had upheld the conviction and sentence. We were amazed and giddy with relief. But the thing we remember laughing about most that night is that, in Philadelphia, they had actually interrupted *Fridays with Frank.*

The following day the *Philadelphia Daily News* ran with a front-page headline that succinctly encapsulated the importance of the ruling to Philadelphians: "SABO'S RULING ON NEW TRIAL FOR MUMIA: NO!"

The *Daily News* had the "NO!" taking up half of the front page. Sabo issued his 154-page Opinion, stating that Abu-Jamal "Fails to prove by a preponderance of evidence each and every claim presented to this court."[179]

The other side wasn't happy. Defense attorney Rachel Wolkenstein said, "The judge gave any number of statements throughout the hearing that we would have to take something up on appeal. It was very clear he had already made a determination." Long time Abu-Jamal supporter Ramona Africa said, "Would anyone expect a man who has acted as Sabo has [to] do anything else? This has never been an issue of the murder of Dan Faulkner. It has always been an issue of this system, of Lynch Mumia."[180]

I naïvely believed the battle was finally won.

2 0

AMERICAN LAWYER MAGAZINE

On the cusp of Judge Sabo's ruling, I experienced a period of renewed spirits and actually believed that the tide was turning toward Danny and away from Abu-Jamal. Emblematic of this refreshed outlook, we held an extraordinary event on September 16, 1995, in honor of Danny, the day after Sabo ruled on the PCRA hearing. This is the event, organized by the Fraternal Order of Police, that I previously mentioned in connection with Pam Lychner, who stole the show in front of five thousand supporters. Never before had we hosted an event of that size. The Abu-Jamal supporters were quite successful in drawing crowds for their out-of-town events, and we had never seriously attempted to match them. Glowing with the outcome of the PCRA hearing and comforted by the outpouring of support, the event for Danny was truly inspiring and filled me with hope where only anxiety had resided for so long.

Mike O'Sullivan captured the scene beautifully when he wrote in *The Peace Officer*, the Philadelphia FOP official publication:

> September 16, 1995 was a day the law enforcement community can look to with pride. We were represented by uniformed and plainclothes officers from the southern states to New England. Fraternal Order of Police representatives from as far away as New Mexico attended. We had the unity of the officers, families and friends of those who were directly involved. We were fortunate enough to have the support of those who were involved in the successful prosecution of the convicted and sentenced slayer of Peace Officer Daniel Faulkner in 1982. We had each other. If you were there, nothing else needed to be said. This was one proud moment. We can all share the accomplishment, which occurred on a late afternoon in September. We were fortunate enough to be there to honor and not be honored.[181]

Mayor Rendell was there and gave his recollections of the five-week trial in 1982. Joseph McGill also made passionate remarks. So did Michael Smerconish and Police Commissioner Richard Neal. City Managing Director Joseph Certane was there; so, too, was City Controller Jonathan Saidel. Gil Gallegos, the president of the national FOP, and, as I mentioned, Pam Lychner from Justice For All; they were all in attendance. When I finally spoke, I said to the group, "Danny always told me that the department was like a family. I never knew what Danny meant until he was gone. Philadelphia is my home. You are my home."

Things were looking cheerier, indeed. Yes, by the end of the summer of 1995, I thought we had weathered the onslaught.

But back in California, I barely had the chance to catch my breath before there was another challenge in the offing. In December, 1995, the *American Lawyer* magazine published a lengthy article written by Stuart Taylor Jr., entitled "Guilty and Framed."[182] This publication would come to be one of the most widely cited documents by defenders of Abu-Jamal. It was certainly better written and more cogent than most of what his lawyers were filing on his behalf. As the title made clear, Taylor reached an interesting conclusion: that Abu-Jamal was both guilty and framed. He asserted that Abu-Jamal was a victim of police misconduct that included witness coercion and the manufacture of an admission. He also believed he was subjected to a biased judge. The piece is intelligently written, and although I obviously disagree with its conclusion, I do believe a hearty rebuttal to this article's findings is necessary to truly appreciate the absolute guilt of Mumia Abu-Jamal.

Taylor contends that while Jamal is "probably an unrepentant killer," his trial was "grotesquely unfair and his sentencing hearing clearly unconstitutional," claiming police misconduct and perjury, an inadequate defense team, a biased judge, and a racially imbalanced jury. He argues that the jury that convicted Jamal lacked some important evidence, including a police report that casts doubt on Jamal's confession. In addition, he claims the jury did not see evidence that suggested the testimony of prosecution eyewitnesses changed between their initial interviews and their trial testimony.

Taylor also argues that, even if Jamal did kill Danny, there were mitigating circumstances:

> When Jamal came on the scene, what he saw was a big (6-foot) white police officer beating Jamal's much smaller brother bloody with a 17-inch flashlight; and when Jamal rushed to his brother's aid, the officer probably shot Jamal in the chest before Jamal shot the officer—perhaps before Jamal drew his own gun . . .

> The prosecution's theory—and, probably, the reality—is that it was Jamal who fired the fatal shot into the fallen Faulkner's face. But the testimony undergirding this theory was far shakier, less credible, and less consistent with the eyewitnesses' initial reports to police than the jury could have known.

Taylor was more inclined to believe the defense theory—that, faced with a life-threatening situation—Danny fired the first shot. He argues that would be reason enough for a jury to reject the first-degree murder charge, which requires proof beyond a reasonable doubt of unprovoked killing with "deliberation and premeditation."

> Is it clear beyond a reasonable doubt that Jamal killed Faulkner? I lean toward that conclusion, but with some ambivalence. I still have a nagging little question about whether the real killer may have gotten away. And the evidence that tips me toward finding Jamal guilty beyond a reasonable doubt is supposed to be irrelevant (under Fifth Amendment case law), and would be inadmissible at any retrial.

> That evidence is the 14-year-long silence of both Jamal and his brother, William Cook, about what happened . . .

> The most Jamal has ever said about the murder was his statement to the jury during the sentencing phase that "I am innocent of these charges."

> What's that supposed to mean? Jamal's lawyers say it means Jamal didn't shoot Faulkner. I'm not so sure. This is a man who chooses words with care. If he were truly innocent, wouldn't he have found at least one occasion, in the 5,000 days since Faulkner's death, publicly to say something like: "I didn't shoot him." And to explain who did?

When the *American Lawyer* article was published, Paul and I both remembered being taken aback and ill prepared to respond to Taylor's articulation of the case. We didn't have our Web site where it needed to be and Paul was not nearly the fact expert on the case that he would later become.

We also had to deal with the fact that Stuart Taylor did not fit the standard pro-Abu-Jamal profile. His reputation was not that of a card-carrying lefty, thus his words enjoyed greater credibility and force. Taylor had been to Philadelphia to research his piece and had met with Hugh Burns in the DA's office; Hugh Burns had become the key person for us there. It was Burns who had assumed responsibility for maintaining the verdict that Joe McGill won at the 1982 trial. He is a razor-sharp, amiable litigator who has been as diligent in preserving the verdict as Joe McGill was in winning it. These gentlemen are amazing. I am extraordinarily lucky that individuals like Joe McGill, Hugh Burns, and Arlene Fisk are willing to be prosecutors when their talents would be worth far more in economic compensation if they were in private practice.

With regard to *American Lawyer*, here is what I have pieced together: Assistant DA Hugh Burns, on the job for nine years, was working on Abu-Jamal's ongoing appeals along with Assistant District Attorneys Arlene Fisk and Joey Grant when he received a call from his boss, First Assistant District Attorney Arnold Gordon. Mr. Gordon informed Burns that a writer doing an article about the case would be contacting him for information. He added that Taylor was a decent man, he was "OK" and should be given whatever he needed. Burns complied, although it is his recollection that Taylor did not interview anyone in the District Attorney's Office. He simply reviewed the records from the original trial for several days and then left as swiftly as he arrived.

Burns later received a telephone call from Stuart Taylor in which he sketched out one of his more obtuse theories for the article: Faulkner "faced a life-threatening situation" because Cook "allegedly" struck him, it was "dark," the neighborhood was "unsettling" and he saw "another individual running toward him," he "shot Jamal first" and then "got spun around and shot in the back by a man who ran away," Burns said, "I couldn't help laughing out loud when I heard that. "I said, this seems rational to you? A cop shoots somebody just because he's walking toward him?" Well, Taylor explained, maybe the officer was afraid because the neighborhood was bad or maybe Abu-Jamal looked dangerous to him. "The cop thought a guy was so dangerous he had to shoot him," Burns asked, "but then he turns his back on him?" Burns also was quick to add: "Daniel Faulkner patrolled this area regularly, and regularly did so in the small hours of the morning. There is no evidence that he found the area 'unsettling,' or that he was afraid of the dark." In fact, Burns reports that the area was actually very well lit!

According to Burns, Taylor was displeased by anyone who displayed a healthy skepticism regarding his outlandish theory that Danny shot first. Taylor never asked about bullet trajectories, distance of one shooter from the other, or any of the questions an experienced investigator might ask when trying to determine the order of several unfortunate incidents occurring simultaneously on that cold, dark, early winter morning.

Hugh Burns is extraordinarily knowledgeable about the intricacies of Danny's case and, in his capacity, has been a compelling and commanding force in refuting Taylor's fictionalization of the events. With both precision and punch, and at my request, Burns has repudiated Taylor's claims:

> The conclusion that Abu-Jamal fired first does not, as Taylor writes, depend on an "assumption" that the officer, "while staggering and falling onto his back, with two assailants right on top of him," was able to turn and fire one shot at Abu-Jamal. There were not "two assailants right on top of" the officer, but one assailant, Abu-Jamal, behind him. Cook was being handcuffed at the time and had his back to the officer, and so was neither an "assailant" nor "on top of" the officer. Moreover, that Abu-Jamal attacked the officer is not an "assumption," but rather a fact established by the testimony of witnesses who actually saw the shooting—Michael Scanlan, Cynthia White, Robert Chobert, and Albert Magilton.

> These eyewitnesses did not know each other. Each of them testified to seeing the gunman, Abu-Jamal, do the same things. Though other people were in the general area, the only ones at the shooting scene were the officer, Cook, and Abu-Jamal. No one ran from the shooting scene. [183]

> Another eyewitness, though he did not testify, was Abu-Jamal's brother. Cook did not claim, as Taylor now speculates, that the officer shot Abu-Jamal and that Abu-Jamal (or someone else) shot the officer (in the back and then in the face) in "self-defense." Cook's one and only comment was, "I ain't got nothing to do with this." [184]

Perhaps Taylor would have reached a conclusion more consistent with Burns's findings if he had actually taken the time to sift through the most recent information available about the case. Taylor claimed that, in addition to the 1982 trial records, he reviewed the "evidence brought out in the much publicized [1995] Post-Conviction Hearing." Yet, throughout his article, it's clear that he preferred to ignore most of the 1995 evidence, as he repeatedly omitted testimony that might refute his speculations or provide answers to his so-called "unanswerable questions." It should be remembered that the 1995 testimony was given months before Taylor's article went to press and was readily available to him, yet he consciously chose to ignore it. If one reviews that same testimony today (posted on www.daniel faulkner.com), one will find that all of Taylor's ballyhooed speculations were addressed and promptly deflated months before his article was written by the 1995 PCRA testimony. His lingering "unanswered" questions had all been unambiguously answered at the time his article printed.

Why didn't Taylor include this information? One can only guess. My assumption is that he had become so deeply invested in his fantasized version of the events that by the time the PCRA transcripts became available, he was unwilling to abandon his work despite the abundant evidence disproving its plausibility. Taylor instead chose to soldier on. Perhaps Taylor published his article assuming that nobody would ever have easy access to the trial and PCRA transcripts in the future. But the advent of the Internet age and the Justice for P/O Daniel Faulkner Web site proved him wrong. The answers are available to anyone with a modem and a mouse.

The passage of time has brought additional insight regarding the refutation of Taylor's theories. More than a dozen Appellate Court Judges addressed accusations similar to those embraced by Taylor—police corruption, judicial bias, perjury, and Abu-Jamal's innocence, and attested to their extreme improbability. Nevertheless, given the article's acclaim, I do think a thorough re-review of it is apt. Allow me to provide the answers to the so-deemed unanswerable.

Throughout most of his article, Taylor made the same arguments that were rampant in the press prior to the 1995 PCRA hearing. In the beginning of his article, Taylor states that the trial "was grotesquely unfair and his sentencing hearing clearly unconstitutional." Since the time Taylor's article was written, however, at least twelve different judges (actually, when you consider that the U.S. Supreme Court has three times denied Abu-Jamal's requests for review, the number is easily over twenty) have reviewed the trial and the sentencing hearings and failed to find them "grotesquely un- fair" or "clearly unconstitutional." In 2001, Federal District Court Judge William Yohn did find that the wording used on the sentencing verdict form "*might have*" confused the jury; this remote possibility proved to be the basis for the grant of a new sentencing hearing (currently being ap- pealed by the district attorney).

Despite Judge Yohn's decision, one should know that the trial jury never asked for clarification of the form and never expressed any confusion to Judge Sabo. That hardly qualifies as "grotesquely unfair." Despite this seeming mini-victory, Judge Yohn went on to reject all of Abu-Jamal's arguments alleging an unfair trial. His opinion is now pending an appeal before the Third Circuit Court of Appeals in Philadelphia. To this date, not one of the many judges who reviewed the case has been able to discern what seems so obvious to Taylor.

Taylor's article further stated: "Jamal was prejudiced by police miscon- duct and *probably* rampant police perjury." If police misconduct and per- jured testimony were "rampant" and caused Abu-Jamal's case to be prejudiced, one would expect that Abu-Jamal's attorneys would have been able to easily expose that fact. And one would think that at least one judge out of more than a dozen who reviewed the facts would have found this to be the case. Yet, eleven years after the article's publication, there has still been no evidence of "police perjury" found by the courts nor has any one of Abu-Jamal's numerous attorneys substantiated any "police misconduct." In retrospect, maybe Mr. Taylor should have stepped in as a friend of the court and helped Abu-Jamal's attorneys if he so clearly saw evidence of "rampant injustice." The accusation is convenient. However, it is simply unfounded.

Taylor's accusation that Abu-Jamal's defense was "under-funded" and his lawyer "ineffective" is another baseless figment of Taylor's imagination. While you wouldn't know it from reading Taylor's article, Anthony Jack- son, Abu-Jamal's 1982 attorney, specifically addressed these allegations while testifying at the 1995 PCRA hearing. The fee was $13,062.50 plus $900 in expenses, for a total of $13,962.50. The point here is that this is high compared to other cases of that day and it overlooks that Abu-Jamal had other sources of money, including the Mumia Abu-Jamal Defense Committee, the Association of Black Journalists, and numerous volunteers. And so what? In 1995 at the PCRA hearing, he had unlimited resources and he failed to present any credible evidence.

The record shows that Judge Sabo told Jackson that he could have additional court funding if he needed it, but Jackson had no such need. Not surprisingly, Jackson never asked for additional funds. He was supported by the Association of Black Journalists and the MOVE organization, plus a loose association of Abu-Jamal's family, friends, and supporters. If no additional funds were requested of the court (especially considering the abiding offer that such funds would be provided), this fact alone should more than amply dispel Taylor's notion that Mumia's team was suffering financially.

Anthony Jackson was not exactly the overburdened, inexperienced associate one might assume from Taylor's article. Once a Private Investigator, Jackson had also worked in the Philadelphia District Attorney's Office. He was a seasoned defense attorney who had tried twenty cases involving first degree murder before he took Abu-Jamal as a client. Of the twenty cases, he lost only six; there were no death sentences. Jackson was not "foisted" upon Abu-Jamal by a "biased" Judge Albert Sabo, and Jackson stated outright in his 1995 testimony that he was referred to Abu-Jamal by his friends at the Association of Black Journalists, and that Abu-Jamal interviewed him a short time after the shooting and personally selected him as his defense attorney. Because Abu-Jamal was indigent at the time, Jackson approached Judge Paul Ribner and asked to be appointed as Abu-Jamal's attorney at the court's expense.

The Taylor article stated that Judge Albert Sabo was "notoriously biased" in favor of the prosecution. This unsubstantiated proposition has been put before many judges, not one of whom could find evidence of any "bias" on the part of Judge Albert Sabo. To the contrary, in their Opinion of October 29, 1998, which unanimously rejected Abu-Jamal's second appeal, the Pennsylvania Supreme Court praised Sabo for his handling of the case in the face of an onslaught of outbursts and insults from both Abu-Jamal and his lawyers. Bias on the part of Sabo would certainly be convenient. It's too bad that it is entirely untrue.

Like many journalists before and after him, Stuart Taylor could not resist the urge to play the race card. He seemed to think that the court, somehow, in the full light of day, racially stacked the jury that convicted Mumia Abu-Jamal and sentenced him to death. Taylor's article states that there were "questionable *voir dire* stratagems," then offers some very misleading statistics that appear to support his argument. While never actually identifying such "stratagems," Taylor stated that the jury was 83 percent white while the racial makeup of Philadelphia in 1982 was 40 percent black. The conclusion to be drawn by the reader is that the prosecution must have used some sort of trickery to racially stack the jury against Abu-Jamal. The math seems to work. The theory does not. It is Taylor who is employing the trickery. Potential jurors are selected one at a time and there is no way to guarantee that the twelve people selected are going to be a perfect mathematical mirror of the racial makeup of the city. Our justice system, for better or for worse, simply does not work that way. Further, both the prosecution and the defendant get to remove potential jurors who are accepted by the other side.

Joe McGill knew what he was up against. He was a trial prosecutor familiar with the demographics of the city and determined to qualify as many black jurors as possible. The first juror he selected was black. As it turned out, this juror was later disqualified because of misconduct and was replaced by a non-black alternate. Furthermore, Taylor also failed to reveal that at least one black juror accepted by McGill was struck by Abu-Jamal who, at the time, was temporarily acting as his own lawyer. Yes, it is true—circumstances created a final jury with only two black people. If the first juror selected had not been thrown off the case for misconduct and had Abu-Jamal not struck one black juror that McGill had accepted, there would have been four black people on the jury. Would Taylor consider a 30 percent black jury in a 40 percent black city sufficiently pleasing to his politically correct sensibilities?

As to the Taylor statement that there is a "Police report strongly supporting Jamal's claim that his 'confession' was a complete fabrication," Taylor is referring to a report written by Officer Gary Wakshul in which he wrote, regarding Abu-Jamal's transport to Jefferson the night he murdered

Danny, "The negro male made no comments." But Wakshul later stated that he had heard Abu-Jamal shout out "I shot the Mother Fucker and I hope he dies." Had Wakshul testified to the confession at trial, he might have been impeached by what he had written. But that's not what happened. What Taylor leaves out is that two *other* witnesses testified at trial that they heard Abu-Jamal bragging about the murder, one of whom was Danny's partner, Officer Garry Bell. The other witness was Priscilla Durham, a black woman who was a Jefferson Hospital security guard and not only heard Abu-Jamal confess, but immediately made a report to a supervisor about hearing that confession. Her reportage was produced at trial and Durham confirmed that it correctly stated what she had heard: Abu-Jamal bragged about shooting Danny. So, which is it? Are the witnesses lying—even Durham, who reported the confession the next day and had no conceivable axe to grind—or did Wakshul temporarily forget the confession because he was distraught over Danny's murder? Don't ask Taylor. He apparently never heard Durham, or Durham's report.

Taylor's next argument was that there is evidence *suggesting* that three prosecution eyewitnesses changed their stories at trial from the ones they had given to police that morning. This sounds pretty sinister until one looks at the record to see exactly how the eyewitnesses "changed" their testimony. In each instance, Taylor focuses on trivia, like the precise distance that Abu-Jamal staggered before he fell or how tall he is, while disregarding the salient facts eyewitnesses *consistently* stated each time they told their stories. Taylor also failed to tell his readers that these eyewitnesses had no opportunity or reason to coordinate their accounts. No eyewitness had any association or relationship with any other eyewitness. Each eyewitness independently stated that, from distances of less than sixty feet, each saw Abu-Jamal stand over the fallen Danny, shoot him in the face, then run or stagger a short distance and fall to the ground. Furthermore, it seems as if Taylor's preoccupation with *theories* of police corruption distracted him from the fact that, within less than an hour of the shooting, four eyewitnesses told four different police officers, in four different locations, that they saw Abu-Jamal shoot Danny, try to run away, and then sit down at the scene. Police later picked up the injured Abu-Jamal where he sat, where lying beside him was an empty gun registered in his name. Talk about taking your eye off the ball! Who cares about how tall Abu-Jamal is or how much he weighed!

One need only look at the evidence offered at the 1995 PCRA hearing to dispel any notion suggesting that the prosecution's eyewitnesses lied. Verification came from a *defense witness*, Robert Harkins, yet another witness to Abu-Jamal firing the shot that killed Danny, called by the Defense Dream Team for Abu-Jamal, who was driving his cab directly past the shooting on December 9, 1981. He had an unobstructed view of the entire shooting and, according to Leonard Weinglass, Harkins might have been the closest person to the shooting. Harkins gave a written statement to police within an hour of the shooting. Interestingly, Joe McGill had decided not to call Robert Harkins as a prosecution eyewitness at trial because he knew that the more people he put on the stand, the greater the likelihood that they would disagree about peripheral details, to the detriment of essential truth. In 1995, Abu-Jamal's attorney chose to call Robert Harkins, apparently in the hope of uncovering some minor inconsistency and/or to take focus off the pertinent facts. But, while being questioned by Abu-Jamal's own attorney, Dan Williams, Harkins stated that he had seen a man shoot Danny, saw Danny fall to the ground, and then watched as a struggle ensued. A stunned Williams asked Harkins, "And you told them [the detectives] that the person, the police officer fell down and that's when the shooting happened?" Harkins replied, "Well, he leaned over and two, two to three flashes from the gun. But then he walked, sat down on the curb." An even more stunned Williams asked, "The guy that done [*sic*] the shooting walked and sat down on the curb?" Harkins replied, "On the pavement."[185] This is exactly where the police found Abu-Jamal with his empty five-shot Charter Arms handgun at his side, less than two minutes after the murder. So Abu-Jamal's own eyewitness testified to Abu-Jamal's guilt and, in so doing, verified the credibility of the prosecution's eyewitnesses. This information was all available to Stuart Taylor when he wrote his article. Yet, Taylor continued to "suggest" that the prosecution's eyewitnesses offered perjured testimony.

In Taylor's wildly distorted version of the events of December 9, Abu-Jamal is cast as the brave savior to his defenseless brother who was being attacked and "beaten bloody" with a flashlight by the "bigger" Danny. Taylor fictionalizes: "The officer *probably* shot Jamal in the chest before Jamal shot the officer—perhaps before Jamal drew his own gun." This story, unsubstantiated by one iota of evidence, reads more like a fantasy than anything that resembles the confirmed story line. Where did Stuart Taylor find the evidence in the record to support that theory? He didn't. It's simply a self-indulgent fairy tale dreamed up at my husband's expense. Even the most unhinged members of Abu-Jamal's radical-left fans do not make arguments this absurd.

In a de facto concession to the improbability of the "Danny as perpetrator" theory, Taylor alternatively considers the defense theory that someone else shot Danny and ran away before police arrived. This story is equally preposterous. Bear in mind that the time between the shooting and the police's arrival was approximately seventy seconds. Yet, Taylor concludes that this explanation of the events is "more plausible" than the prosecution's. In so contending, Taylor again ignores the fact that, whether he likes it or not, the prosecution's theory is based on the testimony of people who were there and saw the murder happen. Meanwhile, Taylor's conspiracy theories about "who shot first" and "a real killer" are based on little more than his inventive musings. While Taylor's article certainly demonstrates creativity and provides a riveting read, its unsupported nature renders it more of a work of fiction that anything that should be seriously considered in determining the culpability of the man who murdered my husband.

At the article's conclusion, Taylor attempts to leave the reader with more reasoned observations, perhaps in the hope that they will be more willing to overlook the outlandish nature of his previous speculations. Taylor writes about Abu-Jamal's word games and weasel-speak. He calls attention to Abu-Jamal's "rules of engagement" when granting interviews and his unwillingness to tell anyone what happened the night he shot my husband. After all his speculation, Taylor finally came to the conclusion, for him a startling one, that "Mumia Abu-Jamal murdered Officer Daniel Faulkner." One marvels at the meandering maze of rumors he walks through to come to the same destination that every objective journalist has arrived at over the past twenty-five years. I'm sorry, Mr. Taylor, but it just wasn't worth the trip.

Needless to say, I was very upset when the Stuart Taylor article was published. He hammered at each and every minute adjustment in the prosecution's side of the case and grossly exaggerated the import of such trivial changes. He confused human beings for surveillance cameras and cast undue doubt on strong eyewitness accounts. I sent him a letter pointing out the imbalance in his reporting and the lack of attention he gave to the utter failure of the defense to prove any of the article's theories during the PCRA hearing that had just ended. I remember saying to him that, if he were taking the position that Abu-Jamal was poorly represented at trial and that the witnesses were coerced and changed their story, then please tell me why, when given the chance to prove it, the defense failed so miserably?

Unfortunately, the *American Lawyer* piece written by Stuart Taylor Jr. breathed new life into a demoralized Abu-Jamal defense. Despite their bitter defeat in the PCRA process, the Taylor interpretation served to reinvigorate their efforts. On balance, as 1995 ended, I think we had a pretty good year. We had emerged triumphant from the Summer of Hell, successfully quashed the defense's outlandish speculations in a court of law, and convincingly maintained our case. We were exhausted and emotionally wearied, but there was great comfort in knowing we had faced the enemy and won. Yet, the *American Lawyer* piece was a chilling reminder of the capricious nature of our Mumia-saturated lives. We were not sure what the future might bring.

2 1

THE BRUDERHOF

If the Abu-Jamal efforts were white-hot in 1995, the coals were certainly still simmering in the spring of 1996. Although Judge Sabo had dealt Abu-Jamal a setback after the first of what would be three PCRA hearings, Stuart Taylor's *American Lawyer* description of the case was being widely circulated to maintain and generate Abu-Jamal support. Keep in mind that he said Abu-Jamal was guilty, but framed. The first part of his analysis— the guilt part—was ignored in the Abu-Jamal circulation of his article. The Internet was ablaze with a growing number of national and international Web sites for Abu-Jamal and word on the street in Philadelphia was that the BBC was interested in filming a documentary about the case. Much like a political campaign, it was a battle being waged simultaneously on many different levels. By the spring of 1996, I thought I had seen it all: book and radio deals bestowed upon a cop killer; phony witnesses emerging from the shadows; celebrities commanding national platforms and speaking about a case despite an admitted lack of knowledge. And then, just when I thought things could not get any more bizarre, the theater of the absurd expanded its cast of characters. The newest entry was a group of German pacifists, a totalitarian religious cult who call themselves the "Bruderhof"—German for "Society of Brothers."

I had never heard of the Bruderhof before they got involved in the case. As I later found out, they are an extremely private society. The sparse information available about them is provided mostly by members who have rejected the group's rigid ideology and managed to escape. My first recollection of their involvement is seeing them at the 1995 PCRA hearing. Their distinctive dress made an instant impression. The men all sported blue shirts and the women dressed in pinafores. At the time, they seemed just another feature of the backdrop of madness, a few more actors present to participate in the folly. I remember drawing parallels between the Bruderhof and the Amish, the Pennsylvania Dutch, who are a presence in Lancaster County outside of Philadelphia. But, unlike the Amish, the Bruderhof do not reject modern technology[186] and instead embrace it as part of their mission and perpetuation. That mission now included support for Mumia Abu-Jamal.

As their presence in the case grew increasingly vigorous, I decided to do a little research on the Bruderhof history. I recall reading in the newspaper that they had begun in Germany in the 1920s and had an association at times with the Hutterians, another pacifist strain of Christianity. Members were supposedly forced out of Germany in the Nazi era because of their refusal to join Hitler. As of the mid-1990s, they supposedly had about two thousand members who lived in six small communities in the northeastern United States. They also had active branches in the United Kingdom, Germany, and Australia.

According to their own literature, their stated goal was to create a society where self-interest yields to the common good. No member receives a salary or has a bank account. Income from all business is pooled and then used for the care of the members and for various communal outreach efforts. In the commune, two meals a day are eaten together, and several evenings a week the group gets together for fellowship, singing, prayer, and/or decision-making. To generate income, the Bruderhof own several companies, most notably Plough Publishing.

Their faith ostensibly is based on Jesus's teaching from the Sermon on the Mount, "Love Your Brother as Yourself." Their beliefs are supposedly structured around the tenets of non-violence, the refusal to bear arms, and a staunch practice of never condoning the killing of another human being for any reason. Members do not serve in any country's armed forces. "God's will is for community and his will is done most completely in community."[187] Possessions are seen as sinful and all income and wealth is shared freely. "To do God's will, we must free ourselves from the sin of possession."[188]

So what did the Bruderhof now have to do with Abu-Jamal? Their leader, J. Christoph Arnold, said that "Mumia has, in a sense, become one of us . . . Even though he is not a believing Christian, his writings have brought the Gospel of Christ alive to us in a new way. He reflects the same faith in the possibility of redemption despite terrible suffering."[189] Abu-Jamal was said to be in constant contact with Bruderhof children through letters that he affectionately signed "Papa Mu." A picture of Abu-Jamal smiled at the children from a windowsill in a school converted into their headquarters for the "Children's Crusade from Death Row."[190] A few years after the Bruderhof first got involved in this case, Plough released one of Abu-Jamal's books, *Death Blossoms*. The group also has some radio involvement, and Abu-Jamal's radio show is broadcast on Bruderhof Radio.

After Judge Sabo granted Abu-Jamal a stay of execution in 1995, he received a letter from Bruderhof member Richard Thomson dated July 5, 1995. Thomson thanked Judge Sabo for granting the hearing and made an unusual request. He wrote: "My request is that if this hearing does NOT result in a fresh trial, or at least a reversal of the death warrant for Mumia, I want to offer my own life in place of Mumia's and accept the lethal injection in his place so that he may live and your law be satisfied."[191] Thomson went on to cite the "Let him who is without sin cast the first stone" parable to show his opposition to the death penalty. This sixty-one-year-old Bruderhof member, father of eight and grandfather of fifteen, offered to terminate his own life to save Abu-Jamal as part of a political statement and disapproval of capital punishment laws.

In between the 1995 PCRA hearing and the events I am describing now, the Bruderhof joined forces with a group called the James E. Chaney Foundation, which was created to honor the civil rights worker who was slain in Mississippi in 1964. The two groups formed what they named the very official-sounding National Commission on Capital Punishment. Despite their ostensible air of broad concern, the greatest indicator of their profound partiality is made obvious by reading their roster; one of their advisory board members is none other than Team Mumia superstar lawyer Leonard Weinglass. Under the banner of anti–death penalty advocacy, the Bruderhof sought to hold "hearings" on the death penalty in the ornate chambers of Philadelphia's City Council. They wanted Abu-Jamal to be a participant!

Rich Costello, president of the Fraternal Order of Police, was fit to be tied. Based on some research he had done, he believed the Bruderhof was a cult. Rich has never been one to mince words. At the time, Rich was quoted as saying that the Bruderhof was "nothing more than a thinly veiled Abu-Jamal support group. We're not going to give them what they want, which is violence, so that they can get on the news. They're blood-thirsty parasites and their hearing is like a drug seminar sponsored by the Colombian drug cartel."[192]

Rich Costello was not the only one at home in Philadelphia who was offended by the group's plan to take control of City Council Chambers. Many members of City Council were disgruntled and frustrated that their workplace had become the constant backdrop for the Abu-Jamal effort. They did not want to see their formal work environment used as a forum for anti–death penalty crusades for the second year in a row. Councilman James Kenney was one of seven City Council members (Anna Verna, Frank Rizzo, Richard Mariano, Frank DiCicco, Thacher Longstreth, and Joan Krajewski were the others) to sign a letter protesting the use of their chambers for this anti–death penalty forum. Initially, Council President (and future mayor) John Street stayed out of the fray; but not councilman Jimmy Kenney. He was not afraid to take a stand, and argued: "I don't want to deny a group the right to hold a hearing but having it here somehow gives them legitimacy and approval. And, in my opinion, this group doesn't deserve that legitimacy."[193] Kenney echoed the FOP position saying, "It's not fair to the members of the police department that we're going to allow a government building and the main room in it to legitimize a group, some of whom believe it's OK to shoot police officers."[194]

Sadly, Council President John Street ultimately gave permission for the Bruderhof's death penalty hearing to take place. This time, I was determined to stay away. It was probably the only time in twenty-five years that I refrained from personally appearing in Philadelphia to confront people I regarded as Danny's detractors. They announced their intention to hold three straight days of "hearings" in City Hall, including Abu-Jamal via videotape as well as other so-called luminaries and "legal heavyweights" such as Bianca Jagger. My instincts told me that if I stayed away, they would receive less publicity. Rather than attend, I decided to write a letter that I would submit to Michael Smerconish to read aloud. I knew I could not stop their effort and feared that my arrival would give their kangaroo court added publicity. In this vein, the letter was the perfect solution. Michael dutifully delivered. I think he was the only person who actually confronted the group and unapologetically presented them with his pro–death penalty view.

During this time, I remember Michael was particularly emboldened by the recent results of a criminology study at Wayne State University. The study revealed that following widely publicized executions, there are fewer murders committed on the third day thereafter. Death penalty opponents have persistently claimed that the death penalty is not a deterrent. Well, Michael had research that said otherwise. With fervor and conviction, Michael presented the evidence to the group.

I have long believed that the death penalty opponents' claim that capital punishment serves no deterrence value is only valid insofar as potential criminals perceive such sentences as empty threats. Danny's case is a prime example. If Abu-Jamal's death sentence is ever carried out, it will be done more than a quarter century after his crime. To the extent the death penalty is not a deterrent, perhaps it is because of the lag time between sentencing and the punishment. As a society, we have got to do something to stop the endless cycle of appeals. No one has learned this the hard way more than me.

The first two days of the Bruderhof confab in Council Chambers consisted of myriad experts and crusaders who gave raw emotional testimony that the vengeance wrought by the death penalty was empty and did nothing to ease the suffering of victims.[195] Children whose fathers were on death row spoke, and a statement in opposition to the death penalty was read on behalf of Bianca Jagger.

On the third and final day, the hearings were moved to the Friends Meeting Room because City Council needed its chambers. On this day, my husband's murderer, Abu-Jamal, was shown on videotape, saying: "the death penalty is being used by politicians as a stepping stone for higher office. They say [people sentenced to death] are the worst of the worst. But, actually, money, race and rank determine who gets on death row."[196]

As expected, the backdrop of the Bruderhof event proved to be yet another missed opportunity for Abu-Jamal to quash uncertainty and discuss exactly what he was doing at about 4:00 a.m. on December 9, 1981—if not murdering Danny. He was not present, mind you, but the spectacle created by the Bruderhof returned the limelight to the man who has never answered for himself. I am not questioning Abu-Jamal's Fifth Amendment right. Our Bill of Rights guarantees that he need not testify on his own behalf. But you would think that, after a jury has delivered its verdict, a rational public would require at least some type of explanation before pledging their unwavering adoration and even offering to take his place for execution. This, however, has never been the case. Abu-Jamal receives many visitors in jail; before visiting him, many of these doting "fans" are cautioned not to ask him about the case. This *should* trigger immediate suspicion. Yet, despite this unsettling forewarning, his devoted brethren file through the prison doors, glowing with a false sense of righteousness, to greet their persecuted prisoner.

22

HBO

In early 1996, just around the time of the Bruderhof fiasco, there were simultaneous rumblings in California that people back in Philadelphia were being contacted to submit accounts for a "European" documentary about the case. Some heard it was the BBC. This news was unfortunate but not totally unexpected. The Internet was ablaze with international expressions of support for Abu-Jamal, especially in Britain, Germany, and France, among other countries. Misinformation and wacky conspiracy theories in support of Abu-Jamal had been translated into many different languages; it was truly an international campaign. Thus, news of a proposed foreign film project featuring the Abu-Jamal story was hardly shocking, and if it arose from these origins, I doubted I would get a fair shake. As I would later learn, however, the true origin of the project was much closer to home.

By the time we learned the true nature of the film project, Rich Costello, Garry Bell, and Joe McGill had already been duped into believing that they were contributing to a "British documentary" for airing on the BBC. They were never told that their assistance was actually in support of a project for American television. Although produced in part by a British company, Otmoor Productions, the project was under the direction of American media powerhouse HBO.

Now, those same devious producers who had recorded interviews with my most ardent supporters invited me to appear on camera. They provided me with no assurances. I flatly rejected their requests when they refused to give me any paperwork. All I wanted was something in writing explaining the parameters of the project. Over a decade of misrepresentations and spin had made me extraordinarily circumspect, some may say paranoid. I was not uttering a word without some legal guarantees.

Those who had already been recorded under false pretenses were very upset. FOP President Rich Costello was particularly angry about his participation. He claimed that Otmoor Productions had misrepresented themselves so he would cooperate with their efforts. According to Costello, the reporters and producers of the program claimed to be with the BBC and said that they were making a film that sought to retell the "police version" of the case.[197] It was not until I was scanning the "Events" section of my newspaper that I put the pieces together. There, I saw the mention of a documentary, not a foreign film, to be aired on HBO. Immediately, I sought an advance copy of the program just like those that were already being supplied to members of the media. I soon learned that the widow of the victim did not hold the same position as media pundits in the eyes of HBO.

I started working the telephone. My inquiry led me to a man named Richard Plepler who worked as an executive vice president for HBO. (In the spring of 2007, he would be named copresident of HBO.) I contacted him, and to my great surprise, he took the call. I told him who I was and that I was interested in seeing an advance copy of the film, which they were calling *The Case for Reasonable Doubt*, before it aired. By now, I knew that people in the media were getting teasers of it because they were calling me and telling me that it was totally one-sided and that I had to see it. When I got in touch with Plepler, he told me he would fly to California from New York and personally speak to me about it. And, true to his word, he did. He stayed at the Beverly Hills Hotel, where I met him for lunch. He tried to assure me that the piece was very factual and that they had checked everything carefully. He said lawyers had been involved in the review process. I again asked him if I could please have a copy of it so I could watch for myself. I even offered to view it with him at the hotel if he wanted to screen it there, but he refused this simple request. Not only would he not give me a copy, he wouldn't even let me see it! Basically, he had flown out to California only to tell me I would see it when the public saw it and he could do nothing else. I told him that I was offended that members of the media had advance access when I did not, even though the subject of the narrative was the brutal murder of my husband. All that he would say was that he thought I would be very pleased with the finished product.

About a month prior to the show's airing, I sent a letter to Time-Warner's chairman, Gerald Levin, warning him of the potential problems with the documentary. Time-Warner owned HBO. I also tried to call Gerald Levin to personally speak with him. I remember talking to his assistant on the phone and trying to reason with him. Levin had no idea what I was going through. He could never understand unless he walked in my shoes and lost a loved one. It is ironic that his son was murdered just a few years later. I have often wondered whether, after receiving that news, he reflected on what happened to me, and the way that I was treated by HBO. In my letter, I expressed my displeasure and criticized the documentary's use of alleged new eyewitnesses who were never used in the trial:

> It has been brought to my attention that Home Box Office, a Time-Warner Company, intends to air a British made documentary concerning a man named Mumia Abu-Jamal, and also has plans to produce a movie about this same individual. This is very troubling to me as I am the widow of the police officer this man executed in 1981.
>
> By all reports, this documentary is very one-sided and contains little fact. I have even been told that it borders on tabloid journalism. Instead of presenting the true facts of the case as they have been testified to in court, an attempt is made to sensationalize the case and the murder by allowing so-called surprise witnesses to make unchecked testimony about the murder they claim to have seen. There have been nearly a dozen appeals of my husband's case presented by quite literally dozens of attorneys defending Mr. Abu-Jamal. Where have these "surprise" witnesses been for the past 15 years and, if they are at all credible, why hasn't Mr. Abu-Jamal's defense team put them on the witness stand in court? The facts of my husband's murder are brutal and crystal clear. All physical evidence and eyewitness testimony has demonstrated over and over again that Mumia Abu-Jamal shot my husband in the back and, while he lay face up and conscious on the sidewalk, Abu-Jamal emptied his gun into my wounded husband's face. He was sentenced to death nearly fifteen years ago.[198]

HBO didn't blink. Instead, on July 7, 1996, one year after Judge Sabo rejected every one of Abu-Jamal's outstanding legal claims, HBO televised the one-hour documentary titled *A Case for Reasonable Doubt*. At home in our living room in Southern California, Paul and I watched together; we were horrified. The film opened with the hauntingly mellifluous voice of Abu-Jamal: "I am a journalist, a husband, a father, a grandfather, and an

African American. I live in the fastest-growing public housing tract in America." The camera then focused on a sign outside his "residence," the State Correctional Institute of Greene County, Pennsylvania. It went beyond our worst expectations. We both knew that the battle was far from over and that this HBO production would be a huge setback.

The program included the following disclaimer: "This program looks at a complex and controversial legal case which has generated much debate on both sides for over 14 years. This documentary examines that controversy."[199] Just as soon as the disclaimer faded from the screen, however, the bias seeped in. HBO was not blatantly telling lies; they were way too clever for that. Rather, it was more of a careful distortion of the truth. They cunningly manipulated fact and circumstance in order to avoid outright lying. They took bits and pieces of transcripts and partial sentences out of context. They artfully edited, cut, and pasted in order to paint Abu-Jamal as the unfortunate victim of the justice system gone awry. They included much of the material that had been rejected at the PCRA hearing one year previously. As repugnant as it may have been to the informed, it certainly made for good controversial TV for the masses.

Because of HBO's assurance to me that the program had been thoroughly fact-checked, Paul and I assumed that the end result would be far more accurate than it turned out to be. As we sat there on the couch together, we expected reasonableness and respectful restrain. Our amazement soon turned to deep annoyance as we continued to watch. At various points during our initial viewing, one of us would leap off the sofa and exclaim, "That's not true!" or "That's been disproven!" Most enraging of all was the sly way in which the producer used the interviews of Joe McGill, Garry Bell, and Rich Costello to provide the illusion of balanced coverage. However, instead of giving these men "on the other side" the full opportunity to present their case, they aired only snippets of their interviews— never enough to tell the whole story. The overall effect was a misleading narrative thinly veiled in a cleverly crafted impression of impartiality.

Early in the program, the producers flashed scenes from Danny's funeral. These images were accompanied by a voice-over clip of Philadelphia radio station KYW Newsradio's coverage of the events. The pictures showed me, and the rest of Danny's family, experiencing mind-numbing grief. The scenes were then juxtaposed with scenes from an Abu-Jamal protest. It continued with Dr. Anthony Colletta, the surgical resident who worked on Danny and Mumia Abu-Jamal at Jefferson Hospital the night of the murder, December 9, 1981. Dr. Colletta was unhappy with the police response to Abu-Jamal. Colletta claimed that he was the only person who seemed to care about attending to Abu-Jamal's wounds.[200] Lydia Wallace, Abu-Jamal's older sister, was then shown discussing the physical state her brother was in when she saw him at the hospital. She recalled that she could hardly recognize him as his face was so badly bruised and gashed from the force used in arresting him. She then claimed that her brother cried out, "I'm innocent. I'm innocent. They're trying to kill me."[201] Missing, of course, was the police response to the beating allegations.

The ballistics evidence was one of the main focuses of the HBO presentation. HBO relied upon a ballistics expert who claimed that the evidence was poorly handled during the 1981 investigation and 1982 trial. From watching the documentary, one would come away believing that the police and prosecution had truly dropped the ball and failed to do legitimate tests. This, however, was not the case.

HBO relied on a guy named Herbert McDonnell, a ballistics expert in Philadelphia. They didn't give him all of the information about what tests had been done at the original trial; thus, his so-called expert opinion was missing huge chunks of vital information. When he made his statement, it sounded very authoritative: "They didn't do this test," and "They should have done that test." He contradicted himself because he said that no ballistic testing was done, and then claimed that a test was done that indicated Abu-Jamal was shot from farther away than twelve inches. By that point in the show, Paul and I were in shock. We were literally screaming at the television.

The erroneous ballistics claim has been repeated endlessly by the Abu-Jamal defense. As I have already explained, supporters of Abu-Jamal contend that the caliber of bullets in Danny's body did not match that of Abu-Jamal's gun. They also claim that some ballistics tests that they say should have been done were never completed. This is just not true.

Despite conclusive evidence that the bullets in Danny's body were .38 caliber, the cold hard facts did little to deter HBO from regurgitating and propagating the ballistics myth. The Abu-Jamal defense team still continues to disseminate this twisted tale.

In addition to the ballistics misinformation, HBO's made-for-TV version of Abu-Jamal's "campaign for justice" gave prominence to three other often repeated but amazingly unlikely Mumia Myths having to do with ballistics tests that "should" have been performed:

First, HBO contended that a trace metal detection test should have been done on Danny's jacket to determine the distance from which the bullet in his back was fired, in the vain hope that a shot from a considerable distance would support the defense's claim that Danny had been shot by an unknown assailant who fled the scene.

A trace metal detection test *was* done. It confirmed that gunpowder residue was present on Danny's jacket and also on Abu-Jamal's clothes. This confirmed that Danny had been shot in the back from a range of less than twelve inches.[202] Only two people were seen by the five eyewitnesses to have come that close to Danny—William Cook and Mumia Abu-Jamal. This clearly contradicts the theory proposed by Abu-Jamal's attorneys that an unknown man shot Danny from several feet away prior to fleeing the scene.

Second, HBO related that supporters of Abu-Jamal contend that a neutron activation test should have been done on his hands to determine if he had recently fired a weapon. They then contradict their own claim by saying that Abu-Jamal's hands were tested but the results of such tests were hidden by the prosecution. They want it both ways. It is interesting to note that his supporters argue both sides and that Abu-Jamal himself, the person whose hands are in question, can't seem to remember what happened. Amazing.

As it turns out, a neutron activation test was not done on Abu-Jamal's hands for a very good reason. Abu-Jamal compromised the accuracy of such a test when he struggled with the police officers attempting to arrest him. Heavy particle residue (gunpowder residue) that can be found by neutron activation is easily contaminated or lost by any kind of jostling, brushing, or energetic conduct by the shooter. Expert Charles Tumosa, supervisor of the police crime lab, testified that any such test done after the arrest would have been inconclusive due to such contamination.[203] In his

1995 PCRA testimony, Abu-Jamal's own ballistics expert, George Fass-nacht, agreed that a neutron activation test would have been "very difficult to perform" on Abu-Jamal's hands given his struggle with police.[204] It should therefore be perfectly plain and obvious why a neutron activation test was not done. Even if it had been, its results would have been murky and inconclusive. In a case where even the crystal clear has been tainted with outlandish theories of doubt, inconclusive neutron activation test results would have only complicated matters more.

Also bear in mind that when Abu-Jamal was brought into the emergency room at Jefferson Hospital that night, he had been shot and was in need of immediate medical attention. One can only imagine the furor and racially charged accusations that would have been flung around if treatment had been delayed while police personnel analyzed his hands.

Third, Team Mumia fatuously asserts that the police should have "sniffed" the barrel of Abu-Jamal's gun to determine if it had been fired that morning.

If this seems wildly unscientific to those of you not trained in ballistics (myself included), you would be correct. In fact, Abu-Jamal's own ballistics expert, George Fassnacht again, testified in the 1995 PCRA hearing that the "Smell Test" is completely subjective,[205] irrefutably rendering such a test scientifically invalid. Therefore, there was no way to prove in a court of law the accuracy of the sniffing officer, male or female, with or without sinus problems or a head cold coming on. Even if such a "Smell Test" had been done, you can only imagine the claims that would have erupted from Abu-Jamal's defense if their client had been convicted due to something as subjective as one Philadelphia police officer's sensitive sense of smell. There is little doubt that had that "Sniff Test" been done at the scene and its results been entered into evidence against Abu-Jamal by the prosecution, the defense today would have one more thing to holler about.

Another troubling aspect of the HBO piece was the way it portrayed Abu-Jamal himself. Mumia Abu-Jamal had been on death row for some fourteen years and convicted of killing a police officer. Nevertheless, HBO chose to refer to him as an "award-winning freelance broadcaster." They even had the audacity to assert that, at the time of Danny's murder, Abu-Jamal was enjoying the pinnacle of his career. Abu-Jamal himself admitted that he had to drive a cab because working as a freelance journalist did not pay enough. What he did not mention was that he had recently been fired from his permanent broadcasting job at WHYY.

And, once again, just like at the recent Bruderhof "hearing" in City Council Chambers, HBO gave the "award-winning" Abu-Jamal the opportunity to speak on camera about his life behind bars. And, once again, as perfectly expected, he was not asked what he did the night of December 9, 1981.

Up until this point, our battles had been largely waged in Philadelphia. Although the campaign for Mumia Abu-Jamal had invaded the national and even global discourse, the case's intricacies were still primarily discussed and debated on the East Coast. The HBO special thus marked an unfortunate and tectonic shift. The so-called documentary was aired for a national TV audience that included many of our friends with whom we had always been reluctant to discuss the details of the case. Paul and I had desperately needed some place we could go and be removed from the tumult that raged on the East Coast. Our social circle in California had provided that refuge. But now, just as I had been forced to adjust to the withering away of so many aspects of my personal life, my social sanctuary, too, was stolen from me.

As Paul and I sat in our living room that night, we were hyper-aware that our friends sat on their own cozy couches with their families, also viewing the HBO debacle. After all, we'd even recommended the program, as we believed Richard Plepler's repeated assurances that this would be a fair presentation. By the end of the HBO program, my initial grunts of disapproval had escalated into incoherent yelping at the television. I was disgusted. I was angry. I felt hurt and misled. Right after it aired, the phone started ringing with friends calling to say they were impressed by what they had seen on TV. They wanted to know if we were absolutely sure it was Mumia Abu-Jamal who murdered Danny. As the program had prompted them to do, they also questioned the fairness of the trial. I was really hurt. How could they possibly be concerned about Abu-Jamal? There has never been any doubt in my mind who killed my husband. I was right there immediately following the killing when both the murderer and his victim were being treated at Jefferson Hospital. I was deeply offended that some of our friends had chosen to rely on the carefully edited speculations of a group of people so far removed from the legal maneuverings of the actual trial.

It was like a tale of two coasts. In California a small group of friends and I were putting out fires. But back in Philadelphia, my old friends knew better. By now, they had seen and heard it all before. You have heard me say that it has always been the case that Abu-Jamal's support diminishes the closer you get to Philadelphia or, said differently, it grows the farther you get from where it happened. My Philadelphia friends were calling me and saying how angry they were and how one-sided the HBO documentary was.

Veteran *Philadelphia Inquirer* columnist Steve Lopez, who has since joined the *Los Angeles Times* and is not exactly a conservative summed up the hometown sentiment best:

> I realize HBO is new at this, but you don't have to be Mike Wallace to know what stone to look under. Instead of asking the question, HBO rehashes the same questions that have been out there for nearly 15 years. It also gives us a lot of special effects, flashing lights and haunting music, all of which will probably attract even more people to Mumia Abu-Jamal's internal flock of movie stars, left wing burnouts and other dingbats.
>
> Abu-Jamal, interviewed in prison, says he is innocent. He does not elaborate and is not asked to. His brother, the only other living person who knows what happened that night, and who has refused to talk about it, is not interviewed and is barely mentioned.
>
> Near the end of the HBO piece, a narrator lets Abu-Jamal off the hook with this weasely line: Abu-Jamal now says that if he can get a retrial before a jury of his peers, he will finally give a full account of the night of December 9, 1981.
>
> That's very big of him. But after waiting more than 5000 days (more than half of Danny Faulkner's lifetime) for him to pull his story together, I wouldn't go to the bank on it.[206]

I contacted Richard Plepler at HBO the day after the program premiered. He told me the show had had a small audience and its subsequent airings would be during off-peak hours. He assured me that it would air only a few more times. Paul also had a conversation with Plepler, calling him in New York the next day. Plepler told Paul that if HBO had left out significant facts, he would write a personal apology to me and air a retraction. He also said, "Look we got the results in from last night and the viewing was very,

very low. Nobody saw it. Don't worry about it." He said it was only going to run for a week in off hours, so if the first viewing didn't get any viewership, then the subsequent airings were unlikely to attract interest. He said he couldn't take it off the air but would put a disclaimer on the front end explaining, in so many words, "This is one side's view of the situation." What else could we do but accept that?

In truth, we later learned that *A Case for Reasonable Doubt* did not receive the anemic numbers that Plepler alleged. The program actually attracted a vast amount of attention during its first week of airing and became an HBO success. They received so much attention, in fact, that they extended it for another month and ran it in contradiction of everything that Richard Plepler told us.

Moreover, the program was repeated on Court TV, followed by a one-hour panel discussion on the same network titled *Fair or Foul? The Case of Mumia Abu-Jamal.* The panel for the discussion featured a retired New York City cop who confessed to knowing nothing about the Abu-Jamal case. Another panel member was Stuart Taylor Jr., whose article in *American Lawyer* concluded, as I have detailed, that Abu-Jamal was framed for a murder he *did* commit. I called Plepler and blasted him again. I was disgusted and wanted him to know. How dare he lie to me, fly out to California, sit in front of me, look me in the eye, and tell me this piece was factual when, in fact, it was just propaganda for Abu-Jamal, to free Mumia Abu-Jamal? I called him every name in the book.

Five days after the program aired, Paul wrote to Richard Plepler and thanked him for having generously spent an hour on the telephone with him listening to his concerns. Plepler offered to meet with Paul and me. Paul then sought to clarify the content of that meeting by articulating thirteen places in the program where he believed errors existed that implied "reasonable doubt." HBO declined such a meeting.

Rich Costello and the Fraternal Order of Police organized a boycott against HBO. Costello asked his nearly thirteen thousand members to cancel their HBO subscriptions and requested other state and national FOP organizations to join the cause.[207] After the airing of the HBO piece, the effort gained additional momentum as more police officers viewed the piece and became enraged. The *Philadelphia Inquirer* reported at the time that "Dallas and San Diego intend to pass resolutions joining the boycott. It looks like this thing is catching on."[208]

The experience did not end when the program finally stopped airing on HBO. *A Case for Reasonable Doubt* was subsequently released on video and quickly became the mandatory must-see recruiting and training tool for the radical leftist supporters of Abu-Jamal. One day at Blockbuster I had the unfortunate surprise of stumbling upon a copy as I browsed through the racks. I was later made aware that the program was also circulating around the Internet. The video was quickly becoming the staple of Abu-Jamal supporters on college campuses around the country. There were repeated airings of the documentary at universities as part of lectures and programs centered on the case. Supporters invaded academia and frequently touted the video as support. They would often sell copies of the video upon the program's completion, hand out information packets that tuned in to the video, and extol the information contained within the video as if God himself had delivered it on the witness stand. With the documentary as their centerpiece, the movement was quickly transforming into a cult. Mumia Abu-Jamal had become their martyr. HBO had facilitated the spread of the gospel and added a mainstream air of legitimacy.

The HBO program also resulted in the loss of one of our strongest supporters in the media. The "documentary" was so persuasive that African-American talk radio host Ken Hamblin, the so-called "Black Avenger," who had previously been sympathetic to our cause and even had me on his show a few times, now joined the doubters and began questioning the fairness of the trial. His producer was a woman named Cecily Baker. She often called me for information about the case. Suddenly, that phone line was silent.

Talk radio was not then what it is today. Early on in the case, I was able to solidify relationships with a small but strong contingency of sympathetic talk radio personalities. To this end, Ken Hamblin was a big help. Hamblin had a national program and was a big figure in radio in 1996. I was deeply grateful that he was willing to take on Danny's cause in a big way. As a result of his endorsement, I got additional support from a wide audience. I would frequently hear from complete strangers saying things like: "I was driving my truck in Iowa and heard you on the radio. I don't have that much money, but I felt so bad that I pulled over and wrote down your Web site. Here's a five dollar bill and God bless you."

All of this changed, however, with the HBO airing of *A Case for Reasonable Doubt,* and I was again forced to confront the harsh sting of betrayal. After the HBO piece aired, Hamblin invited me on his show to discuss the case and my reactions to the program. Thinking that I still had an ally, I dialed in for an interview. Instead of the support and encouragement that I had long appreciated, Hamblin surprised me with a series of probing questions indicating his newfound doubt. He announced that he now believed that Abu-Jamal did not receive a fair trial, that there were too many questions left unanswered, and that he felt generally unsettled about the case. I felt completely disarmed. After that appearance, I completely shut down and never again appeared on Hamblin's show. I blame HBO. With a robust flex of its programming muscle, a thick layer of showbiz gloss, and a few clever cuts and edits, HBO's *A Case for Reasonable Doubt* caused an uproar of unreasonable suspicion. The battle continued. Richard Plepler and HBO had breathed new life into an appropriately moribund effort. Often in the years since, I have wondered whether Plepler feels remorse for the heartache that he inflicted on my family and me. I doubt it.

2 3

THE 1996 PCRA HEARING

In 1996, Abu-Jamal's legal defense team was still licking its wounds from their stinging defeat in the 1995 Post-Conviction Relief Act hearing, but they were emboldened by their media successes. They now sought an appeals hearing to add to the record following Judge Sabo's rejection of Abu-Jamal's bid for a new trial. His lawyers claimed they had new information about Veronica Jones, a twenty-one-year-old hooker who at the time of the murder had been "on duty" about a block away from where it happened. On September 4, 1996, the Pennsylvania Supreme Court granted Abu-Jamal's request. As I was quickly discovering, it takes remarkably little for a man in Abu-Jamal's position to get a "gig" on the legal stage.

Allow me to tell you about Veronica Jones. On December 15, 1982, approximately one week after Danny's murder, Veronica Jones provided her first written and signed statement to police at her home. In that statement, she placed herself two blocks from the shooting, in front of a bar where she admittedly had been drinking and smoking marijuana all night. She characterized herself as "high" and "intoxicated." She stated that she heard gunshots whereupon, after waiting "a few minutes," she looked around the corner to investigate. She told police that, from a distance of roughly one hundred yards, she saw two men leaving the scene. "After I saw the policeman fall down, I saw two black guys walk across Locust Street and then they started sort of jogging."[209] In reality, Jones couldn't have seen Danny "fall down," as she was around the corner with absolutely no view of the shooting and she had, admittedly, stayed at the place of obstructed view until minutes after the shooting stopped. This is the first of many lies told by Veronica Jones. In an attempt to extract truth from this statement and assuming Veronica did see "two black guys," they were most likely Dessie Hightower and his friend Robert Pigford, who, like Jones, had waited until the shooting stopped to emerge from a parking lot and then headed over to see what had happened.

Jones was called as a defense witness in 1982, apparently in the hope of planting a seed of doubt about Abu-Jamal's guilt in the mind of at least one of the jurors. Despite knowing Jones's whereabouts (Abu-Jamal's investigator frequently observed her working as a prostitute), Abu-Jamal's trial attorney, Anthony Jackson, relied on her written statement and expected her to say that the two men she had seen "jogging" had run from the scene. But Jones told Jackson that the two men had actually "just stood there" and that she had never told the police that anyone had jogged away.

Jackson specifically asked Jones, his own witness, about the two men who, in her original statement, she said "started sort of jogging" after the shooting.

> **Jackson:** By the way, so I understand you clearly you are saying that you never saw two men walk across Locust Street, or jog?
> **Jones:** No, I didn't.
> **Jackson:** When you saw two men at Locust Street—did you see two men on Locust Street?"
> **Jones:** There was two men where the policeman was at. A man by the soda machine. A soda machine on Thirteenth Street. Almost, you know, near the Speedline entrance.[210]

Veronica Jones was then asked about her original statement concerning the physical proximity between Danny and the two men who remained at the scene. She had stated that they did *not* come close enough to be the "real killers." Jackson read back the statement to Jones:

> **Jackson:** How close did the two men who jogged across Locust Street get to the fallen officer?
> **Jones:** Not close enough. Maybe two or three steps away.[211]

When asked by Jackson if she remembered this question and answer, Jones again denied that she had said the men "jogged across Locust Street" in her written statement,[212] apparently to Jackson's surprise. After she was further reminded by Jackson of her initial statement to police and asked about the sudden change in her story, Jones told Jackson that she was "high" the night she had given her statement.

Jackson: By the way, on [*sic*]I guess it was the 15th of December were you intoxicated when the detectives interviewed you?
Jones: I was high.
Jackson: You were high?
Jones: Yes.
Jackson: How high?
Jones: How high?
Jackson: Yes.
Jones: Say half a nickel bag high.
Jackson: How high that is I don't really know. I mean you knew what you were saying?
Jones: I wanted to know how they knew where I lived at.
Jackson: That was your primary concern?
Jones: Yes.
Jackson: But aside from wanting to know that the question is, did you know what you were saying to them?
Jones: Everybody was questioning me.
Jackson: Again, did you know what you were saying to them?
Jones: According to this right here it is a bunch of bull.
Jackson: Again, did you know what you were saying to them?
Jones: Somewhat, yes.[213]

In addition to admitting to dishonesty and/or drug-induced confusion, Jones further revealed that police had sought her help regarding Abu-Jamal shortly after her own brush with the law. Although she did not say so, the obvious inference to be drawn was that the statement she provided was primarily motivated by her own self-interest, which she allegedly had reason to believe would be bettered through providing an incriminating report. The Veronica Jones episode was thus swiftly settled in 1982. She gave no further testimony, although she did say Danny had once saved her from being beaten and robbed.

After the 1982 trial, Veronica returned to the streets and a life of virtual anonymity for almost a decade. Veronica Jones Second Edition did not debut until months after the 1995 hearing ended. At that time, like pirates hunting for lost treasure, Abu-Jamal's lawyers found Jones and discovered she was willing to star in their latest conspiracy tale. Veronica Jones was ready to announce that the police promised her leniency on criminal charges pending against her at the time of the murder in return for her false testimony. This was the purported "new" information that led the defense lawyers to ask the State Supreme Court for a chance to allow Veronica Jones an encore performance. The high court agreed.

Thus, I found myself once again on a cross-country flight to Philadelphia in October of 1996 to hear yet another vain attempt to prove Abu-Jamal's innocence. Keep in mind that these appellate hearings are meant to be a one-time presentation by the defense to display all of their "new" evidence against guilt and to make all of their legal arguments regarding procedural error. It is highly unusual for a defendant to be granted a second PCRA hearing but the Pennsylvania Supreme Court did just that for Mumia Abu-Jamal. This time around, I was accompanied by Paul, who had not been there with me to experience the full madness of the first PCRA hearing; he had attended closing arguments only. This new hearing lasted three days; true to character, it was, as described by the *Philadelphia Inquirer*, "bizarre."[214]

Remember, the cornerstone of Abu-Jamal's 1995 defense was a story about another man killing Danny and then running from the scene east on the south side of Locust Street before police arrived. I've heard this since derisively called the "some other dude" defense. In order to support this myth, Abu-Jamal's attorneys had to find a way to discredit the testimony offered by the eyewitnesses who testified for the prosecution in 1982. Each of those eyewitnesses clearly stated that they saw Abu-Jamal run from the parking lot, pull his gun and shoot Danny, and then fall to the ground. To discredit them, Abu-Jamal's attorneys developed a series of allegations about police coercion and intimidation of witnesses. They alleged that two eyewitnesses, Cynthia White and Robert Chobert, were intimidated by the threat of prosecution for minor offenses they may have committed and that each witness was enticed into offering testimony against Abu-Jamal in return for leniency from the police. In fact, in their 1995 closing argument, the defense stated:

> For almost 13 years the prosecution has promoted the false representation that the evidence in this case is overwhelming. In fact, it is more like a house of cards that has been propped up by prosecutorial and police fabrication, coercion, alternatively coercion and promises made to witnesses. And misrepresentation, destruction of evidence.[215]

Despite Leonard Weinglass's bold pronouncements both inside and outside the courtroom, none of the evidence presented by Abu-Jamal at the 1995 PCRA had shown any alleged police coercion of witnesses. So now, in 1996, Abu-Jamal's lawyers were given the opportunity to take another crack at it. And, with his usual bluster and fanfare, Leonard Weinglass declared that Veronica Jones would blow the top off the prosecution's case by exposing allegedly rampant police coercion. Jones was cast in three roles by Abu-Jamal: (1) by stating that the two black men she had seen actually ran away and had not "just stood there" as she had testified in 1982, she would bolster their discredited theory that another man shot Danny and ran away; (2) she was to state that she had been intimidated by police into offering perjured testimony against Abu-Jamal in 1982; and (3) she was to allege that she had spoken to a prosecution witness, Cynthia White, who allegedly told her that she, too, had accepted a deal for her favorable testimony. The passage of time certainly allows for the robust workings of the creative mind. Veronica Jones had never before mentioned anything regarding the last two allegations.

Veronica Jones wins no points as a model citizen. She has a long rap sheet and she had been arrested for taking part in the robbery of a bar in Philadelphia and was facing up to ten years in prison if convicted. In her 1996 testimony, Jones claimed that two detectives visited her while she was awaiting trial and offered to have her armed robbery charges dropped if she cooperated with them. In addition, though she had never mentioned it to anyone including her family, her attorney, or the court before she met with Abu-Jamal's attorneys, for the first time ever Jones claimed that the two detectives had "intimidated" her by telling her that if she were convicted on the armed robbery charge, she could go to jail for up to ten years and that "Children's Services" would likely take her children away from her. In addition, for the first time ever, Jones alleged that these detectives told her that prosecution witness Cynthia White, a fellow prostitute, had accepted a deal in return for favorable testimony. Leonard Weinglass also noted that the armed robbery charge was dropped after Abu-Jamal's conviction. Each of these new revelations worked nicely to support Abu-Jamal's claim of police intimidation and coercion of witnesses. Abu-Jamal's lawyers had crafted quite the clever tale.

Although she had plenty of fanciful allegations to hurl, Veronica Jones circa 1996 never fully revisited her recollection of the events the morning of the murder. Instead, Leonard Weinglass carefully led Jones to vaguely admit that she had been "untruthful" about one portion of her lengthy 1982 testimony. In so doing, Jones admitted that she was "untruthful" when she told Anthony Jackson that the two men she had seen "just stood there." In dutifully following Weinglass's leading questions, Jones conveyed to the court that, contrary to her 1982 testimony, she had actually seen the two men "run from the scene."

> **Weinglass:** And do you recall in what respect the testimony that you gave was untruthful?
> **Jones:** I told them that I didn't see two men leave the, umm, run away, leave the scene.
> **Weinglass:** And, Miss Jones, in fact did you see two people run from the scene?
> **Jones:** Yes, I did.[216]

Things were certainly looking peachy for the defense after their direct examination of Veronica Jones. Veronica had painted the picture of a now mature black woman who found her way in life after her younger years as a drug-abusing prostitute. She told the court that she was terrified to come forward but felt she had to testify for her children's sake, so that they could be proud of their mother. Abu-Jamal's attorneys had been able to artfully manipulate Jones's testimony to allow for the possibility that Jones had witnessed the shooting and saw the real killer run from the scene, as had several other alleged "eyewitnesses."

The chipper spirits of the defense attorneys quickly turned dour when Jones was cross-examined. Their starlet was revealed as little more than a fickle criminal. Jones admitted to holding numerous aliases and to being arrested several times in the last decade. Her new story was that two detectives had visited her in 1982 while she was in jail, where she was being held on weapons and robbery charges, and offered to help her get back on the street if she helped them convict Abu-Jamal.[217] Arlene Fisk, the assistant district attorney, did an excellent job with the cross-examination. While Jones was trying to present herself as a reformed mother embarking on the path of virtue, Fisk was quick to emphasize Jones's persistent bad behavior: robbery, welfare fraud, and passing bad checks. Frisk also made a mockery of Veronica's abrupt reemergence after years of silence. According to Fisk, the defense claim of an arduous search for and discovery of the missing Jones was highly unlikely, especially since the 1995 hearings were subject to national headlines and TV coverage.

Furthermore, when cross-examined about the murder, Veronica Jones admitted that *she never saw the shooting*. She was around the corner, drunk and stoned with "some guy" and admitted that, when she did look around the corner, two guys "sort of jogged across the street." She also admitted that she couldn't say whether or not the men she saw—minutes after the shooting had ended—were the shooters because she never saw the shooting.

It was also made clear that Jones was never granted any favorable treatment after submitting her statement. Jones never accepted any kind of deal; nothing ever happened in regard to addressing her case. Fisk had court documents proving that Jones's stepfather paid her bail, whereupon Jones left the state and failed to appear for her own trial. Moreover, when she was arrested yet again in 1985, on a different charge, the outstanding warrant was discovered; she pleaded no contest and was sentenced to five years probation. Arlene Fisk argued that if she had really cut a deal with the police, she would have stuck around to get the benefit of her bargain.

The prosecution was also quick to note that, if any deal regarding Jones's felony case had been struck, it would have come from the district attorney, not the police. The police have no authority to manipulate cases in the courts. They would never have been able to hold up their end of any alleged deal and their failure to produce the desired effect would have sent Jones immediately to the shelter of her attorney or to Abu-Jamal's attorney and/or the press. But it didn't happen. There was no record of any deal being negotiated at any time for either Veronica Jones or Cynthia White.

Jones's previously vivid recollection of events in 1982 suddenly turned murky. She was now unable to remember when or where the alleged meeting with police occurred. She also admitted that she had never really discussed the specifics of a "deal," although she had claimed otherwise earlier in the day.

Fisk: How long before you were brought in to testify did these men come to see you in prison?
Jones: I don't remember.[218]

Jones admitted that she had never mentioned to anyone in 1982 anything about either this alleged police pressure or the offer of a deal connected to her pending armed robbery case. Most notably, Jones never told David Rosen, Esq. about the deal. Rosen was the Public Defender who was representing Jones in her 1981 robbery case. The very case that would have been impacted by any deal made on Jones's behalf.

Fisk: Your attorney that you spoke to at your preliminary hearing, that is after the visit of the police officers—I'm sorry—the detectives to the prison, did you report that visit to your attorney?
Jones: I don't remember. I don't remember.[219]

Jones admitted that she was arrested again in 1988 and was represented by the same public defender. Once again, the older and admittedly wiser Jones failed to mention the police threats or the alleged deal she was offered.

Fisk: Okay. At that time you were reunited, were you not, with the same attorney who had represented you at the preliminary hearing some six or seven years earlier?
Jones: Yes, ma'am.
Fisk: Did you at that time in 1988 report to your attorney that you had been threatened or intimidated by detectives' [*sic*] and as a result had perjured yourself under oath?
Jones: I was 20 years old.
. . .

Fisk: You will agree with me that in 1988 you were six years older and therefore you were 26 years old?
Jones: Well, I was 26. Still I was a very naïve person not knowing the Court system as I do a little now.
Fisk: Now, is your answer that you did not report it to your attorney or you do not remember whether—
Jones: I don't remember reporting it to him.[220]

In fact, Rosen, who represented Jones in 1982, testified at the 1996 PCRA that Jones had never mentioned this deal to him.

Veronica Jones also admitted that the police had never told her what it was that she was supposed to say in return for the leniency she was to receive from them. In direct contradiction to what Abu-Jamal's attorneys had alleged, Veronica Jones then admitted under cross-examination that she never actually reached any deal with the police.

> **Fisk:** Oh, all right. Did you say anything to these detectives when they visited you in prison?
> **Jones:** I never said too much, I just listened.
> **Fisk:** Well, did you tell them you would do it or did you tell them you wouldn't?
> **Jones:** I just wanted to, I had them reassure me about my charges being dropped. And they kept reassuring me, reassuring me. Then they started saying how my kids could be taken from my mom being I was sent up for all this time. Yeah, so I remember talking to them but I don't recall what I told them.[221]

Fisk steadily dismantled Veronica Jones's claims; one by one, her extravagant allegations were deflated. We were confident in our position and expected a swift victory. However, no Abu-Jamal legal episode is complete without high drama. We were not disappointed. On day one of the hearing, Arlene Fisk produced an outstanding warrant for Jones's arrest for attempting to pass a bad check in a Woodbury, New Jersey, liquor store in 1992. The warrant was from 1994. When Fisk presented the document to the court, two New Jersey detectives marched to the witness stand, identified Jones (who had been arrested under one of her aliases), put her in handcuffs and walked her out of the room. The Abu-Jamal crowd went crazy! Adding a snazzy spin to their well-honed "Free-Mumia" chant, the Abu-Jamal supporters now erupted in a "Free Veronica Jones" cheer. On day two of the trial, the defense revealed that MOVE member Pam Africa had paid Veronica Jones's $1,000 bail.

Jones was thus embarrassingly discredited. Once again, the defense was forced to watch the withering away of another outlandish conspiracy theory. Accompanying the now-familiar story line of wild accusations turned to rubbish, the customary courtroom antics persisted. I saw Abu-Jamal smile at Veronica Jones on the day of her testimony. She was quoted in the newspaper as saying, "He's cute."[222]

There was also a battle between the two sides as to what they could wear during the hearing. The judge did not want "Free Mumia" buttons in his courtroom. The Abu-Jamal people said that if their buttons came off, the police should have to take off their FOP pins. A forum designed to decide the fate of Danny's murderer had turned into a sartorial spat!

A month after the three-day hearing, Judge Sabo, as he had done in 1995, rejected the defense's request for a new trial, finding in a fourteen-page Opinion that the testimony of Veronica Jones was not credible: "This court, after observing the witness testify, found her testimony to be incredible and worthy of little or no belief. Moreover, even if believed, the testimony of Veronica Jones would not be likely to change the result if a new trial were granted. Veronica Jones was not a key witness in the defendant's trial. She did not offer testimony that she saw the killer of the police officer, nor did she recant testimony concerning same."[223] This Opinion was later upheld by the same Pennsylvania Supreme Court that had enabled Veronica Jones her second chance in the spotlight.

Veronica Jones was uncovered as a fraud. The defense's fanciful theories had once again collapsed. The hearing ultimately accomplished very little. In my mind, it did, however, prove one thing: the appalling hypocrisy of the defense. Remember, the defense team was essentially alleging that Veronica Jones had been paid off, not with money but with leniency, in return for her false testimony. This we know. What many do not know is that the record of the 1996 hearing shows that Jones and "her man" had failed to pay the rent for two years on the apartment that they shared. Soon after Jones's first meeting with Abu-Jamal's attorneys, however, Jones and her friend miraculously began making regular rent payments, which totaled several thousand dollars. These payments continued to be made in various amounts up to the day of Jones's 1996 testimony. Not only was she suddenly able to make rent payments after two years of delinquency, she was able to pay her back rent as well!

2 4

TEMPLE RADIO

For a man who has never offered a word regarding his conduct the night of Danny's murder if he had *not* pulled the trigger, Abu-Jamal is certainly vociferous behind bars. By 1997, Abu-Jamal had published two books, *Live from Death Row* and *Death Blossom*, neither of which offers an account of his behavior. He also continued his work as the death row superstar for Pacifica Radio.

Early in 1997, I learned that Pacifica intended to expand Abu-Jamal's reach by airing his taped essay commentaries as part of the radical program *Democracy Now!* hosted by a woman named Amy Goodman. This was intended to be similar to what was attempted by NPR three years prior. These new segments were promoted by Pacifica as "an insider's look at life behind bars." The initial segment ran during a radio pledge drive the last week of February 1997.[224] People in Philadelphia were livid when they discovered that WRTI-FM, a station owned by Temple University, intended to run the segments as part of its 9:00 a.m. weekday version of *Democracy Now!* As pressure quickly mounted, WRTI-FM boldly decided not only to cancel its contract with Pacifica for the Mumia spots but for the entire *Democracy Now!* program, as well as a half-hour evening news broadcast produced by the same outfit. Not surprisingly, the decision by Temple was met with criticism by Abu-Jamal supporters. With unrelenting vigor, they once again cried "foul" and claimed it was a blow to the free-speech rights of a convicted cop killer. Go figure. Dan Coughlin, the producer of *Democracy Now!*, whined that Temple "caved to pressure from opponents of Mumia Abu-Jamal, and these included very powerful forces in Pennsylvania such as the Fraternal Order of Police." In his eyes, such a decision "amounts to censorship."[225]

Temple's decision had broad ramifications. By canceling its contract, Temple also ensured that the program would not be aired on eleven other stations in Pennsylvania, New Jersey, and Delaware, as WRTI controlled their programming. Consequently, Pacifica's participating stations were reduced from thirty-six to twenty-four.[226]

The controversial radio essays were produced by the Prison Radio Project, the same group that made the NPR tapes in 1994, and were recorded by Abu-Jamal in October 1996, prior to the implementation of a new Pennsylvania Corrections rule that banned all inmates from participating in taped or filmed interviews. Its principal purpose, according to Pacifica, was to confirm the rights of prison inmates to gain access to the media.[227]

Democracy Now! host Amy Goodman claimed that her program was the top fund-raiser for WRTI but that it was the station's grants from the State (whose governor, Tom Ridge, had issued Abu-Jamal's death warrant) that caused the cancellation. She pondered: "If public radio won't air this man's voice, where can he go?"[228] How about hell?

My proposed itinerary for Abu-Jamal was not shared by all. Amy Goodman garnered some support, particularly at Temple University. College campuses had long been hotbeds of uninformed Mumia Abu-Jamal support. Temple, despite its Philadelphia location, was no exception. Several Temple students jumped on Abu-Jamal's bandwagon. Their uninformed clamor was supported by a small collection of faculty members. As part of their effort, they hosted a campus symposium on censorship where law professor Burton Caine declared: "Temple is a public institution bound by the Constitution of the United States. Even if it weren't a public institution, freedom of speech is an academic value of the highest degree." Caine invited members of MOVE, Pacifica, and university officials to respond.[229] University Vice President George Ingram did just that, declaring that the decision to cancel WRTI's contract with Pacifica and the *Democracy Now!* program was due to a change in the programming format in favor of music. He did, however, acknowledge that the change was "accelerated when [he] heard that *Democracy Now!* was planning to broadcast Mumia tapes."[230] Ultimately, much to its credit, Temple did not cave in to protests. But this was not the end of Abu-Jamal's broadcasts. The essays were aired as scheduled on Pacifica's remaining affiliates, who had outlets in Washington, D.C., and New York City.

I was watching this one from afar but I had to weigh in and so, on March 3, 1997, I published a column in the *Philadelphia Daily News*, saying:

> Mumia Abu-Jamal and those who promote him lament that he can't touch his children and grandchildren because he lives in a "concrete hell." Who is really oppressed by our court system and prison system? The prisoner who is able to achieve his hopes and dreams at taxpayers' expense, or survivors and victims of his crime, forced to listen to, watch and accept this situation? Abu-Jamal has children and grandchildren. He can see his wife and communicate with her. He's had the opportunity to complete college courses and receive a degree. He has written two books. And in the country he so loathes, within the system he feels is so oppressive, he can voice his opinions and "practice his trade."
>
> My husband, Danny, had many of the same goals and aspirations—college, a legal career, children and grandchildren—but Abu-Jamal denied Danny his right to those things on the night he shot him in the face. How important is it to add one more voice to the national debate over the death penalty? When that voice is the voice of a remorseless murderer, I say that voice has no right to be heard.
>
> Pacifica Radio determined to air the so-called commentaries of Jamal. The people at Pacifica and the host of their program "Democracy Now!" feel Abu-Jamal should be heard. George Ingram, associate vice president of university relations at Temple University, had the courage and moral judgment to choose not to air the Pacifica program on WRTI, Temple's radio station. Because Ingram chose to exercise his personal and professional right not to listen to or air this program, the host of "Democracy Now!" gave out Ingram's phone number on the air and encouraged listeners to bombard him with personal attacks. It seems that those quick to protect Jamal's rights are less apt to accept someone else exercising theirs.
>
> Should you choose to listen to Jamal's ramblings, you will find he brings nothing new to the so-called "debate" on the death penalty. He adds his personal style to the same tired arguments that many before him have long since worn out. When the question of whether to air a heartless murderer's personal thoughts arises, a high level of moral outrage should make the answer clear, as it did for Ingram. Beyond that, one should look to the content of the material to determine its merit. By any standard, Jamal's insight is not worthy of the taxpayers' money that would pay for the indulgence of airing his commentaries.[231]

Remarkably, as I write this, Abu-Jamal's taped reflections continue to be broadcast on nearly one hundred stations as part of Noelle Hanrahan's Prison Radio Project.

2 5

SANTA CRUZ

My fight against Abu-Jamal zealots had long been a bi-coastal endeavor. Shortly after our Temple University victory, I was summoned for a new battle in California. The city of Santa Cruz, California, one of the most beautiful places in the country, is located on the northern part of Monterey Bay, about seventy-four miles south of San Francisco. On March 25, 1997, the Santa Cruz City Council passed a formal resolution calling for a new trial for Abu-Jamal. The resolution asked Pennsylvania to give the convicted cop killer a new trial, stating: "There is widespread support for a new trial in this case, particularly because of the witnesses for the prosecution who now recant their earlier testimony which was used to convict Mumia in his first [only] trial."[232]

I first heard about the Santa Cruz campaign after a friend forwarded me an Associated Press article announcing the decision. As had become my routine when confronted with fresh opposition, I quickly contacted the mayor of Santa Cruz, Cynthia Matthews. Like virtually every other high-profile supporter of Abu-Jamal I have questioned over the years, Mayor Matthews was unable to provide an explanation for her support and was unable to intelligently relate the basic facts surrounding Danny's murder. She candidly told me that she knew nothing about the night of Danny's murder. Still, her name is on the bottom of the proclamation asking for a new trial for Mumia Abu-Jamal, and she admits to knowing nothing.

After she conceded her own ignorance, I inquired about the intentions of the City Council. Like so many others before her, she was willing to lend her name and public position to a case she knew nothing about. She told me that a group of interested citizens had come to the council and expressed concern that much of the original testimony against Abu-Jamal had been recanted and, therefore, he deserved a new trial. When I asked her who those witnesses were, she told me she had no idea. I was enraged. I asked Mayor Matthews to take a day and get the facts of the case straight. I told her I would call the next day and ask her again why she signed her name to a petition calling for a new trial for Abu-Jamal. Mayor Matthews left town the next day for a long weekend and never called me back.

I soon learned that the group who encouraged the Santa Cruz City Council to adopt the resolution in support of Abu-Jamal was called Refuse and Resist, headed by a Maoist named Clark Kissinger. Apparently, Refuse and Resist had given a presentation to the City Council regarding the supposed improprieties of Abu-Jamal's case and the need for a new trial. The Santa Cruz City Council was clearly convinced. I did manage to speak to Santa Cruz Councilwoman Celia Scott, who informed me that she had done "extensive" research on Abu-Jamal's case and that, based on her research and the information presented to the Santa Cruz City Council by Abu-Jamal's supporters, she believed Abu-Jamal deserved a new trial. She was quoted at the time as saying: "I fully understand why the widow of the slain police officer is upset. It's a terrible thing when one's husband is killed in the line of duty—but the issue is a fair trial."[233]

When I questioned her, Councilwoman Scott claimed that she had received her information on the case primarily from reading a book by Abu-Jamal's attorney, Leonard Weinglass, and that she found no alternative sources available. I volunteered to fill the gaps! I offered to serve as an alternative resource and told her I was willing to share my side of the story with her. My offer was declined; the councilwoman responded that she was "too tired." No one from the Santa Cruz government ever called me again.

Soon thereafter, I was alerted by a local Santa Cruz reporter, Karen Clark, that an article had appeared in a local University of California–Santa Cruz newspaper discussing the facts of the murder. Clark volunteered to send me a copy. Surprise, surprise: It was written by none other than Abu-Jamal's attorney, Leonard Weinglass. In retaliation, I provided an interview to Clark, refuting every point Weinglass had made. My statements were published in a follow-up. A day or so later, the same reporter called me back and told me that Weinglass would be speaking at UC Santa Cruz the next day to refute the lies of the widow. Of all people, Leonard Weinglass was calling *me* a liar.

Paul and I decided that we would attend the Weinglass event at UC Santa Cruz. This was a party we needed to crash. To get to Santa Cruz on such short notice, we would have to fly. We were going to fly commercial, but there was no scheduled service to make it in time. Luckily, a friend, Stuart Fischbein, offered to let us use his private plane and have a friend of his, Nick Ullman, fly us up. However, the night before the event, the Santa Ana winds began to blow so hard that I could hear the house popping and cracking all night. We were forced to make a decision—fly in gale-force winds in a four-seat single-engine airplane or stay home. At the last minute, Stuart solved our problem by arranging for us to fly up in a larger plane. So off we went. The flight was like being on a roller coaster ride for four hours because of the turbulence caused by the strong headwind. It was a long, windy flight up the California coastline.

Upon arrival at Santa Cruz, we were interviewed by the *Santa Cruz Sentinel* before we headed for the Santa Cruz Civic Auditorium. We were both dressed in business attire and stood out like sore thumbs in a sea of pro Abu-Jamal supporters, much like Paul had stood out at UCLA when he went to hear Leonard Weinglass speak a few years prior. As we approached the room where Weinglass was scheduled to speak, I told Paul that it looked like a Grateful Dead concert—kids in tie-dyed "Free Mumia" T-shirts and dreadlocks, none of whom knew who we were. Inside the room, a large mural-type banner was hanging on the wall with Abu-Jamal's likeness printed on it. We immediately spotted Leonard Weinglass talking to the event's organizer, Refuse and Resist's Dwight Fry, who was not a student but the leader of the local R&R chapter, the same folks responsible for the Santa Cruz resolution.

We entered the pre-talk reception and were about to slyly saunter into the main event. No one knew we were attending and no one had invited us. I'm sure Weinglass had anticipated that the event would be something akin to preaching to the choir. As we made our way into the main room, we stood out not only because of our appearance but also because we were carrying about two hundred fliers on which we had printed the real facts of the case in bullet-point form to be handed out later to the otherwise misinformed attendees. We decided not to immediately distribute the materials.

Suddenly, Weinglass realized I was there and was overheard by Paul to say to Dwight Fry, "Oh shit, the widow is here." No pleasantries, no hello. Weinglass knew me, of course, and must have realized he was in for a fight.

We walked past Weinglass and made our way to a couch in the middle of the room and sat down. Although Weinglass and Fry knew who we were, the other attendees were oblivious. We positioned ourselves about ten feet from where Weinglass would be addressing the crowd. We were front and center. I couldn't have gotten closer to the enemy if I'd tried. This was ground zero in the fight for Danny. Our pilot, Nick, sat in the background on the windowsill, not knowing quite what to expect next. The night began when a speaker asked how many in the audience supported the death penalty. Ours were the only two hands in the air.

Just prior to Weinglass's speech, Dwight Fry alerted the crowd of 150–200 zealous pro-Abu-Jamal supporters about our presence. He said, "We're all here to learn the facts of the case from Mr. Weinglass. I want everyone here to extend courtesy to a guest who is here. The person I am referring to is sitting here in the front. This is Maureen Faulkner, the widow of Officer Daniel Faulkner." I then placed a tape recorder on the table in front of Weinglass. The minute he started speaking, I clicked on the recorder right in front of his face. I watched with great glee as his eyes darted from the recorder and then straight to my face. He knew he was trapped. He began to profusely stumble and sweat. Throughout his speech, he had to continually wipe his brow.

I believe that the presence of the tape recorder successfully compelled Weinglass to tone down his presentation. He didn't exactly lie, but he was certainly twisting the truth. At one point, the reporter who had originally contacted me nailed Weinglass on the bullets. Weinglass said that Abu-Jamal was carrying a gun that evening but it did not have any bullets in it. According to Weinglass, it was an empty gun he just carried. When the reporter questioned this logic, Weinglass reasoned that Abu-Jamal was a peaceful person who didn't believe in violence. He carried the gun as a cab driver to intimidate anybody who might try to rob him but that he would never actually shoot somebody.

Clearly uneasy with our presence mere feet in front of him, Leonard Weinglass then told the crowd—just forty-five minutes into what was supposed to be a talk of an hour and a half—that he had to leave shortly to catch a plane. I suspected that his abbreviated speech was due to the presence of the tape recorder. He decided to take a few quick questions. At first, we remained silent during the questioning. Just as the session was about to end, Paul raised his hand and requested the opportunity to speak.

He said something like, "I know we crashed your party and we're probably not welcome here. You guys have been very polite and courteous up to this point and we can leave it at that or, if you are open to it, I would like to ask Mr. Weinglass a few questions about our perspective of the facts that he presented." Certain people grumbled and mumbled, but Dwight Fry stepped in and said, "I am the moderator, the one running the show here, and I would like to hear what they have to say. So as long as everyone is OK with it, and Mr. Weinglass is willing to answer the questions, I would like to give them their time to ask their questions." Weinglass agreed to do it.

Paul began to question Weinglass on the facts of the case. Weinglass literally started dripping sweat and scratching his head profusely. By the time Paul was done talking to him and asking him questions, his hair was standing up like Dr. Brown in *Back to the Future*. We both recognized this twitch as a habit that Weinglass had, which came out in court when he was annoyed and losing an argument.

Finally, after about twenty minutes of discussion with Paul, Weinglass decided to exit: "Oh my God, look at the time. I would love to stay and talk, and you're welcome to stay here and continue to talk to the people, and Mrs. Faulkner can speak to them, but I have to catch a plane. I am going to have to leave now."

When Weinglass left the event, Dwight Fry asked me if I wanted to address the crowd to explain my side of the story and my reasons for attending. I did. I focused on the personal side of the case—my relationship with Danny, the impact of losing him, the funeral and ultimately the trial. Then I told the students that I went into the courtroom with a clear conscience, just wanting to know who murdered my husband, and when I came out there was absolutely not a doubt in my mind that it was Mumia Abu-Jamal who did this. People yelled out or screamed a few times while I was talking, whereupon Dwight Fry would get up immediately and say, "If anyone is going to be disrespectful to Mrs. Faulkner, they need to leave," because they were screaming, "You liar! You're not telling the truth!" Despite the disruptions, Fry kept control of the room.

After I spoke, Paul told them about the informational pamphlets he had brought and proceeded to discuss the factual evidence of the case for nearly an hour. When we both finished, we spoke with some students and other attendees, mostly girls, who sympathized with my pain and loss and who were visibly upset. I vividly remember one girl in particular who came up to me afterwards, bawling and overcome with sadness. "What happened to your husband is awful," she told me. Her compassion ended there, however. Still sobbing, this girl now started to plead with me: "Please don't let them kill Mumia. He can't be killed. You need to be the one to step up and beg the courts and say that you don't want him to die. It's your responsibility to do that," and on and on and on about how he was such a wonderful man and the world needs him so much. "You're the only one, who can do this, and you must do it, and you have to do it." I was shocked.

Dwight Fry finally offered his insight. He said, "I personally believe that Mumia Abu-Jamal did not get a fair trial and is innocent, but I must tell you I have a family, I have a wife and children, and if anyone ever murdered my wife, I would want the same to happen to them that you want for Mumia Abu-Jamal. I would want justice to be done and justice to be carried out. If twelve people had given the death penalty to someone who had murdered my wife, I would want justice carried out to the letter of the law."

All the while, pilot Nick had been observing the event from the back of the room. He was clearly rattled by the intensity of the experience. On the plane ride home later that night, high above the chaos below, Nick confided that it was the most intense two and a half hours he'd ever spent in his life. He thought they were going to kill us.

2 6

THE 1 9 9 7 PCRA HEARING

Two months after the showdown in Santa Cruz came another in Philadelphia. Yes, the bi-coastal battle raged and showed no sign of settling down. Yet another hooker with a drug problem was being trotted out to save Abu-Jamal. As had become custom, the Pennsylvania judicial system was willing to give the cop killer yet another day in court. The case was, by now, a permanent fixture in the national media. By way of example, the June 16, 1997, edition of *Time* magazine featured Oklahoma City bomber Timothy McVeigh on the cover with the headline "Should He Die?" Inside, as a part of a discussion of the death penalty in America, there was a color photograph of Abu-Jamal along with a write up in which he was described as "perhaps the most publicized death-row case outside of 'Dead Man Walking.'"[234]

The hooker du jour in the summer of 1997 was Pamela Jenkins. She had been a confessed crack addict for ten years who did not testify at the 1982 trial or the subsequent Post-Conviction Relief Act hearings.[235] She was not present the night of the murder. I first heard about Pamela Jenkins in March when Leonard Weinglass held a press conference outside of Mayor Ed Rendell's office. Here, Jenkins told the media a story supposedly told to her by Cynthia White, who *did* witness the murder and *did* testify at the 1982 trial. According to White's supposed story, as told by Jenkins, police had threatened to kill White unless she testified against Abu-Jamal. Jenkins claimed that she had a sexual relationship with a young cop in 1981 and that he had tried to convince her to testify against Mumia Abu-Jamal.[236]

This was now the third straight year that Abu-Jamal was being afforded an opportunity to provide the court with new evidence to support his innocence. More time was being added to Abu-Jamal's clock. I was emotionally frayed at the prospect of returning to Philadelphia for another charade, which is exactly what this had become. Paul believes that one of the reasons Abu-Jamal has received so many appellate hearings is because the State is actively endeavoring to prevent any possible appearance that they are limiting Abu-Jamal's rights. In a case with so much national and global coverage, everything and everyone involved is under a microscope. I guess it makes sense that the State would try to do whatever possible to keep from being criticized but it is also an unfortunate manifestation of how our system is often too perpetrator-oriented and unsupportive of victims. At what point should our judicial system finally swoop in and impede this endless cycle? At what point should they say, Wait a minute, the man has had every conceivable chance to prove his innocence after a jury determined his guilt and has failed? As the years pass, it is clear that this point has not yet come. Abu-Jamal's lawyers continue to make a mockery of our entire judicial system and to this date, continue to ask for even more PCRA hearings to trot out several new witnesses.

For the 1997 hearing, the prosecution was captained by Hugh Burns and Arlene Fisk, two of the most able attorneys I have ever met. Tireless. Fearless. Articulate. Arlene has a terrific courtroom presence, as was in evidence at the PCRA hearing in 1996. Hugh J. Burns Jr. is one of the great unsung heroes of my world, the keeper of the flame over the span of many years, one who has resiliently remained a champion in the face of a neverending barrage of challenges from a well-orchestrated and -funded defense team drawing on international support. Have you heard the expression, "slow and steady wins the race"? That is Hugh. Unassuming. Competent. Committed.

Once again, the Honorable Albert F. Sabo presided, as required by law. Since 1995, his title had been "senior judge," another sign that we'd been at this too long. The setting was the city's new Criminal Justice Center across the street from City Hall. The spectators were the same assortment of police officers in support of Danny and a hodge-podge of anti–death penalty types for Abu-Jamal. Not everyone could get into the courtroom. Several busloads of Abu-Jamal supporters had come from New York, as had representatives from a group called the Student Organization for Social Justice, the Quixote Center in Maryland, and a Pittsburgh contingent of the Bruderhof. Missing, as usual, was any significant show of support from Philadelphians for the cop killer except, of course, from some remaining stragglers from MOVE. Nation of Islam Minister Khalid Abdul Muhammad also showed up, the same minister who had appeared at Kean College in New Jersey four years earlier and referred to Jews as "bloodsuckers."[237] Julia Wright, daughter of novelist Richard Wright, flew in from France as a member of the International Friends of Mumia Abu-Jamal. Given what was to come, Ringling Brothers and an Elvis impersonator should have been there too!

Jenkins testified that she had met Cynthia White while working the streets, and that White allegedly told her before the Abu-Jamal trial in 1982 that she had been coerced by police. According to Jenkins, Cynthia White's testimony that she saw Abu-Jamal shoot Danny was false. Jenkins claimed that the last time she spoke with White was in March of that year (1997) in a north Philadelphia crack house and she "looked like she'd seen a ghost."[238] Well, she would have had to have seen a ghost if she saw Cynthia White in March of 1997, because Cynthia White had been dead for five years!

The prosecution promptly produced a New Jersey death certificate stating that a woman named Cynthia Williams, a known alias for Cynthia White, died in 1992. The stunned expressions on the faces of Abu-Jamal's lawyers in response to this revelation were priceless. Police testified that the dead woman had the same fingerprints as White.[239] Sgt. Elizabeth Welch of the New Jersey State Police testified that direct comparison of the recorded fingerprints of Cynthia White with the fingerprints of the dead woman in New Jersey conclusively established that they were one and the same person, prompting Arlene Fisk to say to the court: "The defense put on perjured testimony. Pamela Jenkins testified, among other things, that she saw Cynthia White and chased her out of a drug house in March. Cynthia White has been dead since 1992."[240] Judge Sabo had heard enough. When the defense lawyers asked permission to call a private investigator in the hopes of producing people who had seen White recently, the Judge told them, "If she's alive, go out and get her. Bring her in! I have heard evidence that she is definitely dead." Needless to say, the dead woman couldn't make it.

The Jenkins episode was a supreme embarrassment for the defense, even by their usually low standards. Following the event, I heard Leonard Weinglass on radio station KPFK doing some much-needed damage control. He announced to the radio world that, despite how it may have seemed, the defense had always been aware of the existence of that death certificate. He claimed that they still allowed Pamela Jenkins to testify because their belief was that the death certificate was fraudulent. Weinglass continued that Cynthia White's remains were cremated; he also alleged that nobody had ever identified her body. Mr. Weinglass, once again, this is just not true! The obvious implausibility of this latest conspiracy theory aside, we know for certain that Cynthia White's dead body was identified by her mother. In his aforementioned book, *Executing Justice*, Abu-Jamal defense lawyer Dan Williams admitted that the "Jenkins debacle really shook Len and me up."[241] It also sounds like it was the beginning of the end, or the end of the end, for the defense team. Williams wrote that in the aftermath of Jenkins, he hoped the embarrassment it caused would heal the rift between himself and the ultra-left PDC contingent, but that this was "naïve." By the spring of 1999, Wolkenstein and Piper were back with yet another "explosive new eyewitness." This one would claim that Danny was an inside informant for the federal authorities investigating corruption in the department, who was killed at the behest of corrupt Philadelphia police officers in order to silence him. Please—Mike Farrell, Ed Asner, Whoopi Goldberg, and every other individual who has blindly lent their name to a convicted cop killer—read what Abu-Jamal defense lawyer Dan Williams wrote in *his* book about this event: "When I heard the story at a defense team meeting at Len's [Weinglass's] loft, I bit my lip to avoid another unpleasant argument with Rachel. Actually, I was enraged, convinced that bona fide lunacy had set in."[242] He further writes that Weinglass also believed the story to be insane. Wrote Williams about his own view, "I have to admit, I also wasn't about to embarrass myself by running with such a patently outrageous story on the most visible death penalty case in the world." Wolkenstein and Piper left the defense team in August of 1999. Abu-Jamal fired Weinglass and Williams in March of 2000.

And so, for a third time, a Post-Conviction Relief Act hearing ended with Abu-Jamal's request for a new trial being denied. Do you think that Weinglass & Co. finally decided to retreat? Hell no! And why should they? Support was still pouring in from such disparate locales as Oakland, California, and Paris, France.

27

A SAN FRANCISCO TREAT

Three losses in Post-Conviction Relief Act hearings could not deter Abu-Jamal devotees. A thick shell of oblivion insulated them from the burning shame of loss, and they persisted in their rabble-rousing ways. At the end of the summer of the "dead hooker defense," the City of San Francisco nevertheless joined the pro-Abu-Jamal parade and actually honored the man who murdered my police officer husband. And they did it in grand style.

Three thousand supporters gathered at Mission High School's auditorium on August 16, 1997, for the event. The key speakers at the function were Geronimo ji Jaga (Pratt), a former Black Panther who spent twenty-seven years behind bars (as a "political prisoner" if you believe the pro-Abu-Jamal literature) for murdering a couple; Abu-Jamal's attorney Leonard Weinglass; and author Alice Walker. Over all, the event raised $30,000 to help pay for Abu-Jamal's ongoing defense bills.[243] The usual suspects behind most left-leaning affairs were present and participating. The ACLU, the National Conference of Black Lawyers, Refuse and Resist, and students from UC Berkeley all joined hands in organizing it.[244] San Francisco Mayor Willie Brown Jr. presided at the event.

In addition to gaining praise and support from labor unions at the event, Mayor Brown and the City Board of Supervisors joined in with a special proclamation and awarded a certificate of honor for Abu-Jamal. The certificate of honor read to the crowd is as follows:

> The Board of Supervisors of the City and County of San Francisco hereby issues, and authorizes the execution of, this Certificate of Honor in appreciative public recognition of distinction and merit for outstanding service to a significant portion of the people of the City and County of San Francisco by: Mumia Abu-Jamal, In recognition of his struggle for

justice, and the community rally calling for his freedom from imprisonment and honor of this struggle designate August 16, 1997 Mumia Abu-
Jamal Day in San Francisco.

Signed: Supervisor Tom Ammiano[245]

You may wonder, besides murdering Danny, what particular outstanding service to a significant portion of the City and County of San Francisco
did Abu-Jamal provide? The story actually gets worse. Mayor Brown's
proclamation, which was also read aloud at the San Francisco high school
event, is also extremely classless:

> Whereas, on August 16, 1997, an evening of solidarity in support of
> Mumia Abu-Jamal will take place at Mission High School here in San
> Francisco; and
>
> Whereas, many believe that Mumia Abu-Jamal has been wrongly im-
> prisoned for the past 15 years; and
>
> Whereas, many of us are working toward securing a new trial for Mumia
> Abu-Jamal in the Pennsylvania Supreme Court; and
>
> Whereas, the evening of solidarity has drawn support from the labor
> unions, leaders of African-American religious organizations and govern-
> ment officials;
>
> Now, Therefore, be it Resolved, that I, Willie L. Brown, Jr., Mayor of the
> City and County of San Francisco, in recognition of the efforts to find
> justice for Mumia Abu-Jamal, do hereby proclaim August 16, 1997, as
> Justice for Mumia Abu-Jamal day in San Francisco.[246]

Talk about an abuse of power! When I heard the news, I was nauseated.
The rest of the event was par-for-the-course as were most other pro-Abu-
Jamal events prior to and following it: speeches discussing police wrong-
doing in handling the evidence and the fact that too many Americans
(many of them black) are in prison.[247]

Again, the major problem was a complete lack of factual evidence. A
perfect example of this was the fact that a widely distributed article from
Revolutionary Worker about the event named the police officer who was
killed in Philadelphia in December of 1981 as "William Faulkner." How
typical! Although seemingly innocuous, distortions were rampant. Fueled
by a hearty heap of misinformation, fury over the so-called injustices inflicted upon Abu-Jamal raged with enduring intensity. Few had any ideas

about the true facts of the case, not even the correct name of the murder victim. We had just concluded the third Post-Conviction Relief Act hearing at which Abu-Jamal's latest, zany claim was blown to bits, none of which was known to, or mattered to, these supporters.

As it later turned out, this was only the beginning of San Francisco's dalliance with Abu-Jamal. Two years later, on Saturday, April 24, 1999, pro-Abu-Jamal supporters organized simultaneous events in San Francisco and Philadelphia coined as the Million Person March for Mumia to honor the killer's forty-fifth birthday. They drew about fifteen thousand demonstrators in San Francisco—significantly more than usual, according to Police Lieutenant Mary Stasko, who observed, "Most of the protests we get have between 500 and 1,000 people." The great majority of them appeared to be students, mostly high-school and middle-school students from Oakland.[248] Also in attendance and scheduled to deliver speeches to the crowd were actors Danny Glover, Ed Asner, and Peter Coyote. One student, a fourteen-year-old named Rashaud Richardson of Oakland, summed up the degree of factual knowledge about the case that the demonstrators usually possessed: "They're trying to execute an innocent black man, trying to say he is a murderer. They're trying to say a man who helped the community—my hero—is a criminal."[249]

When a young Oakland girl shared her sentiments with the press, she unwittingly captured the attitude of the rally. Sixteen-year-old Dominique Moore was eager to add: "I feel strongly that Mumia needs me, and we need him. He is a champion of African-American culture."[250]

Also in attendance was Larry Faulkner, Danny's brother. Larry had been planning a trip to California at the same time and figured that he might as well attend the demonstration and pass out some real information to the protestors as one way of getting Danny's story out. Not surprisingly, his efforts were largely ignored. He told me that "Most of them said, 'No, thanks.' Nobody hassled me and I didn't hassle them. I let them know I was there to let people converse with me if they wanted to hear the other side and know what really happened the night my brother was murdered."

San Francisco's "sister event" held in Philadelphia on April 24 (billed as a protest to "shut down the city") garnered only about three thousand supporters. "I said we wanted to shut down this city. In fact, we want the world to stop and take notice of a government in conspiracy," Pam Africa, head of International Concerned Family and Friends of Mumia Abu-Jamal, had said.[251] The Philadelphia crowd was also seething with protestors who seemed to have about as much of a handle on the facts of the case as Rashaud in San Francisco. This unfortunate dearth of information was overwhelmingly evidenced when Obanion Gordon of Camden, New Jersey, told the press: "The state has always lynched black males, especially black males who have been passionate about the liberation of their people."[252]

Groups of protestors marched at Philadelphia's City Hall that day with, of all things, a police escort. Can you imagine what was going through the minds of the officers charged with that thankless task?

Danny at age five and his brother, Kenny (left), at age six in a visit to Santa Claus during Christmastime.

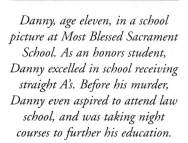

Danny, age eleven, in a school picture at Most Blessed Sacrament School. As an honors student, Danny excelled in school receiving straight A's. Before his murder, Danny even aspired to attend law school, and was taking night courses to further his education.

A photo of me taken at the age of seven.

A picture of me taken in one of the bedrooms of the Butt Estate at Listapada Farms in Valley Forge before my wedding ceremony on November 8, 1980.

Wedding photos courtesy of Michael Foley

Danny and I about to cut our wedding cake with my sister-in-law, Cathy Foley, and best man, Hugh Gallagher.

Walking into the Kimberton Inn, where our reception was held, for the first time as husband and wife.

*Danny and I on a sunset cruise in Maui during our
Hawaiian honeymoon in November of 1980.*

*A moment of affection Danny and I shared in the Muir Woods
of San Francisco during our honeymoon.*

Danny, in front of the Golden Gate Bridge in San Francisco, during the final leg of our honeymoon. Our travels took us from Los Angeles, and then to Hawaii, with a final stop in San Francisco before returning home to Philadelphia.

When reminded about this photograph, Danny would always tell his friends, "I was just listening to my earpiece," overlooking that he was not wearing an earpiece.

William F. Steinmetz/*Philadelphia Inquirer,* reprinted with permission

Danny receiving a commendation from Captain Merrick.

The house that Danny and I shared together, located at 6236 Harley Street in Philadelphia. This is the house where I last kissed Danny goodbye before he went to work on that fateful day in December.

Me in front of the tree taken just before the only Christmas we would spend together as husband and wife. This picture was taken by Danny in our Harley Street home in 1980.

WRITTEN BY MUMIA ABU JAMAL - APRIL 18, 1970

A DAY IN THE LIFE OF THE COLONY

Date: April 8th, Wednesday
Time: night-time
CHARACTERS INVOLVED:

NIGGER ....youthful Ricardo
Smacks (Carlos)
pig #1: ....White racist pig
pig #2:...........White racist
pig #3: ....American nigger
pig

...and the over-familiar scene again unfolds, like a movie where you can easily guess the ending. Where the cats in the White hats run rings around the hairy, filthy, onery 'Black barts' in the cowboy flicks.....

Only this is for real.

Carlos is another nigger on a South Philly block where the gestapo plays their games - "GENO-CIDE" (made in U.S.A.).

Why must it be said that he is 16? Where is the importance? Would a world of difference be made if I said he was an ebony elder, an old Black man, of 61, or 3? We Black people having been faced with countless cases of legal murders, street executions, by the racist pig police and their lackies, know that things will get a lot worse before they get better, And that the only insurance that we

have is the blackprint of self-defense. That every Black home equip itself with 12- gauge shotgun security, and 45 self defense. We remember the Joey Brooks', the Harold Brown's, even if you appear to have forgotten.

We will either rewrite the racist script, or we will blow up/burn down, the decadent theatre which insists upon showing that murderous flick. We intend to put the Indians where the Cowboys were.

The scales have been tipped, in fact, tugged, against us from way back. White racist America must not for a single moment believe that the manifesto (about Chairman Bobby) relates only to Bobby. Every Black man is our Bobby, and the pigs must suffer the same relentless rebuttal from us for executing him as for any of us. The Philly fascist faggots have, after Harold Brown and Joey Brooks, found it easier to slide into the colony with "nigger tickets", Black pigs, thinking that the brothers and sisters wouldn't get uptight if it was a "brother'. Well, pain is pain, torture is torture, and murder is murder, a pig is a pig. And the bullets that await the night raiders will effect the

Black nigger bootlickers, the endorsed spokesmen, in the same meaningful manner

A people who have suffered-so much for so long at the hands of a racist society, must draw the line somewhere. We believe that the Black communities of America must rise up as one man to halt the progression of a trend that leads inevitably to their total destruction.

Huey P. Newton
Minister of Defense
Black Panther Party

'What do we do?' is the major 1619 -to- 1970 question, which we can no longer ask Malcolm. The answer lies in doing what we wish to do, what we must do...doing it! For Joey Brooks, Harold Brown, and Ralph Featherstone and all our Black dead-

"Upwards to 20,000,000 Black people, knowing you for the rotten, racist, murdering nation of White thievish hypocrites that you are, are no longer interested in explaining anything to you, America. Indeed, we understand that you already know what it's about. We know that your investigations into the disorders are just a bunch of

maneuvers designed to give you time while you multiply and perfect your machinery of repression, which you have already unleashed upon us. In fact, your investigators themselves are amongst your chief and shrewdest criminals."

To you, the House of Babylon, the international rapist, and universal criminal, our promise is "Bigger and better fires, one flame for all America, an all American flame."

Quotes by Eldridge Cleaver, Minister of Information.

In the base of Ricky Smarks, a nigger "Guardian" of the Law" and "Peace Officer", Owens, pulled the trigger that now leaves Carlos hospitalized in critical condition.

Read the 7th point of the 10 Point Program of our Party written in the back. Then read "WHAT WE BELIEVE."

The fateful list of fascism grows longer. How many more Black names need be added?

I for one, feel like putting the pen.....

LET'S WRITE EPITAPHS, FOR PIGS.

Mumia
Philadelphia Branch
BLACK PANTHER PARTY

I for one feel like putting down the pen...........

Lets write epitaphs for the pigs

An article written by Mumia Abu-Jamal in an April 18, 1970 Black Panther publication. In it he writes, "Let's Write Epitaphs, For Pigs."

Mumia Abu-Jamal posing in front of idols of his youth. He adopted the time tested and overused moniker "Political Prisoner" after killing Danny.

Photo courtesy of Temple University Libraries, Urban Archives, Philadelphia, PA.

MOVE members armed to the teeth outside their compound. Not long after this picture was taken, MOVE members killed Philadelphia police officer James Ramp during a gun battle with police in 1978. A short time later, Jamal began openly supporting MOVE and espousing the teachings of John Africa, MOVE's founder. These are the people who jeered and spit at me during the 1982 trial. And these are the people that Mumia Abu-Jamal supports and works closely with today.

Photo courtesy of Temple University Libraries, Urban Archives, Philadelphia, PA.

A young Mumia Abu-Jamal shown in his first arrest at the age of eighteen.

Photo courtesy of the Philadelphia District Attorney's Office.

PHILADELPHIA DAILY
NEWS
The People Paper

THURSDAY, DECEMBER 10, 1981

Our 214th Issue in Our 67th Year; © 1981, Philadelphia Daily News

4 ★

20¢   Sports

Death of a Cop

4 Tell Police of Shooting

Photographed by Norman Y. Lono

Officers stand straight at roll call after death of comrade Daniel Faulkner. Four pages on the shooting, the victim and the suspect begin on Page 3.

The front page of the Philadelphia Daily News *on December 10, 1981,
the morning after Danny's death.*

William Cook's car and Danny's hat at the scene of the murder.
Photo courtesy of the Philadelphia District Attorney's Office.

Police Officer Danny Faulkner's patrol car.
Photo courtesy of the Philadelphia District Attorney's Office.

Above, the intersection of 13th and Locust Streets, circa 1981.
Photo courtesy of the Philadelphia District Attorney's Office.

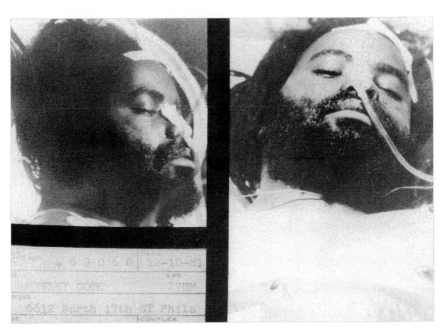

One of the first pictures taken of Mumia Abu-Jamal after murdering my husband. Abu-Jamal's life had been spared, unlike that he had so mercilessly taken from Danny.
Photo courtesy of the Philadelphia District Attorney's Office.

Our friends console one another in front of Danny's casket. We were all so young then. We're 25 years older now, but still extremely close.

Photo courtesy of Temple University Libraries, Urban Archives, Philadelphia, PA.

Danny's mother and I at the funeral. I gave Danny's mom the flag that was draped over his casket. Danny's murder and the insanity of the trial afterwards were devastating to her. She never fully recovered.

Photo courtesy of Temple University Libraries, Urban Archives, Philadelphia, PA.

My parents and I leaving Danny's funeral. My heart was broken and they felt so helpless because there was nothing they could do to ease the pain of their only daughter. If a picture is worth a thousand words, this one says pain, loss and grief. It was the worst day of my life.

Photo courtesy of Temple University Libraries, Urban Archives, Philadelphia, PA.

The front cover of The Philadelphia Inquirer *on Saturday, July 3, 1982, the day after Mumia Abu-Jamal was found guilty of murdering Danny.*

*Eerie foreshadowing of what was to unfold. This is a photo taken of my
mother (center right) and her friends at a restaurant known as "The Cove."
In a stunning coincidence, not only was this restaurant located at
1234 Locust Street, the site of Danny's murder, but the photo was also taken on
December 9, 1942, exactly thirty-nine years before Danny was murdered.*

*My parents, James and
Annamae Foley, in a
photo taken on their
anniversary only a year
after Danny's murder.*

*A photo of Paul Palkovic, my constant companion
and champion, and me taken in 1992.*

A photo from the first Mid-Atlantic Law Enforcement Survivors weekend held in North Wildwood, New Jersey in 2000. Danny was honored at this event. Some of the friends that joined me included (left to right) Thomas Hoban, Garry Bell, Dave Bell, Edward Frederick, and Dan McCann.

Me speaking at the Union League tribute for Danny on April 23, 1999.

Photo © Fgallo@francisgallo.com

Former mayor of Philadelphia and present governor of Pennsylvania, Edward Rendell, speaking at the Union League event for Danny.

Photo © Fgallo@francisgallo.com

Some members of the Faulkner and Foley families who attended Geno's Day for Police Officer Daniel Faulkner on June 4, 2000.

This picture was taken at the Daniel Faulkner Memorial Motorcycle Run started for Danny in May 1999. I am pictured with some loyal supporters of the cause including (left to right), Joey Vento, Michael Smerconish, and Les Young, who was responsible for organizing the first Motorcycle Run.

2 8

K G O · T V

T he support and celebration of Abu-Jamal in San Francisco was more repulsive than surprising. Circumstances demanded that I grow accustomed to misguided allegiance to Abu-Jamal. Of all cities in America, San Francisco seemed an appropriate headquarters for the Abu-Jamal effort, probably the only city in this country where an elected mayor would honor a cop killer. Thus, when KGO-TV, an ABC-affiliated television station in San Francisco, aired a detailed report on May 7 and 8, 1998, refuting the lies of the Abu-Jamal case, it caused an enormous stir.

The report was written by Tim Beecham, who had once worked in Philadelphia, and was delivered by anchorman Dan Ashley. It was broadcast in two parts, during two different nights. Although it is difficult to say with certainty, the report seems to have been prompted by the somewhat mystifying mass of support for Abu-Jamal in San Francisco, in a city where, despite its liberal leanings, there were no actual ties to the killer. The mystery is compounded by the fact that the murder had occurred sixteen years prior and three thousand miles away. Ashley did a terrific, fact-based job in unraveling and exposing the pro-Abu-Jamal movement, including an excellent exposé of lead attorney Leonard Weinglass.

Having re-watched Ashley's program recently, I am still impressed with the way in which it discusses, point by point, Abu-Jamal supporters' claims and then examines what really happened based on the evidence from the trial. The result is a piece of reporting that shows the glaring deficiencies of the pro-Abu-Jamal camp's fantastical assertions. Allow me to give you a recap.

DAY 1: MAY 7, 1998
The report begins by asking a simple question: "Why are so many so willing to donate so much money and energy to a case they seem to know so little about?"

207

Dan Ashley: He is touted as America's number one political prisoner. Mumia Abu-Jamal. A death row inmate convicted of killing a police officer. Thousands of people right here in the Bay Area and around the world have rallied to his cause, raising money and demanding a new trial. It's a case that plays right into some people's fears that the government should not be trusted. But, as you'll see as we begin a special assignment report, you also can't trust everything you hear about this case.

He's big in the Bay Area, rallies protesting his conviction and death sentence for killing a police officer routinely draw thousands. His book, in its sixth printing, has been translated into seven languages. There is another book by his lawyer, as well as CDs and videos.

His essays air on more than a hundred radio stations, his face is on posters, his case is on the Internet and his name is a mantra.

So, who is this Mumia, and how did he become so popular? Why are so many so willing to donate so much money and energy to a case they seem to know so little about?

Well, our story begins sixteen years and three thousand miles away in the wee hours of the morning, on a street corner in Philadelphia. Everyone agrees that somebody killed a police officer that night. Officer Daniel Faulkner was shot in the back and in the face at close range. Mumia Abu-Jamal, a former radio reporter turned cab driver, was found sitting on the curb a few feet away. A bullet from Faulkner's gun in his chest. On the sidewalk between them, a .38 caliber hand gun registered to Jamal. It contained five spent shells.

Sixteen years later, a Saturday in San Fran and true believers are organizing.

The story line here is conspiracy. Jamal, a Black Panther as a teenager, a frequent critic of the Philadelphia Police as a radio reporter, was set up. His politics his only crime. Police coerced witnesses and concocted evidence. An eloquent voice of the voiceless is on death row and about to be silenced.

The record shows it all began with a traffic stop. A blue Volkswagen driving the wrong way on a one-way street, no lights. Officer Daniel Faulkner makes the stop and calls for backup. There is a scuffle. Witnesses say the driver, William Cook, punched Faulkner. Faulkner is cuffing Cook, Jamal's brother, when four witnesses say they saw Jamal.

Assistant District Attorney Hugh Burns: Jamal coming across the street, shooting the officer in the back. The officer gets off one shot, he falls to the ground, he's disarmed, he's lying there face up. Jamal fires into his face and kills him.

Dan Ashley: Jeff Mackler heads the Bay Area's Mobilization to Free Mumia Abu-Jamal. He claims to have spent years studying the case, organizing protests, and lobbying churches, unions, and city councils for resolutions of support. He now admits he's never even read the trial record.

Jeff Mackler: Four eyewitnesses said that the murderer of this policeman went that way.

Dan Ashley: In fact, the record shows four eyewitnesses saw Jamal shoot the officer and then sit down on the curb.

Jeff Mackler: There was no ballistics evidence ever presented in court.

Dan Ashley: In fact, there was extensive ballistics testimony, and though the bullets were mangled, tests showed them to be .38 caliber, with markings consistent with Jamal's gun.

Jeff Mackler: His attorney said, "I am not competent to defend this man."

Dan Ashley: The trial attorney, seen here at a 1995 hearing, had twenty capital cases under his belt in 1982 and came highly recommended. He did, however, tell the judge his client was uncooperative.

The '82 trial was chaotic. Jamal asked to defend himself, then challenged the legitimacy of the court. Though he helped pick a jury, which included two blacks, frequent outbursts caused the judge to remove him as counsel. The outbursts continued. Jamal was removed from the courtroom on thirteen different occasions.

Marc Kaufman (*Philadelphia Inquirer* Reporter): From the beginning, Mumia's style and I think his strategy was to try to disrupt the trial.

Dan Ashley: Mark Kaufman of the *Philadelphia Inquirer* covered the '82 trial and subsequent appeals. Like many Philadelphians, he is mystified by the flourishing Mumiamania. Particularly so in the face of the physical evidence and the fact that in sixteen years, neither Jamal nor his brother have ever offered another version of what happened.

Marc Kaufman: He [Cook] certainly knows what happened that night and boy, if I was going to advocate for the guy, I'd sure want to know what he has to say about what happened that night.

Dan Ashley: Several California cities and dozens of celebrities are demanding a new trial for Mumia Abu-Jamal. And tomorrow night, we'll investigate what they know about this case and we'll hear from Officer Faulkner's widow, who came to California to escape her bad memories only to say that they followed her here.[253]

You get the picture, I am sure. Imagine how this played in the city where honorary status had been presented to a man on death row. It was devastating to the Abu-Jamal supporters. And there was more to come the second night of the report.

DAY 2: MAY 8, 1998
Dan Ashley: It begins in one hour in Palo Alto. A so-called "commission of inquiry" to free a man sitting on death row for killing a police officer.

His name is Mumia Abu-Jamal. His many supporters believe he is the victim of a legal lynching, a miscarriage of justice in a racist system. In tonight's special assignment, a closer look at the facts of this case and the orchestrated campaign to turn a convicted killer into a folk hero.

From Philadelphia to the Bay Area, Mumia Abu-Jamal has passionate supporters. According to them, American justice is racist and the heavy hand of the state is trying to silence its harshest critic.

According to transcripts of his 1982 murder trial, prosecutors had four eyewitnesses, three of which positively identified Mumia Abu-Jamal as the gunman who murdered Philadelphia Officer Daniel Faulkner. They had ballistics evidence, a confession, and a defendant who offered no alternative theory of innocence.

For many, Mumia Abu-Jamal's conviction is crystal clear based on the evidence. But the farther you get from Philadelphia, the murkier the details of the case become. As a result, here in Los Angeles, Mumia Abu-Jamal is a marquee name, a box office sensation in the anti–death penalty movement.

Mike Farrell: When you learn the facts of the case, you become embarrassed about the criminal justice system in this country.

Dan Ashley: Actor Mike Farrell heads an impressive list of celebrities who have taken up the cause, including Ed Asner, Alice Walker, and Whoopi Goldberg. They insist Jamal was targeted by police; evidence manufactured; and the trial rigged. Farrell claims to know all this from reading the trial record.

Mike Farrell: The issue of the confession, the so-called confession, was that it didn't come up until two months after the event.

Dan Ashley: In fact, a hospital security guard reported hearing Jamal boast of shooting the officer outside the hospital emergency room the next day. Two police officers later claimed to have heard the same confession.

Mike Farrell: He [Jamal] was not allowed funds for investigation to come up with witnesses.

Dan Ashley: Actually, $14,000 of public money was spent on the defense, including customary fees for an investigator and expert witnesses. In addition, a private group of supporters also contributed money.

Mike Farrell: It would seem to me then that the person you ought to be speaking to then is Len Weinglass.

Dan Ashley: When confronted with the facts, Jamal's California supporters repeatedly referred us to this man, Leonard Weinglass, Jamal's lead attorney. Their information, they say, comes from him.

Leonard Weinglass first hit the national stage thirty years ago as defense counsel for the Chicago Seven. For the past six years, he has handled two cases for Mumia Abu-Jamal, one in the halls of justice, the other in the court of public opinion. In the first, there are rules of evidence. In the second, anything goes.

Leonard Weinglass [at a pro-Mumia event]: We now have evidence. We have proof.

Dan Ashley: The proof, according to Weinglass, consists of new witnesses who either contradict what they told police sixteen years ago, or say they saw something that night, but never told anyone until now. Weinglass spoke with us from New York via satellite.

Doesn't it disturb you that so many people representing your interests and Mumia Abu-Jamal's interests are here on the West Coast spouting misinformation about this case they said they got from you directly? Doesn't that bother you?

Leonard Weinglass: I don't think that happens at all. I think there are people who don't know every detail that's in ten thousand pages of transcripts, but I think they do understand very well the substantive issues and the essence of this case. And I think what they say is entirely accurate.

Dan Ashley: Hugh Burns is the assistant district attorney in Philadelphia now handling the Jamal case.

Hugh Burns: These people basically are willing to say anything. I mean if they thought it would be to their advantage to say that Martians came down and killed Officer Faulkner and framed Jamal they would say that.

Dan Ashley: There is at least one person living in California who has followed this case very precisely: Officer Faulkner's widow.

Maureen Faulkner: I was driving down the road and I saw poster after poster after poster on my way to work: Free Mumia Abu-Jamal. And I thought, here I am out in California looking at this. I just can't believe it.

Dan Ashley: Maureen and Danny Faulkner had been married only thirteen months that December night. He kissed her goodnight before going to work. She never saw him again.

Widowed at twenty-five, Maureen Faulkner has spent the past sixteen years trying to bring balance to the Mumia publicity barrage.

Maureen Faulkner [in courthouse footage]: Mr. Jamal is guilty of executing my husband.

Dan Ashley: She says she's been denounced, screamed at, and spat on by Jamal's supporters. To her, it all has the eerie ring of history.

Maureen Faulkner: I believe there was a person by the name of Goebbels who said, "Tell a lie, tell it big enough, tell it often enough, and it becomes truth." Well that's just what's happened in this case.

Dan Ashley: Meanwhile, sales of books, buttons, T-shirts, and posters keep generating cash for the cause. Direct contributions to the defense effort are now tax-deductible if funneled through two nonprofit organizations: The

Black United Fund in Philadelphia and the Bill of Rights Foundation in New York.

Dan Ashley [to Weinglass]: And, do you know how much money has been raised for the Mumia Abu-Jamal campaign? How much money have you raised?

Leonard Weinglass: I don't know and if I did know I wouldn't tell you.

Dan Ashley: Why?

Leonard Weinglass: Like all practicing lawyers, I never reveal what my client pays me.

Dan Ashley: The Bay Area is a long way from the street where Daniel Faulkner died, yet Jamal's California supporters have persuaded city councils here to adopt resolutions calling for a new trial.

Jamal Supporter [at a rally]: This is a certificate of honor from the Board of Supervisors of the City and County of San Francisco.

Dan Ashley: San Francisco joined the list last year and Mayor Willie Brown declared a "Justice for Mumia Abu-Jamal Day" here. The mayor chose not to discuss the case with us, so we're not sure what he knows about the facts. Whatever the reason though, his official endorsement seems to have completed Mumia Abu-Jamal's transformation into an American folk hero.

One more claim made about Mumia Abu-Jamal that we'd like to get straight. On the cover of his book *Live from Death Row,* he is said to have won the Peabody Award, one of the most prestigious honors in broadcast journalism. Well, the University of Georgia, which presents that award, has no such record.

And one more thing as I mentioned in the beginning, rallies to support his demand for a new trial are scheduled for Oakland tomorrow and tonight in Palo Alto.[254]

And there you have it. That was the KGO-TV report as aired in full on May 7 and 8, 1998. Verbatim. Very surprising that it came from San Francisco. You can imagine the rage that must have consumed Leonard Weinglass and the rest of the pro-Abu-Jamal crowd when they saw or heard about KGO-TV's report. For years, they had dominated the media war; KGO-TV was challenging their supremacy.

As expected, Weinglass was outraged when he saw the KGO-TV report and immediately sought to retaliate. In response to the program, Weinglass and C. Clark Kissinger put together a document entitled "A Case Study in Irresponsible Journalism," which was distributed to supporters and posted on a pro-Abu-Jamal Web site, Refuse and Resist. The masterminds of manipulation struck again! The thirteen-page report claims:

On May 7 and 8, 1998, KGO-TV broadcast a two-part series attacking the international movement to prevent the execution of Mumia Abu-Jamal. This series, which totaled 12 minutes in the local news segment, purported to present the true facts on this important public issue. In reality, it presented incorrect and false information on virtually every point. What is most disturbing is that this was not done from ignorance. Although opposing parties in this case presented KGO with conflicting information, the public record of the court proceedings was available for anyone who honestly wanted to determine the truth.

Here we cannot retrace the whole story of the shooting, arrest, and conviction of Philadelphia journalist Mumia Abu-Jamal. For this we refer the reader to the many books, articles, and Internet Web sites dealing with the case. Our purpose here is to dissect a deliberately false story presented by KGO-TV in order that the ABC network and the management of its San Francisco affiliate can take the appropriate action to correct the public record and discipline those responsible.[255]

Each carefully phrased line of Weinglass and Kissinger's response artfully conceals volumes of truth. It is especially interesting to note that Weinglass and Kissinger claim that they "cannot retrace the whole story of the shooting, arrest, and conviction." They instead refer the reader to other sources, "books, articles, and Internet Web sites," to gain a further factual understanding. Think about that. If you were writing a rebuttal that you were trying to make as convincing as possible, wouldn't you include all of the information you had available? Surely you wouldn't need alternate sources. You wouldn't merely refer readers to alleged proof for your case somewhere in cyberspace and library archives. You would lay it on thick right then and there. Weinglass and Kissinger did not. They were quick to point the finger but not so swift in backing up their accusations. Furthermore, the books, articles, and Web sites to which Weinglass and Kissinger refer are also telling. Surely, these are the very same sources that have been spreading half-truths and circuitous logic about the Abu-Jamal case from the beginning.

In their self-righteous rage, Weinglass and Kissinger's report spared no venom when it came to me. Here's the text of what they say regarding my character:

> The KGO attack includes an interview with Maureen Faulkner, the widow of Officer Faulkner. Mrs. Faulkner accuses the supporters of

Jamal of acting like Nazi propagandist Josef Goebbels by repeatedly telling lies in the hope of their eventual acceptance as truth.

It would have been helpful if KGO had asked Mrs. Faulkner about a claim she made that when a ballistics expert held up her dead husband's shirt in court to display the bullet holes, Jamal turned around and smiled at her. This is a real crowd-stopper. It seems to capture the very essence of the prosecution's claim that Jamal was a cold-blooded killer.

The only problem is, it isn't true. A simple examination of the transcript shows that, on the day the ballistics expert presented his testimony, Jamal was absent from the courtroom. Also, the first time we heard her make this claim was in 1995, 13 years after the event in question. In the court of law, the prosecution has had Judge Sabo to protect them. But in the court of public opinion, Mrs. Faulkner has no such protection. Her erroneous statements were quickly exposed.

I have already explained, in detail, the bloody shirt incident, and all that I will say here is thank goodness the event was documented by court transcripts and by Marc Kaufman from the *Philadelphia Inquirer*.[256]

The pro-Abu-Jamal forces did not stop with the rebuttal by Weinglass and Kissinger. The bully had been publicly punched in the nose. They were so enraged that the media would question their credibility that they waged retaliatory battles throughout the entire summer of 1998. On Saturday, August 1, 1998, at 1:00 p.m., the Mobilization to Free Mumia Abu-Jamal, a San Francisco group headed by Jeff Mackler, organized a picket demonstration outside KGO-TV headquarters to protest its so-called biased reporting. According to Mackler, the KGO-TV report was: "A slanderous attack on Mumia and his supporters [that] presented false information on virtually every point made in the report."[257]

At the bottom of the press release was a description of Abu-Jamal that described him, not as a murderer or cop killer, but rather, as "An award-winning African-American journalist and radio commentator who has been on death row for over 17 years for the shooting death of a Philadelphia police officer."[258]

I decided to respond to Leonard Weinglass's attacks on my credibility by addressing his claims much in the same way he attempted to refute KGO-TV's. I especially sought to emphasize the haphazard way in which

Weinglass throws around the terms "fact" and "truth." So in a letter to the station, I said:

> Mr. Weinglass regularly presents his version of the "facts" and "truth" about this case. More often than not, these alleged "facts" are nothing more than self-serving misrepresentations of the court record. In dealing with Mr. Weinglass regarding the Mumia Abu-Jamal matter, we feel it's important to define the words "truth" and "fact." We define the TRUTH as that which is testified to while under oath by an individual in the courtroom and is deemed credible by the court. We feel this testimony remains true until it is proven false in the courtroom, by someone the court deems "credible." The truth is not simply what Leonard Weinglass tells us it is. We define a FACT as something known to be real or true. A fact is also not what Leonard Weinglass tells us it is.
>
> As your reporters discovered while doing their research, the real story here does not involve the guilt or innocence of Mumia Abu-Jamal; that has already been determined beyond any reasonable doubt in the court-room. The real story about this case, as you correctly reported, involves the ongoing misinformation campaign currently being directed by Leonard Weinglass and Abu-Jamal's support groups. We have known this for years, but KGO is one of the first media outlets to bring it to the public's attention.[259]

The KGO report thus began a very important chapter in my fight for Danny. As I look back over the many milestones in a long and emotionally trying journey, I remember how uplifting and vindicating it was to finally be treated with fair and factually accurate media coverage. It was a much-needed turning point away from spin and hyperbole and onwards towards fact and honest recollection.

2 9

THE *NEW YORK TIMES*
AD FOR DANNY

It was now *seventeen* years since Danny's death. On the heels of three Post-Conviction Relief Act hearings and the KGO-TV report, I finally had reason for optimism. While our financial resources still lagged behind Abu-Jamal's (no wealthy celebrities, no book deals to support our fund), we were working tirelessly to get our message heard.

A few years after the ad in support of Abu-Jamal appeared in the *New York Times*, we, and our loosely affiliated supporters, under the banner of "Justice For Danny Faulkner," were ready to respond. We figured that we would take the facts of the case and present them to the American public in an easy-to-read format that would clearly convince detractors how ridiculously false the defense claims were. The KGO-TV piece would serve as a model. I was floored to learn that a full-page ad in the *New York Times* would cost approximately $40,000. Assuming that we could raise the money, we knew there was absolutely no room for error. Everything had to be perfect. Paul and Mike Lutz of the FOP were in disagreement as to what the content of the ad should be. Paul wanted to use the 1995 PCRA findings in the ad, while others wanted to make it more "in your face hard-hitting."

The more Paul began to understand the facts of the case, the more he realized that the best way to convince people about Abu-Jamal's guilt was to educate them on the facts. Remember, in 1998 the Internet was in its infancy and neither Paul nor I were well versed in computer technology. However, Paul got help from a technologically savvy friend, Mark Van-Leewen, who convinced us of the informational powers of the Internet, and the Web site for Justice for P/O Daniel Faulkner became the starting point of our reinvigorated efforts. We were convinced that anyone who took the time to read the whole site would be easily convinced of Abu-Jamal's guilt.

Compared to what we have now, our first Web site was rudimentary, and it showed, but we were nevertheless proud and justifiably so. The site was the product of many weeks, months, and even years of research and effort. Paul especially poured his heart into it. Our goal was to get our Web site online for the first time simultaneously with the printing of the *New York Times* ad. My goal for the ad was simple: I wanted the world to know that Abu-Jamal murdered my husband in 1981 and that he has been misleading the public about his supposed innocence ever since. I wanted to urge readers that the cop killer's death sentence should be executed immediately. While the message was straightforward, we needed to have the appropriate facts to back it up. I was determined that our integrity not be questioned. Not only was I trying to dethrone a hero, I was aware that any public pleas in favor of capital punishment were inherently controversial.

When the *Times* ad went to press, it cost the Justice for P/O Daniel Faulkner group $34,500.[260] It was the best thirty-four grand I ever spent. The money was raised in small amounts from supporters across the country; it was amazingly gratifying to receive support from so many. Many of our donations came in $5, $10, and $25 increments. We have never had the luxury of celebrities or rock bands willing to donate huge sums of cash to our cause; it has always been completely bottom up, not top down.

Here is the way we ran the ad:

JUSTICE FOR POLICE OFFICER DANIEL FAULKNER

Philadelphia Police Officer Daniel Faulkner—Executed by Mumia Abu-Jamal December 9, 1981

On December 9, 1981, a young bride lost a loving husband, a Mother lost a son, and the Philadelphia Police Department lost one of their finest. At approximately 3:40 a.m. on that day, 25-year-old Police Officer Daniel Faulkner, who was on duty and in full uniform, observed a vehicle traveling the wrong way on a one-way street. Faulkner was conducting an investigation of the vehicle, which was operated by William Cook, who is the brother of Mumia Abu-Jamal. The scene of the car stop was 13th and Locust Streets in Center City Philadelphia. While being questioned, William Cook assaulted Officer Faulkner. Without warning or provocation, Mumia Abu-Jamal ran up behind Officer Faulkner from a parking lot, and shot the Officer in the back, at close range. Although critically wounded, Officer Faulkner turned and managed to shoot his attacker in the chest. At this point, the Officer fell to the ground, wounded, disarmed and unable to defend himself. Abu-Jamal now stood over Officer Faulkner and fired 2–3 more shots, point-blank, at Officer Faulkner's upper body. He then bent down and fired the fatal shot, which entered Officer Faulkner's head, above his eye. The bullet came to rest in his brain, killing him instantly. Abu-Jamal, who tried to flee the scene, but was unable to do so because of the wound he sustained, was found several feet from his victim, Police Officer Daniel Faulkner.[261]

A large quarter-page picture of Danny was included in the ad to finally show the world that the story here was not the plight of Mumia Abu-Jamal but that of a young man who had been murdered, and who had a name, Danny Faulkner. The rest of the page discussed the case against the murderer, Mumia Abu-Jamal, and presented the facts with actual trial testimony. The bottom of the ad directed readers to the Web site www.justice 4danielfaulkner.com and asked for donations to help the cause.

We were incredibly excited the day it was published. I will never forget June 14, 1998. Paul and I drove together to Borders to pick up our copy. On this ride to the bookstore, I was consumed with excitement and anticipation. All the months of planning and years of raising money in anticipation of our retaliation were coming to fruition! I wondered what it was going to look like—what page would it be on—what would be the response. After we purchased the paper, we were too anxious to look right away. We waited until we got back to the haven of our living room before opening it up. I remember the elation: Oh my God, it's actually there! It's real! We saw right away this was going to agitate the maniacal Mumia crowds. Excitement soon turned to paranoia: What if they found out where we lived?

My fear was not completely unfounded. After more than a decade of boorish behavior and vicious taunts from them, I was justifiably scared. For the next couple of weeks, every time the phone rang or someone knocked at the door, I worried that "they" were going to be there.

In addition, as a result of increased media exposure of the case, this had become a particularly stressful time for me, an aspect of my situation that often still gets lost in the media coverage. For some reason, the media expects that, after a certain amount of time, one is supposed to let go or move on according to their timetable; to someone whose sunlit days were turned into endless shadow and grief, it's an impossible task. I have never let go. And I have no intention of doing so.

After the Web site was launched and the ad hit, Leonard Weinglass came out swinging on KPFK radio. As expected, he was antagonistic and even threatened to sue me for defamation.

Weinglass sent a letter to the Editor of the *New York Times* voicing his anger at the ad. As you read what he wrote, keep in mind that it was the Abu-Jamal side that first established the *New York Times* as a battleground for advertising about the case. While their ad was founded on spin and hyperbole, ours was based on facts and trial transcripts. Weinglass was up-in-arms. He wrote:

> In a startling, and even disgraceful, effort to hasten and insure the execution of an innocent man whose substantial legal claims that he never received a fair trial are just now being reviewed by the highest court of Pennsylvania, a previously unknown group speaking for the Fraternal Order of Police, and apparently headed by a slain police officer's widow, took out a full page unsigned ad on the most prestigious page of the Sunday *New York Times* of June 14th entitled, "Justice for Police Officer Daniel Faulkner." The target of this attack, Mumia Abu-Jamal, a renowned journalist from Philadelphia who has been on death row for 16 years for the alleged shooting of Officer Faulkner, and who was known as "the voice of the voiceless" for his award winning reporting on police abuse and other social and racial ills that afflicted the minority communities of Philadelphia, had received worldwide support in his effort to overturn his unjust conviction. At the time of his arrest in 1981 Jamal was serving as the President of the Association of Black Journalists and had previously been a founder of the Black Panther Party in Philadelphia and a supporter of the Philadelphia MOVE group.

> The advertisement for death, taken out at the cost of tens of thousands of dollars, selectively quotes from witnesses at Jamal's 1982 trial, all of whom have been thoroughly discredited in subsequent court hearings beginning in 1995. Omitted are the evidence and witnesses who have come forward to establish facts which were kept from the jury during the 1982 trial. The ad claims as a "fact" that two police officers heard Jamal

confess to the shooting of officer Faulkner the night of the killing. Yet the police officer who guarded Jamal reported that very morning that Jamal had made "no comments." That officer reportedly was on vacation and unavailable at trial, when in fact, he was at home waiting to testify.

Similarly, the charge that the shot which killed Faulkner came from Jamal's legally registered .38-caliber weapon contradicts the medical examiner's report—first entered into the official record in 1995—that the bullet removed from Faulkner's brain was a .44-caliber. That fact was also kept from the jury. Moreover, a weapons expert found it incredible that the police at the scene of the shooting failed to test Jamal's gun to see if it had been recently fired or to test his hands to see if he had fired a weapon.

The testimony cited in the ad of "eyewitnesses" who claimed to identify Jamal as the shooter was equally flawed, coming from witnesses whose testimony has now been exposed as false. One of these witnesses, a white cab driver named Robert Chobert, first reported to police that the shooter was 225 pounds and "ran away" from the scene. This couldn't have been Jamal, who weighed 170 pounds and was found by the police sitting on a curb at the scene of the shooting, bleeding profusely from a shot fired by Faulkner. Why Chobert changed his story did not become clear until 13 years later when, at a court hearing in 1995, he admitted that at the time of the shooting he had been driving his taxicab without a license while still on probation for felony arson—throwing a Molotov cocktail at a grammar school. The jury which presumably found Chobert truthful never heard these facts. Furthermore Chobert revealed in 1995 that he had asked Jamal's prosecutor to help get his driver's license back. Years later he was still driving, unhindered by the police, without a license.

The main witness cited in the ad, Cynthia White, was someone no other witness even reported seeing at the site. In return for her testimony that Jamal shot Faulkner, White was allowed to continue to work the streets as a prostitute for years, apparently with police protection. In a 1997 hearing, another former prostitute, Pamela Jenkins, who was a friend of White at the time, testified that White was acting as a police informant, a fact not given to the defense, and that she had testified only after the police had threatened her life.

Other sworn testimony revealed that witness coercion was routinely practiced by the police as they pursued their investigation against Jamal. In 1995, eyewitness William Singletary testified that police repeatedly tore up his initial statement—that the shooter, not Jamal, ran away from the scene—until he wrote something acceptable to them. The following year, another former prostitute, Veronica Jones, courageously came forward to testify that she had also been coerced into changing her initial true eyewitness account that two men had fled the scene of the killing; again, not Jamal. To anyone familiar with the notorious practices of the Philadelphia Police Department, this pattern of police misconduct is not unique to Jamal's case.

At the 1982 trial and every subsequent hearing in Jamal's case information was withheld from the defense by the prosecution in a courtroom presided over by Judge Albert Sabo. In an unrelated proceeding, six former Philadelphia District Attorneys swore under oath that no accused could receive a fair trial in Sabo's court. Jamal presented over a score of separate constitutional violations to the Pennsylvania Supreme Court, from the withholding of evidence to the racial exclusion of jurors. Eleven qualified African Americans were rejected by the prosecution, a standard practice as was recently revealed in the exposure of a "training tape" for excluding blacks from juries prepared by the Philadelphia District Attorney's office in the mid-1980s. On this basis alone, Jamal should be given his freedom.

In a country where the racial bias inherent in the death penalty was recognized by the U.S. Supreme Court in 1987 (even as it ruled that such bias provided no basis for appeal!) Philadelphia reigns as the "capital of capital punishment." A 1998 study by the Death Penalty Information Center, titled "The Death Penalty in Black and White," notes that blacks make up 84 percent of those on death row from Philadelphia and that black men from that city are almost four times more likely to receive a death sentence than other defendants.

Since this sinister ad only repeats old, discredited tales and completely ignores the evidence presented in Jamal's appeals, one is left to ask, "Why now?" The Pennsylvania State Supreme Court is about to render a decision on Jamal's appeal of Judge Sabo's predictable denial of a new trial for Jamal. Pennsylvania Governor Tom Ridge, who signed Jamal's death warrant in June, 1995, has vowed to once again order Jamal's execution should he lose his appeal. Anticipating the possibility of a repeat of the massive protests that succeeded in saving Jamal's life in August, 1995, the pro-death penalty and law enforcement forces now seem more determined than ever to defeat and deflect the strength of that movement.

In a country awash with commodity advertising, the many thousands of dollars spent in this false and misleading ad will not subvert or detract from the public outcry in support of Jamal. The rush to judgment back in 1982, fueled by sensational media reporting that echoed police demands for the death of Mumia Abu-Jamal irrespective of the evidence, has produced an historic injustice which has kept an innocent man in prison most of his adult life. The effort to now seal his fate through advertising is equally reprehensible and must be rejected in favor of immediate freedom for Mumia Abu-Jamal.

—Leonard Weinglass
Attorney for Mumia Abu-Jamal[262]

The Abu-Jamal camp couldn't allow itself to be beaten. Just three months later, on October 16, 1998, Abu-Jamal's supporters paid for another ad to run on A-23 of the Friday *New York Times*. Their second ad was much like the first, spouting lies and half-truths. By the time of the second ad, the three PCRA hearings had taken place, leaving gaping holes in the defense's some-other-dude theory. With little else to rely upon, the defense adopted a new strategy—celebrities over substance. While always Hollywood-conscious, Team Mumia now more than ever operated under the assumption that, if they could attract enough big names to join their cause, everyone would believe them regardless of their numerous legal defeats. The new ad contained the name of longtime Abu-Jamal supporter Ed Asner and the Asner Family Foundation. How preposterous—a "Family Foundation" supporting a man who destroyed several families through murder—the Faulkners, the Foleys, and his own!

The ad contained nothing new or startling. Nothing groundbreaking. Nothing illuminating. It was just more of the same old: an arrogant flex of their financial muscle and a celebrity-sprinkled web of lies.

3 0

HOLLYWOOD'S UNLIKELY HERO

The passage of time could not dampen the spirit of controversy. Seventeen years after Danny's murder, 1998 was a wild ride. First, there was the KGO-TV report in San Francisco. I made my second trip to the National Police Memorial in Washington, where T-shirt sales in support of Danny were the rage. Our *New York Times* ad followed shortly thereafter, whereupon the shenanigans of Weinglass & Co. were launched in full force. Within days of our ad, our Web site was hit with a virus that cost us $500 to repair. Someone sent to us several pages on which was written the word "pig" thousands of times. Then, on October 30, 1998, the Pennsylvania Supreme Court unanimously rejected Abu-Jamal's appeal. Not surprisingly, the story does not end there. The battle was slated to continue for many more years inside and outside the courtroom. On November 3, 1998, a new Massachusetts governor's acceptance speech was interrupted by Abu-Jamal supporters. And finally, culminating the year of bedlam, 1998 ended with the news that Sam Donaldson was investigating the case. Needless to say, this made me a bit nervous.

My many years of struggle and tumult have taught me that it is not always easy to predict just exactly who will be on my side. One would think that representatives of the U.S. government, including congressmen and mayors, would be quick to support me. While most do, a handful (Rep. Dellums, Rep. Rangel, Rep. Fattah—from Philadelphia, and Mayor Willie Brown of San Francisco) have stepped up in support of Mumia Abu-Jamal. Mayor John F. Street of Philadelphia, the mayor of the city in which Danny was employed and murdered, has been a great disappointment. Nevertheless, over the years, support has snuck up on me from unexpected places. Now, with Sam Donaldson sniffing on the trail, we were completely vulnerable. We had no idea what to expect.

Exactly seventeen years after the murder, December 9, 1998, ABC News filed a *20/20* report under the title "Hollywood's Unlikely Hero," produced by Harry Phillips with Sam Donaldson as the correspondent. Phillips was my initial point of contact. He called and asked if I would be willing to meet with him to discuss the facts surrounding Danny's murder. His only assurance to me was that he would tell our side of the story along with Abu-Jamal's side and that he would let the facts speak for themselves with the audience.

I'd heard that before, and I was nervous. The bad experience with Richard Plepler at HBO and their bogus piece of pseudo-journalism was still fresh in my mind. I was uneasy about doing the interview.

But something about Harry Phillips and his ABC News team inspired trust and instilled confidence. Perhaps I was more optimistic after the KGO-TV surprise in San Francisco; for whatever reason, I sensed an air of extraordinary professionalism and fair-mindedness from the ABC representatives. I have always admired Sam Donaldson. I know that many people assumed that he was a loyal member of the so-called "liberal media." However, I never did place him in this category. I always thought he was capable of delivering a fair report. This is not to say that I was unconcerned about his aggressive nature; I was. But I hoped that, to whatever extent he was confrontational with me, he would be with the other side, too. Harry Phillips told me that Sam would be great for the case because one side was clearly lying, and Sam would figure it out. I was happy to have him try.

When the segment finally aired, *20/20* lived up to its promise and presented both sides of the case in an even-keeled and exactingly detailed manner. This was no superficial report. The ABC crew spent months immersing themselves in the facts of the case and the finished product reflected their meticulous ethics. They cut me no breaks. They simply presented the full picture. Anytime you present the full picture, you are benefiting Danny and his memory. The facts are on the side of Abu-Jamal's guilt.

I have the transcript of the show. I won't cherry-pick, but I want to give you an idea of what was broadcasted on national television by one of the most respected news magazine programs in the country. Pay special attention to the questions posed by Sam Donaldson to Abu-Jamal's celebrity supporters and attorney Leonard Weinglass. He asks the tough questions and finds out that there is little real substance behind the hoopla created by those who claim Abu-Jamal is an innocent philosopher being framed by a corrupt government. Here is how it began:

> **Voice-over:** Tonight—he's on death row for murder, but Hollywood celebrities and world leaders say he shouldn't die.
>
> **Joseph McGill, Prosecutor:** People are making something of a hero of somebody who runs over and shoots a cop in the back.
>
> **Announcer:** Rallies take place around the world for a man convicted of killing a police officer, and the officer's partner says the convict even confessed to the crime.
>
> **Garry Bell,** police officer: He just shouted out that "I shot the MFer. I hope he dies."
>
> **Announcer:** So why have some of the most recognized names in entertainment and politics taken up his cause?
>
> **Maureen Faulkner,** victim's wife: Mumia is nothing but a cold-blooded murderer. And they have been duped.
>
> **Announcer:** And why is the slain cop's widow still haunted by the voice of her husband's killer?
>
> **Mumia Abu-Jamal:** From death row, this is Mumia Abu-Jamal.
>
> **Announcer:** Tonight, Sam Donaldson returns to the scene of the crime and examines the evidence. Is this man a cold-blooded killer or America's last political prisoner? The compelling story of "Hollywood's Unlikely Hero."

The piece opened with some repartee between Sam Donaldson and Diane Sawyer. From the outset, Diane Sawyer challenged viewers: "He has generated international fervor, support from all kinds of celebrities and politicians. Do they know the whole story? Are they in for a surprise?" Watching at home in California, Paul and I were optimistic about what was to come.

Shortly after Diane Sawyer's introduction, the piece featured Abu-Jamal in jail saying: "I'm fighting every day, not just for my freedom, not just for my liberation, but for all of our liberation." What about my liberation, Mumia? What about the liberation of truth? Do you think that your hyperbolic revolutionary bellows are a satisfactory proxy for an explanation of what occurred on December 9, 1981? I wondered if he would use this interview as the forum to finally explain himself. And if not, would that fact be pointed out?

Sam Donaldson then provided an overview of the murder from the crime scene:

> It began here on Locust Street in downtown Philadelphia on a cold December night seventeen years ago. Officers responding to a call for backup found a squad car, its lights still flashing, behind a blue Volkswagen parked right here. And, on the sidewalk, they found one of their own lying face up in a pool of blood. Officer Daniel Faulkner was dead, shot once in the back, and then right between the eyes. And a few feet away, sitting on the curb, they found Mumia Abu-Jamal beside his gun.

> Witnesses said Officer Faulkner had been trying to arrest the driver of the blue Volkswagen, William Cook, who happens to be Jamal's brother. Three eyewitnesses, one stopped in that intersection, one standing on a corner there and one sitting in a cab here right behind the squad car, all say they saw Jamal run from across the street and shoot the officer in the back. As the officer spun around, he grabbed his revolver and, as he fell to the sidewalk, fired a shot that wounded Jamal in the chest. It was then that Jamal, according to the witnesses, executed Officer Faulkner. The backup officers arrived within forty-five seconds, too late to save Officer Faulkner's life, but not too late to arrest Mumia Abu-Jamal."

Prosecutor Joe McGill then offered his view: "What you have is eyewitness testimony, not one but three. You have a weapon, clear. And later at a hospital, he blurts out what he did in an arrogant way."

Next, Donaldson addressed the HBO scandal. He first introduced a clip of Abu-Jamal, commenting on it by saying: "Seen here two years ago in a sympathetic British documentary, he repeats the only thing he has ever said about the murder."

> **Mumia Abu-Jamal:** I am absolutely innocent of the charge I was charged on.

Aha. Once again, the death row darling falters; this was all he had to offer. Bizarre circumstance had transformed him into an international celebrity but, as of the airing of the *20/20* special on this unlikely hero, he had lost three Post-Conviction Act Relief hearings and had been denied his appeal by the Pennsylvania Supreme Court. In addition to our legal victories, we had started fighting back in the public arena, and were getting results! Here, Abu-Jamal was given another chance to turn things around.

He could have gone on camera and proclaimed to the world, "OK, at long last, I want you to know what happened that night. Here it is." Alas, he did not do it. Instead, he left it to Leonard Weinglass to throw a barrage of mud at the wall in a vain hope that something would stick. Of course, Weinglass's recipe for defense and rebuttal always included a couple of celebrities for dramatic flavor. On cue, Ed Asner and Mike Farrell appeared:

> **Ed Asner,** actor: I just know that the trial stunk. And the police malfeasance is sufficient. Witness flip-flopping all over the place is sufficient.
>
> **Sam Donaldson** (voice-over): Ed Asner and Mike Farrell are just two of many Hollywood actors who believe the police, the prosecution, and the judge, Albert Sabo, stacked the trial against Jamal.
>
> **Mike Farrell,** actor: The president of the criminal justice bar, for example, was quoted as saying, "When Judge Sabo walks into the courtroom, the Constitution dies a little."

Farrell and Asner were soon followed by a French professor. In a perverse sense of homage to Mumia Abu-Jamal, the professor actually said: "I feel so little compared to him."

Finally, Sam Donaldson asked Weinglass what happened that fateful night if it were something other than Abu-Jamal committing murder. Paul and I wondered which fantasy version of events Weinglass would take off the shelf for the big event. All his outlandish theories had been disproved in a court of law. This had never deterred Weinglass in the past.

> **Leonard Weinglass:** Mumia ran to a scene where his brother was being beaten. That is true. As he got there, gunfire erupted. That is also true. But it was Mumia who was shot. Then the officer was shot. It is our contention that the person who shot the officer fled the scene, as reported to the police that night.

So, Weinglass had decided on "The Tale of The Mystery Man," an oldie, but what a goodie! I came on air next, telling the listeners and the world exactly the same thing that was racing through my head at home as I watched Weinglass's inane blabber.

> **Maureen Faulkner,** victim's wife: Leonard Weinglass is a liar.

After a commercial break, Donaldson plunged into the evidence. "We conducted a four-month investigation and here is what we found," he said. "First, ballistics: Jamal's supporters say the bullet that killed Officer

Faulkner was .44-caliber, not a .38 like the gun found at the scene," said Donaldson. And then he blasted the defense spin on this issue.

> **Claude Pujol:** The bullet is not the size of the gun, first thing. They never did any tests.
>
> **Ed Asner:** The fact that no ballistics tests were done, which is pretty stupid.
>
> **Sam Donaldson** (voice-over): But ballistics tests were done and proved the bullet was fired by a .38-caliber revolver. The claim that the bullet was a .44 rests solely on a hasty note scribbled by a pathologist at the autopsy. However, the pathologist later testified that he had no expertise in ballistics, that he had only been guessing. But Weinglass refuses to believe that.
>
> (On camera) You don't think it was a guess?
>
> **Leonard Weinglass:** I don't think he would guess.
>
> **Sam Donaldson:** The police say that that slug has the lands and grooves consistent with being a .38 slug.
>
> **Leonard Weinglass:** It does.
>
> **Sam Donaldson:** But if it's a .38, then your contention that it was a .44 is wrong.
>
> **Leonard Weinglass:** Well, I think that issue is very much something that should be played out in front of a jury.
>
> **Sam Donaldson** (voice-over): But it had already been played out in front of a judge, when, three years ago, Weinglass's own ballistics expert testified the fatal bullet was a .38.

The investigative work was masterful: Never—outside of court—had Weinglass been confronted with such a barrage of truth in such a powerful way. By now, we were cheering as we watched! Even better, all the information the public was hearing was 100 percent accurate. All ballistics experts agreed that Danny was murdered with a .38, the type of weapon Abu-Jamal had himself purchased and was carrying that night.

Next came the subject of Abu-Jamal's confession.

> **Leonard Weinglass:** And that testimony was produced by the officer's partner, plus a security guard who wanted to be a police officer. More than two months later, they remembered that Mumia said that.
>
> **Sam Donaldson** (voice-over): It is a fact that the confession surfaced only after two months. And that one officer present originally reported, "The Negro male made no comments."
>
> **Voice-over:** But hospital security guard Priscilla Durham told the jury she reported it to her supervisor the next day. And another security guard, James Legrand, says he, too, heard the confession. The slain offi-

cer's partner, Garry Bell, says the shock of the shooting suppressed his memory.

Garry Bell: I've searched my soul. I've beaten myself up wondering how I could not have gone at a sooner date, immediately even, and report what I had heard.

Sam Donaldson (voice-over): Finally, if there was a plot to fabricate a confession, then it had to include at least the eight people involved in reporting and investigating it, an idea rejected by two separate appeals courts in the last three years.

Again, "from the sofa," we relished the swift presentation of facts. We had never before heard such a thorough, if brief, analysis of the confession issue. For years, we had wished that somebody would say what Sam Donaldson just did. Our elation continued as Donaldson discussed the eyewitness issue.

Donaldson: Then there are the defense eyewitnesses. Leonard Weinglass says four people saw the real killer running from the scene. But his number-one witness William Singletary waited more than a decade before testifying to a story so bizarre even Weinglass has trouble defending it.

(On camera) He said the shooter emerged from the Volkswagen, yelling and screaming, shot Officer Faulkner in the head and ran away. Whereupon, according to Singletary, Abu-Jamal approached the scene and said, "Oh, my God, we don't need this," bent over Faulkner, who'd been shot between the eyes, and asked, "Is there anything I can do to help you?" Whereupon, according to Singletary, Faulkner's gun, which was in Faulkner's lap, miraculously discharged, hitting Jamal in the chest. Now, that's incredible.

Leonard Weinglass: He might be wrong on some of his timing. There's no doubt about that.

Sam Donaldson: Timing? He's telling a story here which clearly, from the forensic evidence, couldn't have happened.

Leonard Weinglass: This is my point. The jury should have heard from Singletary.

In my opinion, Sam Donaldson had made a complete ass out of Leonard Weinglass, and there was still more to come.

Sam Donaldson (voice-over): Defense eyewitness number four was a prostitute standing on this corner two blocks away, who, after fourteen years' silence, claimed she saw two men jogging from the scene. She also admits to being, in drug lingo, "half a nickel bag high."

At this point, Donaldson reported about the scene of the murder with prosecutor Joe McGill. McGill explained that a defense witness was "beyond a football field" away from the crime. Finally, Donaldson brought out the fact that the closest eyewitness of all was Abu-Jamal's brother, William Cook, and that the only thing Cook ever said about the murder was, "I ain't got nothing to do with this." Period.

Donaldson then echoed what I had been trumpeting for years, namely that Cook has *never* said, "Well, my brother didn't do it either." Even as Abu-Jamal's life stands in peril, never has William Cook come forward to say someone else committed the crime. Weinglass unconvincingly attempted to say that Cook, informally, did give the defense team such a denial. Weinglass also tried to justify Cook's silence by offering that he was wanted on a minor theft charge and therefore was reluctant to come forward. Perhaps Weinglass, too, should have remained silent; he sounded like a fool, or like he was trying to fool you.

Former Philadelphia district attorney, then mayor, and future governor Ed Rendell was also shown on camera. Mayor Rendell told Sam Donaldson, "It's just plain sad how this has become a cause celebre around the world." Rendell said that, before San Francisco Mayor Willie Brown Jr. signed a proclamation in support of Abu-Jamal, he should have called him. "Willie should have picked up the phone and called me." This was not the only blow to the celebrity bandwagon. Ed Asner and Mike Farrell were next. Donaldson cornered the two regarding Abu-Jamal's guilt. He questioned their involvement and forced viewers to consider the hidden agendas and larger purpose behind their interest in the case. With true Hollywood panache, Farrell sidestepped the issue and delivered a self-serving reply.

Mike Farrell: You know, Ms. Faulkner, bless her. I really wish for her peace at some point. And if, in fact, a new trial holds that Mumia Abu-Jamal committed this crime, I hope he is punished appropriately.

Unfortunately, Mr. Farrell, peace will only come to me with the proper execution of justice.

As you can imagine, the leftist supporters of Abu-Jamal were bewildered and bruised that night, uncomprehending how such a damning piece would be aired on television. Their protests were for naught. The broadcast was factually sound. The truth hurt. The battle was far from over, but no longer were our troops being mercilessly slaughtered in the field. Gone were the days when our friends would call us and wonder aloud whether I might be mistaken in the belief that Abu-Jamal murdered my husband. Reasonable people would no longer openly question his guilt. A few weeks after the report aired, after the initial pro-Abu-Jamal barrage against ABC News had died, I sent letters of thanks to Harry Phillips, Sam Donaldson, and Robert Igor. I did this, not to thank them for being one-sided and ignoring the problems Abu-Jamal supporters had with the case, but to thank them for simply keeping their promise and being fair. That is all that I have ever asked for.

In my letter to Harry Phillips, the producer of the *20/20* piece, I wrote:

> You are one of the few people who understands how long I've waited and how hard I've fought, asking nothing more than to have an accurate accounting of the facts surrounding my husband's murder presented and to have Abu-Jamal's supporters exposed for what they really are. In 22 minutes you accomplished all of this. In doing so, I hope you have begun to push the pendulum of public opinion and support in a direction away from Abu-Jamal.
>
> At no time have I ever felt the real facts needed to be spun in our favor. From the first time I heard the testimony against Jamal in the courtroom, I've never doubted that he murdered Danny. All I've ever asked of the media is that they do their homework and that a reasonable degree of professionalism be shown in presenting the facts to the public. While the local media in Philadelphia has usually lived up to this modest standard, the national media has failed to do so for years. Then you came along. Finally, things have been set straight. I am simply unable to express on paper how the layers of anger and frustration were stripped away as I watched your program. These feelings had built up within me for years. Your hard work and honesty has helped to lift their burden.[263]

I also wrote to Sam Donaldson.

> I understand that Mumia will always be seen as a saint or a prophet by some of his more rabid supporters. However, my greatest source of frustration has been the fact that Jamal's supporters have misled so many good people into believing he is innocent. Since the time when Mr. Weinglass took Jamal's case over and gave the first push to the tiny snowball that has become the Mumia misinformation avalanche, all I've ever wanted was to have the truth about the trial facts and testimony to be

heard. It's always been my feeling that if presented fairly, these facts would speak for themselves and point beyond any doubt to Jamal's guilt. I wanted the world to know the truth, but I was just one tiny voice standing alone against the Mumia propaganda machine. Through your efforts and talent, you have fulfilled my wish, and for that I will always be grateful.[264]

20/20 received a heavy outpouring of positive responses to its piece. The report was so successful that, a year later, they updated the material slightly and rebroadcast a new version in August of 1999. In the rebroadcast, they added an interview with Philip Bloch. Philip Bloch is a pacifist and anti–death penalty advocate who had been a volunteer at the prison where Abu-Jamal was incarcerated. Bloch is an incredibly honest and brave man. When he saw the 20/20 piece, he realized that he had to come forward and tell his story. I will soon share it with you here. In a word, what Bloch would offer was stunning.

31

THE OAKLAND TEACH-IN

The *20/20* program filled us with expectation and hope. The glow did not last long, however. There were new challenges ahead as Team Mumia persevered with vengeance. The newest manifestation of the Mumia machine was setting up shop in Oakland, California, and came in an unlikely form: a "teach-in." In a shattering jolt to my consciousness, I learned through an AP reporter who e-mailed our Web site that a so-called "teach-in" was being organized in support of Abu-Jamal in Oakland's public schools. Not a legitimate role model such as Martin Luther King Jr., but instead, a convicted cop killer. It was first suggested that the teach-in was the zany brainchild of a high school history teacher, Sara Fuchs, who had been using the Abu-Jamal case to teach about the criminal justice system and the death penalty.[265] Sara Fuchs, however, cannot claim full credit. After more complete research, I learned that the real force behind the teach-in effort was a radical activist group, The Coalition to Defend Affirmative Action and Integration and Fight for Equality By Any Means Necessary. BAMN, the acronym for "By Any Means Necessary," was founded in 1995 and has close ties to a Detroit-based radical political party known as the Revolutionary Workers League.[266] Together, their coalition had a strong presence at the University of California–Berkeley.

The organizers of the events surrounding the Teach-In for Abu-Jamal were Craig Gordon and Bob Mandel. Both were teachers in the Oakland school district and both were members of the executive board of the teachers union and members of BAMN.[267] Mandel claimed the teach-in was a "fundamental issue of the right to teach, the right to learn and the right to discuss issues that are pertinent."[268] They deliberately scheduled the event to coincide with Martin Luther King Day. The teach-in was expected to involve all five high schools in Oakland, fourteen middle schools, and possibly some elementary schools. Participation was to range from a single class to all day. Parental permission was being required. Then, fate interceded.

On Saturday, January 9, 1999, a forty-one-year-old Oakland police officer named James Williams was gunned down in the line of duty, shot by a sniper.[269] He was a rookie cop who left behind a wife and three children. Williams's funeral was scheduled for Thursday, the 14th, the same day as the teach-in for the Philadelphia cop killer. Given this development, Carole Quan, superintendent of the Oakland school district, made the call to cancel the district-wide teach-in. Susan Piper, the district spokeswoman, stated: "The Superintendent felt at this point, because we could not guarantee balance and because of the fact that we had a tragedy in the community, she should cancel the Teach-In."

But several Oakland teachers held the teach-in despite the superintendent's cancellation of the events. There was a mock trial of the Abu-Jamal case, a History/World Culture class discussion of the Abu-Jamal case being a lesson on race and class bias, another lesson about the death penalty using the Abu-Jamal case as the subject for elementary students, and finally, a round-table general discussion of police brutality and the death penalty.[270] The curriculum included recommended reading, graphs, and the HBO documentary about Abu-Jamal. The *20/20* program was noticeably absent, despite having been aired one month before and, as of that date, still the focus of great discussion about Mumia Abu-Jamal.

The teach-in resulted in nearly two weeks of daily coverage in various Bay Area newspapers. Nationally, the school district was treated to a much-deserved black eye by becoming the recipients of much negative publicity.

3 2

RAGE AGAINST THE MACHINE

In 1999, back on the East Coast, an event of epic proportions was in the making. The Abu-Jamal celebrity base now included rock stars, most of whom I had never heard of. Abu-Jamal's most ardent musical supporter was a band called Rage Against the Machine. Like many celebrities, the group's members were not content with their position in the world of music and felt compelled to use their celebrity status to advocate causes they knew nothing about. One of these causes happened to be the effort by Abu-Jamal to receive a new trial. With their exhaustive legal training, the band members combed through the trial records and analyzed each piece of evidence prior to joining the effort. Through their highly trained eyes, the case seemed like a slam-dunk. Abu-Jamal was innocent. Pardon the sarcasm. In reality, Rage Against the Machine was content to rely upon sensationalized lies, just like the rest of the celebrity supporters of Abu-Jamal.

I may never have heard of Rage Against the Machine, but I was soon to become very familiar with the band, which was indeed successful. They had No. 1 albums, videos, and Grammys to their name. The group had four members: Zack de la Rocha, vocalist; Tom Morello, Harvard-educated guitarist; Brad Wilk, drummer; and Tim Bob, bassist. In doing research for this book, I have learned that Rocha's father was Beto, a Chicano political artist.[271] Beto was a member of the group Los Four, who were most well known for their work on the early Chicano mural movement, which included the dull slogan at the bottom of each of their works "Chicano Art Existe!" or "Here We Are!"[272] In 1983, Beto suffered a mental breakdown, which turned him into a fanatical Christian. Beto became obsessive and, when Zack went to visit him on weekends in Lincoln Heights, he was forced to faithfully preach with his father for days at a time. Zack and Beto would sit in a room with the curtains closed and the door locked in total silence, studying. It was said the thirteen-year-old boy would eat on Friday and not again until he got back to his mother on Monday. When Zack was with his father, Beto forced him to destroy paintings and murals that had established a Chicano identity for him. Eventually, Zack ran away from Beto and permanently lived with his mother.[273] Too bad Dr. Phil didn't intercede with young Zack and spare me his pent-up frustration.

Rage's involvement with the Abu-Jamal movement in 1999 was not new—back in August of 1995, there was a sizeable benefit concert at the Capitol Ballroom in Washington, D.C. There, Rage played alongside Handsome, the Sullivan Brothers, and others. The $8,000 the show raised was given to the organization called International Concerned Family and Friends of Mumia Abu-Jamal.[274] And now, the band was planning a colossal Free Mumia concert to be held on January 28, 1999, at the Continental Airlines Arena in the Meadowlands, New Jersey, with proceeds again going to the International Concerned Family and Friends of Mumia Abu-Jamal. The other bands performing with Rage were Black Star, Bad Religion, and the Beastie Boys.

Rage has even intertwined Abu-Jamal's name into some of their lyrics. In "Guerilla Radio," one of the lines is "Sound off, Mumia Guan Be Free . . . All you pen devils know the trial was vile." In "Voice of the Voiceless," a line says, "True Rebel, my brother Mumia . . . We are at war until you are free."[275] Alternatively, some of their songs merely refer to some of Abu-Jamal's hobbies, such as—um—killing. Namely, their cover of Cypress Hill's song "How I Could Just Kill a Man" comes to mind.[276] And I even show up in their lyrics. At least, I think that's me, referred to in the song "Calm Like a Bomb" on the album *Battle of Los Angeles* as a "widow pig parrot."

I found out about the concert through our Web site. Since its inception at the time of the 1998 *New York Times* ad, the Web site has served as a clearinghouse for fresh information on the case. As Paul and I became more and more tech savvy, we increasingly used the Web site and e-mail to distribute and receive info on Abu-Jamal to and from people all over the world. We got e-mails from people saying, "Did you know this. Did you know that?" I believe a police group from New Jersey, understandably outraged by the event, first notified us about the concert.

I was particularly incensed that such an event would be happening so close to the place of Danny's murder. Not Philadelphia, mind you, but North Jersey. I immediately contacted Continental Airlines, the company from which the arena got its name, and asked them how they felt about being associated with a convicted cop killer. I got in touch with one of their PR people there and tried to dissuade them from making a profit off of a concert in support of a murderer. They said they would look into it and get back to me if they could do anything about it. I don't recall them following up, but I do think that they put pressure on the organizing parties. I next contacted the manager of the band. He claimed initially that he knew nothing about the benefit concert. Of course, I did not believe him. Infuriated, we exchanged words.

Finally, I called the promoter of the concert and got his office number. After my first failed attempts to daunt the organizers' efforts, I decided to change my strategy. During this time, I did a number of radio interviews in Philadelphia, New York, and New Jersey. While on air griping about the concert, I recited the promoter's number and encouraged listeners to contact him to air their grievances. Within minutes, the guy's phone was ringing off the hook. Sometimes you have to fight fire with fire.

Tom Morello, the lead guitarist and oldest member of the band, understood exactly what he was doing. Morello touted Abu-Jamal as "an outspoken revolutionary and a hero to millions."[277] All of the nearly sixteen thousand tickets made available for the concert sold out within hours on January 14.[278] Based on the telephone campaign that I had launched, the promoter agreed that if people wanted to turn the tickets in, they would get full refunds. I believe six hundred and fifty tickets were returned and refunded; the promoter rescinded his offer before others had the opportunity to do so. To this day I am grateful to those who enjoy the music, but had the courage to return those tickets. The refunded tickets were resold. The concert was sold out.

Morello realized that although his band's goal for the event was to support Abu-Jamal's cause, most of their teenage fans would know little or nothing about Abu-Jamal's case. This fact alone makes their decision to hold such a concert deplorable. While it is nearly certain that most of the concertgoers had no real understanding of Abu-Jamal's case or the details of his life, it could be surmised that the same group would leave the concert with a belief, albeit a misguided one, that Abu-Jamal was innocent. Young, impressionable, and energized by the music and fun, they would believe that they were fighting a righteous cause against injustice. The system was the enemy. Abu-Jamal was their friend.

As one could imagine, New Jersey State officials were displeased by the event. Governor Christine Todd Whitman, the state attorney general, and the state police superintendent all encouraged potential concertgoers to boycott the event in protest of the band's support of Abu-Jamal.[279] Attorney General Peter Verniero spoke out against the event, saying, "I find it deplorable. The sad irony is that police officers lay their lives on the line every day to protect the very freedoms that these [music] groups are able to take advantage of."[280] State Police Superintendent Col. Carl Williams added that the state "should cancel the event, fearing the crowd might clash with troopers who provide its security."[281] Governor Whitman had no legal course of action to stop it. In fact, such a concert, no matter how disgusting, was protected by the First Amendment.

For this latest battle on the airwaves, an unlikely ally emerged; Howard Stern. Stern's flagship radio station, WXRK (K-ROCK) in New York, was initially airing ads promoting the Rage concert at the Meadowlands. An irked listener of Stern's show who later identified himself as a police officer was particularly offended by WXRK's decision to run the ads and called in to question Stern about it. In response, Stern announced that he, too, was offended by the station's decision to run the ads: "There are so many other people I'd rather give money to than a guy convicted of killing a cop. I hear the commercial; it's like 'And he's accused of killing a cop and we're raising money.' Is that something you really want to brag about? That's something that I find very offensive. I think too many cops are getting killed these days."[282] On the same show that Howard Stern expressed his displeasure with the pro-Abu-Jamal concert ad running on his station, WXRK General Manager Tom Chiusano issued an on-air apology: "I apologize to every policeman who can hear my voice . . . for [those ads] having gone on our air. It never should have happened. We have always been a very sympathetic, empathetic supporter of the police department and will continue to be so."

Soon thereafter, I was invited to appear on Stern's program and debate Tom Morello. It happened two days before the concert. I was on the phone from California; also on the phone were Leonard Weinglass and Hugh Burns from the Philadelphia DA's office. Hugh, who is a pretty straight-laced guy, knew little of Howard Stern before the show; when he learned of Stern's reputation, like others, he was justifiably concerned about what might occur. Stern, I have to say, was terrific with me, sympathetic, supportive, and kind. I can't say with certainty that anything significant was accomplished over the course of this "debate." I was pretty much myself, Hugh stuck to the facts, and the other side spun its usual BS. Nevertheless, it was a good feeling to present our side to a new audience, as well as extremely cathartic. Stern got exasperated with Morello, and after going through the facts, said that for the defense to be accurate, Abu-Jamal must have been the most unlucky person in the world.

I remember talking to Gary Dell'Abate, aka Baba Booey, Stern's producer, before the show and sternly instructing him that if Howard so much as uttered a word about the size of my breasts or which sexual position I prefer, I was going to hang the phone up. Gary reassured that he would absolutely not. I was told that Howard supports and respects police and that he would give me the respect that I deserve on the air. My mom had listened to Howard's program a few times before I went on the air. The last show she had listened to, Howard Stern was spanking a woman on the air. She called me with more than a hint of apprehension in her voice: "Maureen, this is your mother. I don't know what kind of radio show you're going on, but that man is doing some unspeakable things to a woman over the airways." Rest assured, my backside remained unscathed.

After the interview was over, it was difficult for me and Paul to gauge the outcome. We decided to check online to see if we had received any responses through our Web site. Up until that time, we'd gotten maybe five hundred e-mails total, ever. In a matter of minutes, our inbox was teeming with two thousand more! They came from all over the country and were 99 percent pro-Maureen: "You kicked his ass." "Tom Morello is a jerk." "I will never listen to Rage Against the Machine again."

Morello responded to the vast amount of criticism regarding Rage's planned Abu-Jamal concert by pointing to the fact that the band had been protested by the Ku Klux Klan and the Neo-Nazis in the past and, now, the Attorney General of New Jersey. He assured fans that, just as in every other case, the band would not cave in to outside pressure and the show would go on as scheduled. "It's not the first time that right-wing knuckleheads have had a problem with Rage Against the Machine and it won't be the last . . . We're not going to back down because of some sniveling politicians."[283]

The concert did indeed occur. It is mind-boggling to me that sixteen thousand young people came together in a manner that supported the man who murdered my husband. To the extent there was a silver lining, it came in the form of the actions of law enforcement. The police who worked security for the event donated their overtime money to Justice for P/O Daniel Faulkner, and the proceeds from the arena were donated to multiple New Jersey survivor's causes.

3 3

MUMIA MONEY

What, you may be wondering, came of all the money raised in support of Abu-Jamal? Rage Against the Machine, by way of example, bloated the Abu-Jamal coffers with their sold-out show at the Continental Airlines Arena. How was that money accounted for? Or better yet, *was* that money accounted for? The answer is rather murky, which itself is rather revealing. It involves the interrelationship between the Black United Fund of Pennsylvania ("Black United") and the International Concerned Family and Friends of Mumia Abu-Jamal ("International Friends").

Some background: Black United is a north Philadelphia–based association that assists other African-American nonprofits with organization and fund-raising. In 1991, Black United agreed to collect and forward donations for the International Friends, itself a west Philadelphia organization led by MOVE member Pam Africa. Although I have told you before, I cannot reference MOVE without reminding you that in 1978, nine members of the group murdered a Philadelphia policeman named James Ramp, and in 1985, MOVE caused a fire that destroyed an entire city block in west Philadelphia where eleven people, five of them children, died. Black United was the recipient of $95,000 from the Rage Against the Machine concert.

In 1999, the *Philadelphia Inquirer* published a number of stories that shined a halogen on these entities. According to the stories, IRS officials raised "serious questions" about the relationship between Black United and International Friends because Black United was supposedly lending its tax-exempt status to the International Friends, which was neither tax-exempt nor a registered charity. Black United said it did not raise money for Abu-Jamal or determine how it was spent. "All we do is collect the money," said Marilyn Jewett, a publicist for Black United at the time. "It's not our money." According to the IRS, however, such arrangements comply with tax law only if a registered charity like Black United directly supervises the use of the money.[284]

There was more. Under Pennsylvania law at the time, any charitable group that raises more than $25,000 in a year must register with the State and file a report each year. Since 1991, at least $280,000 in tax-deductible donations were passed on to International Friends, which Pam Africa admitted had never been registered or obtained tax-exempt status from the IRS or the State before the scandal broke.[285] It was also revealed that nationwide, a variety of organizations had raised nearly $1 million on Abu-Jamal's behalf during the 1990s.[286] Leonard Weinglass, Abu-Jamal's lead attorney at the time, would not comment on his legal fees in the case but "did say that Abu-Jamal's fund-raising had been handled primarily by Black United and a New York City organization called the Bill of Rights Foundation, affiliated with actors Mike Farrell and Ossie Davis."[287] According to the *Inquirer*, "Money pours into the 'Free Mumia' movement from far and wide," including from Web site subscriptions (up to $120 each), college campuses, and worldwide demonstrations. Meanwhile, International Friends' Web sites were telling donors that contributions were tax-deductible.[288] The *Inquirer* revealed that Black United itself had been raising money without its state charity registration since late 1995 and that the group had maintained its ties to International Friends even after removing any mention of the relationship from fund-raising literature.[289]

Sound confusing? Well, from my perspective, based on the *Inquirer* coverage, it was pretty clear that i's weren't getting dotted nor were the t's being crossed—or worse. From the outside looking in, to me it appeared that there were improprieties with the way that money raised in the name of the Abu-Jamal effort was being handled.

Philadelphia Mayor Ed Rendell must not have liked what he saw, either. On May 21, 1999, Mayor Rendell ordered Black United's removal from the Philadelphia City Employees Combined Campaign, an annual charitable fund-raising initiative directed at City employees, because Black United had allowed its state registration as a charitable organization to lapse (after 1995). Deputy Mayor Linda S. Berkowitz stated in a letter to the organization that it "never formally advised the City of the extent of its involvement with" International Friends, adding, "We believe that omission on the part of the Black United Fund was at the very least disingenuous."[290] Of course, some were quick to call the move thinly veiled racism.[291] A state audit ensued and Black United was fined $10,000 for its lapsed registration.[292]

Now here is where the story really takes a turn toward the nefarious, in my opinion. In June of 2000, in the midst of the spotlight being shone on Black United and International Friends, Pam Africa reported a break-in at her west Philadelphia office, home to International Friends. Her group said that politically motivated thieves ignored equipment and valuables and stole only "several boxes of important financial documents, including an international donor list." But a volunteer with the group who was first to arrive the morning after the alleged break-in "found the door locked and the office in order." In other words, there was no sign of forced entry. He said Pam Africa told him later that the files had been removed. The *Inquirer* reported that, "To get [to the MOVE office], you must go inside a massive granite office building, pass a security guard, go up five flights in a creaky elevator, turn left and walk down a hallway. The windowless office has one door."[293]

The supposed theft came "at a key juncture for the organization." A member of the group, Bob Harris, told the paper: "The theft left the group without any records of key financial information." Harris said that Africa told him the break-in took place just before she could photocopy the originals.[294]

How convenient.

In 2000, International Friends incorporated itself and received tax-exempt status from the IRS, but not from the Pennsylvania Bureau of Charitable Organizations. In fact, a lengthy state audit of the group continued and, in August of the following year (2001), the *Inquirer* reported: "The main fund-raising organization for death-row inmate Mumia Abu-Jamal has been ordered to stop soliciting contributions in Pennsylvania, after failing to give a full accounting of its finances." The paper cited a letter sent from the State faulting International Friends for ignoring repeated demands for cooperation in the audit as well as ongoing financial inadequacies. "The July 9 letter from the Bureau of Charitable Organizations of the Pennsylvania Department of State put it bluntly: 'You cannot solicit contributions in Pennsylvania until all the reasons listed above are corrected.'" The *Inquirer* added: "Africa hung up on a reporter seeking comment Friday. 'I'm trying to save my brother,' she said, in an apparent reference to Abu-Jamal. 'Leave me alone.'"[295]

Two months later, in September of 2001, International Friends received its state registration, though ongoing investigations into their years of fundraising were said to continue.[296] As far as I know, the IRS never fully audited their group. I can't imagine that our side would have received the same treatment. I know that when our properly registered nonprofit was late in filing a tax return, the Commonwealth of Pennsylvania very quickly told us not to raise money until our ducks were in a row, so to speak.

The most incredible, and galling, part of the Mumia Money Machine, to me, was that Black United was funded by the United Way. The United Way collected and disseminated money only to those who have received approval as qualified nonprofit organizations. What that means is, the various groups must verify that they are truly nonprofit organizations in good standing; that they are using the money for scrupulous purposes; and that their expenses fall within certain parameters. Black United collected and disseminated money to the groups over which they form an umbrella. Black United was on the Philadelphia City Employees list for the United Way. So, whenever the City of Philadelphia had a fund-raiser for the United Way, one could say, "I want to give money to Black United via the United Way." In other words, money was being donated by City employees to the United Way, which could then direct that all or a portion of the donation would go towards Black United, and Black United would then fund International Friends, regardless of their lack of legal standing. Throughout the whole process, they were going out soliciting donations from celebrities, organizations, Rage Against the Machine's benefit concerts, and so on. And that money was being used to support my husband's killer. That is, until the investigation revealed that Black United was completely out of compliance with any federal or state requirements to be a qualified nonprofit organization.

In the end, Pam Africa's supposed charity also came under scrutiny. It turns out that International Friends had never even sent in a request to become a nonprofit organization. The *Inquirer* investigation showed that

International Friends had taken in more than $1 million. They had some receipts from Leonard Weinglass in excess of several hundred thousand dollars. This is why, on the *Howard Stern Show*, I asked Weinglass to tell us how much money he made off this case. His response was something like, "This is a case that I take no more than what somebody coming out of law school on their first year would be taking; I make virtually no money off this case." He said that on a nationwide broadcast. A couple of years after Weinglass's proclamation of financial modesty, the aforementioned investigation was done. In the process, investigators were able to trace at least two or three hundred thousand dollars per year paid to Weinglass.

34

PHILIP BLOCH

I wish YOU were shot. Fucker. Die. You're NOT influencing anyone, you are just proving how ignorant you are. IF you think you can make a change anything [sic] *then you are even stupider than I thought. Fuck you. Make the world a better place, kill yourself. Nobody cares about you or that piece of shit cop that deserved to die, and did. One less cop. You can't cheat karma. Fuck you.*

This hateful message greeted me in my inbox late in 1999. Although I can't say it's typical of the majority, it is certainly representative of a fairly consistent, small stream of abusive messages that comes through our Web site. However, in addition to angst and frustration, e-mail has also delivered valuable information regarding the case. On April 3, 1999, at 6:07 p.m., I received the message below. While hate mail is expected, this e-mail was downright shocking. With my mouth agape and my head spinning, I read the following message:

> There is at least one person to whom Mumia has admitted killing Officer Faulkner and that person may be willing to break his silence on the matter. He was a close friend of Mumia during the early 1990's. He was not an inmate, but rather a student at Juniata College. He has a history of affiliations with left-wing causes and has been an outspoken opponent of the death penalty. However, he has been disenchanted for a long time with the willingness of many on the left to use dishonesty and deceit to advance their causes. His sympathies are extended to the widow of Officer Faulkner. If he can be of any comfort or assistance he is willing to discuss the matter further.
>
> Phil Bloch

When I opened this e-mail, I wasn't sure what to make of it: a left-wing friend of Mumia with knowledge of a confession?

At first, Paul suspected the e-mail was a set-up by the Abu-Jamal forces to somehow embarrass me. The name Phil Bloch did not sound even remotely familiar, and we thought it was probably a pseudonym anyway. Paul cautiously wrote back to the sender expressing our intent to further investigate the matter and thus began a delicate dance over the Internet. The person e-mailing us was understandably evasive. We were skeptical but curious, and acted accordingly.

My first question to my mysterious correspondent was whether he would provide the name of the person to whom Abu-Jamal had confessed. About a week went by before he responded. He was the man. He told me that one day he had said to Mumia Abu-Jamal, "Do you regret killing Officer Faulkner?" Abu-Jamal responded, "Yes."

I immediately picked up the telephone to call him. He sounded legitimate, credible, and convincing. He told me he was a forty-seven-year-old substitute high school history and social studies teacher who, as a volunteer prison social worker, had befriended Abu-Jamal. Bloch told me he was a pacifist who was opposed to the death penalty. I had yet to meet him but I envisioned him as a kind-hearted aging hippie; when we did meet, this was an accurate description, Birkenstocks included. This status actually afforded credibility. Unlike many of our supporters, he was not cut from the law enforcement cloth.

I quickly recognized that Phil Bloch's story was very big news and I asked him if he would be willing to speak publicly. He had understandable misgivings about being in the public eye but, after consulting his wife, he called me back to say yes, he would come forth. His willingness to do so was motivated by his disturbance over the way in which the opposition was vilifying me. He was similarly disgusted by the way in which Abu-Jamal was becoming a martyr in prison. He was morally repulsed. I warned him: "If you do come forth, Philip, you know you are going to have a lot of people attacking you and you really should think about it carefully before you do." He was not intimidated. At this point, I put him in touch with three people: Michael Smerconish; Buzz Bissinger, a Pulitzer Prize–winning journalist who was working on an article about the case for *Vanity Fair*; and Harry Phillips of ABC, who had done the *20/20* show and was preparing for a rebroadcast.

I had never heard of Buzz Bissinger before Michael Smerconish told me about him. Michael had come to know Buzz in 1987 when Michael was involved in a political campaign in Philadelphia, working in a high-level position for Frank Rizzo, who was seeking to return to City Hall as mayor. I remember Michael telling me that Frank Rizzo hated Buzz Bissinger, believing Bissinger's biased reporting on the 1987 mayor's race had cost him the election. This is why it was all the more puzzling when Michael, Frank Rizzo's former political director, was recommending that I cooperate with Buzz.

Michael told me that he thought Buzz was a bright guy with well-known liberal credentials and, if Buzz really committed himself to studying the case, anything supportive he might write would be more powerful than anything generated by a more conservative figure.

Buzz Bissinger first came out to California to meet me and immediately asked if he could have a couple days of my time. He stayed in a hotel nearby and for three days, all day long we sat and talked about the case, what had followed, and my feelings from the time Danny was killed up until the day of our interview. I had no idea what was going to be written in *Vanity Fair*, but I felt as though I was truthfully telling what exactly went on in the courtroom and what had happened to me personally through the years. Buzz was already in the process of extensively researching the case and speaking to Abu-Jamal's defenders. Throughout his time in California, he never really showed his hand but I had a good feeling about him; I thought he was a quiet man and a good interviewer.

Meanwhile, as Bissinger was doing his work, I was growing more comfortable with Philip Bloch. I put him in touch with the DA's office, and he was cooperating with them. Now the question arose as to how and when his story would become public, and I decided that *Vanity Fair* offered a great opportunity. I decided to put Bloch together with Bissinger, thinking that if Buzz Bissinger found Phil Bloch credible, this would add an enormous element to a national story. That is exactly what happened. Buzz found him to be extremely reliable. The article was scheduled for the August issue, which actually hit the stands in July. Fireworks ensued!

Bissinger's piece in *Vanity Fair* told the Philip Bloch story in a national magazine to an international audience. The title of the piece was "The Famous and the Dead," and Bloch was a big part of it. Bissinger explained that Philip Bloch was a volunteer worker for the Pennsylvania Prison Society, a prison reform organization. Abu-Jamal sought out Bloch and the two became friends. Bloch and Abu-Jamal had at least ten conversations through which he and Abu-Jamal developed what he called an "intellectual friendship."[297] Both had similar backgrounds in the left-wing movement. In one conversation that Bloch had with Abu-Jamal in the early 1990s, they talked about the use of violence and whether or not it might be an acceptable alternative in the advancement of a cause. With candor and concern, Bloch then asked Abu-Jamal that fateful question. Abu-Jamal bluntly confessed with one simple word, "Yes."

Philip Bloch recalled what happened immediately after Abu-Jamal's unwitting admission: "There was a long pause. I think we probably realized what he had just done."[298] Even without elaboration, Bloch says he was positive that Abu-Jamal understood precisely what had been asked. "It was directly implied in my statement that he was the one who did it. I don't think there's any possibility of miscommunication."[299] Bloch said that the conversation just moved along and the two went on to talk about other things not the least bit related to the case. Bloch said that it wasn't planned. "It was just in the flow of the conversation."[300] Bloch maintained that there was, and is, no question about whether or not, by that statement, Abu-Jamal had just confessed to killing Danny. He had. Abu-Jamal admitted to killing my husband to his prison confidant and friend.

For the next seven years, Bloch kept this to himself. Some would attempt to diminish his credibility because he harbored the knowledge of Abu-Jamal's supposed confession for so long. Philip Bloch then realized how much I was "being subjected to such calumny." He said that people were trying to "make it seem like he [Danny] was some rogue cop that was out beating Mumia's brother." Bloch was so disgusted by all of the hatred against me that he was finally compelled to share with the world Abu-Jamal's confession. And that is why, in April of 1999, Bloch wrote the e-mail. Soon after, Bloch gave an official statement to a detective from the Philadelphia Police Department.

Bloch's coming forth was no easy decision. He said that he had not been in contact with Mumia Abu-Jamal for five years, after Abu-Jamal did not answer his letters. The letters Bloch sent were written just because Bloch and Abu-Jamal were friends. Even after coming forth with Abu-Jamal's confession, Philip Bloch says that he "still has a lot of respect for him [Abu-Jamal]."[301]

Buzz Bissinger's article in *Vanity Fair* was comprehensive and enlightening. By now I was very familiar with the press and what impressed me about *Vanity Fair* was the level of fact-checking they did before it came out. The article probed the important areas and treated Danny fairly. Our supporters were pleased with it; the Abu-Jamal supporters were outraged. But more than anything else, it was really Bloch's story that generated the most waves around the world. There is no doubt that Team Mumia was rattled by the fact that a prison social worker with left-wing leanings was willing to tell the world that Abu-Jamal had confessed while in prison and that the story was being told in a magazine with Hollywood clout. Supporters of Abu-Jamal called Bloch's statements "too dubious for a responsible journalist to run with"[302] and a "far-fetched, subsequently debunked tale."[303] But the *20/20* program that re-aired shortly after the *Vanity Fair* article called Bloch a "significant development"[304] in the Abu-Jamal case.

Abu-Jamal himself wrote a response to the Bloch revelations contained in the *Vanity Fair* article that was, in turn, published on many pro-Mumia Web sites. In the letter, Abu-Jamal made the accusation that Bloch just wanted his fifteen minutes of fame:

> Once again we hear about a so-called confession, but instead of two months later this comes over a decade later. We don't hear it from a priest, from a lawyer, or from a personal friend but from an official Visitor of the Pennsylvania Prison Society; over ten years later. A lie is a lie, whether made today or ten years later. But I suppose Mr. Bloch wanted his fifteen minutes of fame in which case I hope he has received it. I find it remarkable that this rumor turned lie was never brought to my attention by the author, by Mr. Bloch himself or by *Vanity Fair* magazine, which never contacted me. Welcome to snuff journalism.

> I look forward to the State producing this witness, Mr. Bloch, after I am granted a new trial! The only thing worse than "a forgotten confession" is one allegedly born on the "false wings" of harassment. If ever one

needed proof of the State's desperation, here it is. I thank *Vanity Fair,* not for their work but for stoking this controversy, because controversy leads to questioning and one can only question this belated confession.

On a *MOVE!*

—Mumia Abu-Jamal[305]

With his characteristic rage and readiness to attack, Abu-Jamal also commented: "Perhaps he [Philip Bloch] is frustrated that he is still a substitute teacher and wants a push from his friends in high places. Perhaps he seeks the warm glow of limelight. Who knows? Who cares?"[306]

My reaction to all of this was to point out that, once again, Abu-Jamal had weighed in on his own case without offering an accounting of his actions on December 9, 1981, assuming he was doing something other than murdering Danny.

35

AMOR PATRIAE DUCIT

The e-mail from Philip Bloch arrived on April 3, 1999, but that story did not hit until July when *Vanity Fair* was released. The interim months of that spring of 1999 allowed no respite. On April 24, 1999, there was a Millions for Mumia March planned for Philadelphia and San Francisco. Plastered on utility polls in both cities was a call-to-arms for supporters of Abu-Jamal to show their solidarity. We did a little planning of our own. The night before the march would be ours.

Michael Smerconish did a lot of planning. He was determined not to cede the media spotlight. He wanted to have a preemptive event of our own, not a protest march or a confrontation, but a Tribute Dinner for Danny. This event would double as a fund-raiser for our not-for-profit in Danny's name, which we were now using to fund scholarships for murder victims' children. The night ended up being one of the greatest moments I have had in the twenty-five-year battle. As little as I knew about dealing with the media, Michael was an expert.

Michael was then a full-time lawyer under the tutelage of famed trial attorney James E. Beasley and a part-time broadcaster with his own talk show on the Big Talker, 1210-AM, WPHT. Together with his legal secretary, Mary Russel, and his legal assistant, attorney Michael Katz, Smerconish turned his law office into "Danny Central" for several weeks in the early spring as he busily planned the tribute. The tribute was to be held at the famed Union League of Philadelphia, a historically significant private club where Michael was a member. The Union League is a spectacular facility. The club motto is Amor Patriae Ducit, or "love of country leads." As Michael planned the event with the Union League's catering chief, Barbara McLaughlin, the event continued to grow. At first, we said we would need seats for 150–200 people. We planned to charge $100 per person (with $70 per person going to the not-for-profit) and hoped that we could fill those seats. We had no idea what the response would be. We thought our audience would be mainly cops, and $100 is not chump change to a police officer. The seating capacity was quickly reached for that first room and I remember an enthused and relieved Michael calling me in California to say that he had added another room, an adjoining room with another one hundred seats. Soon that, too, was full. Then, the entire first floor was filled and, finally, Michael asked Barbara, "How many can you serve for dinner?" She told him that the building could serve a maximum of eight hundred for dinner but that would fill every space, and not in one room. In other words, we would be using every nook and cranny in the building, which is several stories and encompasses a city block. We ended up gathering before and after dinner in a magnificent ballroom on the second floor, where the formal program was held.

Michael had another edict that night. He would not "comp" any guests except me and the Faulkner family. If there were people who paid for seats that they could not use, Michael made sure that they were given to police officers for free. There were also many politicians that wanted to be present at the event. Michael insisted that they each pay, and they did! In attendance that night were not only members of the Faulkner family, police officers, my friends, Danny's friends, and citizens who felt drawn to show up and be supportive, but also Philadelphia Mayor Ed Rendell (now Governor of Pennsylvania); U.S. Senator Arlen Specter (a former Philadelphia district attorney); W. Thacher Longstreth, a city councilman who was really Mr. Philadelphia; Police Commissioner John Timoney; Pennsylvania Lieutenant Governor and future Acting Governor Mark Schweiker; Pennsylvania Attorney General Mike Fisher; Pennsylvania Auditor General Bob Casey (now U.S. Senator); Philadelphia District Attorney Lynne Abraham; Joseph McGill, the former assistant district attorney who had prosecuted Abu-Jamal for his brutal crime; and the U.S. Attorney based in Philadelphia, Mike Stiles. To this day I am moved by the breadth of the support Danny and I received that evening.

I have repeatedly avowed that the people closest to the facts of the case understand the propriety of Abu-Jamal's conviction. The diverse assemblage of devotees present at dinner that night is truly indicative of this fact. To me, it says that the citizens of Pennsylvania believed in Abu-Jamal's guilt. If this were not the case, you would never see elected officials showing up at this event all spiffed up, much less writing their own personal checks to be there. We could have sold the building out several times over.

That's why the night was one of the highlights of my life. So many times over the span of twenty-five years I have felt as if it was me against an infinitely better funded, organized, and staffed army. Paul and I, I should say. But on this one night, I recognized with acute clarity the magnificent level of support we had engendered.

Michael was the Master of Ceremonies, but he did not offer a prepared speech. Instead, in between introducing the speakers, he stood at the podium and, in a very matter-of-fact fashion, read different passages from the 1982 trial transcripts. He would give the name of a witness, the date of testimony, and then read a paragraph or two of their testimony about the murder. I know the words he spoke floored many of the people who were now seated for the program. These were my most ardent friends and supporters and yet I know that many of them were still taken aback by the incriminating testimony that had been offered at trial. People sat in dead silence on each word. This was not the usual banquet speech with murmurs and clanging plates. This crowd was transfixed. The Appendix to this book is comprised of what he read that night.

The night was picture-perfect. Everyone elegantly dressed, focused, sympathetic, and united. There was a spectacular, enormous (four-foot-tall) ice sculpture in the shape of a police badge with Danny's number on it, No. 4699, in the middle of the room. Richard Zapille was a former deputy mayor and deputy police commissioner who is deserving of special recognition. He worked the event tirelessly along with Michael. And I have to tell you one thing that touched my heart. We had a raffle for a door prize—a beautiful gold bracelet that was donated to the event by a merchant named Richard Hoch. The winner was an African-American police officer named Asbury Johnson. He slowly came forward and accepted his prize. Then, he caught everyone, especially me, off-guard by offering the expensive bracelet to me. He was the epitome of class. I did not want to accept it; I wanted him to keep it, but he was insistent. Now, I never take that bracelet off. I later learned that he was a police officer who had survived after he was shot several times in the line of duty.

I will never forget how the night ended: the Philadelphia Police and Fire Pipe & Drums entered the room in full regalia, playing "Danny Boy" with bagpipes. I know it is a cliché, but it's true—there were no dry eyes in the building. It was the perfect way to end the perfect evening on a day that had been proclaimed (thanks to City Council members James Kenney and Joan Krajewski) as Danny Faulkner Day in Philadelphia and (thanks to State Representative Denny O'Brien) Danny Faulkner Day in Pennsylvania.

Earlier I mentioned the scholarship monies. Below are the names of the first sixteen recipients, each of whom has experienced the worst kind of tragedy life can offer—losing a parent to murder. Each was given a $5,000 educational grant on behalf of Justice for P/O Daniel Faulkner:

Aking Beverly (Cabrini College)
Justin Frisby (Cabrini College)
Erma Aponte (CHI Institute)
Dana Dutch (Community College of Philadelphia)
Charles Ritterson (Wesley College)
Zilika Meade (Art Institute of Philadelphia)
William Billy Kite (Kutztown University)
Michael Selby (Frankford Hospital School of Nursing)
Edward Fields (University of Pittsburgh)
Nicole Ballard (Peirce College)
Kaitlin Eichhorn (Philadelphia University)
Angela Ahmarov (Gwynedd Mercy Academy)
Gina Capriotti (Jean Madeline Institute)
Nora R. Rafferty (LaSalle University)
Anthony Bruno (college to be determined)
David Capriotti (college to be determined)

I cannot recount here each of the tragedies endured by these young people, but allow me to at least give you an example. Erma Aponte's personal tragedy is illustrative of those endured by Faulkner scholarship recipients. Her father was murdered close to Christmas in the year 2000 while driving a taxi in north Philadelphia. Before reporting for work the night he was murdered, he'd told Erma that he'd try to earn the $50 she needed for an application to a computer school. Erma is one of six Aponte kids now fatherless.

Jerry Watkins, another wonderful man, who unfortunately has since left this Earth, was then administering the scholarship grant program and told me: "When I called Erma to tell her she was the recipient of $5,000 from Maureen Faulkner to continue her education, she told me she had been in court that very day to hear a jury find her father's killer guilty of murder. "It shows my dad is still watching over me."

Our event was a complete success. The next day, it was front-page news in all the local newspapers. Meanwhile, the Millions for Mumia March being planned for Philadelphia was a complete bust. The crowds were sparse and the support weak.

3 6

H O G   W I L D

My spirits were soaring in the spring of 1999. The crisp May air brought along with it renewed vigor and the promise of relief. The Pennsylvania Supreme Court had twice unanimously rejected Abu-Jamal's appeals; our *New York Times* ad was providing momentum for a nation-wide, grassroots movement; the media had been consistently kinder; and a credible confession had surfaced, effectively spreading seeds of doubt in the hearts and minds of former Jamal-believers. Team Mumia's Million Person March was a dismal flop, while we packed the Union League in tribute to Danny, and almost every major elected official in Pennsylvania supported our side.

As the gusts of progress and optimism eased our journey that sunny spring, many of our supporters embarked upon a journey of their own. In May of 1999, thousands of motorcyclists partook in a motorcycle run in Danny's honor.

What would be the first of three Daniel Faulkner Memorial Motorcycle Runs occurred one month after the Union League event, on Sunday, May 23, 1999. It was an effort to raise support for Danny born of the outrage that many bikers felt after hearing of the Rage Against the Machine concert some months prior. I remember that I got a call from Rich Costello, who told me that two men, Les Young and Jeff Campbell, had reached him with their idea of having a bikers' event for Danny. Les's wife, Sue, was also an incredible force. These folks were Harley riders from South Jersey, and they proposed doing a run from Hamilton Township, New Jersey, to Philadelphia.

Les Young and Jeff Campbell were no career philanthropists; they had never been inspired to organize anything of this sort before. Like so many of our supporters, they simply heard about Danny's story and their anger and frustration provoked action. They got their wives and friends from the motorcycle clubs to work with them. They had no idea how to file with the City or even to get the route cleared. I remember one of them sort of asking me rhetorically: "All of these assholes do concerts for killers but who does a concert to support a dead cop's wife?"

We had no idea what the turnout would be, and I grew even more skeptical the morning of the event when I saw the weather—rainy and cold. Paul and I had flown in from one of his company's sales trips in San Diego. I remember my brother, Michael, driving me to the event in the pouring rain, and us wondering who in the world wants to ride a motorcycle in this weather. When Paul and I arrived at about 8:00 a.m., the Faulkner family was already present preparing to sell pro-Danny T-shirts and distribute ID bands to the registrants, the only problem being there were no registrants! Les, Jeff, the Faulkners, and my brother, Mike Foley, despondently idled around the gigantic empty parking lot in a New Jersey industrial area.

And then, like a sudden stampede, this all changed. You could hear them coming: first tens, then hundreds, then several thousand men and women on motorcycles emerged from the downcast morning like a harbinger of hope—all there to support Danny. I still get goose bumps when I think about it. When I saw the sea of bikers approaching, with the sound of their roaring engines filling the air, it really took my breath away. The rain continued to fall but it didn't matter. You should have seen the looks on Les's and Jeff's faces; they went from absolute abject disappointment to beaming satisfaction. The sound of the approaching bikes was magical. They just kept coming and coming.

The newspapers estimated the biker participants as numbering just over twelve thousand![307] Each of them had paid a $10 entrance fee. Many sported emblems and T-shirts supportive of Danny. They were an incredibly diverse bunch. They were all ages, all appearances, all weights, and lengths of hair. They rode a ten-mile route from Westhampton, New Jersey, into Philadelphia. On the New Jersey side of the Delaware River, the New Jersey State Police provided an escort and at the Benjamin Franklin Bridge heading into the city, the Philadelphia Highway Patrol took charge. Police Commissioner John Timoney led the caravan.

The event was so successful that Les Young and Jeff Campbell ended up starting a nonprofit organization, Bikers Allied to Commemorate Uniformed Police, Inc. (B.A.C.U.P.), which they used to collect and distribute money to police charities. After the first run, they spread the proceeds of the event to Justice for P/O Daniel Faulkner, the Hero Scholarship Fund of Philadelphia, the Burlington County 200 Club Scholarship Fund, and the Camden County Hero Scholarship Fund. Due to the incredible success of the first run, Les and Jeff began plans for the second annual run and set the date for May 21, 2000. The Third Annual Run on June 3, 2001, finally was held under rainless skies. It was estimated that between ten thousand and twelve thousand riders were in attendance. By 2001, the event had more than just a regional presence. Bikers from all around the nation paid tribute to the nation's fallen officers. B.A.C.U.P said that ten charities would receive the funds from the 2001 ride and that they had donated $62,000 to charities up to that point.[308] I was heartened to know that despite my struggles and hardships, good things were being done for others in Danny's name.

3 7

BACK TO SCHOOL

While I was heartened by the growing outpourings of support for Danny, there were also frequent frustrations coming from the Mumia camp. One of the worst occurred in the spring of 1999, when the mystique of Mumia earned Mumia Abu-Jamal a gig as commencement speaker!

Students at Evergreen State College in Olympia, Washington, are given the opportunity to select their own commencement speakers. The class of 1999 wanted Abu-Jamal. What kind of college invites someone of this ilk to participate in graduation? Evergreen State College describes itself as "a progressive, public liberal arts and science college located in Olympia, Washington, in the beautiful Pacific Northwest . . . Evergreen values a student-centered learning environment, a link between theory and practice, and a multicultural community of diverse faculty, students and staff working together."[309] Over time, I learned that Evergreen had long been known by critics as "Earthshoe U."

After making my displeasure known to university administrators, I decided to organize a protest of my own. I said that if they were insistent on moving forward, I wanted to be a part of the graduation ceremony myself.

Paul and I had posters made with pictures of Danny on them. One said: "My husband, Daniel Faulkner, was murdered by Mumia Abu-Jamal." As we journeyed to Washington, the media followed. Even the *Today* show featured me in a piece aired on the day of commencement.

The graduation exercises were held outdoors for roughly eight hundred students. At the ceremony, prior to the airing of Abu-Jamal's address, President Jane Jervis advised the attendees that they "should be aware of the pain and outrage" that would be expressed by me, the victim's widow, but it was important to have diverse voices heard.[310] I was "politely applauded" by the graduates. With the announcement of Abu-Jamal's address, students "whooped, cheered and gave a standing ovation to the man convicted of murdering my policeman-husband" while I stood by silently.[311] Abu-Jamal tried to be philosophical via Memorex: "Why was it right for people to revolt against the British because of taxation without representation and somehow wrong for truly unrepresented Africans in America to revolt against America? For any repressed people, revolution, according to the Declaration of Independence, is a right."[312]

After the speech, we had to walk up a winding path. To my delight and surprise, the path was lined with people holding signs of support and police officers in full uniform.

One year after his address at Evergreen State, students at another bastion of higher learning, Antioch College in Yellow Springs, Ohio, long a hotbed of student activism, decided to ask Abu-Jamal to be a speaker at their commencement on April 29, 2000. The students' selection of Abu-Jamal, a murderer, as their commencement speaker was especially troubling as only a few months earlier two of their fellow students had been murdered in Costa Rica. As he did at Evergreen, Abu-Jamal was to deliver his address on tape to the students, sagely dispensing his advice for the next phase of their lives. He taped the six-minute talk in a telephone call he was allowed to make from his prison in southwestern Pennsylvania[313] and the message was similar to the one he recorded for Evergreen. The other speaker who shared the stage with Abu-Jamal that day was Leslie Feinberg, the transvestite social activist who founded the Gay and Lesbian Abu-Jamal Support Group called Rainbow Flags for Mumia.[314]

Needless to say, I was disheartened. I sent a letter addressed to the graduating class and explained my disappointment at their decision to include Abu-Jamal in their commencement, calling on their better judgment in hopes of changing their minds.[315] But when it was clear that this show was going to go on, I decided to make the trip to Ohio, just as I had done to Washington. This time, I planned a vigil one hour before the commencement ceremony.

The President of Antioch decided to hold a forum in an off-campus building an hour before the ceremony began to discuss Abu-Jamal's inclusion and the issues surrounding his case. He invited me, the FOP, and Refuse & Resist. But he knowingly scheduled it for the same hour as my vigil. I was sure this was intended to defuse my protest. Even more twisted, I soon learned that Evergreen State College President Jervis had e-mailed the Antioch president, warning him that I was a "highly-polished public relations professional who has made a career of her husband's death." A reporter got hold of it and faxed the letter to me. In the letter, Jane Jervis said that I was profiting from Danny's murder, that I was making money and putting money in my pocket. That's not true, and there was no way I was going to sit idle and allow my name to be dragged down by such a cruel assessment and unfair allegation. I picked up the phone and left her a message stating I was not only going to sue her but also the college for defamation of character. I demanded both a public apology and a letter of apology; she called me on the telephone and left me a verbal apology.

At Antioch, more than five hundred supporters from law enforcement groups and crime victims' groups joined my vigil as I stood up for the memory of my husband.[316] The tranquility, however, did not last long. When I was standing at the podium, some student supporters of Abu-Jamal, with their faces shielded by bandanas, cursed, jeered, and shouted, "F-you, pigs," and "Pigs belong in the grave" at our group of off-duty officers and families of murder victims. The crowd turned and started toward the protestors. I had to plead with my supporters not to do anything further and that we needed to preserve Danny's memory in a non-violent manner.

After our vigil, we were ushered to the actual graduation to be quarantined in a specific area, far from the actual ceremony cordoned off by a blue ribbon. I had planned on attending a graduation ceremony at a college, but (I'm not exaggerating) it was like one of the rallies the Nazis staged in Nuremberg. The buildings surrounding the open-air stage and spectator seats were adorned with streaming banners. Oversized posters with Abu-Jamal's haunting grimace were everywhere and "Free Jamal" banners waved in the wind.

As had happened at Evergreen, during the Abu-Jamal speech, many officers turned their backs on the stage. Not surprisingly, the throngs of supporters cheered wildly. As the crowd roared, Garry Bell, who had made the trip from Philadelphia to be present at the commencement, said to me: "Our goal is to educate people. There are a lot of people who don't know the facts."[317] I was proud of the restraint he showed. I know it was not easy for Dan's good friend who had seen Mumia's handiwork close up.

Once again, Abu-Jamal did not talk about his trial or Danny's murder. That was done with a flourish by Leslie Feinberg prior to Abu-Jamal's speech. He focused instead on the impact one person can have on the world, which was the topic the Antioch students had requested. He pointed to the lives of Nelson Mandela, Malcolm X, W. E. B. DuBois and civil rights activist Angela Davis, and explained: "We admire these people because, at critical times of their lives, they cast their lots with the poor, the oppressed. Their lives have extended what freedom means . . . You at this Commencement at Antioch are in similar positions . . . show your admiration for them by becoming like them."[318]

Senior Erin Michelle Otten of Columbus was quoted as saying: "I thought his speech was great, and it's important to have this dialogue. I'm glad that this was my graduation. If you disagree, let's talk about it. But don't try to sweep everything under the rug. We were threatened and intimidated and we didn't give in, so I'm proud."[319]

However, one student speaker, Kevin Franck, a senior from Annapolis, Maryland, was sympathetic to our cause. Having researched the case during his time at Antioch, Franck said he believed Abu-Jamal was guilty. He wore a button with Danny's picture on it during his speech and paid tribute to the slain officer with a moment of silence. With characteristic rancor and vulgarity, the supporters of Abu-Jamal interrupted the moment of silence with loud coughing and heckling. I will not forget the courage of this young man, only a few years younger than Danny when he was slain by Mumia Abu-Jamal.

3 8

CHEESESTEAKS
AND JOEY VENTO

Philadelphia is the cheesesteak capital of the world. This is not just
tourism hype. Studies have actually shown that Philadelphians eat
more cheesesteak sandwiches per person than people anywhere else on
Earth. And, just as sure as Philadelphians are fans of cheesesteaks, they
tend to be fiercely loyal to a particular cheesesteak shop. In most of the sur-
veys conducted by magazines and other media outlets, there are usually
two at the top: Geno's and Pat's. The two establishments sit opposite one
another in south Philadelphia, at the intersection of Ninth Street and Pas-
sayunk Avenue. You could walk from one to the other, although no one
does. You are either a Geno's person or a Pat's person. The competition is
as fierce as the loyalty is deep. Pat's was founded by the Olivieri family;
Geno's by Joe Vento. It's been one of the longest-running and most successful competitions in American business history. Neither one appears to
be suffering. There are usually lines outside both of their service windows
at all hours.

I'm a Geno's person. In my opinion, Joe Vento not only has the better
steak, but the cleanest restaurant I have ever visited, and he is one of my
most loyal supporters and one of Philadelphia's most memorable characters. In a city full of zany personalities, this says a lot. You've probably seen
him on TV, cooking steaks on the *Today* show, with Regis or in some other
interesting spot, talking his talk. Or maybe in connection with the controversial sign he hung in his window that reads: "This is America. When
ordering, speak in English." The media people know he's always great
company and most celebrities that come to Philadelphia stop by for a sandwich. Their autographed photos line his establishment. Alongside the smiling shots of celebrities, Vento hangs honors for members of law

enforcement. As a matter of fact, in the spring of 2007, he unveiled a sidewalk memorial in front of his establishment to Philadelphia cops and firefighters who died in the line of duty. Every fallen firefighter and officer has their name on a brick. On a sunny day in a ceremony attended by the city's police and fire commissioners and hundreds of other onlookers, Joey dedicated the walkway by saying to me, "Maureen, Danny is now with his friends." Joey is probably the greatest supporter of law enforcement I have ever met, which is pretty amazing given his background.

Joey Vento is the grandson of Italian immigrants, and son and brother of some pretty tough guys. Joey started his business back in 1966 with $6 in his pocket. The same year, his father, also a restaurateur, had died in prison.

You can find 5'5" Joey Vento in Geno's every day of the year, standing at the grill with his arms covered in tattoos, or managing the books, usually pulling a 4:00 a.m. to 11:00 a.m. shift, and then often returning later in the afternoon.

In early 2000, in the midst of an installment of Mumia Abu-Jamal craziness, Joey Vento made me an incredible offer. By then, we were raising money for a scholarship fund to benefit the children of murder victims and he was anxious to help. He told me he wanted to open his doors one day and donate 100 percent of the gross to our educational grant fund. I remember that I said to him, "Joe, you mean the net," and he said, "Maureen, I'm a business man, I know the difference, I mean the gross. Whatever I take in at the counter that day is yours. I will pay for all the labor and expenses." This was not the only time Joey would be so generous. After the events of 9/11, he opened his doors for seventy-six straight hours and did likewise for victims of that catastrophe, raising $120,000. Because of Joey's support for cops, his "Speak English" campaign, and immense love of Harleys, he sometimes gets portrayed as a right-wing zealot. But that sells him mighty short. In the summer of 2006, it was Joey Vento who gave $100,000 to an Elton John AIDS Awareness Concert in Philadelphia. I am telling you, the man is a prince.

The cheesesteak event for Danny was scheduled on a Sunday, June 4, 2000. Joey said that all proceeds between 11:00 a.m. and 5:00 p.m. would go to the fund and he personally guaranteed $20,000. Paul and I arrived at

Geno's early that day to meet with Joey. He was in fine form, beaming with excitement at the prospect of success and energized to be contributing to our promising new scholarship fund. We had a day of activities planned in a city playground across from Geno's, but Joey had some additional surprises in store. At about 8:00 a.m., as Paul and I sat outside of Geno's munching on cheesesteaks and talking to Michael Smerconish about the day's events, a guy pulled up his car, opened the trunk, whipped out a microphone and amp, and started singing Frank Sinatra songs. Just another day in South Philly! We were in hysterics. (By the way, he was great!)

The community outpouring was invigorating. Shortly after our serenade, I was visited by a former friend and neighbor I had not seen in fifteen years, Lou Giorla. With warmth and understandable pride, Lou handed me $500 in cash he had collected from his friends and neighbors. I was surprised and quite touched by his act of kindness and grace. Nothing moved me quite so much that day. It was a proud moment for him, too. I was very grateful.

The Faulkner family members were present the entire day and I remember them standing in the sun and stifling humidity all afternoon selling T-shirts, with the proceeds benefiting the cause. Eileen Faulkner, Maureen Faulkner (my niece), Kathleen Faulkner, and Jacqueleen Faulkner were terrific and have always been fabulous supporters.

An incredible mix of people showed up that day to fill their bellies and pledge their support: cops, firefighters, nuns, young, old, black, white. The diversity was wonderful and truly emblematic of the diversity of the city. The two-block-long line for cheesesteaks snaked right past the service window of Pat's! I think that Joey enjoyed that part the most even though he was not making a dime for the day. There were Hooters girls on roller skates serving cheesesteaks, a beer truck on Ninth Street, and live music in the park. When all was said and done, $60,000 was raised for the educational needs of kids whose parents were murdered.

The event firmly established Geno's as the Danny Faulkner clubhouse. Ever since that day, we've held meetings there: rallies, BS sessions. Joey has outfitted his place in Danny Faulkner memorabilia and I never come back to Philadelphia without stopping by to thank him and have a steak.

39

BERKELEY BOOK BURNING

C'mon. You just knew that somewhere in this story there was going to be something about Berkeley, and indeed there is. Mumia Madness had reigned for too long without the participation of Berkeley, the official training grounds for the liberal leaders of tomorrow. Their involvement was past due when, in September of 2000, they finally decided to join the circus. Berkeley's involvement was fueled when Dan Flynn, the executive director of Accuracy in Academia (AIA), was scheduled to speak to the students about his recently released booklet *Cop Killer: How Mumia Abu-Jamal Conned Millions Into Believing He Was Framed,* a thirty-eight-page presentation of the facts pointing to Abu-Jamal's guilt. Dan traveled to college campuses discussing topics of importance to AIA and the excellent pamphlet he wrote about Abu-Jamal, and was invited by Cal-Berkeley Young Republicans (yes, even Berkeley has *some* Republicans) to speak to the students on campus. Dan asked if Paul would join him if he made the trip.

When Paul and Dan arrived at the lecture hall, hardly anyone was there except a handful of Rastafarian-looking students in dreadlocks standing outside the five-hundred-seat hall with boom boxes blaring anti-establishment music.

Ten minutes before the event was set to begin, both Paul and Dan anxiously wondered if anyone was going to show up. Aside from the small group of nervous Republicans seated in the first few rows, the hall remained eerily empty. Suddenly, this all changed. With boisterous exuberance, the pro-Jamal camp soon arrived en masse after having gathered at another location so they could march in spectacularly at the last minute. Almost instantly, the place went from empty to full of angry, unruly students. Most of them stood on the arm rests of the fixed movie-theater-style seats so they towered over the crowd. They pointed fingers at Dan and Paul and screamed things like "These are the bastards who executed our friend so and so. I don't know where they think they are, but this is Berkeley, this is our house, and no racist mother fucker is going to speak in our house." And worse.

Undeterred by the growing number of students protesting his presence, Dan Flynn began to outline the main points of his lecture. One of the students who had been shouting obscenities stormed to the stage, and went to the wall-sized chalkboard behind Dan and wrote them instead. He wrote "KKK" and "Fuck you, Nazis" in huge letters, then drew an arrow so it appeared to be pointing at Dan as he spoke at the podium. Another came up front wearing a trench coat. Paul was momentarily afraid this psychotic looking kid might have been concealing a weapon and that he might have to tackle the kid to protect Dan. The kid ambled down the aisle to a spot immediately in front of the podium at which Dan continued to speak. He silently stared at Dan for a moment, turned his back to Dan, threw his overcoat up over his hips, dropped his pants to his ankles and with cheeks spread wide for full effect, assumed the position taken by inmates about to have a cavity search. Dan was unaffected, but forced to endure the disgusting scene before him for about a minute as the security detail supplied by Berkeley did nothing to remove the protester. The antics of the pantless protester sent howls of laughter and encouragement through the hall and served to energize their furor. Others took a run at the sound system in an attempt to pull the plug on Dan.[320] Despite the fact that there had been threats towards Dan and the Young Republicans written on posters all over campus that day, UC Berkeley had sent a contingent of just two female security guards to maintain order at the event, each of whom couldn't have weighed much more than 100 pounds. They showed up after the crowd had entered the building and wanted nothing to do with controlling their fellow students.

The din continued throughout Dan's entire presentation but instead of asking for questions, he unexpectedly introduced Paul and asked him to come to the podium and say a few things to the students. After witnessing the treatment Dan had received, Paul expected to endure the same verbal abuse. But Paul found a way to temporarily defuse the tension in the room and deliver some of the facts to the students without being attacked. He accomplished this by focusing his request for questions toward a group of aging hippie-types sitting in the first few rows that seemed to be genuinely interested in hearing about the case. Paul told the sea of seething students that while they may not want to hear what he had to say, the group of their friends up in front did. He admonished the students to "respect their elders" the "people who blazed the Free Speech trail for them" and to "let them ask their questions and hear the answers without interruption." Much to Paul's amazement they actually did.

But when Dan came back on stage to conclude, the rioters erupted from their dormancy. "F-you, bastard," and other foul-mouthed epithets once again filled the room. Paul was concerned that the security guards appeared to be missing. Finally, a lone security representative reentered the room to report that they were burning Dan's book in front of the building! It was true. This liberal bastion of free speech was actually hosting a Nazi-style book burning that night, and pamphlets attempting to educate students regarding the violent murder of an innocent cop were being thrown into a bonfire that was encircled by UC Berkeley students. Incredible.

Things were clearly out of hand. The security guards asked Paul and Dan to leave via the back door leading to a hidden alley, and they were told to leave the campus immediately.

Paul and Dan didn't know it but the Young Republicans who had hosted the event went outside to where Dan's books were being burned and took pictures of one-hundred-plus burning books and wearing shirts proclaiming: "Fight Racist Censorship: Free Mumia Abu-Jamal."[321] And in an ironic twist, this antiquated form of hate-motivated censorship took place a stone's throw from the Free Speech Café.

Free speech was dead on arrival at America's most liberal university.

40

GERALD NICOSIA

Gerry Nicosia is a liberal writer from California best known for *Memory Babe: A Critical Biography of Jack Kerouac* and *Home to War: A History of the Vietnam Veteran's Movement*. He's a self-described "peace activist and death penalty opponent."[322] Based on those credentials, it should come as no surprise that he initially lent support to Abu-Jamal. But over time, Gerry Nicosia's view of the case began to change. When Gerry's changed position became known to the Abu-Jamal defense team, all hell broke loose.

In the late 1990s, Gerry asked for my assistance in a research project he was completing on the case. I was naturally skeptical, but over time Nicosia convinced me that he planned to write an impartial narrative of the Abu-Jamal saga. For months, he interviewed me once a week on Tuesday evenings at 8:00 p.m. In November 2000, Nicosia submitted an eighteen-page book proposal to his agent, Ellen Levine, under an agreement of strict confidentiality. Included in the proposal was the sentence: "Could an unjust, unfeeling, flagrantly racist society have pushed that young man far enough to murder a young white police officer, Daniel Faulkner, in cold blood?"[323]

Details of the proposal were somehow leaked in the publishing community and one of the publishers was a friend of Leonard Weinglass. Frances Goldin, the literary agent representing Mumia Abu-Jamal at the time, learned about Nicosia's plans. Nicosia claimed that once Goldin heard about his proposal, his access to people within Abu-Jamal's support group, which had previously been readily available, became nonexistent. No longer could he wander the hallowed halls of Jamaldom and access the inside of the camp. The gates were closed.

Nicosia started receiving frightening messages from people he knew and had worked with years earlier. At one point, somebody had called and put a clock up to the phone: Tick, Tick, Tick. An ominous threat without words can be terrifying.

The book remains unpublished.

41

JUDGE YOHN'S DECISION

In 2001, we marked the twentieth anniversary of Danny's murder with a special event. A Philadelphia lawyer—and I use those terms with the reverence they used to command—named James Binns (everybody calls him Jimmy) decided he wanted to dedicate a plaque in Danny's honor at the corner of Thirteenth and Locust Streets, right where Danny died. In fact, he wanted to start with Danny, and then honor the life of every slain cop by doing likewise, wherever they died in the line of duty.

Danny's plaque featured a replica of his badge and these words: "In memory of Daniel 'Danny' Faulkner. Murdered at this spot in the line of duty protecting the citizens of Philadelphia on Dec. 9, 1981. Dedicated Dec. 9, 2001, by his family and friends." Since that first plaque, Jimmy's program has dedicated dozens of plaques in memory of Philadelphia's fallen heroes.

I was sitting behind my desk at work in California on December 18, 2001, when the telephone rang. On the line was Hugh Burns from the District Attorney's Office in Philadelphia. He had news that would drain the blood from my face. Burns was calling to tell me that he had just learned that a federal judge named William H. Yohn Jr. had ruled on Abu-Jamal's habeas corpus petition, and that while he had upheld the conviction and rejected all but one of twenty-nine legal arguments raised by the defense, he had also overturned the death sentence. Judge Yohn found that the jury may have mistakenly believed it had to agree unanimously on what are called "mitigating circumstances," where unanimous agreement was not needed, and that this may have swayed their determination toward a death sentence instead of life in prison. To me this was a ruling based on a total technicality and not something that had originally been argued by the Abu-Jamal defense.

I felt sick. This was truly the first loss we had sustained in a courtroom in twenty years. Immediately when that call ended, the phones started ringing from reporters. I finally decided that I needed to speak to Michael Smerconish to get his counsel as to how I should respond to the onslaught, but not before I said the following to one of the reporters:

> I'm angry, outraged and disgusted. I think Judge Yohn is a sick and twisted person after sitting on this case for two years and making this decision just before Christmas. He wants to walk the middle of the road and try to appease both sides, and it doesn't work.[324]

I was mad. And for good reason. And I want to clear something up. When I used the words sick and twisted, I was referring to the fact that this process had gone on for so long, and now, my family and I were having this emotional hand grenade thrown in our laps just days before Christmas. It was not my intention to say that Judge William H. Yohn Jr. was sick and twisted. To the contrary, he has a solid reputation throughout the legal world as being a "fair-minded" law-and-order judge, and I often regret using those words to describe my feelings about the timing of his decision.

Abu-Jamal had been turned down by the State Supreme Court three times. Now, at the federal level, his lawyers claimed that dozens of constitutional violations had occurred during his trial and direct appeal. The federal judge hearing the petition, Judge Yohn, could have potentially ordered a new trial or thrown out the death sentence if he found that any of those claims were valid. I never believed that ordering a new trial was a possibility and thought that the idea of the death sentence being overturned was a long shot, hence my surprise when Judge Yohn overturned Abu-Jamal's death sentence after accepting only one of his twenty-nine claims. The Opinion and Order was handed down one week before Christmas and just nine days after the twentieth anniversary of Danny's murder. I thought the timing was tasteless, given how long the case had been going on.

I was not alone in my pain. Philadelphia District Attorney Lynne Abraham vowed to appeal the decision in order to have the death sentence reinstated. She said the judge's decision was "legally flawed and unsupportable by the law" and added that the guilty verdict "has withstood 20 years of appeal after appeal, and it's still standing after today."[325] In a separate statement, Abraham criticized the judge's reliance on precedents which became law many years after Abu-Jamal's trial, saying that no judge or prosecutor "could have known of some new rule that would not even be announced by the Federal Court until over a decade and a half later."[326]

At a news conference on the day of the ruling, FOP President Richard Costello called Judge Yohn a "political hack" and "a smiling hyena sitting in his [Abu-Jamal's] lap." He went on: "This is one hell of a Christmas present to every police officer throughout this nation. It endangers every police officer out there."[327]

The Abu-Jamal side wasn't happy either. While the judge had cast doubt on the implementation of the death sentence, he also rejected Abu-Jamal's claim of an unfair trial and absolute innocence. Since Abu-Jamal had been granted a new sentencing hearing rather than a new trial, his attorneys also planned to appeal the Order. If and when the sentencing hearing moved forward, lawyer J. Michael Farrell indicated that he would argue that his client's innocence itself was a mitigating factor he would introduce: "A penalty hearing in this case would be a full-blown trial as to guilt and innocence. A witness list might read like a Who's Who."[328]

The federal decision was huge news. I appeared on the *Today* show with Michael Smerconish opposite some of the Abu-Jamal supporters. Newspapers across the country covered the development. Many editorial pages and columnists were critical of the decision. Joseph Perkins wrote in the *Washington Times*:

> This week, the cop killer got an undeserved Christmas present. . . . The only injustice is that the convicted cop killer has been able to work the legal system for the past two decades, filing appeal after dubious appeal, endlessly delaying the punishment he so richly deserves for taking the life of a peace officer.[329]

Judge Yohn's 272-page Opinion is available at www.danielfaulkner.com. It begins with a short recap of the case history in the Pennsylvania courts from the original 1982 jury trial to the failures of Abu-Jamal's direct and Post-Conviction Relief Act appeals to the Pennsylvania Supreme Court. Judge Yohn acknowledged that the nearly twenty-year gap between the original trial and his decision on Abu-Jamal's habeas corpus petition might be "difficult to understand," and that "it is clearly painful to the petitioner, his family and friends, and the family and friends of the victim to have this issue renewed and reinforced in their memories after the passage of so much time."[330] He went on to note that such drawn-out proceedings would be unlikely to recur with recent changes in the law, most notably a one-year statute of limitations on the filing of such petitions. (Judge Yohn was wrong. It would take the 3rd Circuit Court six years to hear argument on the timely appeal of Judge Yohn's Opinion.)

Beyond its overturning of the death sentence, the decision was on target in many other respects. Judge Yohn upheld the jury's finding that Abu-Jamal killed Danny after he meticulously dissected and rejected twenty-eight of Abu-Jamal's twenty-nine claims that his constitutional rights had been violated during the guilt and direct appeal phases of his case.

The basis for Judge Yohn's decision as to the death penalty was his finding that Abu-Jamal's constitutional rights had been violated by the instructions the Trial Judge (Sabo) gave the jury during the sentencing phase of the trial.[331] Judge Yohn agreed with Abu-Jamal's argument that both the instructions and the verdict sheet improperly led the jurors to believe that they needed to agree unanimously when finding any mitigating circumstances that might lead them to sentence Abu-Jamal to life in prison rather than to death. Following the guilt phase of a capital murder trial, jurors weigh aggravating circumstances—here, murdering a police officer acting in the line of duty—against mitigating circumstances like a traumatic upbringing, when trying to determine whether to sentence a convicted first-degree murderer to death or to life in prison. During the penalty phase of the trial, the jurors found the aggravating circumstance and one mitigating circumstance, that Abu-Jamal had no significant prior criminal record. The jurors were properly instructed that under Pennsylvania law they were required to sentence Abu-Jamal to death if they *unanimously* found one or more aggravating circumstances and no mitigating circumstances, or if they unanimously found that the aggravating circumstances outweighed any mitigating circumstances. If the jury deadlocked, Abu-Jamal would be sentenced to life imprisonment.

Citing a pair of U.S. Supreme Court decisions in which ambiguous jury instructions may have prevented jurors from considering constitutionally relevant mitigating evidence, Judge Yohn determined that the verdict sheet and the Trial Judge's instructions in Abu-Jamal's trial could have led the jury to believe that a mitigating circumstance was not to be considered unless all jurors agreed that it was present.[332] He concluded by contrasting his own "reasonable" application of Federal Law to the Pennsylvania Supreme Court's "unreasonable" application and ordered that Abu-Jamal's death sentence be overturned and, further, that he be sentenced to life imprisonment if a new sentencing hearing is not held.

So what does it all mean? It means that the legal battle isn't over, much less the contest that I have waged outside of the courtroom. Now, both sides are appealing. The prosecution is appealing the overturning of the death sentence and the Abu-Jamal lawyers are appealing the conviction. Argument was held in the spring of 2007 on these appeals. I need to say again that Hugh Burns, head of the Appellate Section of the DA's office, is the latest hero in this most recent battle of our crusade and I continue to marvel at his legal skills, street savvy, and patience. I lost my husband. I will not let this matter rest. It is people like Hugh, people who never had the pleasure of knowing Danny but take to his cause and champion his defense, who keep me energized. Hugh is a brilliant, unassuming lawyer. I look at him with the same level of respect with which I do a police officer.

4 2

THE FRENCH

Europe has always been a hotbed of support for Mumia Abu-Jamal but France, in particular, seems to idolize him. France's support for Mumia Abu-Jamal reached the height of absurdity when it was formalized and sanctioned by governmental authorities. On December 4, 2001, the Paris City Council voted to name Pennsylvania's famous death row inmate an "Honorary Citizen" of Paris. The last time such honor was bestowed was to famed artist Pablo Picasso in 1971.[333]

The formal ceremony for Abu-Jamal's citizenship did not take place until 2003. On October 4 of that year, the City of Paris finally made good on its offer to honor Abu-Jamal and the convicted cop killer became the city's newest citizen.[334] In his comments during the ceremony, Mayor Delanoe said: "As long as there is a place on this planet where one can be killed in the name of the community, then we haven't finished our work."[335]

Abu-Jamal thanked his French supporters for their generosity with his usual whiney, propaganda-peppered banalities via audiotape:

> My friends, comrades, brothers and sisters. I want to take this opportunity to thank our good friends in France, to the many good people who are deeply opposed to the modern barbarity of the death penalty, and for those who have retained the taste of liberty that sparked the great French Revolution over two hundred years ago.
>
> I have been forced to think about what it means to be a citizen, even an honorary one. I have often wondered what such a thing meant for I have seen precious little of what it means in my life and in the lives of many of my contemporaries. It must mean far more than the empty right to vote. Does it mean the so-called right to have Black jurors summarily removed from your jury? The right to have openly racist judges appointed to decide whether you shall live or die? The right to a trial that violates the laws of the land and indeed international law?

If that is so, then I am an American citizen and it has become virtually meaningless. I am hoping that an honorary citizenship may mean something more. What more? I don't have the experience to know. But I do have the knowledge to thank you and the French Republic for—since the time of Mitterand, 1981, taking the side of life.

There are indeed over three thousand men, women, and juveniles who, if they could, would surely thank you all for such a choice.

I am but one of them. So I thank you all. Merci, On a *MOVE!* LONG LIVE JOHN AFRICA![336]

The French dalliance with Abu-Jamal didn't end there. The love affair continues to this day. As recently as February 14, 2005, French politicians and activists traveled to Philadelphia to support Abu-Jamal's cause. Even more grotesque than the French display of adoration, Philadelphia Mayor John F. Street actually welcomed them as visiting dignitaries! Mayor Street's staff representative actually invited the crowd into the mayor's ornate Reception Room on the second floor of City Hall. There, they sauntered and schmoozed in the wood-paneled den, under the watchful gaze of portraits of past Philadelphia mayors, as they took command of the city's official podium. A man named Jacky Hortaut of the National Unit Collective, a coalition of pro-Abu-Jamal groups, addressed the crowd outside with galvanizing remarks: "We are here to denounce this discriminatory and racist justice!" he roared. Subsequently, Mjenzi Traylor, the city's first deputy director of commerce, told the crowd that he was there to "make certain that we are receiving the message that you would like for us to deliver to Mayor Street." He then proceeded to distribute replicas of the Liberty Bell, the Philadelphia icon and America's symbol of freedom! "We welcome you to Philadelphia. Thank you very much for coming," he finished.[337]

I've long suspected that Mayor Street was an Abu-Jamal sympathizer; his involvement with witness Cynthia White offers the most revealing evidence to support this supposition. I don't think this story has ever been fully told.

Remember, White was one of three key eyewitnesses at trial (the others being Michael Scanlan and Robert Chobert) who testified to seeing Danny stop William Cook, and Abu-Jamal run out of the parking lot across the street and shoot Danny.[338] In 1982, prior to Abu-Jamal's trial,

Cynthia White was in jail. She complained to Joe McGill, the man who prosecuted Abu-Jamal in the 1982 trial, that, without notice, she had been visited by two lawyers who were not her own.[339] One of these lawyers was John Street, not yet mayor of Philadelphia.

According to White, John Street (who was not representing Abu-Jamal in any way) attempted to convince her not to testify. His diligent persistence is revealing of his character. The following interview statement of Cynthia White, where she describes her encounter with John Street, truly speaks volumes:

> **Question:** Miss White, will you go on in your own words and tell us about that visit?
>
> **Answer:** It was around lunch time, I think about 11 a.m. on Monday 6–14–82, Flag Day. Ms. Sherry, a guard at the Detention Center Hospital, told me I had a special visit. I asked her who and she said, it's a lawyer. I was taken to where they interview you and I was told by one of the male guards it was John Street, a lawyer. I signed and said that I would see him. I thought he was from the Public Defender's Office to represent me for my case in Philly. When I went back to where Mr. Street was sitting he said, "You are Cynthia White, aren't you." I said yes. He said, "I'm John Street, a lawyer, and this is Arlene Bell, an Attorney. He then asked me where I live, my mother live, if I had any other living relatives, and how many times I've been arrested. He also asked me why I was here in jail. I told him where I lived, my mother's address and I gave him a false name and address for other relatives because I didn't want him to know where my sister live. I don't know why I gave him the bad name and address for my sister. I told him I was not arrested here in Philly. I was here in jail because I had some charge in Boston, Mass. Mr. Street then said, "I'm here to represent you in the Jamal case." I asked him for what. Mr. Street then said that the police and DA could charge me with something if they didn't like my statement and Jamal was found not guilty. He stated he was there to keep the police and DA from arresting me. He asked if the police or DA had made any deals with me and I told him no. He asked me this about four times. I don't remember exactly when, but he asked me four times. Mr. Street asked me if I could tell him what I saw when the incident happen. I told him I didn't want to talk about it. He asked me why and I told him I just didn't want to talk about it. He asked me if I voluntarily walked up and tell the police what happen and I told him yes. He said "well the police didn't come up to the corner and grab you, you had enough time to walk away." I told Mr. Street I didn't think it was right what he (Jamal) did so I went up and

told the police. He asked me if I like the MOVE People and I told him I had nothing against them, I didn't know them. Mr. Street said to me, "I don't know why he would run up and shoot the police officer because I've seen my brother Milton arrested many times and I didn't run up and shoot the police."

Question: What did you do after your conversation with John Street?

Answer: Mr. Street said he was going to contact the DA and I told him I didn't want him to represent me. After he left I called Detective Thomas immediately and then Mr. McGill.

Question: Was Mr. Street's representation for free?

Answer: No, he told me it would cost $300.00.[340]

The date on the Investigation Record was June 16, 1982. The date of the meeting with John Street was June 14, 1982. This was the week that Mumia Abu-Jamal's trial began (June 17, 1982). This all suggests that John Street, the future mayor of Philadelphia, spoke to Cynthia White with the intent of silencing her damning testimony against Abu-Jamal. For reasons undisclosed, John Street was on Abu-Jamal's side. John Street has suppressed his support for over two decades. The Liberty Bell incident confirmed, at least for me, his true colors. John Street was uncovered.

I asked Joe McGill about the Cynthia White episode recently. He told me that in his view, White was a critical witness in our case. Although we had three additional witnesses, she was the one witness who, because of her location, saw the entire incident from start to finish. He said, "Any negative influence on her testimony would be critical to the case. I was very proud of her courage to respond to this incident the way that she did. As a matter of fact, given the time and her exposure on the streets, I found her actions to be courageous. She was what she was but she tried to do the right thing."

Joe also told me that during John Street's campaign for mayor, supporters of John Street's opponent knew generally about this incident. "They had pumped me for details and wanted me to go public. I told them that I would not discuss it and definitely would not go public since I did not want the Faulkner case to become a 'political football' in that hard-fought primary."

I still wonder how John Street got in to see Cynthia White. He certainly did not represent her and only attorneys or their investigators were allowed in to see prisoners. What did he have to say to be allowed in?

In more than two decades of fighting for Danny's memory, I have resisted any temptation to mix politics with my case. I am proud to have supporters who are both Democrat and Republican. My spite towards Street has nothing to do with his politics and everything to do with the fact that he displayed gross disrespect to not only me but to the memory of Danny, the city of Philadelphia, and the brave men and women who serve to protect it.

I telephoned Mayor Street's office to complain about the red carpet his office had rolled out for the foreign communists. A staffer offered me an obligatory and insincere apology and, as I requested, he left a message for the mayor. A few hours later, Mayor Street personally returned my call.

Mayor Street apologized if his actions were taken the wrong way. He told me that he knew that there were dignitaries coming into the city. He did not know where they were coming from; he had a very busy schedule. He did not really know too much about the replicas of the Liberty Bells that were given out. He said, "Look, Maureen, Mumia Abu-Jamal is still guilty of murdering your husband. He was tried and convicted by a jury and he is serving his time in prison where he belongs." He assured me he was always a staunch supporter of police.[341]

But Street was singing a different tune to the press than what he had said to me privately. The next morning, an article in the *Daily News* stated:

> Street offered a more qualified apology in public yesterday. "To the extent that anybody misunderstood the actions that were taken here, then we certainly apologize for that," Street said. "Other than that, we're a government that holds itself open to people from all over the world and who have different views."[342]

What drivel! Any time an apology begins with "To the extent," it really isn't an apology. John Baer's reporting in the same edition of the *Daily News* was even more illuminating. Baer covers Harrisburg, the Pennsylvania state capital, for the *Daily News*. Street was in Harrisburg that Monday to lobby for funding for Philadelphia mass transit when Baer caught up with him to ask about the French Connection. Reported Baer, "I simply ask, 'Wasn't it a mistake?' And he goes off about how it's routine for international visitors to get gifts from City Hall, and I'm thinking, yeah, but these are not routine visitors, these are people calling for the freedom of a man who murdered a city police officer and I ask, 'Why not just admit it was a mistake?' Because, he says, 'I don't want to criticize people who are trying to do the right thing.'"343

Despite renewed debates in the media, the Paris suburb of St. Denis dedicated one of its streets in Abu-Jamal's honor, which received both praise and condemnation from across the world. Abu-Jamal's faithful followers saw the dedication in France as an appropriate way to honor their movement. His opponents, however, saw the street dedication as a reprehensible political statement that condones the murder of a police officer. I was back in LA and told the media that the entire thing was disgusting. "This is so unnerving for me to get this news. It's insulting to the police officers of Philadelphia that they are naming a street after a murderer."344 My concern was heard by two Pennsylvania members of Congress who introduced legislation to deal with this issue. Controversy surrounding Mumia had new legs and soon became a focal point in Washington, where on May 19, 2006, Republican Congressman Michael G. Fitzpatrick introduced a bill to combat the decision of St. Denis. Mr. Fitzpatrick and his original cosponsor, Pennsylvania Democrat Allyson Schwartz, urged Congress to take a unified position in condemning the St. Denis government and requesting the French government to order the street to again be renamed.

On December 6, 2006, by a vote of 368 to 31, Congress passed the resolution condemning the naming of a street for Abu-Jamal in St. Denis, France.345

43

THE O'REILLY FACTOR

The French fiasco renewed national interest in the case. Bill O'Reilly was among those who presented the update to a national audience. O'Reilly already had a boycott underway against the French and could not believe that they had latched onto such vermin. When I received a call from *The O'Reilly Factor* asking me to appear and talk about the fact that Paris was making Abu-Jamal an honorary citizen, I readily accepted the offer. On air, we discussed our mutual disgust over the way in which Abu-Jamal had risen as a celebrated hero among very unlikely segments of society. We also talked about the celebrity element of the case. I spoke of my oft-repeated offer to have Mike Farrell, Ed Asner, or any of the celebrity supporters speak to me on camera about the case. Bill O'Reilly seemed keen on the idea.

A few days after the first appearance on O'Reilly's show, which was focused mainly on the proclivities of the French, I received word that my presence was again requested on *The Factor*. Mike Farrell was willing to appear with me. This time, the show would emanate from Los Angeles, where Bill O'Reilly was scheduled to do his show. This was shaping up as a significant appearance because the Hollywood celebrities are loath to be anywhere near me.

This appearance on *The O'Reilly Factor* was in the fall of 2003. O'Reilly gave Farrell a chance to speak his side of the story before including me, and in that time, Farrell explained that he is an adamant opponent to the use of the death penalty in all cases. He conceded that he doesn't know whether Abu-Jamal is innocent or guilty, but after reading "significant pieces" of the court transcripts, he believes that Abu-Jamal did not receive a fair trial.[346]

Once I became involved in the dialogue, Farrell and I argued about the fairness of the 1982 trial. I told Bill O'Reilly: "In 1982, 1995, '96, '97, and

'98, I sat through the court hearing. If anyone wanted to know who murdered my husband, it was me. I went into that courtroom with an open mind. I saw eyewitnesses, ballistics, and I had no doubt in my mind that it was Mumia Abu-Jamal that murdered my husband. He had control of his own destiny in that courtroom. He did receive a fair trial." Mike Farrell responded by telling me how sympathetic he was for me, and that he knew what I had gone through being that he lost a dear friend.[347]

Another contentious part of the interview was when O'Reilly questioned Mike about indicting the system. Farrell argued that "the system indicts itself" and when asked whether he was doing so at the expense of me, he responded "not at all."[348]

Farrell and I disputed the issue of the jurors as well. Farrell spoke about the lack of black jurors, despite the fact that there were "11 perfectly qualified . . . black jurors." When I responded that these eleven were struck because they either didn't believe in capital punishment or had previously known Abu-Jamal, Farrell said, "I'm sorry. Eleven of the people who were struck by the D.A. peremptorily did say they could try this case fairly and they did not oppose the capital punishment." The exchange continued as I told him that that is not what the court record states and offered to sit down and go over it with him one day.[349] And so it went. We both said our piece. Bill O'Reilly officiated.

What is perhaps most interesting about this exchange is what came three and a half years later, when Michael Smerconish was contacted by a publicist for Mike Farrell and asked whether he would be willing to interview Farrell regarding his recently released book titled *Just Call Me Mike: A Journey to Actor and Activist*. Michael Smerconish told me that he is routinely asked by publishers and publicists to interview authors of new books, but that he took a particular interest in this one, correctly assuming that Farrell would have dealt with our case in his memoirs. The book is mostly a collection of anecdotes about Farrell's days on the hit shows *M*A*S*H* and *Providence* along with first-hand accounts of international tragedies such as war and oppression in Cambodia, El Salvador, and Rwanda, among others. The interview was scheduled before Michael even received the book; he told me that it arrived the morning of the interview and sure enough, he was quickly able to locate those pages where Farrell dealt with the case, in time for his interview with Farrell. Having heard the tape, I suspect Farrell had no idea that he was about to be interviewed by someone vastly more knowledgeable about the case than he. He probably suspected he was just dealing with some random DJ in Philly.

Before I tell you about this most revealing of interviews, let me first tell you what Farrell wrote about me and the case.

Farrell wrote that he was introduced to the Abu-Jamal case through Leonard Weinglass, the former lead attorney. Weinglass asked Farrell to join Ossie Davis in chairing the Committee to Save Mumia Abu-Jamal. (Davis, best known as an actor, director, and playwright,[350] had made a visit to Abu-Jamal in May of 1999, spending over two hours with him. Following the meeting, Davis began to advocate for a new trial for Abu-Jamal, saying that, "it was an extraordinary visit because I was dealing with, I think, an extraordinary man. There was a talent that I respected because I had read his writings before. But in conversations I became aware that this was a deeply spiritual human being who was capable of love, and that love was wide enough to embrace even those who would kill him."[351]) Farrell wrote that he agreed to join Davis in heading the committee on the basis that he "liked Ossie, had faith in Len, and believed the death penalty an abomination."[352] Farrell also wrote that although "facts around the shooting were cloudy . . . there were many problems with the case, including the behavior of the judge."[353]

Farrell was clear to specify in his book that "I thought Mumia Abu-Jamal deserved a fair trial, not that I was convinced of his innocence."[354]

He acknowledges Mumia's supposed confession but cites that it was not mentioned by the police for two months after the occurrence. As he states in the book, "It was hard to believe that two veteran officers forgot such a key piece of evidence until it was needed for the state's cause."[355]

Most important to me was Farrell's claim that I was a pawn of the FOP. He wrote that "The Pennsylvania Fraternal Order of Police (FOP) had taken up the cudgel, using Officer Faulkner's widow Maureen as the up-front figure in their campaign to kill Abu-Jamal."[356] I thought that was offensive. I am a nightstick for the FOP?

Michael Smerconish was anxious to learn from Farrell what level of investigation he undertook before lending his name to a convicted cop killer.

Farrell told him that he "looked into it [the case] to some degree," reading "some of the transcripts" of the trial, different testimonies, and various other things, which he told Michael "were sufficient to me to convince me that it was worth supporting the call for a new trial."[357]

Michael Smerconish then asked him about his willingness to support Abu-Jamal where Abu-Jamal had never supported himself, meaning, he has never offered an accounting of what happened that night, and neither has his brother, who was present.

Farrell said that although the issue "has always been a source of concern," for him, he believes that there are two parts to the issue: "One, I believe everybody deserves a fair trial, I don't believe he got one and two, I oppose capital punishment, and his is one of the . . . preeminent cases in the country or has been made to become those cases in the country that typify for a lot of people some of the problems associated with the capital punishment and it felt to me that all things being equal that it was worth whatever effort I put into it to see to it that enough attention was brought to the case."[358]

Next, when Michael asked Farrell of his impression of me when we met on Bill O'Reilly's show on October 16, 2003,[359] he told him that although he sympathizes with me for my loss and that I "seemed very genuine in [my] concern . . . [I've] been used by the pro-death forces . . . inappropriately."[360] Which I find ironic, given his admission that Leonard Weinglass contacted *him*, simply because of his fame and because he knew he was an opponent of capital punishment. And then he turned around and said that he thinks *I* have been used by the pro–death penalty forces? Now that's the pot calling the kettle black.

4 4

TOOKIE AND
THE TERMINATOR

Every year near December 9, I am tormented with vivid memories of
that foreboding knock on the door. Despite the passage of time, December always brings painful memories of anguish and anxiety, of when
police officers arrived to tell me that my world had crumbled. On the tenth
anniversary of Danny's murder, I believed that I was nearing the end of the
most painful recollections, even as the flood of memories continued. Then,
when the case entered into the national and international spotlight, there
were constant reminders on TV, in print, in public. The case has never left
my consciousness. While I never want to forget Danny, I would be grateful for an improved ability to endure the first week of December.

The week of the twenty-fourth anniversary of Danny's murder was
particularly difficult. Suddenly, Abu-Jamal was back in the news in my
adopted state of California, as California's "Governator," Arnold
Schwarzenegger, wrestled with what to do with a last-ditch plea to stop the
execution of Stanley "Tookie" Williams. Williams was a former gang thug
and executioner. He had been sitting on death row for a long time, and it
finally looked like he would receive his sentence. Living in Southern California, near Tookie Williams' home town, I watched the Save Tookie battle unfold and, as the date drew near, the same activists who supported
Abu-Jamal became vocal for Tookie Williams. It was incredible. The media
was full of the same faces saying the same things they had said about
Danny's murder for two and half decades. In fact, just a week before
Williams's fate was determined, I was driving home from work and heard
on a talk radio station a discussion of Williams and Abu-Jamal, and Mike
Farrell came on saying many of the same things he said in Danny's case. I

pulled over with my heart pounding. It had been twenty-four long years. I am a strong person, but it was a jolt to hear it once again.

Tookie Williams's story sounded eerily familiar to me. The Williams case had been thoroughly reviewed many times over a period of twenty-four years and was the subject of at least eight substantive judicial opinions which reaffirmed Williams's guilt during those years.[361] On December 13, 2005, at 12:23 a.m., Tookie Williams became the twelfth man executed by the State of California since its death penalty was reinstated over twenty-five years ago.[362] In the hour of Tookie Williams's actual death (3 a.m. EST), my friend Michael Smerconish was already awake in Philadelphia preparing for his morning-drive radio show. He was studying the case and decided to read not just the news clips but also Governor Schwarzenegger's written denial of clemency. As part of this endeavor, he stumbled upon a surprising reference to Abu-Jamal. I had just spoken to Michael the day before, when he called me to chat about the similarities between Abu-Jamal and Tookie. At the time, both of us were ignorant of the fact that there was any actual connection between the two apart from the celebrities who supported both. Now, in the wee hours of the morning, Michael read that the governor of California took into account Tookie Williams's support for the man who killed my husband in his decision to deny Williams's appeal for clemency. In his final official decision on the matter, Governor Schwarzenegger found it significant that Tookie Williams supported Abu-Jamal, and he regarded this allegiance as an indication of Williams's lack of repentance for his own crimes. Michael woke me from a dead sleep to read to me from the document. This, I remember telling him, was the kind of news I welcomed in the middle of the night.

Governor Schwarzenegger's denial of clemency is a must-read document. The five pages begin by recounting the facts of the Tookie Williams case:

> During the early morning hours of February 28, 1979, Williams and three others went on a robbery spree. Around 4:00 a.m., they entered a 7-Eleven store where Albert Owens was working by himself. Here, Williams, armed with his pump-action shotgun, ordered Owens to a back room and shot him twice in the back while he lay face down on the floor. Williams and his accomplices made off with about $120 from the store's cash register. After leaving the 7-Eleven store, Williams told the others that he killed Albert Owens because he did not want any witnesses. Later

that morning, Williams recounted shooting Albert Owens saying, "You should have heard the way he sounded when I shot him." Williams then made a growling noise and laughed for five or six minutes.

On March 11, 1979, less than two weeks later, Williams, again armed with his shotgun, robbed a family operated motel and shot and killed three members of the family: (1) the father, Yen-I Yang, who was shot once in the torso and once in the arm while he was lying on a sofa; (2) the mother, Tsai-Shai Lin, who was shot once in the abdomen and once in the back; and (3) the daughter, Yee-Chen Lin, who was shot once in her face. For these murders, Williams made away with approximately $100 in cash. Williams also told others about the details of these murders and referred to the victims as "Buddha-heads."[363]

Governor Schwarzenegger then noted that the basis of Williams's clemency request was not his innocence but, rather, the "personal redemption Stanley Williams has experienced and the positive impact of the message he sends." This was a message, his supporters said, that he had offered in the form of kids books written behind bars.[364]

What Tookie Williams did not count on was that the governor or members of his staff would actually read the books. They did. They found that his 1998 *Life in Prison* tome was dedicated to: "Nelson Mandela, Angela Davis, Malcolm X, Assata Shakur, Geronimo Ji Jaga Pratt, Ramona Africa, John Africa, Leonard Peltier, Dhoruba Al-Mujahid, George Jackson, Mumia Abu-Jamal and the countless other men, women and youths who have to endure the hellish oppression of living behind bars."[365]

Wrote the governor: "The mix of individuals on this list is curious. Most have violent pasts and some have been convicted of committing heinous murders, including the killing of law enforcement," a reference to Abu-Jamal's execution of Danny. Schwarzenegger found this list to be "a significant indicator that Williams is not reformed and that he still sees violence and lawlessness as a legitimate means to address societal problems."[366]

After Williams's execution, I was particularly struck by the words of Lora Owens, a family member of one of Williams's victims who told the press: "The court system has worked . . . Justice has been served."[367]

With great hope and expectation, I yearn for the day when I, too, can deliver such a statement. In the meantime, I thank Governor Schwarzenegger.

45

TWENTY-FIFTH ANNIVERSARY: GONE BUT NEVER FORGOTTEN

There's no playbook for how to commemorate the twenty-fifth anniversary of the murder of your husband. The twenty-fifth anniversary of Danny's death fell on a Saturday. I intended to spend it in church, and with friends, and did both, followed by a visit to Joe Vento at Geno's Steaks. But on the day before, December 8, 2006, Michael Smerconish planned and hosted a luncheon with a threefold purpose. Primarily we gathered in Danny's honor and to raise money for the scholarship fund I'd established to make donations toward the education of the children of murder victims in Philadelphia. Additionally, we honored Philadelphia District Attorney Lynne Abraham as she neared the end of her final term. Lynne Abraham could be elected DA for as long as she wants the job, but she has served notice that she would not seek reelection. The luncheon was memorable, heartening, and inspiring to me all through the dark day of remembering why we had gathered there.

Once again, we congregated at the venerable Union League, where we had taken command of the entire space in 1999 on the eve of what had been billed as the Millions For Mumia March, a protest that ended up falling pitifully short of its objective in both cities where it was held. Our tribute dinner was a huge success then and so, too, was this memorial luncheon. The men and women who comprise the District Attorney's Office usually do not get the recognition they deserve for putting in long hours in an often unglamorous job. That Friday honorarium was a different experience for them. A crowd of four hundred packed the formal dining area, and they cheered with approval for Lynne Abraham; Joe McGill, who prosecuted Abu-Jamal; and Hugh Burns, the appellate attorney who has done more than anyone to keep him behind bars.

I came early and stayed late, talking and talking with old and new friends, fund-raisers, and other supporters, and those whose newfound interest brought them to us for the first time by the good work the scholarship fund was doing. It was such a perfect event that it spurred me on in my quest for justice for Danny.

Wouldn't you know, even as we marked the day of Danny's death, spin and inaccuracy threatened to dampen the atmosphere. Only eight blocks north of where we sat inside the Union League on Broad Street, a *Daily News* reporter, for some unknown reason, was busily crafting a brand-new profile of that old liar William Singletary, the supposed eyewitness whose story was as full of gaping holes as a fish net, especially the part where a dead man talked to him. Fallacies are not unusual, but what was odd is that this occurred in Philadelphia, where the media historically has been more circumspect regarding Abu-Jamal. A simple Google search would have told the reporter how wrong she was. Apparently too busy to fact-check, Valerie Russ reintroduced long-disproved accusations of police coercion and mystery-man theories to her uninformed readers.[368]

As we gathered on Broad Street, the federal court system had yet to act on appeals to Judge Yohn's Opinion from 2001. I was told by lawyers that this was an unusual amount of time to have an appeal pending without a scheduled argument in front of the appellate court, the Third Circuit. The most unsettling part is knowing you are powerless to do anything to bring about resolution. It is a feeling that has pained me for twenty-five years. And so I marked the anniversary date of a quarter century since Danny's death without any knowledge of when something would next happen in a legal sense. Several months later, I was contacted by the DA's office and told the case had finally been set for a hearing in the Third Circuit.

That argument took place on May 17, 2007—it had taken five and a half years since Judge Yohn's decision at the federal trial court level to finally get an airing in front of a three-judge panel of the United States Court of Appeals for the Third Circuit. Remember, in 2001 Judge Yohn had upheld Abu-Jamal's conviction, but had overturned his death sentence. Judge Yohn had overturned the death sentence on what I regarded as a technicality, ruling that because of the way the jury verdict slip was configured, perhaps the jury had mistakenly believed it had to agree unanimously on any mitigating circumstances which might have led them to give Abu-Jamal life in prison, instead of a death sentence. So the DA's office, the Commonwealth, would now be arguing that Judge Yohn was incorrect to overturn the death sentence on that basis. Meanwhile, in addition to trying to uphold that determination, the Abu-Jamal defense would try to argue that the underlying conviction itself was suspect, for among other reasons, they claim the DA's office kept blacks off the jury due to their race. Now, the fireworks would be heard by a panel of three judges at the appellate level, one step removed from the United States Supreme Court.

Judge Yohn had rejected all but one of twenty-nine legal arguments advanced over the years by Abu-Jamal's many defense lawyers, now led by Robert Bryan, Esquire. This was the first time I had seen Bryan. He had replaced Leonard Weinglass a few years prior. Bryan is a San Francisco–based litigant primarily of death penalty cases. He is the former chair of the National Coalition to Abolish the Death Penalty. Before taking on the representation of Abu-Jamal, his highest profile client was Anna Hauptmann, the widow of Richard "Bruno" Hauptmann, the man executed in 1936 for the kidnapping and murder of the Lindbergh baby. Bryan maintains that Abu-Jamal first began contacting him in the mid-1980s and in 1991 formally asked him to take his case, but that Bryan declined because of a full schedule of other capital cases. In 2003, upon being approached again, Bryan agreed to become involved.

Coinciding with the argument, Michael Smerconish wrote something for the *Philadelphia Inquirer* that really put things in perspective.[369] He didn't write about the legal aspects of the case; he wrote about the human toll it had taken. He pointed out that Thomas and Mary Faulkner had raised seven children: Thomas Jr., Joseph, Joanne, Lawrence, Patrick, Kenny, and Danny. And that they were a decent, religious family, united not only by their Catholic faith, but also the hardscrabble lives they each led in southwest Philadelphia and in Delaware County. Thomas Jr. was a cop for five years until he was injured. Joseph worked for a cement company and battled many physical problems. Joanne was a waitress. Lawrence worked as a bartender. Pat has spent forty years working for Acme, and Kenny worked a variety of jobs, including bartender. Of the seven chil-

dren, only Danny became famous, and not in a way that any parent or sibling would ever desire.

He then pointed out that whereas all of Danny's siblings were still alive
at the time of his tragic death, now, as the case was being heard in federal
court twenty-five years later, only two of the seven Faulkner children were
still with us: Larry and Pat. Danny's mother, Mary, was also alive when he
was killed and attended every day of the murder trial but she too was dead,
having passed a few years thereafter. (As I have indicated, Danny's father,
Thomas, a trolley driver, died when Danny was a boy.) It was the same
thing with my family. Both of my parents, who agonizingly accompanied
me to trial in 1982, had since moved on. Indeed, all of these people close
to Danny had died without closure on the case. Meanwhile, as natural
causes continued to take members of Danny's and my families, the man
who heaped tragedy upon everyone related to us was still alive and thriv-
ing, albeit behind bars. Abu-Jamal was now fifty-three. And as far as I
know, healthy.

Pat Faulkner, one of Danny's two surviving brothers, told Michael
Smerconish that he couldn't bring himself to be there in federal court that
week. "I just don't know how I would react after twenty-five years and I
don't want to over-react, and embarrass my brother's memory with my
temper. You can only hold something in so long," he said. No one could
fault him. I respected his restraint. But for me, there was no turning back.
I had attended every single hearing in the case over the span of two and a
half decades and I remained intent on seeing the judicial process to the end.
State court, federal court, the world court—I don't care, I will be there.

Getting ready to walk into the federal courthouse that morning, I was
thinking about something Judge Yohn had written in his exhaustive, several-
hundred-page Opinion a few years prior: "Since its inception this matter
has negotiated a tortuous procedural course, and this pattern continues
today." Tortuous indeed. The murder was in 1981. In 1982, Abu-Jamal
was afforded a trial by his peers, which led to his conviction and death sentence. In 1989, his conviction and sentence were upheld by the Pennsylvania State Supreme Court. The Commonwealth's highest court also
rejected subsequent appeals. (In 1995, 1996, and 1997, his case was the

subject of Post-Conviction Relief Act hearings, which afforded him the opportunity to raise new evidence; each time he had no credible new evidence, the court concluded.) And now, with the state appeals just about exhausted, Abu-Jamal had turned his attention to the federal courts, where he was seeking what's called habeas corpus relief. Way back in 1982, when Abu-Jamal was unanimously sentenced to death by a jury that he helped pick, I never could have even imagined that seven years into the next century my family and I would still be taking time from our lives to attend appeals hearings.

This process is obscene in the way it taints the survivors' lives for so long. You can never move on. There's never any closure: just endless rounds of hearings and motions made by new batches of crusading attorneys. This case has now even tainted the lives of Danny's nieces and nephews, who were just little children when Abu-Jamal murdered Danny. It gets out that you are the niece or nephew of Danny Faulkner, and people treat you differently. Sometimes better, sometimes worse, but you can't get away from it. And now some of them will be standing in the courtroom in place of their uncles, who have lived their lives and passed on. And Jamal is still alive on death row writing books and mugging for the camera. It's all so wrong. And although mine is the most high-profile case, I am not the only survivor that has gone through this. I talk to victims all the time who are going through the exact same sort of thing I go through, appeal after appeal after appeal for technicalities, and always trying to get murderers off death row or out of prison.

The William H. Green Federal Courthouse is located on what is called Independence Mall at Sixth and Market Streets in Philadelphia. The Mall is home to the Liberty Bell and Independence Hall. The federal courthouse is a far cry from City Hall, located just nine blocks due west down Market Street. To begin, it's a modern office building, both formal and sterile at the same time. Also, although Judge Sabo did his best to control the antics of Abu-Jamal, the atmosphere of trial in 1982 and subsequent hearings often took on a circus atmosphere. Not federal court. I had been told to expect a no-nonsense, business atmosphere that would tolerate no shenanigans and that is what I found. Given the interest in the case, the Third Circuit used a ceremonial courtroom located on the first floor of the building instead of a normal, appellate courtroom. This was no doubt due to the over-flow crowd that had gathered. The courtroom was packed from the moment the federal marshals opened the doors first thing in the morning, and outside, several hundred Abu-Jamal supporters gathered in his name. They had all congregated at the Sixth Street entrance to the building. I entered around the corner, on Market Street, so as not to get caught in the crowd.

The case was heard by a three-judge panel, which for our case consisted of Chief Judge Anthony J. Scirica, who was appointed by President Reagan; Judge Thomas L. Ambro, appointed by President Clinton; and Judge Robert E. Cowen, also appointed by President Reagan. Judge Scirica was in the middle, and I sat directly opposite him in a seat reserved for me in the front row. They had afforded each side one hour for argument, beginning promptly at 9:30 a.m. To my right was the table for the Commonwealth, where Hugh Burns sat with Ronald Eisenberg, the deputy of the DA's law division, and Tom Dolgenos, the chief of the federal habeas unit. To my left were the Abu-Jamal defense lawyers, including Robert Bryan.

Joining me in the front two rows of the audience were a number of close friends. Of course, Paul was at my side. So was Trish Faulkner (Tommy Faulkner's wife), Maureen Faulkner (Danny's niece and Trish's daughter), Eileen Ware (Danny's niece and Trish's daughter), Debra Reed (Maureen Faulkner Jr.'s friend), Garry Bell (Danny's partner), Carol and Dan McCann (great friends to Danny and me), Grace Burns and Gracey Burns (prosecutor Hugh Burns's wife and daughter), Rich Costello, Mike Lutz, Joe McGill, and Michael Smerconish. Joe McGill was the prosecutor in the 1982 trial, whose conduct was the focus of those seeking to get Abu-Jamal's death sentence overturned. Again, the narrow issue on the death sentence was whether the jury had mistakenly believed that it had to agree unanimously on any mitigating circumstances which might have led them to give Abu-Jamal life in prison, instead of a death sentence. While unanimous consent is required for aggravating circumstances, it is not required for mitigating circumstances. The Abu-Jamal defense was arguing that the jury verdict slip failed to distinguish the level of consent required as between the two. At a certain point in the hearing, I was listening to a back and forth as to how many words away from "mitigating" the word "unanimous" had appeared on the verdict slip. This was mind-boggling to me.

Twenty-five years after Danny was taken from me, and twenty-four years after a jury wasted no time in determining that Abu-Jamal did it and should himself die, and this was what they were arguing about? Frankly, as one who sat through the 1982 trial, and remembered well the short nature of their deliberations on sentencing (under four hours), I doubt any of this would have mattered. After hearing from the eyewitnesses to the murder and other trial witnesses, I don't care who was on that jury, they would have come in with the same verdict because it was so obvious that Abu-Jamal murdered Danny and he did it with premeditation.

Joe McGill's role during the Third Circuit argument was the same as mine—to sit silently while others argued about a matter of great importance to both of us. In my case, we were talking about the murder of my husband; in his case, the subject was his professional conduct as the prosecutor of Abu-Jamal. Several times I looked at him while there was argument about his jury selection, and whether he deliberately excluded African Americans, or whether the jury verdict slip had been misleading, and I thought how difficult it must be for him to sit silently. I was sure he was fighting some internal desire to jump up and make himself heard, as I know I was. In hearing after hearing, I have had to sit like a church mouse when I wished I could stand up and confront the lies used to defend the man who murdered Danny. Well, in the case of Joe McGill, I want to give him that chance right here, right now. Who better than him to offer an explanation of what was at stake in the case, and he shared his thinking with me on both the issue of whether blacks had been deliberately kept off the jury, and the construction of the jury verdict slip, as follows:

> Jury selection is a process in which the attempt is made to get a fair and equitable jury for the purposes of deciding the case, or another way of stating it is, to exclude any kind of juror who is unable to be fair. To facilitate that process, both the prosecution and the defense have plenty of opportunities to strike jurors basically for any reason as long as it is not an illegal reason. The process begins when a judge will come and instruct a panel of prospective jurors, and a panel in Philadelphia in the early 1980s could be as many as forty or fifty or even sixty. The judge will instruct the panel at length regarding their responsibilities, what they will have to do day-to-day, and whether they have any particular problems relative to service. The prosecution and the defense will then have the opportunity to ask questions of that panel in front of the other panelists,

to determine whether they will later ask them more questions individually to determine whether they can be fair. This was done in the Abu-Jamal case in 1982 and it was uneventful. I remember that in this case, it was several panels, and there were a lot of prospective jurors who were struck by one side or the other. You can be struck in two ways: you can be struck for "cause," which means for some reason you are unable to follow the law or you just simply could not be fair. That is what would be called striking for cause. Then there is a "peremptory" challenge, and that word means you can strike them for any reason whatsoever as long as it's not an illegal reason. In a capital case, you are permitted twenty peremptory challenges by Court Rule. When you have a highly visible case like the Abu-Jamal case, you need many strikes at your disposal because you can expect to get a lot of people that may have problems either with the death penalty or other reasons that prevent them from being fair and so sometimes it takes a long time to get a jury.

In this case, I didn't use all twenty strikes available to me. I used fifteen, so I had five additional challenges which I did not use. And I never struck anyone because of their race. If I were acting with a racist intent, or with a racial motivation, why would I have left five arrows in my quiver, so to speak, if I had African-American jurors? Presumably, I would have used some of those five remaining strikes to get rid of all minority jurors, right? Of course, the defense never seems to acknowledge that argument. And, as a matter of fact, the first juror that I chose—and that's out of the entire panel—the very first juror that I chose with many, many peremptories left, was an African American. And, as a matter of fact, the second juror I selected was also an African American but Jamal struck him. Now, Abu-Jamal has a right to strike him. I'm not saying he doesn't, but the fact is that the first two would have been African American. What this is *not* is an example of intentionally discriminating against black jurors. I went on to choose one additional African-American juror out of the first six, so you have six jurors on the front row and six jurors on the back row and of the six in that front row, fifty percent would have been African American had Jamal not struck one.

Ultimately, after the jury selection process and before the openings there were three African-American jurors chosen. We were about to start the opening arguments and there were three African-American jurors. But right before the opening there were hearings and there was a decision by the court and jointly agreed to by defense and myself that the first juror needed to be excused because she had violated the Court order of sequestration. That is the rule that the Court may order, upon motion by counsel, that requires jurors to remain in a hotel separated from the public and outside information. She, for a number of reasons, had violated that and the judge was upset and was concerned that she would do it in the future. It was a joint excuse. In the end, there were ten whites on the jury, and two blacks.

It was frustrating for me to sit and hear what was said about the jury selection process at the Third Circuit argument. The things that really upset me were the inaccurate statements about the process and my motivation. There was no discrimination against black jurors. You are not prohibited from striking black jurors; you just cannot strike a black juror because of his or her race, but there may be other reasons. Hugh Burns, who is the chief of appeals and who argued the case, did a tremendous job and was really in command of his facts and law and did an excellent job for the District Attorney's Office. But there were times when I really wanted to jump up and make some comments to try to clarify or say something.

As for the verdict slip, people need to understand that there is a place on all verdict slips for the jurors to note down whether or not they find that there are aggravating and/or mitigating circumstances from the evidence presented at the sentencing hearing as well as evidence that was incorporated into the hearing from the trial. That means in order for there to be a death sentence, there has to be one or more aggravating circumstances, and no mitigating circumstances; or one or more aggravating circumstances, and one or more mitigating circumstances—and that the aggravating circumstances outweigh the mitigating circumstances. The one in this case (aggravating circumstance) which is number one and most serious, killing of a police officer in the line of duty. As for mitigating circumstance, no criminal record is an example. For that matter there could be a number of other reasons. Mitigation really covers a broad spectrum. Examples include character testimony and employment, as long as it is presented as evidence.

The issue in front of the Third Circuit is really a very technical issue and that is whether or not the verdict slip, as it was set out, left the jury with the inference that they had to find mitigating circumstances. The law states that they would have to find aggravating circumstances unanimously. It does not say and it is not needed for the mitigating circumstances to be found unanimously by the jury. The whole situation comes down to how the words were written, believe it or not, how many words away from the word mitigating was the word unanimous. It comes down to a very technical basis. The bottom line is, was the jury confused? And as a result of being confused, did they somehow believe that there was a unanimous requirement for mitigating circumstances. But there have been decisions in other federal circuit courts which indicate that what the

Pennsylvania trial court did here was correct, and not confusing to the jury. There is even a Third Circuit decision that says so, even though there were later cases in the Third Circuit which said the opposite.

There is no question in my mind that the jurors knew exactly what they wanted to do based on the evidence. You could just tell, and that's why they were out so briefly. There was absolutely no confusion. The issue in the appeal was hyper-technical, and it's unfortunate that sometimes words can be used to override common sense. At no time did the trial judge say that the jurors had to be unanimous regarding mitigation. It's now being claimed that the word "unanimous" may be inferred because it was used earlier in a different context.

After the conclusion of the Third Circuit hearing, my family, Joe McGill, several friends, and I went to the FOP lodge so that I could respond to some media requests in a quiet environment. Joe, Trish Faulkner, two of her children, and I were seated at a long table, with a large group of radio and TV news crews opposite us. Their questions were initially directed towards Joe in reference to the relentless allegations made that morning by Abu-Jamal's attorneys, in which they accused Joe of being a racist and of having acted on his racism by systematically excluding blacks from the jury simply because of their color. They knew Joe had to be seething inside and they wanted him to open up. But calm is a Joe McGill trademark, and calmly as ever, Joe stuck to the facts about how, in direct contradiction to his alleged racist intentions, he had actually accepted four blacks to the jury, that he had five unused peremptory challenges that he could have used to exclude the four blacks he accepted had he wished to racially rig the jury, that Abu-Jamal himself had struck one of the black jurors Joe had accepted, and how another black juror accepted by him was released with the agreement of Abu-Jamal's attorney for violating sequestration after the trial had begun. As is always the case, Joe factually refuted each and every racially charged assertion that had been made.

After Joe had finished dismantling Abu-Jamal's attorneys' arguments, the reporters began to question me. I was asked about my feelings on how long it had taken to get to this point, and I mentioned how I had known many of them when this all started in 1981 and how we had all kind of grown old together waiting for the case to move forward. That comment drew a pained laugh from a few of the older folks in the group. Then I was asked if, given all the time that had passed, it wouldn't be better for me and my family if the Third Circuit decided to give Abu-Jamal life in prison (Life Without Parole or LWOP) and have this all end. This idea was not new. In the past I had often thought of or been asked by friends about the same thing. I had never been asked this question in public, but I knew my answer before the reporter had finished the question. I explained that I was wise enough to know that in our legal system, LWOP is not what it seems. I explained to the reporters that unless Jamal is executed, my family and I will have to live every day of the rest of our lives knowing that a future governor could set Jamal free with the stroke of a pen, and that I had no doubt that Jamal's misguided and uninformed supporters and friends would relentlessly lie about the facts to future generations in order to perpetuate the myth that Jamal is a victim of a racist justice system, then demand his release. To support this idea, I noted that over the years I had repeatedly seen governors commute the sentences of murderers—especially those who had grown old in prison—simply because they cut a sympathetic image of a harmless old man, a grandfatherly type, with grown children and grandchildren, or someone who was terminally ill, a person who committed a crime in a bygone day who had been "punished enough." One such case in Louisiana stuck in my mind as the murderer was greeted by his children and grandchildren in Los Angles after his release. I told them I wanted to be certain that Jamal could never be free again—that he would die alone in prison away from his family like Danny had died alone on the street on December 9. I also explained that first degree murder—the crime that Jamal had been unanimously convicted of by a jury of his own choosing—is different from any other crime. I told them that in my heart, I firmly believe that a person who knowingly and violently takes the life of another person, especially a police officer, should forfeit their own life. We owe that to our law enforcement officials, the knowledge that criminals know and see that if they choose to kill a police officer, they *will* forfeit their own life in return. Police officers need and deserve that protection.

After the press conference, I walked away feeling uplifted by the fact that I had not only expressed my desire to see Jamal executed, but that I had a chance to explain why I felt that way. I also felt good about expressing my feelings, as a survivor, about capital punishment and why my family and I need to see Jamal executed. I had thought long and hard about these things and I was comfortable with my feelings and my rational need for closure that all survivors have. Having put my feelings into words in public, I was more confident than ever in the righteousness of my struggle.

So where does all of this leave me today, as I draw near the twenty-sixth anniversary? As of this writing, I am awaiting the decision of the Third Circuit. Whatever that decision, it will not be the end of the road, as one side (or both) could ask the entire court to hear the case, and then the Supreme Court of the United States will certainly be approached. In the immediate decision, the Third Circuit could: 1) reverse Judge Yohn with regard to the death sentence but uphold his denial of a new trial, which would reinstate the death sentence; 2) uphold Judge Yohn on everything, which would result in a new sentencing hearing; 3) grant a new trial to Abu-Jamal; or 4) send the case back to Yohn for further proceedings. Some will no doubt say I am fighting in vain given the national mood regarding the death penalty, and in particular, the trends in Pennsylvania. In the last seven years in Pennsylvania, an estimated fifty inmates who were facing execution have gotten new leases on life behind bars as state and federal judges overturn death sentences at a rate that is buoying opponents of capital punishment and infuriating prosecutors. Since the death penalty was reinstated in Pennsylvania in 1978, only three individuals have had a death sentence carried out and each of them asked for it![370] I am fighting for a jury sentence to be carried out in a state that for all practical purposes has no death penalty. Still, the only thing I know for sure is that my sequel will continue to run until the process finally grinds to a halt. There is nothing more frightening to me than the thought of Mumia Abu-Jamal alive and maybe even walking the earth a free and dangerous man, and in Danny's name, I will never allow that to occur.

ACKNOWLEDGMENTS

Maureen Faulkner

When I first met my co-author, Michael Smerconish, I was desperately try-ing to beat back the lies about Danny's murder that were spreading like wildfire. Michael saw that I needed help and without hesitation he stepped beside me. From that day on, without fail, he has been there for me when I needed him.

I have so many things to thank him for the list seems like it could go on for pages. But first, I have to thank him and his beautiful and gracious wife Lavinia, their children, and Winston—God rest his soul—for wel-coming me into their lives and for sharing him with me. Michael has been my voice when I was not able to speak for myself and has helped me un-derstand how to wage my battle against those who would say and do any-thing to free Danny's killer. He has introduced me to so many generous and supportive people and has brought his friends and listeners to my aid. He has used his talent and influence over the airwaves to get my story out and has countered the misinformation that flourished before he arrived with a constant drumbeat of truth and fact. He embraced and cared about Danny's family, never doing anything without first considering how it might affect them. His patience and understanding were unwavering when I was upset, and he helped me find the inner strength to believe in myself and in the righteousness of my cause. For all these things I will be forever grateful.

Most importantly though, I have to thank Michael for dedicating three years of his life to help me fulfill my dream of telling my story in writing so the world can never forget that on a cold December morning in 1981 a young Philadelphia police officer was brutally murdered and left dead on the frozen pavement and that his name was Danny Faulkner.

Michael Smerconish

My heartfelt and grateful thanks to the family and friends of Danny Faulkner who were invaluable in helping me in my effort to tell his tragic story, especially his close friends Bill Dorsch, Hugh Gallagher, Thom Hoban, Ed Kelly, Danny McCann, Ed McGrory, Jude McKenna, Mike McCullough, Mike Petrucci, and Dan Sobolewski. All took the time to speak with me personally. Along with Maureen, they are Danny's living memorial. Rich Costello from the Fraternal Order of Police was also kind in taking time to review an early draft of the manuscript and offer his suggestions as well.

A very sincere thank you to each of the following whose assistance has been invaluable.

James E. Beasley, Esquire, left this earth on September 18, 2004. He was one of the best trial lawyers of his generation and he was my boss. Jim always knew of the amount of time I was dedicating on a pro bono basis to Maureen Faulkner one door down from his office, and he never complained. He was always supportive of whatever I believed necessary to tell her story. I miss him greatly and think of him often.

Josh Belfer is a high school student in suburban Philadelphia who is wise beyond his years. His legwork was terrific. Remember his name.

Lauren Rose Bennett is a brilliant University of Pennsylvania Law School student whose father is a former legal colleague of mine. She was invaluable in focusing the later drafts of the manuscript, tightening the language and fine-tuning the research.

Grace Blazer was the program director of my radio station, the Big Talker, 1210-AM, WPHT. I thank her for always permitting me to speak my mind about this case over the span of many years on the radio, and for being a good friend to Maureen Faulkner. I will never forget her support in accompanying me to Antioch College where I did a live radio broadcast. In similar fashion, David Yadgaroff and Mike Baldini, the radio station brass, have always been equally supportive of my efforts on behalf of Maureen Faulkner, most of which have emanated from their airwaves, and I thank them, too.

Hugh J. Burns Jr., chief of the appeals unit of the District Attorney's Office in Philadelphia, is one of Maureen Faulkner's greatest champions. Hugh has worked tirelessly to successfully protect the conviction that was won by Joseph McGill. He was invaluable to me in ensuring that the representation of Abu-Jamal's court activities are properly reflected herein.

Alexandra Carella is yet another exceptional high school student who has provided tremendous support for many of my radio endeavors and this manuscript, for which I am grateful.

Patrick Carney, a St. Joseph's University student, was very helpful with research for this book. One of his professors, Sal Paolantonio, told me he was a hard-working and gifted young man, proving that Sal can spot talent on the gridiron *and* in the classroom.

Patrick Faulkner, Danny's brother, was especially helpful in giving me family history and unique insights into the man we lost.

Bart Feroe has been a wonderful supporter of each of my manuscripts, always content to remain quietly in the backdrop while willing and able to serve upon request.

Dan Giancaterino is an Internet librarian who hangs his hat at the Jenkins Law Library in Philadelphia. He's a master at finding any and everything that exists in cyberspace. His skills were reserved for the truly troublesome search issues, and when called upon, he never disappointed, for which I am grateful.

Ben Haney, the pride of St. Joseph's Prep and Notre Dame, spent a summer doing research for this project and brought not only a keen intellect to the job but, also, a passion for the cause that cannot be taught.

George Hiltzik represents me in the world of broadcasting. I am fortunate to have such a macher in my corner. I might not be a yiddisher kop but even goyim like me can recognize that George is a mensch.

Gavin Johnson is headed for Bucknell University as of this writing; he is another late edition who provided some much-appreciated fact-checking.

Michael Katz is a former legal colleague who was selfless in support of Justice for P/O Daniel Faulkner, our not-for-profit, which Maureen created to provide scholarship monies for the children of murder victims. For a period of years, it was Michael who kept all of the paperwork in order and, like me, provided counsel on a pro bono basis.

Cathy Kelley spoke to me about being the young policewoman whose unhappy task it was to notify Maureen that her husband had been shot, but in following orders, was unable to tell her he did not survive.

Larry Kirshbaum is the former president of Warner Books and now the literary agent who represented me on this project. His stellar reputation in the publishing field is well deserved and I was humbled by his willingness to undertake my representation. He saw the merit of this project from our first meeting and I appreciate his ability to see it to fruition.

Anthony Mazzarelli is both a doctor and a lawyer who once interned for me. Now he has a medical practice and radio show of his own but, before he was his own man, he did great legwork on this project.

Stuart McCormick is a Drexel University student on whom I relied to ensure that my quotations of witness statements and trial testimony were 100 percent accurate. I appreciate his thorough efforts.

John McDonald is yet another of this talented pool of young people who surround me. He is an exceptional researcher and writer who was a latecomer to this project, but a welcome addition.

Joseph McGill is the former assistant district attorney who successfully prosecuted Abu-Jamal for murder in 1982. What can I say? He did an exceptional job back in 1982 and has never wavered in his devotion to justice.

Mary Russel was my former secretary at the Beasley Law Firm. Although she has retired from the firm, and I have changed careers, we continue to connect through special projects such as this. She is not merely a typist. She is a trusted friend with a keen eye for the grammatically incorrect whose judgment is valued by both Maureen Faulkner and me. So, too, is her support over the span of many years for, as I have been given the public thanks for assisting Maureen, it was often she who had done the work.

Kurt Schreyer is a University of Pennsylvania PhD candidate studying Shakespeare. Together we are writing a separate manuscript. While his role here was limited, it was in keeping with his superior abilities.

TC Scornavacchi is a Harvard-educated former teacher of my children in a Montessori school whom I was able to convince to join my radio team as my executive producer. Multi-tasking is a term created with her in mind. She can book the radio show, oversee my newspaper column, serve as a sounding board for books, and moonlight at QVC as an on-air talent, all in the course of a day—and routinely does just that.

Brittany Sharkey. Wait. Stop the press. She was a late, but invaluable addition to the team. She is a Georgetown senior who did essential fact-checking and footnote verification with great competency, and at a point where my eyes were cross from having spent too much time re-reading my own work. She came along at the perfect time. I am grateful for her willingness to plow into work that is important but mind-numbing, with such aplomb.

Alex Smith is a talented intern who provided thorough fact-checking during the last stages of the project. A recent graduate of Country Day School of the Sacred Heart, she will be heading off to Catholic University in the fall. Her dedicated efforts did not go unnoticed.

Buz Teacher is the man most responsible for me *ever* having become published and has remained my literary consigliere. I shall always remember fondly the night that he and his wife, Janet, presented my wife and me with the first copy ever printed of one of my hardbound books. That was a great thrill. So too was the day we had lunch as I received an e-mail telling me that this book would happen. He has been a constant source of inspiration for this particular manuscript.

C. Nathan Wood researched court decisions pertaining to this book while a law student at the University of Pennsylvania Law School, for which I am grateful.

Finally, thanks to the other contacts I made whose insight, guidance, and patience made this a reality but, for various reasons, shall go unnamed. I appreciate their friendship, support, and intellect.

APPENDIX

Statements of the Eyewitnesses

Investigation Interview Record
Name: Cynthia White
Date: December 9, 1981, 4:15 a.m.

I saw a Police Officer pull over a Volkswagen. One guy was in the Volkswagen. The Police Officer got out of the car and went over to the Volkswagen. When he got to the Volkswagen, the driver of the Volkswagen got out. They both walked towards the Police car. They got to the front of the car. Another guy came running out of the parking lot on Locust Street. He had a handgun in his hand. He fired the gun at the Police Officer about four or five times. The Police Officer fell to the ground. I started screaming. The guy who shot the Police Officer was sitting on the curb. The guy who got out of the Volkswagen was standing there. A Police wagon came from 12th Street, over Locust St. One of the Officers got out of the wagon and went over to the Police Officer. Other Police Officers arrived. I was trying to tell them who shot the Officer but they would not listen. The Police handcuffed the man who was sitting on the curb, the man who shot the Officer. . . .

Can you describe the guy who fired the gun?
He was a black male, short, in his 20's, he also wore his hair in dreadlocks . . .

. . .

Investigation Interview Record
Name: Michael M. Scanlan
Date: December 9, 1981, 4:24 a.m.

. . . I had stopped at the red light where the Club Whispers is located. I noticed the officer approach a black guy standing outside a car, in front of it. The Officer asked him a few questions and then he spread the guy across the car with his arms out, and the guy turned back around and swung at the Officer. The Officer pulled his billyclub out and swung hard at the guy, hitting him several times on the arm and back. The guy was bigger than the Officer. Then I noticed another black guy come running across the street towards the Officer and the guy he was hitting. Then the guy running across the street pulled out a pistol and started shooting at the Officer. He had the gun pointed at the Officer. He fired while he was running at the Officer, once, and the Officer fell down. Then he stood over the Officer and fired three or four more shots point-blank at the Officer on the ground. I looked around for another police-man and didn't see one so I took off in my car to look for one. . . .

By the time I got there, there were a lot of cars there. They had a guy in a Police van and asked me to take a look at him. I'm pretty sure the guy in the van was the one the Police Officer had first stopped and was fight-ing with. Thcant [*sic*] be positive however. But he did have the same type of hair style, like the MOVE hair style. The guy that shot the Officer had on either a red and yellow, or red yellow and black bright color sweater. I think he had a black hat on, too. The sweater was very distinguishable. . . .

Did you see the male's face, who shot the officer?
No I didn't, just the hat and the sweater.
. . .

Investigation Interview Record
Name: Robert E. Chobert
Date: December 9, 1981, 4:25 a.m.

. . . Did you see who shot him?
Yes.

Who shot him?
A black male. He had knotty hair like MOVE members and it's long, he is dark-complexioned and he is kind of heavy-set. He was about six foot tall and he was wearing a light tan shirt and jeans.

I stopped as soon as I crossed 13th Street and I was letting out my fare. It was a lady. She got out and walked back toward 13th and Broad Streets. I was writing down on my pad how much the fare was. Then I heard a shot. I looked up and I saw the cop who was on the pavement next to his car, his car was parked a little in front of my car. I saw the cop fall to the ground when I looked up and I saw this black male stand over the cop and shoot him a couple more times. Then I saw the black male start running towards 12th Street. He didn't get far, maybe thirty or thirty-five steps, and then he fell. They got him. The cops got him and stuck him in the back of a wagon.

When the police first arrived, they told me to get back in my cab. I got back in the cab. Then an officer came over to me and asked me if I saw the man that did the shooting again, would I be able to recognize him. I told him yes. Then he took me over to the wagon, opened the door and I saw the male in the back of the wagon, and I told the officer it was him that I saw do the shooting.

. . .

Investigation Interview Record
Name: Albert Magilton
Date: December 9, 1981, 5:35 a.m.

. . . [T]his Officer pulled a Volkswagen over at 13th and Locust. He got out of his car. The driver of the Volkswagen got out of his car, from the driver's side. The Officer walked the driver over to the pavement. I noticed a guy walking from the parking lot, across the street. I turned around and the next thing I know is, I heard some shots. I looked and saw the Officer on the ground. The driver of the Volkswagen just stood there. The Police came up and picked the officer up. Other Officers stopped the driver of the Volkswagen. The Police placed the Officer that was shot in the back of the paddy wagon. The Police had the driver of the Volkswagen and another male handcuffed. They held the driver of the Volkswagen there and took the other male away in the wagon.

. . .

Investigation Interview Record
Name: Robert Harkins Jr.
Date: December 9, 1981, 6 a.m.

. . . I was approaching 13th Street when I observed a police car with its dome lights on. And then I looked over and observed a police officer grab a guy. The guy then spun around and the officer went to the ground. He had his hands on the ground and then rolled over. At this time the male who was standing over the officer pointed a gun at the officer and fired one shot, and then he fired a second shot. At this time the officer moved a little and then went flat to the ground. I heard a total of three shots and saw what appeared to me to be three flashes from the gun of the man standing over the officer.

. . .

Interviewed: Priscilla Durham (Security Officer)
Place: Room 109, Main Building, Jefferson Hospital
Time: 2:16 a.m.
Date: December 19, 1981

Miss Priscilla Durham was interviewed by Investigators Bartelle and Begley and she stated that: On December 9, 1981, she was outside the office of the Emergency Room clerk when Abu-Jamal was brought in by the police. She stated he was on the floor with his body half out of the Emergency Room and half in the Emergency Room. She stated the police asked her where they can take him, meaning Jamal. Miss Durham stated she told the police that they can put him back in the Family Room. Miss Durham stated the police took him to the Family Room and about 10 minutes later Mrs. Keating and two doctors went to the Family Room and said that Abu-Jamal needed treatment. She stated the police then took Abu-Jamal to the Cardiac Room.

Miss Durham also stated when Jamal was first brought in and was lying on the floor, she noticed he was bleeding. Miss Durham also stated that Jamal shouted "Yeh, I shot the motherfucker, and I hope he dies."

Excerpts from the Trial Transcript

Trial Testimony of Reginald Thompson
June 19, 1982
Reginald Thompson is the policeman who summarized the Police Audio Log from the night Danny Faulkner was murdered.

Mr. McGill: Mr. Thompson, would you take a look at those—only the top portion of that transcript. Do you see that, sir?
Reginald Thompson: Yes, I do.
McGill: Can you identify that?
RT: Yes.
McGill: What is it?
RT: That's the conversation that went on between me and 612 car on that given night.
McGill: Mr. Thompson, sir, could you read what it was that was played? Okay. "612—
McGill: All right, I said that the wrong way. First of all, say who said it, then say what was said, and then do that for the next person.
RT: OK. This is radio patrol car coming in, 612. Then it's my voice, 12. Then it's patrol car 612 again, I have a car stopped ah 12, 13th and Locust.
　　Radio: Car to back 612, 13th and Locust.
　　RPC: On second though [sic] send me a wagon 1234 Locust.
　　Radio: 601.
　　EPW: Yeah 01 okay, 1234 Locust.
　　RPC: 22 I'll take a ride over.
　　Radio: Okay.
McGill: Okay, that's good enough. Cross examine—by the way, when you say patrol car 612 you mean—that was Officer Faulkner?

RT: Yes, sir.

Trial Testimony of Robert Chobert
June 19, 1982
Mr. Chobert was an eyewitness to the murder.

Mr. McGill: What did you observe, what happened?

Robert Chobert: Well, I let my fare out and I'm marking down on my pad how much it was, and then I heard a shot. I looked up, I saw the cop fall to the ground, and then I saw Jamal standing over him and firing some more shots into him.

McGill: Now, you used the word and name Jamal. I'll ask you this: How many times did you see that individual shooting the Police Officer when he was on the ground after he had fallen down?

RC: What was that again, please?

McGill: You said you heard a shot; is that right?

RC: Yes.

McGill: You looked up, and what did you see the officer do?

RC: I saw the officer fall.

McGill: And then what did you see happen? Just say what you saw happen then.

RC: I saw him shoot him again several more times.

McGill: Several more times?

RC: Yes.

McGill: Now, what then did you see that you referred to as the shooter do?

RC: Then I saw him walking back about ten feet and he just fell by the curb.

McGill: All right, and then what happened?

RC: Then I got—I started getting out of my cab, I started walking to the cop to see if I could help him, and then all of a sudden Police Officers came and told me to get back into my cab.

McGill: All right, and what did you see? Did you see the man at the curb any more, or what did they do to the man at the curb?

RC: They just stuck him in a wagon.

McGill: And where did you say you went?

RC: I went back and got in my cab.

McGill: And what then happened?

RC: And a couple—about—a couple minutes later a police officer came over and asked me if I seen this thing.

McGill: What did you say?

RC: I said yes, I did. He said, Did you see the guy that shot the cop; and I said, yes.

McGill: You have to speak up loud. You may be a little nervous, speak up loud so I can hear you. The officer came to you and asked what?

RC: If I saw what happened, and I told him yes.

McGill: And then what?

RC: Then he asked me if I ever see the guy again, would I know him. I said yes, I would. They took me over to the wagon and asked me, is that the guy. I said yes, it is.

. . .

McGill: Now this individual, sir, that you saw shooting the officer, would you look around the Courtroom and tell me if you see if he is in the Courtroom?

RC: Yes, he is.

McGill: Will you point him out?

RC: He's right there (indicating).

McGill: Would you describe what he has on?

RC: What he got on now?

McGill: Yes.

RC: He has a long shirt, a tee shirt, and a beard and long natty hair.

McGill: Is there any doubt in your mind at all that that man is the man who shot the officer?

RC: That's the man all right. I got no doubt.

Trial Testimony of Robert Shoemaker
June 19, 1982
Robert Shoemaker was the first police officer to arrive on the scene.

Mr. McGill: All right, Officer, do not tell us what the cab driver said, but as a result of what the driver said, all right, what did you do?

Robert Shoemaker: We proceeded westbound on Locust Street, like I said, the wrong way, till we came upon—I saw Officer Faulkner's overhead lights from his car. I stopped approximately two car lengths from his car. I exited the wagon and started to walk between two cars with my gun drawn, a Volkswagen which was on my right, and a Ford, a dark colored Ford, which was on my left. As I proceeded between the two cars, I observed Mr. Jamal sitting on the very end of the curb with his feet in the street, his right arm was crossing his chest, his left hand was approximately six inches from his leg on the ground. I ordered the male to freeze. We made eye contact probably about the same time, and the male did not freeze, his arm started to move to the left. Now at this point I couldn't see what he was reaching for, if he was reaching for anything at all, so I adjusted my stance and I took one side step to the left. At this point I saw a two-inch revolver approximately eight inches from his hand. I again ordered the male to freeze, which he did not, so before he grabbed the gun I kicked the male away from the gun. My heel contacted his throat area and the sole of my shoe hit him on the face. As the male fell backwards he yelled twice, "I'm shot, I'm shot." Still, with my revolver trained on him, I stepped over on top of the male and I kicked the revolver with my right foot away from him to the right. At this point I yelled to my partner to watch this male. At this time I walked over to Officer Faulkner who was lying on his back unconscious bleeding very heavily. He was approximately four feet from the Defendant. Myself and two or three other officers lifted Danny up. We tried to put him in one of those small Horizon cars that we have now on the street, but we couldn't fit him in the car so we took him in a waiting Police wagon, and we put him in the wagon and the wagon took him to the hospital.

McGill: Now, were you the first officer on the scene?

RS: That is correct.

Trial Testimony of Joseph Kohn
June 25, 1982
Joseph Kohn was the manager of the gun department at a sporting goods store in Philadelphia who sold Abu-Jamal the gun he used to murder Daniel Faulkner.

Mr. Jackson: So you don't know that he's the man, do you?

Joseph Kohn: I know that he is the man I sold the weapon to.

Jackson: You know he is?

JK: Yes, sir.

Jackson: How do you know he is the man?

JK: Just like if you would come into my store and buy a weapon, came in two weeks, three weeks or a year later I would remember you.

. . .

Jackson: So, you're saying even though his hair was different and he now has a beard you're sure he's the same person?

JK: Yes, sir.

Trial Testimony of Cynthia White
June 21, 1982
Cynthia White was an eyewitness to the murder.

Mr. McGill: Now, Miss White, I'm directing your attention to December 9, 1981. Do you recall that night?

Cynthia White: Yes.

McGill: On that night at some time shortly before 4:00 a.m. where were you?

CW: On the corner of 13th and Locust.

. . .

McGill: Do you know what corner that was?

CW: Southeast.

McGill: And would you tell the jury exactly what you saw occur?

CW: I was standing on the corner and I noticed the lights on top of the police car and the spotlight in the Volkeswagen [*sic*] was in front of the police car, and they were pulling over to the side of Locust Street. The policeman got out of the car and walked—started walking over towards the Volkswagen [*sic*]. The driver of the Volkswagen [*sic*] got out of the car. A few words passed. They both walked between the police car and the Volkswagen [*sic*] up to the sidewalk. A few more words passed again between them. The driver of the Volkeswagen [*sic*] then struck the police officer with a closed fist to his cheek, and the police turned the driver of the Volkswagen [*sic*] around in a position to handcuff him.

. . .

I looked across the street in the parking lot and I noticed he was running out of the parking lot and he was practically on the curb when he shot two times at the Police Officer. It was the back. The police officer turned around and staggered and seemed like he was grabbing for something. Then he fell. Then he came over and he came on top of the police officer and shot some more times. After that he went over and he slouched down and he sat on the curb.

. . .

McGill: Okay. Now, you mentioned the name and also you pointed a few times. I'll ask you, the man who shot the police officer, Miss White, the man who shot the police officer both in the back and also when he was standing over him, is he in this courtroom?

CW: Yes.

McGill: Would you point him out? Would you tell me what he's wearing?

CW: Striped shirt.

McGill: Is there any doubt in your mind at all that this is the man who shot the police officer?

CW: No, there's not.

Trial Testimony of Priscilla Durham
June 24, 1982

Priscilla Durham was employed by Jefferson Hospital where both Abu-Jamal and Danny were taken after the shooting and heard Abu-Jamal confess to the murder.

Mr. McGill: Now, on that particular day in the early morning hours sometime between four and five a.m. did you have occasion to observe anything unusual in reference to this case?

Priscilla Durham: Yes. I observed Mr. Jamal when he was brought into the Emergency Room.

McGill: And explain exactly what happened and then just basically let the jury know exactly what you observed.

PD: Well, approximately the same time that Jamal was brought into the emergency area I was inside the emergency area behind the double doors. The double doors opened just as Jamal was placed on the mat leading into the Emergency Room treatment area. At this time, I didn't know—all I did was hear him say, "I shot the mother fucker [*sic*] and I hope the mother fucker [*sic*] dies." And it was at this time that I realized who it was in reference to, what was going on.

. . .

Mr. Jackson: Did you know Officer Faulkner?
PD: No, I did not. I—
Jackson: Did you—I'm sorry.
PD: I've seen him several times.
Jackson: Where?
PD: In the hospital.
Jackson: Speak to him before?
PD: As a matter of fact, I had spoke to him about two hours prior to his death.
Jackson: What did you talk about?
PD: Officer Faulkner had just brought in a little seven-year old, I believe she was a seven-year old black rape victim. He apprehended the suspect.

Trial Testimony of Detective Robert Sobolusky
June 24, 1982
Detective Sobolusky identified physical evidence that he seized from Abu-Jamal.

Mr. McGill: Is that the property receipt in connection with the clothing that you seized from the defendant?
Robert Sobolusky: Yes it is.
McGill: Now, would you take that—first of all, identify what you just took out.
RS: A leather holster, shoulder holster.

. . .

McGill: Where did you seize that?
RS: From the defendant.
McGill: Are you able to identify the defendant?
RS: Oh yes.
McGill: Your Honor, at this point, again, there is a stipulation between Mr. Jackson and myself that if Mr. Mumia Abu-Jamal was here, this detective would identify Mr. Jamal as the defendant, as the individual he took the holster from.

Trial Testimony of Michael M. Scanlan
June 25, 1982
Mr. Scanlan was an eyewitness to the murder.

Mr. McGill: What did you observe the officer and this man do?
Michael Scanlan: They were talking. The black man spread-eagle in front of the car, and while he was spread-eagle he swung around and struck the officer in the face with his fist.
McGill: All right. And at that time what then did you observe?
MS: At that point, the officer reacted, trying to subdue the gentleman, and during that time another man came running out from a parking lot across the street towards the officer and the gentleman in front of the police car.
McGill: And what happened?
MS: I saw a hand come up, like this, and I heard a gunshot. There was another gunshot when the man got to the policeman, and the gentleman he had been talking to. And then the officer fell down on the sidewalk and the man walked over and was standing at his feet and shot him twice. I saw two flashes.
McGill: Do you know whether or not any of these shots hit the officer?
MS: Yes sir. I could see that one hit the officer in the face. Because his body jerked, his whole body jerked.
(N.T. 6/25/82, 8.8)

Trial Testimony of Albert Magilton
June 25, 1982
Mr. Magilton was an eyewitness to the murder.

Mr. McGill: And what was this man doing, or this person doing, when he was coming from the parking lot?
Albert Magilton: He was sort of like moving across the—across the street fast, and he had his hands back behind his back.
. . .
McGill: You don't have to come down here. Just indicate to the jury what you mean by his hands behind his back.
AM: He had his hands back like that there.
McGill: Indicating his—
AM: His right arm.
McGill:—right arm.
AM: Towards the back, such like that.
McGill: Sort of cupped?
AM: Yes.
McGill: Behind, on his right side in the direction of his bac [*sic*], more on his back than on his side?

AM: Yes, sir.

McGill: And what did you observe this man doing?

AM: He was moving across the street towards where the officer had stopped the Volkswagen. And—

. . .

McGill: Did you have occasion to identify him at a pre-trial hearing a few weeks ago?

AM: Yes, I did.

McGill: And at that point, where was he seated?

AM: He was sitting next to that gentleman there. While I was—I believe he was sitting in that chair where that gentleman is sitting.

McGill: And this gentleman was sitting where?

AM: He was sitting next to him on his right.

Mr. Jackson: There's a stipulation.

McGill: Your Honor, there's a stipulation. The same stipulation that if the defendant were here, Mr. Magilton would identify him as the man he saw running across the street.

Trial Testimony of Garry Bell
June 24, 1982

Garry Bell was Daniel Faulkner's partner who was not with him at the time of the shooting but rushed to the hospital as the police van was taking him there.

Mr. McGill: All right. And what then occurred?

Garry Bell: I watched for several minutes and I heard from—I don't know who said it—somebody behind me said they were bringing in the guy that shot him. And I turned and several officers brought a male in and laid him on the floor in the hospital just inside the doors.

McGill: Now before they did that you were where? Before that—did you see them bring him in, or just hear they brought him in?

GB: I didn't see actually them bringing him in.

McGill: Okay. And you were with Officer Faulkner, in the room where he was?

GB: That's correct.

McGill: Where he was being attended. Okay. At that time when they brought this man in what did you then do?

GB: I walked over to him. I wanted to see who did it, who shot him. And I looked at him and he looked up at me. He said, "I shot that mother fucker [*sic*] and I hope the mother fucker [*sic*] dies." Those were his exact words to me.

McGill: What did you do?

GB: I said something back to him. I said, "He shouldn't be the one that dies, you should."

Trial Testimony of Anthony Paul
June 23, 1982
Anthony Paul was a prosecution ballistics expert.

Mr. Jackson: Now, if I understand you correctly, the only bullet that you've been able to positively identify is a bullet that was removed from Mr. Jamal. You can positively identify that bullet as coming from C-23; is that correct?

Anthony Paul: That's correct, sir.

Jackson: Now, when you're saying positively I still understand you to say that you're not necessarily saying 100 percent certain but maybe 99 percent; is that fair?

AP: No—well, I'm saying that it came from that gun.

Jackson: Is that fair? No question about it in your mind?

AP: No question about it in my mind.

Jackson: Now with regard to the other bullets that were in Officer Faulkner, you can't tell which weapon it came from; is that right?

AP: That's correct.

Jackson: Now, you indicated on direct examination that the bullet was fired from a gun—well, let me strike that. You first indicate that the markings, the striations, the lands and grooves and all of that, were indeterminable.

AP: That's correct.

Jackson: Would you explain to us—because it seems like I can't reconcile the two things—when you say that it's indeterminable yet it's similar, to get you to believe that it may have fired from a Charter Arms, if it's indeterminable, how can you tell that it may have been fired from a Charter Arms?

AP: Okay. When you look at the bullet specimen itself you will find that the individual significance of the specimen, the individual striations that were engraved that would permit me or permit the Firearms Examiner to say that a specific firearm discharged it, those individual characteristics are gone.

Jackson: Right.

AP: The general characteristics being part of the eight lands and grooves with a right-hand direction of twist, you have a part of that still exposed with sufficient quantity to be able to say that a firearm rifled with eight lands and grooves with a right-hand direction of twist discharged that projectile. But you can't say which firearm with eight lands and grooves fired that projectile. Is that clear?

Jackson: Yes, I understand sir. A Charter Arms has eight lands and grooves; is that correct?

AP: Yes.

Trial Testimony of Dr. Paul Hoyer
June 25, 1982
Dr. Hoyer performed Daniel Faulkner's autopsy.

Mr. McGill: Doctor, on December the 9th, 1981, did you conduct a post-mortem examination on the deceased in this case? Officer Faulkner.
Paul Hoyer: Yes, I did.
. . .
McGill: In connection with what you have referred to as your external examination, in reference to the post-mortem examination did you determine whether there were any remarkable findings in reference to injuries, external evidence of injury?
PH: Yes I did.
McGill: Would you indicate to the jury, please what they were?
The most important injury was that I found two gunshot wounds, one on the face which did not exit and one in the back that did—
. . .
McGill: Go on in terms of the external evidence of injury.
PH: External evidence of injury, on the face, five inches below the top of the head and quarter inch to the left of the midline there is a gunshot wound of entrance, five/sixteen inch high and wide. So there is a gunshot wound of entrance here on the side of the nose. There is a 5½ inch wide, 8 inch high area of focal thermal burns and mechanical injuries from unburned and partially burned powder particles centered about the entrance wound. This is powder stipple. I told you this is evidence of a gun being within about 20 inches of the target.

Trial Testimony of Dr. Charles Tumosa
June 26, 1982
Dr. Tumosa was Supervisor of the Criminalist Unit for the City of Philadelphia.

Mr. McGill: Did you make any kind of findings in relation to any comparison of the primer lead around that particular hole?
Charles Tumosa: Yes.
McGill: What were your results in reference to those?
CT: We determined that the weapon must have been twelve inches or less when discharged.
. . .
McGill: Doctor Tumosa, I am going to now refer you to the jacket that was supposedly Officer Faulkner's jacket. I believe you indicated that without any question the muzzle-to-jacket distance was within twelve inches; is that correct?
CT: That is correct.

McGill: Could it have been two and a half feet away?

CT: No, sir.

McGill: What about six feet away?

CT: No, sir.

McGill: You are certain of that?

CT: Yes, sir. The hole in the back is less than one foot, probably closer to nine to six inches.

ENDNOTES

Foreword

[1] Bill Marsh, "People Stop Fighting Philadelphia City Hall," *New York Times*, July 25, 2006.

[2] Mumia Abu-Jamal, "I for One Feel Like Putting Down My Pen. Let's Write Epitaphs for Pigs!," *The Black Panther*, Apr. 18, 1970.

Chapter 2

[3] Robert J. Terry, Michael A. Hobbs, and Marc Shogol, "Policeman Shot to Death; Radio Newsman Charged," *Philadelphia Inquirer*, Dec. 10, 1981.

[4] Fredric N. Tulsky, "Officers Say Abu-Jamal Hit a Pole," *Philadelphia Inquirer*, June 4, 1982.

[5] David Holmberg, "Judge Tells Jamal Testimony Stands," *Philadelphia Daily News*, June 5, 1982.

[6] Fredric N. Tulsky, "Abu-Jamal's Pre-Trial Plea Refused," *Philadelphia Inquirer*, June 5, 1982.

[7] "Cop Shot to Death; Newsman Arrested; Mumia Abu-Jamal Held in Killing," *Philadelphia Daily News*, Dec. 9, 1981.

[8] Tom Schmidt, "Cop Fatally Shot; Suspect Held," *Philadelphia Daily News*, Dec. 9, 1981.

[9] Ibid.

[10] Ibid.

[11] Ibid.

[12] Terry E. Johnson and Michael A. Hobbs, "The Suspect: One Who Raised His Voice," *Philadelphia Inquirer*, Dec. 10, 1981.

[13] Russell Cooke, "The Victim: One Who Won Citations," *Philadelphia Inquirer*, Dec. 10, 1981.

[14] Mike Freeman and Scott Heimer, "Slain Officer Was 'Tops' with Police, Neighbors," *Philadelphia Daily News*, Dec. 9, 1981.

[15] Ibid.

[16] Tom Infield, Michael D. Schaffer, and Richard Esposito, "Slain Policeman Had No Chance, Eye-Witness Says," *Evening Bulletin*, Dec. 10, 1981.

[17] "Black Newsmen Will Stand by Their President," *Philadelphia Journal*, Dec. 10, 1981.

[18] Tom Infield and Richard Esposito, "Murder Suspect Backed," *Evening Bulletin*, Dec. 11, 1981.

[19] Dorothy Storck, "A Killing Put in Perspective," *Philadelphia Inquirer*, Dec. 13, 1981.

Chapter 3

[20] Bonne L. Cook, "1,000 Mourn Policeman," *Evening Bulletin*, Dec. 15, 1981.

[21] Frank Dougherty, "Dead Too Early . . . Hundreds Honor Slain Officer," *Philadelphia Daily News*, Dec. 15, 1981.

[22] Ibid.

Chapter 4

[23] Sworn Testimony of Reginald Thompson, Police Dispatcher, *Cmwlth. of Pa. v. Abu-Jamal* (N.T. 6/19/82, 106).

[24] David Holmberg, "Why Did Slain Officer Stop Killer's Brother?," *Philadelphia Inquirer*, July 6, 1982.

[25] Sworn Testimony of Reginald Thompson, Police Dispatcher, *Cmwlth. of Pa. v. Abu-Jamal* (N.T. 6/19/82, 106).

[26] Sworn Testimony of Michael M. Scanlan, Witness, *Cmwlth. of Pa. v. Abu-Jamal* (N.T. 6/25/82, 8.18).

[27] Ibid., 8.6; Sworn Testimony of Cynthia White, Witness, *Cmwlth. of Pa. v. Abu-Jamal* (N.T. 6/21/82, 4.93).

[28] Mumia Abu-Jamal, "I for One Feel Like Putting Down My Pen. Let's Write Epitaphs for Pigs!," *The Black Panther*, Apr. 18, 1970.

[29] Sworn Testimony of Joseph Kohn, Gun Department Manager, Pearson's Sporting Goods, Philadelphia, *Cmwlth. of Pa. v. Abu-Jamal* (N.T. 6/21/82, 4.32–4.37).

[30] Sworn Testimony of Cynthia White, Witness, *Cmwlth. of Pa. v. Abu-Jamal* (N.T. 6/21/82, 4.93–4.105); Sworn Testimony of Robert Chobert, Witness, *Cmwlth. of Pa. v. Abu-Jamal* (N.T. 6/19/82, 210–16, 233–34, 255).

[31] Sworn Testimony of Robert Harkins, Witness, *Cmwlth. of Pa. v. Abu-Jamal, PCRA Hearing* (N.T. 8/2/95, 205–28).

[32] Sworn Testimony of Michael M. Scanlan, Witness, *Cmwlth. of Pa. v. Abu-Jamal* (N.T. 6/25/82, 8.62–8.63); David Holmberg, "Witness: Faulkner Hit Abu-Jamal Before Shooting," *Philadelphia Daily News*, June 25, 1982.

[33] Sworn Testimony of Albert Magilton, Witness, *Cmwlth. of Pa. v. Abu-Jamal* (N.T. 6/25/82, 8.75–8.79, 8.88–8.89, 8.102); David Holmberg, "Abu-Jamal Defense Opens," *Philadelphia Daily News*, June 28, 1982.

[34] Sworn Testimony of Anthony Paul, Supervisor, Firearms Identification Unit, Philadelphia Police Department, *Cmwlth. of Pa. v. Abu-Jamal* (N.T. 6/23/82, 6.96–6.100, 6.167–6.168).

35 Ibid., 6.96–6.115, 6.167–6.168; Marc Kaufman, "Abu-Jamal's Wound Tied to Officer," *Philadelphia Inquirer*, June 24, 1982.

36 Sworn Testimony of Dr. Paul Hoyer, Assistant Medical Examiner, *Cmwlth. of Pa. v. Abu-Jamal* (N.T. 6/25/82, 8.164–8.166); Marc Kaufman, "Faulkner Struck Abu-Jamal's Brother, Witness Says," *Philadelphia Inquirer*, June 26, 1982.

37 Sworn Testimony of Charles Tumosa, Criminalist for the City of Philadelphia, *Cmwlth. of Pa. v. Abu-Jamal* (N.T. 6/26/82, 15–32); Marc Kaufman, "Abu-Jamal Defense to Begin Case," *Philadelphia Inquirer*, June 27, 1982.

38 Sworn Testimony of Anthony Paul, Supervisor, Firearms Identification Unit, Philadelphia Police Department, *Cmwlth. of Pa. v. Abu-Jamal* (N.T. 6/23/82, 6.99–6.102).

39 Sworn Testimony of Priscilla Durham, Security Officer, Thomas Jefferson University Hospital, *Cmwlth. of Pa. v. Abu-Jamal* (N.T. 6/24/82, 28); Sworn Testimony of Officer Garry Bell, Witness, *Cmwlth. of Pa. v. Abu-Jamal* (N.T. 6/24/82, 133–136); Sworn Testimony of Officer Gary Wakshul, Witness, *Cmwlth. of Pa. v. Abu-Jamal, PCRA Hearing* (N.T. 8/1/95, 25–26).

40 Producer Harry Phillips with Correspondent Sam Donaldson, "Hollywood's Unlikely Hero," *20/20*, Dec. 9, 1998, ABC Transcript #1879.

Chapter 5

41 Daniel R. Williams, *Executing Justice: An Inside Account of the Case of Mumia Abu-Jamal* (New York: St. Martin's Press, 2001), 329.

42 Petition for Post-Conviction Relief and/or Writ of Habeas Corpus.

43 Daniel R. Williams, *Executing Justice: An Inside Account of the Case of Mumia Abu-Jamal* (New York: St. Martin's Press, 2001), 329.

44 Ibid., 317.

Chapter 6

45 Buzz Bissinger, "The Famous and the Dead," *Vanity Fair*, Aug. 1999, 76.

46 David Holmberg, "'Fool for Client'? Jamal's Role as Own Attorney Presents Problems," *Philadelphia Daily News*, June 17, 1982.

47 David Holmberg, "Jamal Questions Cops on Beatings," *Philadelphia Daily News*, June 2, 1982.

48 Marc Kaufman, "Lesser Role Sought for Abu-Jamal," *Philadelphia Inquirer*, June 9, 1982.

49 Marc Kaufman, "Abu-Jamal Selection of Jurors Halted," *Philadelphia Inquirer*, June 10, 1982.

50 David Holmberg, "1st Juror Chosen for Trial of Jamal," *Philadelphia Daily News*, June 8, 1982.

[51] Marc Kaufman, "Jury Selection Completed for Abu-Jamal's Murder Trial," *Philadelphia Inquirer*, June 17, 1982.

[52] David Holmberg, "Jamal Thrown Out; Brothers Held," *Philadelphia Daily News*, June 19, 1982.

[53] Ibid.

[54] Daniel R. Williams, *Executing Justice: An Inside Account of the Case of Mumia Abu-Jamal* (New York: St. Martin's Press, 2001), 118.

[55] Marc Kaufman, "Abu-Jamal Cannot Defend Self; Judge Says He's Disrupting Trial," *Philadelphia Inquirer*, June 18, 1982.

[56] David Holmberg, "Jamal Thrown Out; Brothers Held," *Philadelphia Daily News*, June 19, 1982.

[57] David Holmberg, "Jamal Again Removed From Slaying Trial," *Philadelphia Daily News*, June 22, 1982.

[58] Sworn Testimony of Maureen Faulkner, *Cmwlth. of Pa. v. Abu-Jamal* (N.T. 6/19/82, 39).

[59] Marc Kaufman, "Witness: Abu-Jamal Shot Officer," *Philadelphia Inquirer*, June 20, 1982.

[60] Sworn Testimony of Robert Chobert, Witness, *Cmwlth. of Pa. v. Abu-Jamal* (N.T. 6/19/82, 213).

[61] David Holmberg, "Jamal Again Removed From Slaying Trial," *Philadelphia Daily News*, June 22, 1982.

[62] Marc Kaufman, "A Second Witness Says Abu-Jamal Shot Officer," *Philadelphia Inquirer*, June 22, 1982.

[63] Ibid.

[64] Ibid.

[65] David Holmberg, "Abu-Jamal Tossed Out of His Trial for Third Time," *Philadelphia Daily News*, June 24, 1982; Marc Kaufman, "Abu-Jamal's Wound Tied to Officer," *Philadelphia Inquirer*, June 24, 1982.

[66] Marc Kaufman, "Abu-Jamal Said He Shot Officer, Two Tell Trial," *Philadelphia Inquirer*, June 15, 1982.

[67] Ibid.

[68] David Holmberg, "Abu-Jamal 'Defied Cops' at Hospital," *Philadelphia Daily News*, June 24, 1982.

[69] David Holmberg, "'I Hope He Dies,' Abu-Jamal Said," *Philadelphia Daily News*, June 25, 1982.

[70] Dorothy Storck, "The Layman vs. the Experts," *Philadelphia Inquirer*, June 3, 1982.

[71] Sworn Testimony of Michael M. Scanlan, Witness, *Cmwlth. of Pa. v. Abu-Jamal* (N.T. 6/25/82, 8.8–8.12).

72 Sworn Testimony of Albert Magilton, Witness, *Cmwlth. of Pa. v. Abu-Jamal* (N.T. 6/25/82, 8.75–8.79).

73 Michael Sokolove, "Attorney a Target of Abuse," *Philadelphia Daily News*, July 3, 1982.

74 Ibid.

75 Marc Kaufman, "Abu-Jamal Found Guilty of Murder; Could Get Death for Killing Officer," *Philadelphia Inquirer*, July 3, 1982.

76 David Holmberg, "Jury Sentences Abu-Jamal Today," *Philadelphia Daily News*, July 3, 1982.

77 Marc Kaufman, "Abu-Jamal Found Guilty of Murder; Could Get Death for Killing Officer," *Philadelphia Inquirer*, July 3, 1982.

78 Ibid.

79 Marc Kaufman, "Abu-Jamal Gets Electric Chair; Slain Officer's Wife Praises the Jurors," *Philadelphia Inquirer*, July 4, 1982.

80 Ibid.

81 Ibid.

82 Ibid.

83 Marc Kaufman, "Abu-Jamal Sentenced to Die, Threatens the Judge," *Philadelphia Inquirer*, May 26, 1983.

84 I'm not sure who first coined the word "Mumidiots" to describe the mindless support of a convicted cop killer but, as best I can recall, it was *Philadelphia Daily News* columnist Stu Bykofsky, so praise be to him.

Chapter 9

85 Mumia Abu-Jamal, "Teetering on the Brink: Between Death and Life," *Yale Law Journal* 100, no. 4 (Jan. 1991), 993.

86 Ibid., 998.

87 Ibid., 993.

88 Ibid.

89 Ibid.

90 Ibid.

91 Ibid.

Chapter 10

92 Buzz Bissinger, "The Famous and the Dead," *Vanity Fair*, Aug. 1999, 76.

93 *American Justice*. Episode no. 131, "Death Row Radical: Mumia Abu-Jamal," first broadcast 1999 by A&E Network.

94 Buzz Bissinger, "The Famous and the Dead," *Vanity Fair*, Aug. 1999, 76.

95 Prison Radio, "Welcome," www.prisonradio.org/index.htm.

[96] Cate T. Corcoran, "Giving Prisoners Some Air," *Stanford Magazine*, July–Aug. 2001, also available online at www.stanfordalumni.org/news/magazine/2001/julaug/departments/onthejob.html.

[97] Prison Radio, "Noelle Hanrahan biography," www.prisonradio.org/noelle.htm.

[98] Mumia Abu-Jamal, "Fujimori Bans the Bar," *Flashpoints*, Pacifica Radio Network KPFA 94.1 FM, Berkeley, Jan. 1993, available online at www.flashpoints.net/mFujimoriBansBar.html.

[99] Mumia Abu-Jamal, "For Young Minds—Two Offerings," *Flashpoints*, Pacifica Radio Network KPFA 94.1 FM, Berkeley, recorded May 27, 2003, available online at www.prisonradio.org/maj/maj_5_28_minds.html.

[100] T. T. Nhu, "Inmate's Voice Is Heard from Death Row," *New York Daily News*, June 13, 1994.

[101] Associated Press, "Public Radio Hires Officer's Killer as a Death Row Commentator," *New York Times*, May 15, 1994.

[102] Ibid.

[103] Elizabeth Kolbert, "Public Radio Won't Use Commentary by Inmate," *New York Times*, May 17, 1994.

[104] Associated Press, "Public Radio Hires Officer's Killer as a Death Row Commentator," *New York Times*, May 15, 1994.

[105] Elizabeth Kolbert, "Public Radio Won't Use Commentary by Inmate," *New York Times*, May 17, 1994.

[106] Arnold H. Gordon, First Assistant D.A., to Mr. Delano E. Lewis, President and CEO of NPR, May 16, 1994. In author's possession.

[107] Ibid.

[108] Associated Press, "Public Radio Hires Officer's Killer as a Death Row Commentator," *New York Times*, May 15, 1994.

[109] Marc Fisher, "Pacifica Stations Bolt Over Convicted Killer's Commentary," *Washington Post*, Feb. 25, 1997.

[110] Buzz Bissinger, "The Famous and the Dead," *Vanity Fair*, Aug. 1999.

[111] Elizabeth Kolbert, "Public Radio Won't Use Commentary by Inmate," *New York Times*, May 17, 1994.

[112] Ibid.

[113] Ibid.

[114] Staff Writer, "Judge Dismisses Inmate's Suit Against NPR," *Washington Post*, Aug. 22, 1997.

[115] Ed Vulliamy, "Former Panther Fights for Voice from Death Row; Mumia Abu-Jamal Argues His Right to Freedom of Speech Has Been Infringed by National Public Radio, but a Judge Disagrees," *The Guardian*, Sept. 1, 1997.

[116] Maureen Faulkner to Eric Breindel, editor of *New York Post*, June 17, 1994.

[117] The Pacifica Network, "About the Pacifica Network," www.pacificanetwork .org/radio/content/section/4/40/.

[118] Statement submitted by Maureen Faulkner for broadcast on Pacifica Radio, June 15, 1994.

Chapter 11

[119] Justice For All, "In Memory," www.jfa.net/memory.html.

Chapter 12

[120] Marc Kaufman, Julia Cass, and Carol Morello, "From Death-Row Cell to Global Cause Celebre: Abu-Jamal's Long Climb to a World Stage," *Philadelphia Inquirer*, Aug. 13, 1995.

Chapter 13

[121] Adam Bell, "Journalist on Death Row Spawns Prison Industry; His Foes Bristle as Bucks Roll In," *Times-Picayune (New Orleans)*, Sept. 10, 1995.

[122] Mumia Abu-Jamal, *Live from Death Row* (Boston: Addison-Wesley Publishing Co., 1995).

[123] Marylynne Pitz, "Attorney Seeks to Let Author Give Interviews on Death Row," *Pittsburgh Post-Gazette*, June 28, 1995.

[124] Adam Bell, "Journalist on Death Row Spawns Prison Industry; His Foes Bristle as Bucks Roll In," *Times-Picayune (New Orleans)*, Sept. 10, 1995.

[125] Marylynne Pitz, "Attorney Seeks to Let Author Give Interviews on Death Row," *Pittsburgh Post-Gazette*, June 28, 1995.

[126] Adam Bell, "Journalist on Death Row Spawns Prison Industry; His Foes Bristle as Bucks Roll In," *Times-Picayune (New Orleans)*, Sept. 10, 1995.

[127] Jim Nolan, "Cop's Widow Fights Killer's Book," *Philadelphia Daily News*, Mar. 23, 1995.

[128] Maureen Faulkner, "Murdered Police Officer's Wife Blasts Publishing Company," *National Fop Newswatch*, Spring/Summer 1995, 7.

[129] Ibid.

[130] Bob Hoover, "Death Row Inmate's Book Stirs Furor," *Pittsburgh Post-Gazette*, June 18, 1995.

[131] Ibid.

[132] Ibid.

[133] Jim Nolan, "Cop's Widow Fights Killer's Book," *Philadelphia Daily News*, Mar. 23, 1995.

[134] Mary Achilles, Office of the Victim Advocate, to Carol Lavery, Director, Pennsylvania Bureau of Victims' Services, Commission on Crime and Delinquency, May 20, 1997.

Chapter 14

[135] Megan Rosenfeld, "Condemned to Silence? Does a Man Lose His Right to Write If He Kills a Cop? A Widow Says Yes," *Washington Post*, May 18, 1995.

[136] Sworn Testimony of John Heftner, Evidence Handler, *Cmwlth. of Pa. v. Abu-Jamal* (N.T. 6/21/82, 4.10).

[137] Sworn Testimony of Joseph Kohn, Gun Department Manager, Pearson's Sporting Goods, Philadelphia, *Cmwlth. of Pa. v. Abu-Jamal* (N.T. 6/21/82, 4.35).

[138] Marc Kaufman, "A Second Witness Says Abu-Jamal Shot Officer," *Philadelphia Inquirer*, June 22, 1982.

[139] Marc Kaufman, "The Rise of Death-Row Chic: How Abu-Jamal, Convicted Cop-Killer, Became the Darling of The Left," *Washington Post*, Aug. 20, 1995.

Chapter 15

[140] F. X. Feeney, "Fight to the Finish: A Widow Vows to Bury Her Husband's Convicted Killer and His Death Row Memoir," *People*, Aug. 14, 1995, 49.

Chapter 16

[141] Mike Ervin, "Leonard Weinglass—Activist Attorney—Interview," *The Progressive*, May 1996.

Chapter 17

[142] Letters to the Editor, "Police History Makes Paranoia About Mumia Understandable," *Philadelphia Daily News*, Aug. 30, 1995.

[143] Ibid.

[144] Richard Jones and Dianna Marder, "Abu-Jamal Rally Draws a Peaceful, Diverse Contingent," *Philadelphia Inquirer*, Aug. 13, 1995.

[145] Associated Press, "7 Busted at London Demonstration," *Philadelphia Daily News*, Aug. 14, 1995.

Chapter 18

[146] E. L. Doctorow, "From Here to Death Row: Did Mumia Abu-Jamal Get a Fair Trial?," *New York Times*, July 14, 1995.

[147] Advertisement, "Mumia Abu-Jamal Must Have a New Trial," *New York Times*, Aug. 9, 1995.

[148] Ibid.

[149] Ibid.

150 Maria Coole, "Taking Whoopi to Task," *Lancaster Sunday News*, Apr. 4, 1999.

151 Tim Robbins, interview by Michael Smerconish, *Michael Smerconish Show*, WPHT 1210 AM, Philadelphia, Dec. 1, 2005.

152 Tucker Carlson, "Mumia Dearest," *The Weekly Standard*, Sept. 18, 1995.

153 Canadian Press, "Calgary Police Officers Join Global Boycott of Ben and Jerry's Ice Cream," *Calgary Sun*, July 30, 2001.

Chapter 19

154 Julia Cass and Marc Kaufman, "Judge Won't Withdraw in Abu-Jamal Appeal," *Philadelphia Inquirer*, July 13, 1995.

155 Editorial, "Mumia Again," *Philadelphia Inquirer*, July 16, 1995.

156 Marc Kaufman, Julia Cass, and Carol Morello, "From Death-Row Cell to Global Cause Celebre: Abu-Jamal's Long Climb to a World Stage," *Philadelphia Inquirer*, Aug. 13, 1995.

157 Mike Ervin, "Leonard Weinglass—Activist Attorney—Interview," *The Progressive*, May 1996.

158 Julia Cass and Marc Kaufman, "Judge Won't Withdraw in Abu-Jamal Appeal," *Philadelphia Inquirer*, July 13, 1995.

159 Suzanne Sataline, "11 Arrested in Protest at Judge's Home," *Philadelphia Inquirer*, July 17, 1995.

160 Marc Kaufman and Julia Cass, "Raucous Appeal Hearing Aborted in Abu-Jamal Case; The High Court Granted a Delay—But Did Not Stop the Execution Clock," *Philadelphia Inquirer*, July 19, 1995.

161 Ibid.

162 *Cmwlth. of Pa. v. Abu-Jamal* (N.T. 6/17/82, 1.44–1.46).

163 *Cmwlth. of Pa. v. Abu-Jamal*, 720 A.2d 79, 9–10 (Pa. 1998).

164 Ibid.

165 Marc Kaufman, Julia Cass, and Carol Morello, "From Death-Row Cell to Global Cause Celebre: Abu-Jamal's Long Climb to a World Stage," *Philadelphia Inquirer*, Aug. 13, 1995.

166 Marc Kaufman and Julia Cass, "Lawyer Overcome in Heated Dispute," *Philadelphia Inquirer*, July 28, 1995.

167 Jim Nolan, "Mumia Lawyer Tossed in Jail Cell; Ignored Judge's Warnings," *Philadelphia Daily News*, Aug. 3, 1995.

168 Ibid.

169 Ibid.

170 Valerie M. Russ, "Another Man in the Car? Defense Suggests Mystery Driver," *Philadelphia Daily News*, Aug. 10, 1995.

[171] Daniel R. Williams, afterword to *Executing Justice: An Inside Account of the Case of Mumia Abu-Jamal* (New York: St. Martin's Press, 2001).

[172] Daniel R. Williams, *Executing Justice: An Inside Account of the Case of Mumia Abu-Jamal* (New York: St. Martin's Press, 2001), 298.

[173] Ibid., 301.

[174] Ibid., 305.

[175] David Holmberg, "Jamal Tries to Shake Witness IDs," *Philadelphia Daily News*, June 3, 1982.

[176] Valerie M. Russ, "Cabbie: Mumia Shot Cop; Denies Deal with DA for '82 Testimony," *Philadelphia Daily News*, Aug. 16, 1995.

[177] *Cmwlth. of Pa. v. Abu-Jamal* (N.T. 6/19/82, 223).

[178] Marc Kaufman and Julia Cass, "Abu-Jamal Hearing Moves to 'Mob Room,'" *Philadelphia Inquirer*, Sept. 11, 1995.

[179] Dinah Wisenberg Brin, "No! Mumia Loses Retrial Bid," *Philadelphia Daily News*, Sept. 16, 1995.

[180] Ibid.

Chapter 20

[181] Mike O'Sullivan, "September 16th: A Day to Remember," *Peace Officer* 3, no. 5 (Oct. 1995).

[182] Stuart Taylor Jr., "Guilty and Framed," *The American Lawyer*, Dec. 1995.

[183] Sworn Testimony of Robert Chobert, Witness, *Cmwlth. of Pa. v. Abu-Jamal* (N.T. 6/19/82, 212–13, 227–28, 233–34); Sworn Testimony of Cynthia White, Witness, *Cmwlth. of Pa. v. Abu-Jamal* (N.T. 6/21/82, 4.106; 6/22/82, 5.134–5.135); Sworn Testimony of Michael M. Scanlan, Witness, *Cmwlth. of Pa. v. Abu-Jamal* (N.T. 6/25/82, 8.21, 8.29–8.30, 8.60).

[184] Sworn Testimony of Officer James Forbes, Witness, *Cmwlth of Pa. v. Abu-Jamal* (N.T. 6/19/82, 155).

[185] Sworn Testimony of Robert Harkins, Witness, *Cmwlth. of Pa. v. Abu-Jamal*, PCRA Hearing (N.T. 8/2/95, 205–10).

Chapter 21

[186] Dave Davies, "FOP: Co-Sponsor of Hearing is a Cult," *Philadelphia Daily News*, Mar. 26, 1996.

[187] Edward S. Smith, *Brethren Life and Thought* 3, no. 22 (Winter 1958), 22–33.

[188] D. Merrill Mow, *Brethren Life and Thought* 5, no. 43 (Autumn 1996), 43–52.

[189] Staff Writer, "News in Brief: Sect Defends Death Row Inmate," *Washington Post*, July 15, 1995.

[190] Ibid.

[191] Richard M. Thomson to Judge Albert F. Sabo, Plough Publishing, July 5, 1995.

[192] Mark McDonald, "2 Sides Await Street Ruling; Pro-Mumia Group Requests Use of Council Chambers," *Philadelphia Daily News*, Mar. 9, 1996.

[193] Mark McDonald, "Mumia Group Hearing Ire," *Philadelphia Daily News*, Mar. 8, 1996.

[194] Ibid.

[195] Julia Cass, "Death Penalty Opponents Begin Forum; The Program Being Run in City Council Chambers Has Drawn Criticism; Some Feel it Will Be One Sided," *Philadelphia Inquirer*, Mar. 26, 1996.

[196] Julia Cass, "Freed By DNA Test; Death Row Survivor Has Cautionary Tale," *Philadelphia Inquirer*, Mar. 28, 1996.

Chapter 22

[197] Mark Faziollah, "Police Say HBO Protest Growing," *Philadelphia Inquirer*, July 9, 1996.

[198] Maureen Faulkner to Gerald Levin, Time-Warner's Chairman, June 5, 1996. In author's possession.

[199] *A Case for Reasonable Doubt.* First aired July 7, 1996, by HBO. Produced by Ottmore in Association with HBO and Channel 4 in Great Britain.

[200] Ibid.

[201] Ibid.

[202] Sworn Testimony of Charles Tumosa, Criminalist for the City of Philadelphia, *Cmwlth. of Pa. v. Abu-Jamal* (N.T. 6/26/82, 15–17).

[203] Ibid., 56–57, 59–60.

[204] Sworn Testimony of George Fassnacht, Ballistics Expert, *Cmwlth. of Pa. v. Mumia Abu-Jamal, PCRA Hearing* (N.T. 8/2/95, 120–21).

[205] Ibid., 179.

[206] Steve Lopez, "Abu-Jamal TV Show Sheds No Light," *Philadelphia Inquirer*, July 10, 1996.

[207] Ibid.

[208] Ibid.

Chapter 23

[209] Eyewitness Statement of Veronica Jones, Investigation Interview Record, Philadelphia Police Department, Homicide Division, Questioned concerning "The Homicide, by shooting, of officer Daniel Faulkner," Interviewed by Bennett/Harmon, Dec. 15, 1981, 9:45 p.m.

[210] Sworn Testimony of Veronica Jones, Witness, *Cmwlth. of Pa. v. Abu-Jamal* (N.T. 6/29/82, 109–110).

[211] Ibid., 112.

[212] Ibid.

[213] Ibid., 122–23.

[214] Julia Cass, "Sparring Goes on at Abu-Jamal's Appeal Hearing; Ramona Africa Paid Bail for a Witness," *Philadelphia Inquirer*, Oct. 3, 1996.

[215] *Cmwlth. of Pa. v. Abu-Jamal, PCRA Hearing* (N.T. 9/11/95, 23).

[216] Sworn Testimony of Veronica Jones, Witness, *Cmwlth. of Pa. v. Abu-Jamal, PCRA Hearing* (N.T. 10/1/96, 20–21).

[217] Julia Cass, "Abu-Jamal Witness Says She Lied; Police Coerced Her Testimony in '82, She Testified," *Philadelphia Inquirer*, Oct. 2, 1996.

[218] Sworn Testimony of Veronica Jones, Witness, *Cmwlth. of Pa. v. Abu-Jamal, PCRA Hearing* (N.T. 10/1/96, 46).

[219] Ibid., 53.

[220] Ibid., 55–56.

[221] Ibid., 46.

[222] Julia Cass, "Hearing on New Testimony in Abu-Jamal Case Comes to Close," *Philadelphia Inquirer*, Oct. 4, 1996.

[223] Julia Cass, "Testimony on Abu-Jamal Rejected," *Philadelphia Inquirer*, Nov. 2, 1996.

Chapter 24

[224] Staff Writer, "Censorship Issues Raised in Silencing of Radio Show," *New York Times*, Mar. 3, 1997.

[225] Marc Fisher, "Pacifica Stations Bolt Over Convicted Killer's Commentary," *Washington Post*, Feb. 25, 1997.

[226] Ibid.

[227] Ibid.

[228] David Hinckley, "PA. Stations Scrap 'Democracy' & Mumia," *New York Daily News*, Feb. 25, 1997.

[229] Kevin L. Carter, "Students Protest Temple's Decision to Take Abu-Jamal Off the Air," *Philadelphia Inquirer*, Mar. 14, 1997.

[230] Staff Writer, "Censorship Issues Raised in Silencing of Radio Show," *New York Times*, Mar. 3, 1997.

[231] Maureen Faulkner, "Oppressed by Mumia's Diatribes," *Philadelphia Daily News*, Mar. 3, 1997.

Chapter 25

[232] Associated Press, "Calif. City Demands New Abu-Jamal Trial; Santa Cruz Says Fairness Is the Issue; Its Resolution Will Be Sent to Gov. Ridge," *Philadelphia Inquirer*, Mar. 27, 1997.

233 Karen Clark, "SC Council Resolution Puzzles Slain Officer's Widow," *Santa Cruz County Sentinel*, Apr. 2, 1997.

Chapter 26

234 Eric Pooley, "Death or Life?," *Time*, June 16, 1997.

235 Marc Kaufman, "Witness Says Police Tried to Get Her to Lie in Court," *Philadelphia Inquirer*, June 27, 1997.

236 Ibid.

237 Staff Writer, "Farrakhan Aide Refuses to Apologize for Remarks," *New York Times*, Feb. 11, 1994.

238 Marc Kaufman, "Witness Says Police Tried to Get Her to Lie in Court," *Philadelphia Inquirer*, June 27, 1997.

239 Ibid.

240 Linda Loyd, "Judge to Abu-Jamal's Lawyers: So Show Me the Witness," *Philadelphia Inquirer*, July 2, 1997.

241 Daniel R. Williams, *Executing Justice: An Inside Account of the Case of Mumia Abu-Jamal* (New York: St. Martin's Press, 2001), 328.

242 Ibid.

Chapter 27

243 "San Francisco: 3,000 Rally for Mumia Abu-Jamal," *Revolutionary Worker* 921 (Aug. 31, 1997), available online at http://rwor.org/a/v19/920–29/921/sfmum.htm.

244 Ibid.

245 Certificate of Honor for Mumia Abu-Jamal, Board of Supervisors, City and County of San Francisco, Aug. 16, 1997.

246 Proclamation Honoring Mumia Abu-Jamal, Mayor Willie Lewis Brown, Jr., City and County of San Francisco, Aug. 16, 1997.

247 "San Francisco: 3,000 Rally for Mumia Abu-Jamal," *Revolutionary Worker* (921), Aug. 31, 1997, available online at http://rwor.org/a/v19/920–29/921/sfmum.htm.

248 Jim Herron Zamorra, "New Generation Turns Out for Abu-Jamal," *San Francisco Examiner*, Apr. 25, 1999.

249 Ibid.

250 Ibid.

251 Associated Press, "Police Set to Protect Rally for Convicted Killer of Officer," *Boston Globe*, Apr. 24, 1999.

252 George Strawley, "Crowd Rallies for New Trial of Man Convicted in Police Officer's Death," Associated Press, Apr. 24, 1999.

Chapter 28

253 "Special Assignment Report (2 Part Series)." Aired May 7 and 8, 1998, by KGO-TV, Channel 7, ABC affiliate, San Francisco. Reported by Dan Ashley.

254 Ibid.

255 C. Clark Kissinger and Leonard Weinglass, "The KGO-TV Report: A Case Study in Irresponsible Journalism," Refuse and Resist, June 18, 1998, www.refuseandresist.org/mumia/1998/061898kgotv.html.

256 Marc Kaufman, "A Second Witness Says Abu-Jamal Shot Officer," *Philadelphia Inquirer*, June 22, 1982.

257 Press Release of The Mobilization to Free Mumia Abu Jamal, 3425 Cesar Chavez Street, San Francisco, CA 94110, July 1998.

258 Ibid.

259 Maureen Faulkner and Michael Dann, Justice for P/O Daniel Faulkner, Inc., to Milt Weiss, News Director, KGO-TV, July 18, 1998. In author's possession.

Chapter 29

260 Advertisement, "Justice for Police Officer Daniel Faulkner," *New York Times*, June 14, 1998.

261 Ibid.

262 Leonard Weinglass, letter to the editor, *New York Times,* June 17, 1998, available online at www.refuseandresist.org/mumia/1998/062398weinglass .html.

Chapter 30

263 Maureen Faulkner to Harry Phillips, Producer, *20/20*, Jan. 1, 1999. In author's possession.

264 Maureen Faulkner to Sam Donaldson, Correspondent, *20/20*, Jan. 1, 1999. In author's possession.

Chapter 31

265 Daniel Fountenberrys, "Ire for Mumia Lesson, Timing a Sore Spot After Slaying of Cop in Oakland," *Philadelphia Daily News*, Jan. 14, 1999.

266 Chris Thompson, "Class Struggle," *East Bay Express,* Apr. 20, 2001.

267 Ibid.

268 Don Knapp, "Convicted Killer Becomes Lesson in Some Oakland Schools," CNN, Jan. 14, 1999, www.cnn.com/US/9901/14/oakland.teach.in.

269 Ibid.

270 Refuse and Resist, "Oakland Schools Teach-In: The Case of Mumia Abu-Jamal," revised Feb. 1, 1999, www.refuseandresist.org/mumia/1999/012799teachin.html.

Chapter 32

271 MTV, "Rage Against the Machine: Full Biography," www.mtv.com/bands/az/rage_against_the_machine/bio.jhtml.

272 Zack de la Rocha Network, "Zack De La Rocha Biography," www.zdlr.net/bio/zdlrbio.htm.

273 Ibid.

274 Ibid.

275 Tom Morello, Zack de la Rocha, and Brad Wilk, "Voice of the Voiceless," in *The Battle of Los Angeles,* Rage Against the Machine (Epic, 1999), lyrics available online at http://lyrics.rockmagic.net/lyrics/rage_against_the_machine/the_battle_of_los_angeles_1999.html.

276 Louis Freese, Lawrence Muggerud, and Senen Reyes, "How I Could Just Kill a Man," in *Renegades*, Rage Against the Machine (Epic, 2000), lyrics available online at http://lyrics.rockmagic.net/lyrics/rage_against_the_machine/renegades_2000.html.

277 Thomas Ginsberg, "Concert for Abu-Jamal Comes Under Attack," *Philadelphia Inquirer*, Jan. 22, 1999.

278 Ibid.

279 Ibid.

280 Ibid.

281 Ibid.

282 Robert Wang, "Howard Stern Sparks Death Row Celebrity Flap," Apbnews.com, Jan. 19, 1999.

283 Thomas Ginsberg, "Concert for Abu-Jamal Comes Under Attack," *Philadelphia Inquirer*, Jan. 22, 1999.

Chapter 33

284 Monica Yant, Craig R. McCoy, Michael Matza, and Larry Fish, "Abu-Jamal Fund May Skirt Tax Laws," *Philadelphia Inquirer*, Apr. 25, 1999.

285 Ibid.

286 Monica Yant Kinney and Craig R. McCoy, "Pa. Halts Abu-Jamal Group's Fund Effort," *Philadelphia Inquirer*, Aug. 5, 2001.

287 Monica Yant, Craig R. McCoy, Michael Matza, and Larry Fish, "Abu-Jamal Fund May Skirt Tax Laws," *Philadelphia Inquirer*, Apr. 25, 1999.

288 Ibid.

289 Craig McCoy and Monica Yant Kinney, "City Plans to Restore Its Ties to Charity," *Philadelphia Inquirer*, Sept. 13, 2000.

290 Monica Yant, Larry Fish, and Craig R. McCoy, "City Drops Charity Tied to Abu-Jamal," *Philadelphia Inquirer*, May 28, 1999.

291 Monica Yant and Larry Fish, "Charity Fights Ouster by Rendell," *Philadelphia Inquirer*, June 4, 1999.

292 Craig R. McCoy and Monica Yant Kinney, "For Abu-Jamal Group, A Question of Cash Despite Its Tax-Exempt Status," *Philadelphia Inquirer*, June 25, 2000.

293 Ibid.

294 Monica Yant Kinney, Craig R. McCoy, and Saba Bireda, "Abu-Jamal Group Tells of Break-In," *Philadelphia Inquirer*, June 15, 2000.

295 Monica Yant Kinney and Craig R. McCoy, "Pa. Halts Abu-Jamal Group's Fund Effort," *Philadelphia Inquirer*, Aug. 5, 2001.

296 Monica Yant Kinney and Craig R. McCoy, "Abu-Jamal Group Is Sanctioned by the State," *Philadelphia Inquirer*, Sept. 27, 2001.

Chapter 34

297 Buzz Bissinger, "The Famous and the Dead," *Vanity Fair*, Aug. 1999.

298 Ibid.

299 Ibid.

300 Ibid.

301 Ibid.

302 Glynn Ash, "Mumia Abu-Jamal: The Frame Continues," *The Ethical Spectacle,* Sept. 1999, available online at www.spectacle.org/999/mumia.html.

303 Ibid.

304 Refuse and Resist, "Press Conference Reveals New Evidence in Support of Mumia Abu-Jamal," Aug. 3, 1999, http://refuseandresist.org/mumia/1999/080399prconf.html.

305 "Vanity Fair Published 'Hit Piece' on Mumia Abu-Jamal; Author Is Publicist for Philadelphia Mayor Ed Rendell," *Revolutionary Worker* 1014 (July 18, 1999), available online at http://rwor.org/a/v21/1010–019/1014/vanity.htm; Seeing Red, "Is Mumia Guilty?," July 9, 1999, www.seeingred.com/Copy/2.5_vanity_mumia.html.

306 "Commentary by Mumia Abu-Jamal: Anatomy of the Lie," *Social Action,* Aug. 1999, available online at www.socialistaction.org/news/199908/mumia.html.

Chapter 36

[307] Suzette Parmley, "Memorial a Common Cause for Bikers, Police; About 12,000 Took Part in the Event," *Philadelphia Inquirer*, May 24, 1999.

[308] Ibid.

Chapter 37

[309] The Evergreen State College, "About Evergreen," www.evergreen.edu/about evergreen/.

[310] Associated Press, "Students Protest Voice from Death Row," *Boston Globe*, June 12, 1999.

[311] Jack Hopkins, "Evergreen Graduates Cheer Convicted Killer's Tape," *Seattle Post-Intelligencer*, June 12, 1999.

[312] Associated Press, "Some Graduates Protested Taped Remarks by Convicted Killer," *St. Louis Post Dispatch*, June 12, 1999.

[313] Francis X. Clines, "Killer or Victim? The Poster Boy For and Against the Death Penalty," *New York Times*, May 21, 2000.

[314] Karen R. Long, "Battle Over Abu-Jamal Shifts to Ohio Colleges," *Cleveland Plain Dealer*, Apr. 6, 2000.

[315] Maureen Faulkner to the Graduating Class of Antioch College, Mar. 27, 2000.

[316] Alice Thomas and Frank Hinchey, "Calm Prevails Despite Tension at Antioch Commencement," *Columbus Dispatch*, Apr. 30, 2000.

[317] Bill Sloat, "Speech Turns Police into Protesters; Death Row Inmate's Address at Antioch Riles Officers Nationwide," *Cleveland Plain Dealer*, Apr. 30, 2000.

[318] "College Hears Abu-Jamal Tape," *Pittsburgh Post-Gazette*, Apr. 30, 2000.

[319] Clyde Hughes, "Abu-Jamal's Taped Talk to College Protested," *Pittsburgh Post-Gazette*, Apr. 30, 2000.

Chapter 39

[320] Eric Langborgh, "Book-Burners Shout Down AIA Speaker at Berkeley," *Campus Report: The Newspaper Of Accuracy In Academia* XVI, no. 3 (Nov. 2000), 3.

[321] Ibid.

Chapter 40

[322] Jim Nolan, "Author Cries Foul, Writer Says Mumia's Camp Shuns Him After Learning About His Book Proposal," *Philadelphia Daily News*, Mar. 22, 2001.

[323] Ibid.

Chapter 41

[324] Sara Rimer, "Cop-Killer's Execution Rescinded; Abu-Jamal Faces Life in Prison or a New Hearing," *Chicago Tribune*, Dec. 19, 2001.

[325] Maida Cassadra Odom, "Death Sentence for Abu-Jamal Overturned," *Boston Globe*, Dec. 19, 2001.

[326] Debra J. Saunders, "Abu-Jamal Finds Safety in Numbers," *San Francisco Chronicle*, Dec. 20, 2001.

[327] Maida Cassadra Odom, "Death Sentence for Abu-Jamal Overturned," *Boston Globe*, Dec. 19, 2001.

[328] Theresa Conroy, "The Abu-Jamal Morass Becomes More Muddied; Judge Affirms Cop Killer's Guilt but Overturns His Death Sentence," *Philadelphia Daily News*, Dec. 19, 2001.

[329] Joseph Perkins, "A Killer's Crusade Against Reality," *Washington Times*, Dec. 28, 2001.

[330] 2001 U.S. Dist. LEXIS 20812 at *5.

[331] Judge Yohn did not address the remaining seven allegations of sentencing phase misfeasance as he believed they were mooted by his decision to grant Abu-Jamal a new penalty hearing.

[332] *Mills v. Maryland*, 486 U.S. 367 (1988) and *Boyde v. California*, 494 U.S. 370 (1990).

Chapter 42

[333] Staff Writer, "France Pays Homage to Mumia; Cop-Killer Is Named an Honorary Parisian," *Philadelphia Daily News*, Dec. 6, 2001.

[334] Free Mumia Coalition, NYC, "Mumia Made Honorary Citizen of Paris," www.freemumia.com/frenchdelegation.html.

[335] Regina Jere-Malanda, "France Honours Black Death Row Inmate," *New African,* November 1, 2003, 61.

[336] Free Mumia Coalition, NYC, "Mumia Made Honorary Citizen of Paris," www.freemumia.com/frenchdelegation.html.

[337] Ibid.

[338] Sworn Testimony of Cynthia White, Witness, *Cmwlth. of Pa. v. Abu-Jamal* (N.T. 6/21/82, 4.92–4.94).

[339] Statement of Cynthia White, Investigation Interview Record, Philadelphia Police Department, Homicide Division, Questioned concerning "John Street's visit on Monday 6-14-82," Interviewed by Bethea/Withers, June 16, 1982, 4:00 p.m.–7:50 p.m.

[340] Ibid.

[341] Maureen Faulkner, interview by Michael Smerconish, *The Michael Smerconish Show,* WPHT 1210 AM, Philadelphia, Feb. 14, 2005.

342 Chris Brennan, "Street Apologizes, Calls Widow Of Cop In Wake Of 'Welcome,'" *Philadelphia Daily News*, Feb. 15, 2005.

343 John M. Baer, "Mayor Street: Admit This Was A Mistake," *Philadelphia Daily News*, Feb. 15, 2005, 5.

344 Jennifer Lin, "Paris Suburb Names Street For Abu-Jamal," *Philadelphia Inquirer*, May 16, 2006, A01.

345 *H. Res. 1082 [109th]: Condemning The Decision By The City Of St. Denis, France, To Name A Street . . .* , GOVTRACK.US, vote on Dec. 6, 2006, *available at* www.govtrack.us/congress/vote.xpd?vote=h2006–527&sort=vote.

Chapter 43

346 Interview with Maureen Faulkner and Mike Farrell, *The O'Reilly Factor*, Fox News, Oct. 16, 2003.

347 Ibid.

348 Ibid.

349 Ibid.

350 A&E Television Networks, "Ossie Davis Biography (1917–2005)," *Biography.com*, www.biography.com/search/article.do?id=9268149.

351 "Ossie Davis Meets Mumia And Calls For New Trial," SOCIALIST ACTION, *available at* www.socialistaction.org/news/199906/ossie.html.

352 Mike Farrell, *Just Call Me Mike: A Journey To Actor And Activist*, Akashic Books/Rdv Books, 2007, 284.

353 Ibid., 283.

354 Ibid.

355 Ibid., 284.

356 Ibid.

357 Mike Farrell, interview by Michael Smerconish, *The Michael Smerconish Show*, WPHT 1210 AM, Philadelphia, recorded June 19, 2007, aired June 21, 2007.

358 Ibid.

359 *The O'Reilly Factor: Guests and Topics: October 16.* Aired on Fox News, Oct. 17, 2003, available at www.foxnews.com/story/0,2933,100404,00.html.

360 Mike Farrell, interview by Michael Smerconish, *The Michael Smerconish Show*, WPHT 1210 AM, Philadelphia, recorded June 19, 2007, aired June 21, 2007.

Chapter 44

361 Charlie Brennan, "Ward Churchill: A Contentious Life," *Rocky Mountain News*, Mar. 26, 2005, available online at www.rockymountainnews.com/drmn/local/article/0,1299,DRMN_15_4757900,00.html.

362 Jennifer Warren, "Watching the Death of Inmate C29300," *Los Angeles Times*, Dec. 14, 2005.

363 Arnold Schwarzenegger, Governor of the State of California, *Statement of Decision on Request for Clemency by Stanley Williams*, Dec. 12, 2005.

364 Ibid.

365 Ibid.

366 Ibid.

367 Jennifer Warren, "Watching the Death of Inmate C29300," *Los Angeles Times*, Dec. 14, 2005.

Chapter 45

368 Valerie Russ, "Witness: Abu-Jamal Didn't Do It," *Philadelphia Daily News*, Dec. 8, 2006, full story rerun Dec. 9, 2006.

369 Michael Smerconish, "Appeals Process Tortures Victims' Families," *Philadelphia Inquirer*, May 27, 2007.

370 Emilie Lounsberry, "Death-Row Reversals of Fortune," *Philadelphia Inquirer*, July 1, 2007.

INDEX

A

Abraham, Lynne, 49, 134, 290
Abu-Jamal, Mumia
  alternate theories of crime and,
    139–41, 142
  American Lawyer article on,
    149–60
  Antioch College commencement,
    261–63
  appeals, 293–94
  background of, 12–13
  broadcast journalism career, 78–80
  Bruderhof and, 161–66
  case facts, 22–25, 29
  celebrity supporters, 121, 123–28,
    200, 205
  confession, 7
  courtroom demeanor of,
    37–40, 102
  courtroom disruptions and,
    34–36, 40, 44, 132–34
  death penalty, 291–92
  death sentence, 272–76
  death warrant, 119
  defense strategies, 182–83
  defense team, 27–28, 33, 44–45
  Evergreen State College
    commencement, 260–61
  evidence against, xiii, 29, 102–4
  federal appeal, 291–92, 293–99,
    301
  fundraising proceeds and, 241–45
  initial media coverage, 11–16
  injuries to, 8, 15, 74, 75, 76
  National Public Radio and, xi, 78,
    80–84, 97
  Pacifica Radio and, 80, 84–86,
    189–91
  Parisian citizenship, 277–78,
    281–82
  Partisan Defense Committee and,
    x, xi, 135
  Phil Bloch and, 246, 247, 249,
    250–51
  political beliefs, 12–13, 23, 44,
    47–48, 78–79
  preliminary hearings, 30
  publishing career, 97–100
  race and, 74–76
  Rage Against the Machine and,
    235–40
  San Francisco, CA and, 203–6
  support of, viii, x–xii, 15–16, 26,
    29, 43–44, 73, 74, 93, 94, 106,
    119–20, 223
  witnesses for, 45–46
  Yale Law Journal and, 72–77
    *See also Commonwealth of
    Pennsylvania v. Mumia Abu-
    Jamal*
Abu-Jamal Defense Committee, 16
Accuracy in Academia, 267
Addison-Wesley, 97–100
Africa, Alberta, 89
Africa, John, 35, 36, 48, 76, 133
Africa, Pam, 31, 89, 205–6, 241,
  242, 243, 244
Africa, Ramona, 89, 147
All Things Censored, 100
All Things Considered, 80–81, 83
Allen, Tony, 89–90
American Lawyer article
  Abu-Jamal as victim, 158–59
  aftermath of, 160
  arguments of, 149–50
  conclusions of, 159

341